ADVANCE PRAISE FOR *CHINATOWN VANCOUVER*

"Lovingly illustrated and written with concision and meticulous research, *Chinatown Vancouver* is a nostalgia-tinged triumph worthy of our Chinese ancestors, who made Canada their home despite so many unwelcoming forces. It shows us how much history still lives in Chinatown's streets and in its buildings' bones. Donna Seto has written a book to treasure."

—**KEVIN CHONG, author of *The Double Life of Benson Yu***

"Utterly unique in blending personal memoir, family history, interviews, and historical commentary with stunning original watercolours and photographs, writer and artist Donna Seto presents a heartfelt, candid, and meticulously researched history of Vancouver's Chinatown. This book offers a thoughtful glimpse of a once vibrant past, a hopeful present, and a future for a vital gentrified location. Nostalgic, informative, and richly detailed, *Chinatown Vancouver* effortlessly transports readers with wonderful visual storytelling and an investigative journey. Necessary and important. I was transported to my own childhood!"

—**LINDSAY WONG, author of *The Woo-Woo* and *Tell Me Pleasant Things about Immortality***

"In *Chinatown Vancouver*, Donna Seto has achieved a rare alchemy: reaching back in time to a Chinatown that now only lives in memory, while simultaneously breathing life into the shared recollections of a community whose deep roots in Canada are often invisible or dismissed. Donna's illustrations made me smile and, sometimes, tear up. Every wash of colour is an emotion. Every stroke is a reminder for us to carry our past into the future. A beautiful, accomplished, gorgeous book."

—**JEN SOOKFONG LEE, author of *Superfan* and *The End of East***

"Donna Seto's vibrant watercolour paintings of historical buildings in Vancouver's Chinatown are deeply rooted in a specific community but will resonate with anyone who grew up near a Chinatown in North America. Her work speaks to the resilience of the loh wah kiu and how they built self-sustaining communities despite anti-Asian hostility. Every building, every story, is a testament to our ancestors and their lasting impact."

—**TERESA WONG, author of *All Our Ordinary Stories***

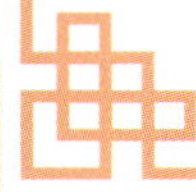
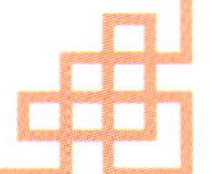

"*Chinatown Vancouver* is an extensive current-day inventory of where the economic, political, and social life of the city's Chinese Canadian community took place. It provides an important document of a once-thriving neighbourhood now struggling to position itself for the future. Donna Seto's delicate, sensitive, and vibrant illustrations of historical buildings are complemented by research and archival photos of each of those sites. They capture not only the facades but also the fragility of Chinatown today as it sits in the crossroads between competing forces and desires."

—HENRY TSANG, author of
White Riot: The 1907 Anti-Asian Riots in Vancouver

"An exquisite book. At a time when Chinatowns are at risk of disappearing forever and anti-Asian racism is rampant, Donna Seto's *Chinatown Vancouver* is an important historical archive of Chinese settlement in Vancouver—not only of the hardships and exclusion but also the vibrant community and legacy. The art is a testament to the unique, sophisticated, and aesthetic beauty the Chinese diasporic community has cultivated in urban spaces. The carefully researched stories folded among the art give voice to the generations before us that have paved the way, teaching us to continue to honour our elders, our past, but to also stand firm and be proud of who we are and where we have come from. As I witness the closures of many places where my family held Red Egg parties and celebrated milestones in my own community's Chinatown, I treasure Donna Seto's work for capturing the fleeting past and providing a beautiful narrative that contests harmful historical depictions of Chinese diasporic communities."

—JAMIE CHAI YUN LIEW, author of *Dandelion*

"Donna Seto's vibrant illustrations, coupled with grainy photos of historical Vancouver, deliver a powerful meditation on the resilience of the Chinese community as it navigates discrimination and hardship, weaving themes of continuity and hope into the visually resplendent pages. This is history that can be tasted, smelled, and embraced. *Chinatown Vancouver* is a profoundly poignant and vital work that will resonate with readers interested in history and human resilience."

—WAYNE NG, author of *Johnny Delivers*

CHINATOWN VANCOUVER

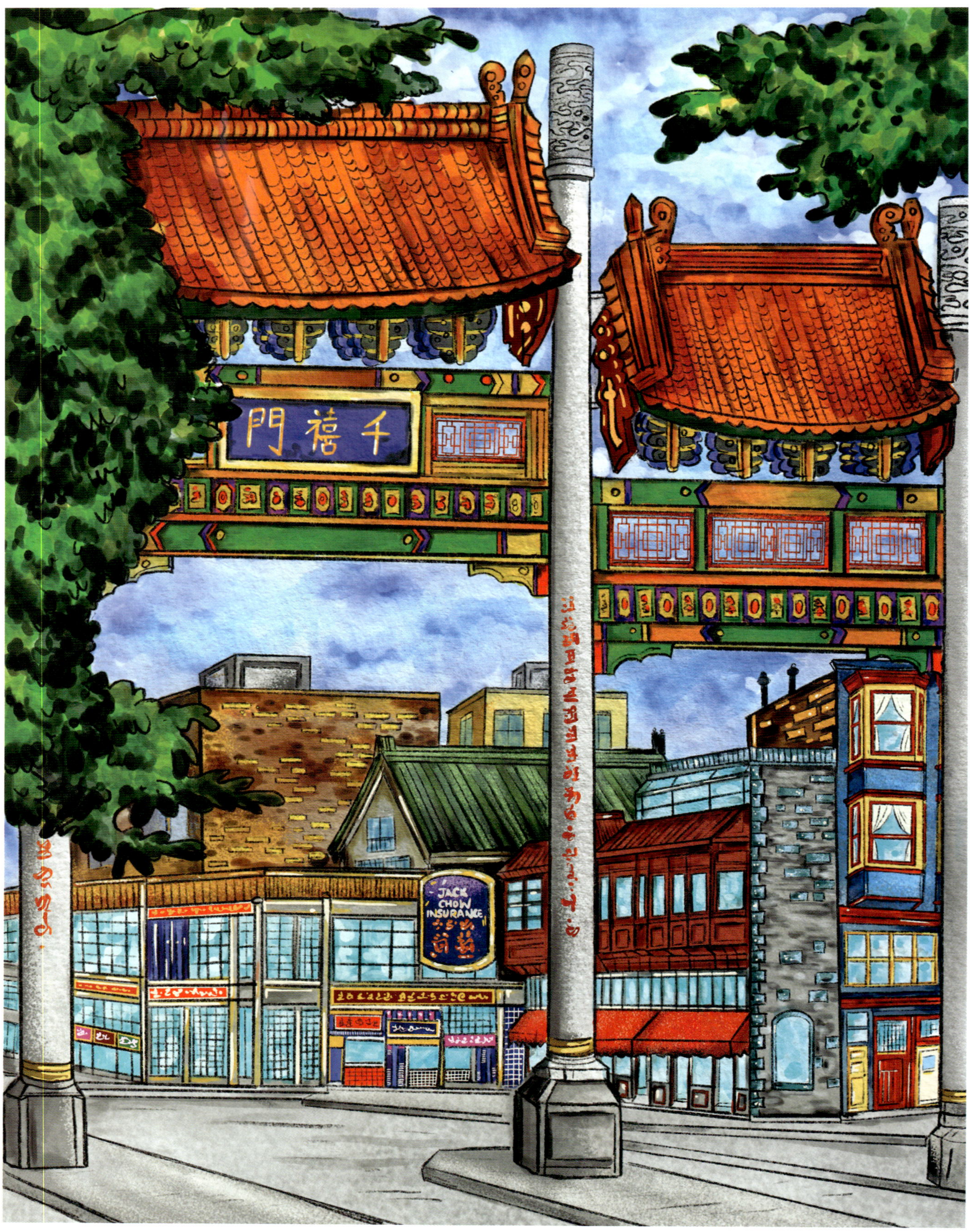
千禧門
JACK
CHOW
INSURANCE

CHINATOWN VANCOUVER

AN ILLUSTRATED HISTORY

DONNA SETO

FOREWORD BY MADELEINE THIEN

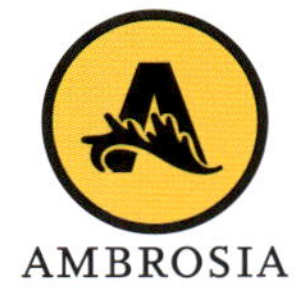

AMBROSIA

**To Chinatown
for the inspiration to persevere
against the odds**

Published in Canada and the USA in 2025 by House of Anansi Press Inc.
houseofanansi.com

House of Anansi Press is committed to protecting our natural environment. This book is made of material from well-managed FSC®-certified forests, recycled materials, and other controlled sources.

House of Anansi Press is a Global Certified Accessible™ (GCA by Benetech) publisher. The ebook version of this book meets stringent accessibility standards and is available to readers with print disabilities.

29 28 27 26 25   1 2 3 4 5

Library and Archives Canada Cataloguing in Publication
Title: Chinatown Vancouver : an illustrated history / Donna Seto ; foreword by Madeleine Thien.
Names: Seto, Donna, author | Thien, Madeleine, 1974- writer of foreword
Description: Includes bibliographical references and index.
Identifiers: Canadiana (print) 2024045555X | Canadiana (ebook) 20240455592 | ISBN 9781487011970 (softcover) | ISBN 9781487011987 (EPUB)
Subjects: LCSH: Chinatown (Vancouver, B.C.)—History—Pictorial works. | LCSH: Chinatown (Vancouver, B.C.)—Buildings, structures, etc.—History—Pictorial works. | LCSH: Vancouver (B.C.)—History—Pictorial works. | LCSH: Vancouver (B.C.)—Buildings, structures, etc.—History—Pictorial works. | CSH: Chinese Canadians—British Columbia—Vancouver—History.
Classification: LCC FC3847.52 .S48 2025 | DDC 971.1/33—dc23

Cover art and lettering: Donna Seto
Book design and typesetting: Lucia Kim

House of Anansi Press is grateful for the privilege to work on and create from the Traditional Territory of many Nations, including the Anishinabeg, the Wendat, and the Haudenosaunee, as well as the Treaty Lands of the Mississaugas of the Credit.

 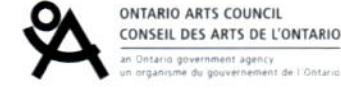

We acknowledge for their financial support of our publishing program the Canada Council for the Arts, the Ontario Arts Council, and the Government of Canada.

Printed and bound in South Korea

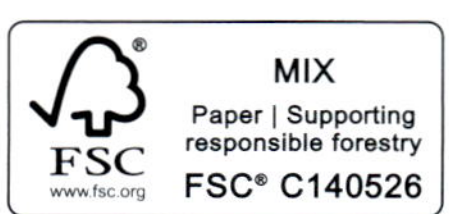

Vancouver's Chinatown is situated on the unceded, ancestral, and traditional lands of the Coast Salish Peoples, in particular the Musqueam, the Squamish, and the Tsleil-Waututh Nations. A full history of the Chinese in Canada cannot be complete without an understanding of how, as settlers, the Chinese also played a role in the displacement of Indigenous Peoples. The relationship between racialized groups in Canada is complex and often mixed with intersectional and parallel struggles, but it is imperative for settlers to understand that meaningful reconciliation is possible only when all groups respect those who came before and who are still here. The revitalization of Chinatown cannot succeed unless we first come to terms with Canada's dark past. Only when these systemic silences are broken can true justice be achieved.

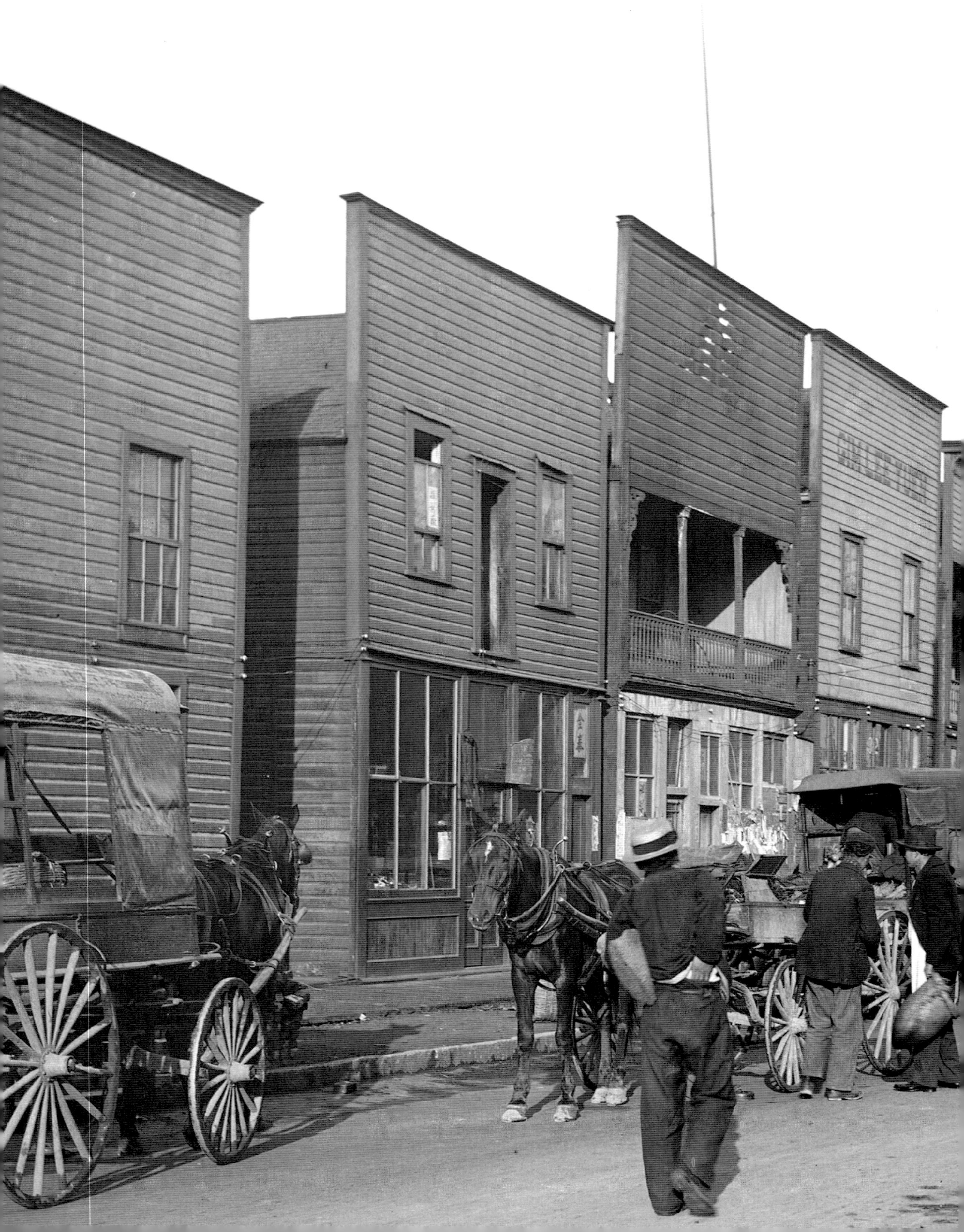

GIM LEE YUEN

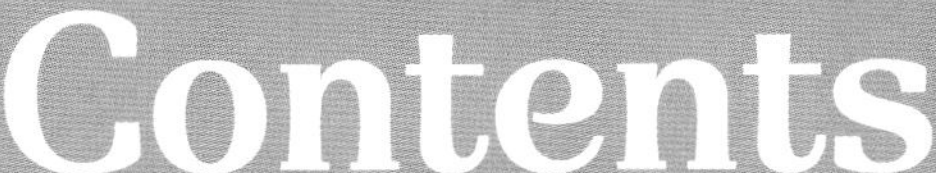

Contents

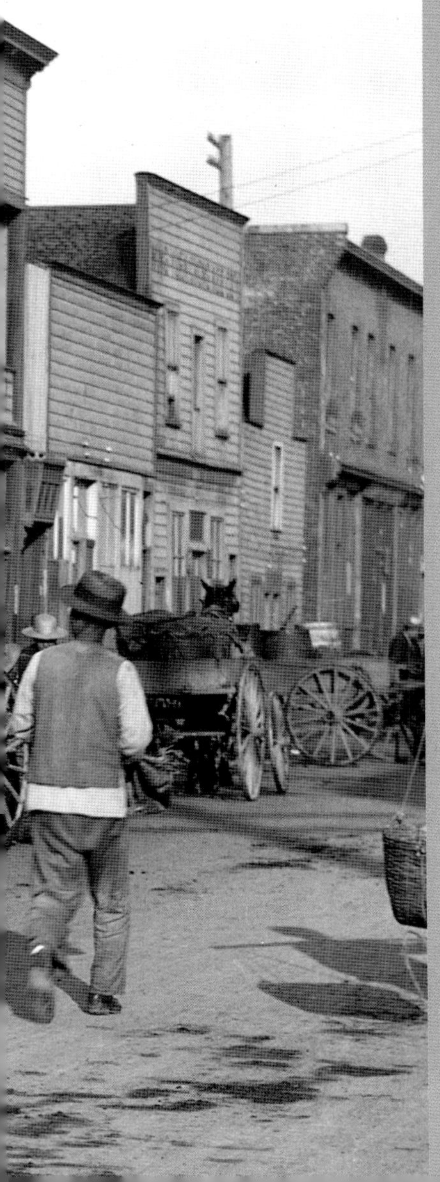

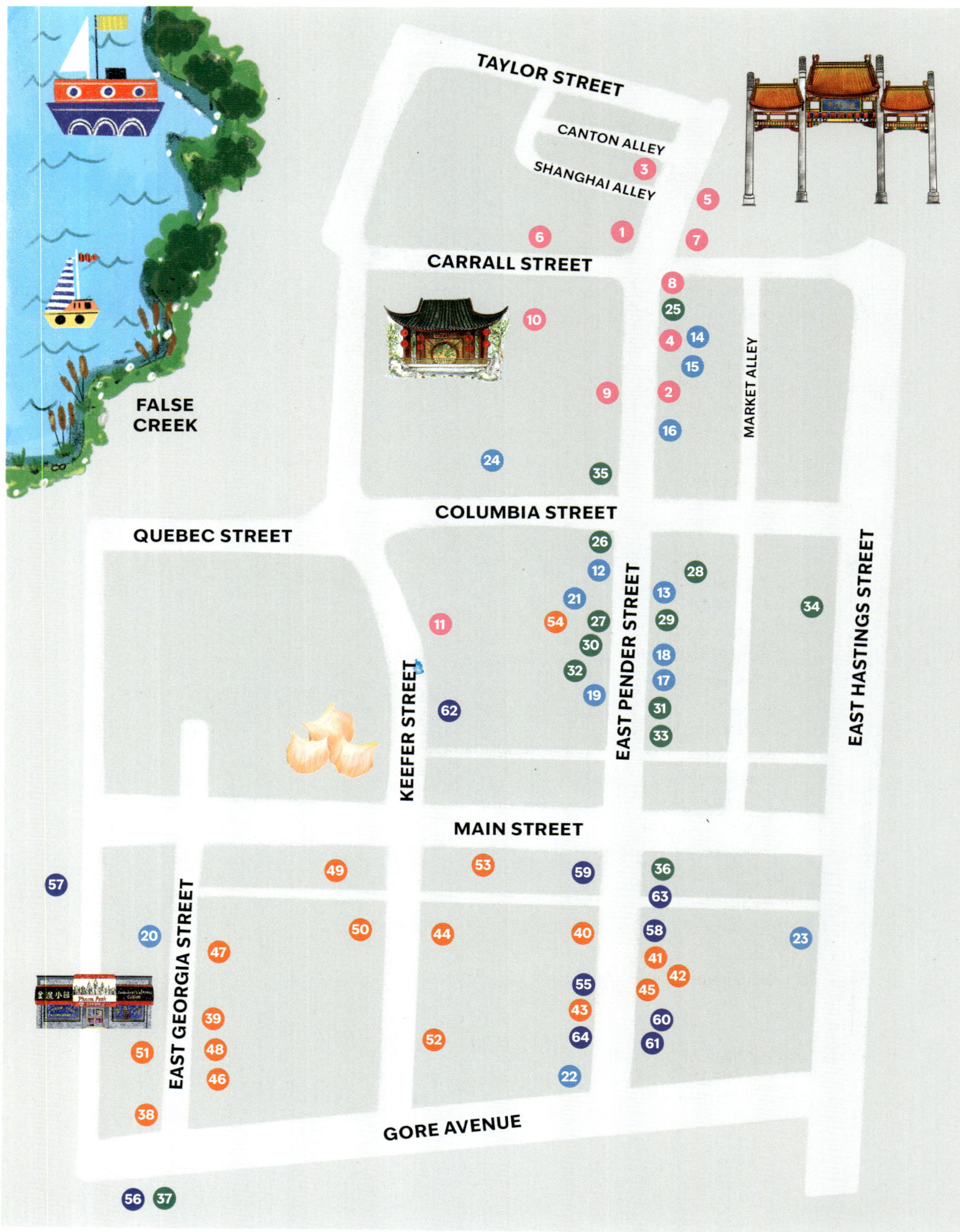

TAYLOR STREET
CANTON ALLEY
SHANGHAI ALLEY
CARRALL STREET
MARKET ALLEY
FALSE CREEK
COLUMBIA STREET
QUEBEC STREET
EAST PENDER STREET
EAST HASTINGS STREET
KEEFER STREET
MAIN STREET
EAST GEORGIA STREET
GORE AVENUE

Map of Chinatown

1. Sam Kee Building
2. Wing Sang Building
3. Shanghai Alley and Canton Alley
4. Modernize Tailors
5. On Wo Tailors
6. Chinese Empire Reform Association/ Lim Sai Hor Association
7. Chinese Freemasons Building
8. Chinese Times Building
9. Wah Sun Stationery
10. Dr. Sun Yat-sen Classical Garden
11. Vancouver Gas Company

12. Chinese Benevolent Association Building
13. Wongs' Benevolent Association Building
14. Hon Hsing Athletic Club
15. Yue Shan Association Buildings
16. Cheng Wing Yeong Tong Society Building
17. Mah Society Building and Jade Dynasty
18. Lung Kong Association
19. Chin Wing Chun Society Building
20. Yee Fung Toy Society
21. Chinese Freemasons and Dart Coon Club
22. Nationalist League/KMT Building
23. China Arts and Crafts
24. Chinese Cultural Centre

25. Ming Wo Cookware
26. Ho Ho Chop Suey/Foo's Ho Ho Restaurant
27. Chinese Theatre
28. Green Door Restaurant and Fuling Gifts
29. Lee Building
30. Chinatown BBQ
31. Ming's Restaurant and the Anglican Chinese Mission
32. Wayen and the South Seas Dining Lounge

33. Bamboo Terrace
34. Smilin' Buddha Cabaret
35. Forbidden City/Marco Polo Supper Club
36. Shanghai Junk/TD Bank
37. Moon Glow Cabaret

38. H. Y. Louie 252–260 East Georgia
39. H. Y. Louie 255 East Georgia
40. Kwong Man Sang
41. Forum Home Appliances
42. Kam Wai Dim Sum
43. Dollar Meat Store
44. Kam Yen Jan
45. Topper Poultry
46. Fresh Egg Mart
47. Treasure Green Tea
48. Ho Sun Hing Printer
49. Tosi and Company
50. Gain Wah Restaurant and Keefer Rooms
51. Phnom Penh Restaurant
52. Maxim's Bakery and Restaurant
53. The Boss Bakery and Restaurant
54. New Town Bakery

55. May Wah Hotel
56. MacLean Housing
57. Georgia Viaduct and Hogan's Alley
58. Shell Service Station
59. Mon Sun Barbershop/ King Hong Chop Suey/ Ten Ren Tea & Ginseng
60. Tai Hing Company/Kissa Tanto Restaurant
61. Mary's Fruit and Vegetable/Sing Tao/Royal Bank
62. Bao Bei Chinese Brasserie
63. Propaganda Coffee/Hong Chong Fish Market
64. Diaz Combat Sports

Timeline of Historical Events

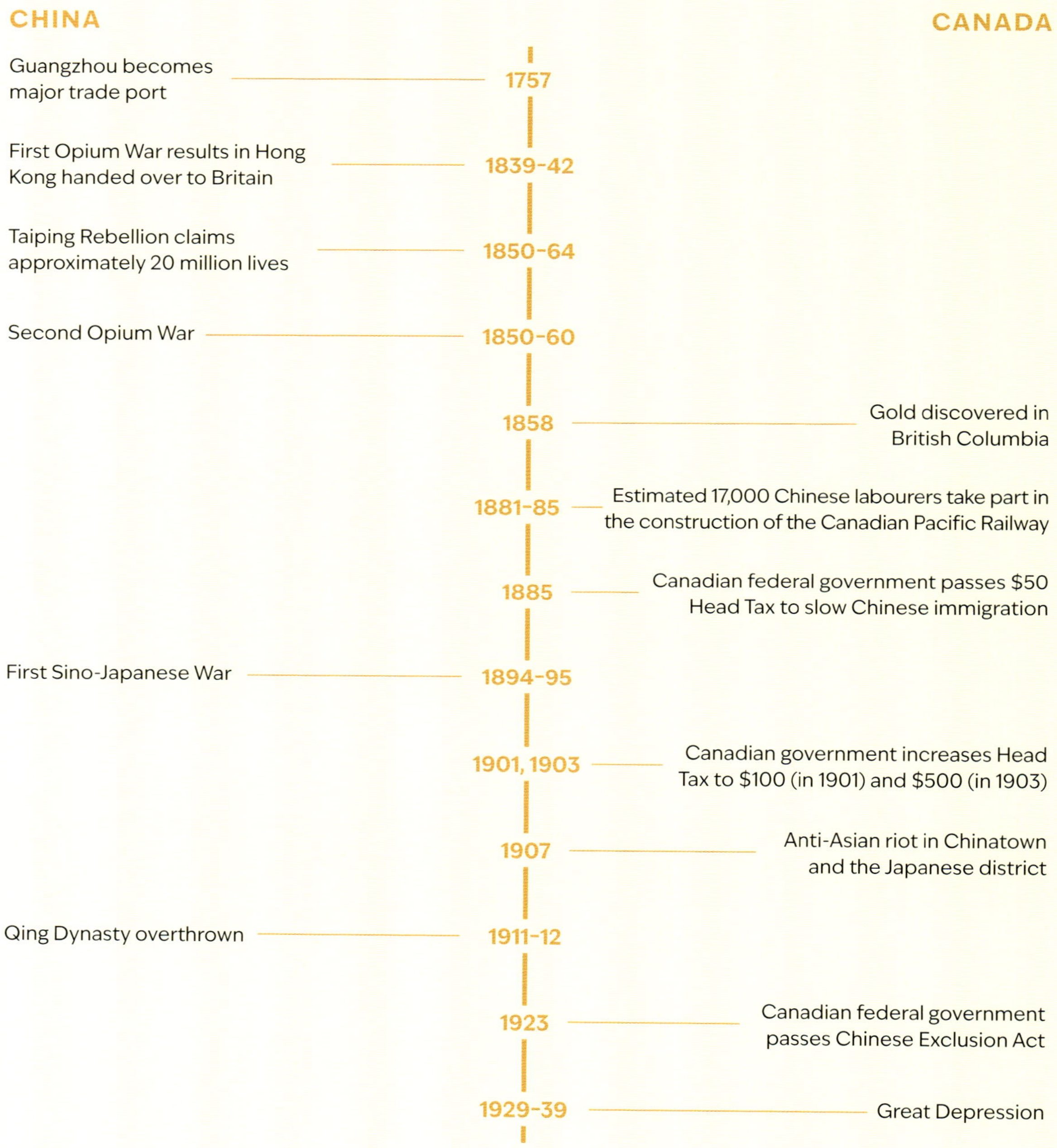

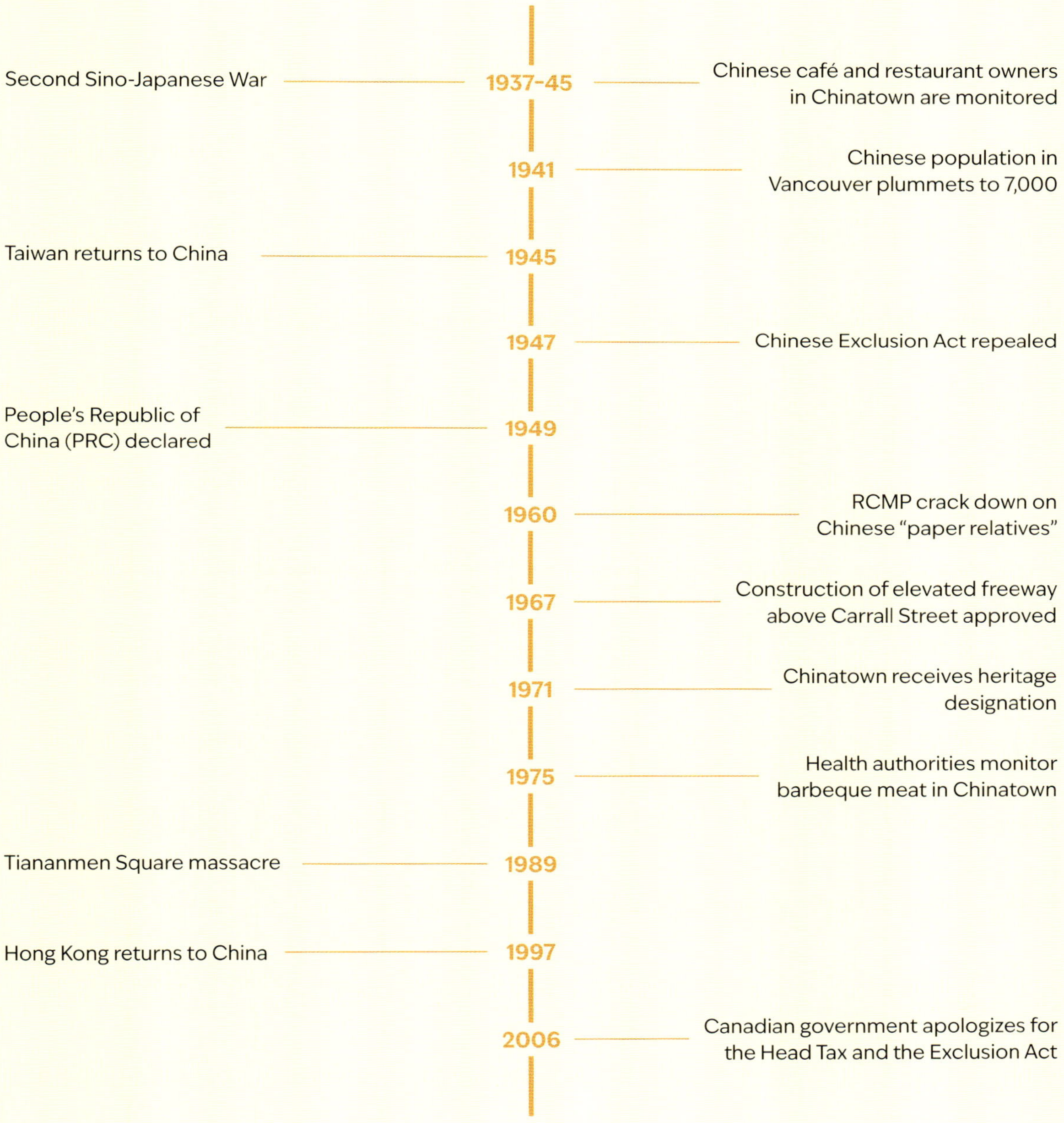

CHINA

CANADA

Second Sino-Japanese War
1937-45
Chinese café and restaurant owners in Chinatown are monitored

1941
Chinese population in Vancouver plummets to 7,000

Taiwan returns to China
1945

1947
Chinese Exclusion Act repealed

People's Republic of China (PRC) declared
1949

1960
RCMP crack down on Chinese "paper relatives"

1967
Construction of elevated freeway above Carrall Street approved

1971
Chinatown receives heritage designation

1975
Health authorities monitor barbeque meat in Chinatown

Tiananmen Square massacre
1989

Hong Kong returns to China
1997

2006
Canadian government apologizes for the Head Tax and the Exclusion Act

Foreword
by Madeleine Thien

A S   I   B E G A N   T O   read *Chinatown Vancouver*, I found myself resisting it. I felt as if I were standing on the shoreline at the turning of the tide, when the sand beneath your feet begins to crumble and give way. Images came to me in pieces—the cornice of a building, the tinkling bell on a shop door, a blue machine grumbling out a 6/49 lotto ticket. As I read, I heard voices on a rainy Vancouver morning, customers lined up in the stairwell of the Park Lock restaurant on Main Street, clutching little paper squares, each scribbled with a number in ballpoint pen. We were waiting to be summoned to that most desired place: a table—covered by a pink cloth and topped by a steaming teapot—between rolling carts of dim sum.

I resisted these pages because I find such memories are both sweet and sorrowful. Here, for instance, was a sharp image of my parents taking me to breakfast on a Sunday when my older siblings were off at Camp Latona, a name which, to me, signified an eighth wonder of the world that I would never see. To console me, my parents ordered all my favourites, one after another, culminating in the thing I most loved, Ma Lai Go, or Malay Cake. In ordinary times, its spongy goodness would be equitably divided using a pair of chopsticks which would walk straight through its plump middle. On this day, the entire cake was mine, and, in fact, I can taste it as I write these words; I can see my parents, in their late thirties and early forties, much younger than I am now. On that Sunday morning, even though they smiled, they were struggling. Six years earlier they had arrived in Canada by way of China, Hong Kong, Australia, and Malaysia. That year, mortgage rates rose to a staggering 22 percent. When I turned eight, they defaulted on their mortgage, losing our home and all the savings they had put into it. One of my most vivid memories is seeing our possessions lined up on the street in garbage bags, waiting to be collected by the dump truck. For the next two decades, my parents became—together and, then, alone—renters in Vancouver, continuously uprooted.

But turn the page of this book and other rivers of memory wash in. The clatter of dishes, the smell of bread and steam, bright rooms with aproned waitresses alerting us to sticky rice and turnip cake. There is my father: in one hand, he holds a white box tied with pink raffia ribbon and filled with egg tarts; in the other, he holds me. I remember my mother's glasses steaming up over a bowl of wonton noodles. If I accompanied my parents, singly, to Maxim's or New Town Bakery, they made sure to choose what the other loved—they did this even after their marriage collapsed and, though living side by side, no longer spoke to one another.

A thought like that reminded me to resist this extraordinary book, where building after building is drawn with care and whimsy and wonder, and most of all, with love. But it was impossible.

Donna Seto's images carried me—pulled me along like a distracted child down a magical street—back to a time when the neon lights still glowed, to the early 1980s and those weekends when my father, growing ever more disgruntled, cursing at anything that moved, would circle and circle Vancouver Chinatown in search of that rarest treasure: a parking spot.

Chinatown was the world of dreams. My sister and I belonged to the community dance troupe, which rehearsed at the Chinese Cultural Centre; we performed at schools, Lions Club dinners, and at every Lunar New Year parade. Our troupe was composed of children who, from Monday to Friday, sweated in classes at Goh Ballet's original tiny attic studio, and, on weekends, transformed into traditional dancers. Our repertoire cast us sometimes as tea pickers, sometimes as peacocks, and once as villagers banding together to harvest a turnip bigger than a house. Our dance master was exacting; we practised hard; we loved these beautiful costumes more than our tutus. I remember my mother's hands weaving my hair into tight French braids, or puffing it up into Princess Leia buns. Our heads, more beautiful than wedding cakes, were adorned with fake pearl pins and wreaths of flowers. Forty years later, when I see children, tenderly costumed, performing—dances of the northwest coast, or Irish and Ukrainian dances, or Palestinian and Lebanese dances— I recognize their solemn and dignified air. To be good at something, to be the bearer of a memory or tradition, was happiness.

My memories needed an outside world—a street of buildings, colours, sounds, and, most of all, the lives of others—to reawaken them. And, so, I kept reading this remarkable book, feeling the sand vanish beneath me.

I recognized some, but not all, of the buildings that Donna brings together in these pages. My clearest memories of Chinatown are street level—the height of a child's eyes. Clearly, I did not look up very often, except perhaps when I caught, from an upper storey, the cymbals and music that heralded lion dancers rehearsing, a sound that elicited the smell of firecrackers, the thrill of smoke, and the infinite awe inspired by a creature, with four or eight or twelve human legs, which leaped from one store to another in order to devour, with its giant clapping mouth, red envelopes suspended in mid-air beside little green leaves of lettuce.

That red envelope reminds me that our community's uneasy relationship with fortune, with luck, has marked our souls. The question *Will the gods smile on us?* is one that has both haunted our community and fuelled its hopes. My parents experienced this question in many forms: Will we find the place where we can be at home? A place where all these sacrifices might be redeemed in the currency of pride and love? Images, long dormant inside me, arose as if they had been sheltering inside Donna Seto's drawings: entering the

Royal Bank on East Pender Street to close my mother's account after her sudden death; the broken fence of my elementary school on Campbell and Pender where I used to hide when no one played with me; the bus stop in front of the Ray-Cam Community Centre on East Hastings where, it seemed, I stood in the sun and wind and rain for endless hours of my childhood, watching the faces of people going by, wondering, always wondering, about the people who shared these streets with me—who they were, what had brought some of them to their knees, why some smiled with a private joy, and whether I was visible to them, whether I really stood there, among the stones and trees.

Turning these pages, a reader might hear my footsteps just as I hear theirs, as we, new-comer, visitor, old-timer, walk these passages that house us all.

It's time for me to close the book, at least for now. These words and drawings of Vancouver's Chinatown arise from the attentiveness of Donna Seto's gaze across time—and her willingness to gaze at time itself.

Creating a painting, drawing, a piece of music, or a piece of writing is, among other things, the willingness to inhabit a full state of attention; we place our faith in the belief that attentiveness is the embodiment of relation. A building wears all its times, all its generations, upon it. Entering, we become aware of, or we remember, or we seek out, the existences in whose wake we are living: those who built these houses, these refuges, this community. We are reminded that everything we are now building, or unbuilding, is creating the world in which our children and children's children will come to face their selves. Perhaps the fear of examining history too closely, a fear so prevalent in our world, is the fear of our responsibility to it; yet the responsibility persists, whether we seize it or not.

Now, looking at the outlines drawn by Donna, I see habitations. These lines give shelter to colour, memory, and personhood. I wish to place this book in the hands of so many people I love, living and gone, and to say: *Do you remember this place, this moment?* I want to reassure them: *I remember.* Or maybe: *This place remembers us.* Or perhaps: *An artist, unable to look away, has breathed us into life.*

CHINATOWN VANCOUVER

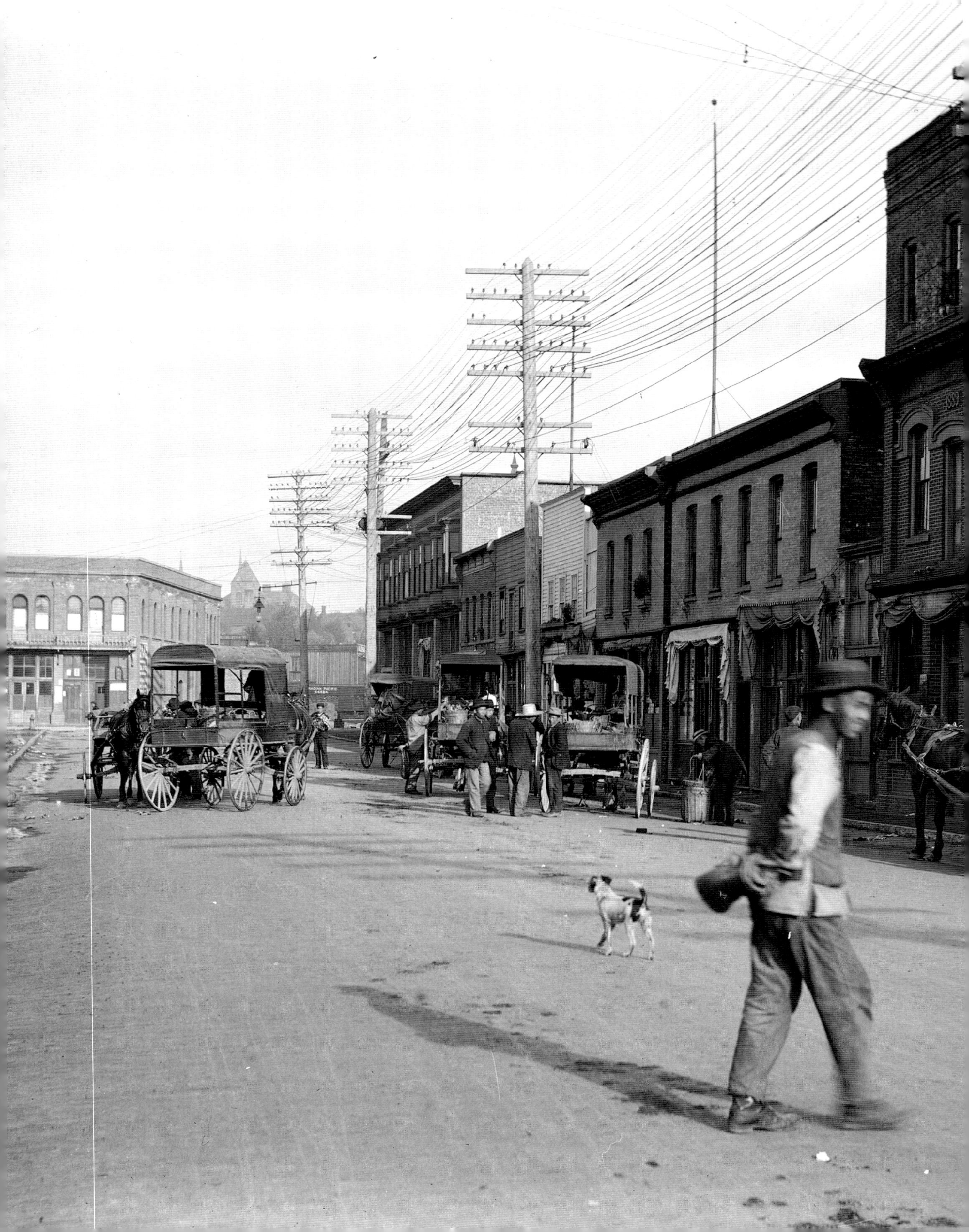

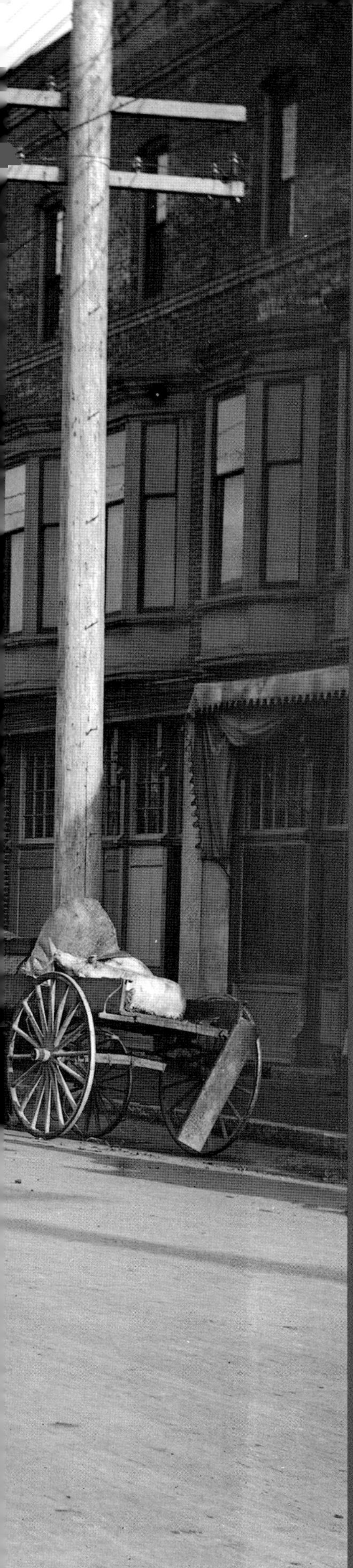

If Chinatown Were a Red Balloon

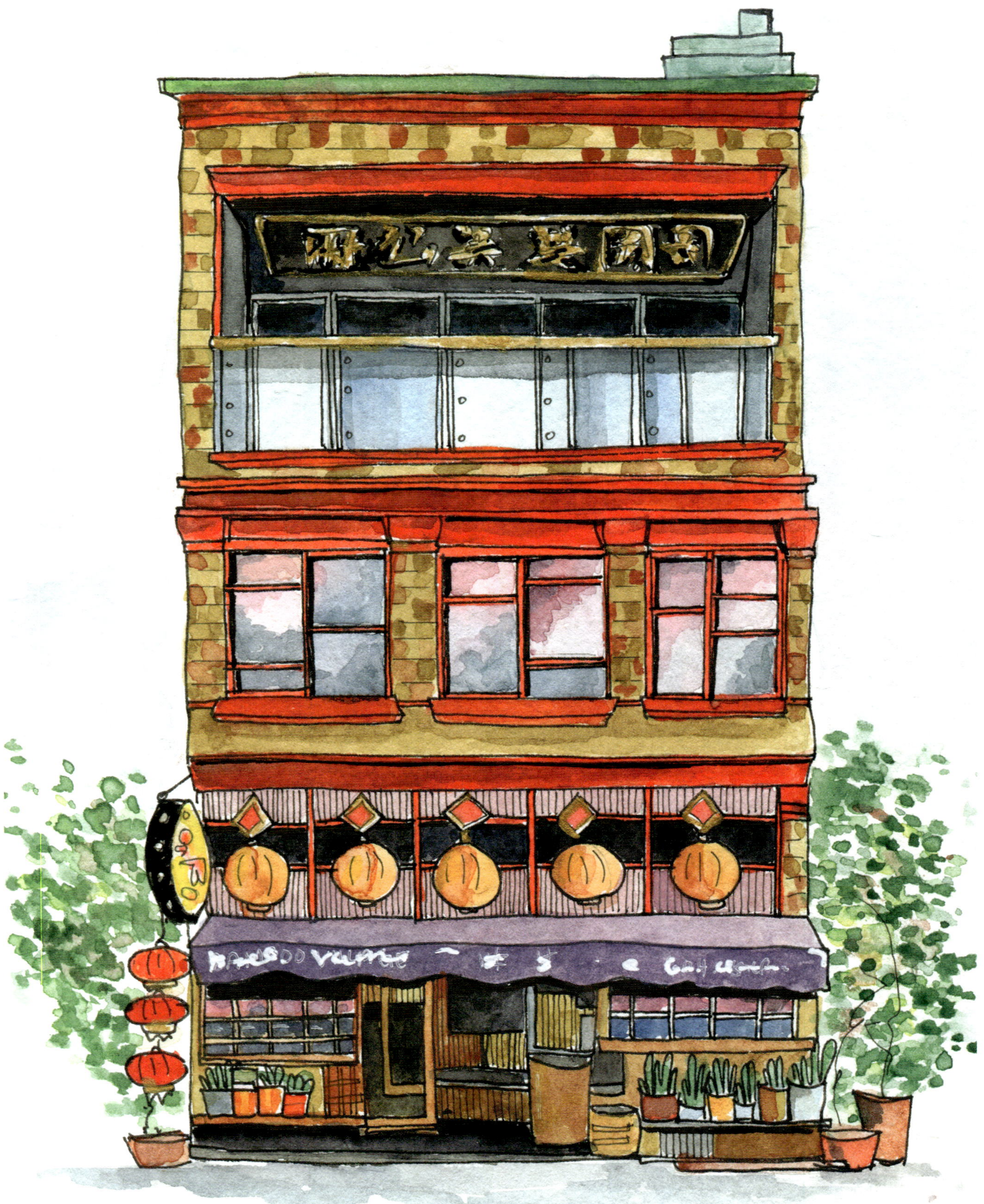

BAMBOO VILLAGE

WHEN I THINK ABOUT Vancouver's Chinatown, the first thought that crosses my mind isn't the freshly roasted ducks hanging in the greasy window of a butcher shop on East Pender. Nor is it the vegetable vendor on Keefer Street who claims his gai lan is cheaper, fresher, and crisper than his competitor's on Gore Avenue. Nor do I think about the otter who broke into the Dr. Sun Yat-sen Classical Garden and ate the curious fluorescent koi that once called the majestic lily pond home.[1]

Instead, these days when I think about Chinatown, I think about a red balloon.

It was 1985 and I was four when I received a bright red balloon during a regular outing in Chinatown. This balloon was special because it was a gift and it was red, a colour associated with luck. A lucky balloon.

My mother and I often wandered through Chinatown's busy streets, ducking into greengrocers and meat shops or visiting the herbalist. I loved following my mother through the crowds as she weaved in and out of the stores, picking up various goods—bok choy, ginger, garlic, oranges, bananas, vermicelli, egg noodles, fermented shrimp paste. If I was lucky, we would make a pit stop at New Town Bakery for an egg tart or meet with a friend at a café, where I'd be treated to a towering glass of red bean ice topped with a scoop of vanilla ice cream. Sometimes we'd visit one of Chinatown's many barbeque meat shops, where we stood in line behind heckling customers as they shouted their orders at cleaver-wielding butchers. My mother and I would then ride the trolley bus up Main Street to our house in Mount Pleasant, where we would deposit the groceries in our overflowing fridge, wash up, and start preparing dinner.

The day I received the red balloon, we wandered through the crowds along East Pender and Keefer like we usually did. It was summer and Chinatown was bustling, buzzing to its own rhythm while the sweet smells of barbeque pork and roast duck scented the humid air. Lyrical dialects filled the streets, each strumming its own tune, while vendors bellowed about how cheap and fresh their produce was. With one hand wrapped around the string of the balloon, I followed my mother, my arms brushing against polyester-clad and nylon-stockinged legs, sticky from the August heat.

"Hold on to your balloon!" my mother warned.

I looked up at the sky, watching the balloon cast its grace against the fluorescent awnings lined with homemade signs scribbled in black marker—half Chinese, half English—advertising ginseng and chrysanthemum tea.

"Let's go," my mother ordered as we weaved through another crowd, my small hand slipping out of hers as I waited for my balloon to follow. The balloon bounced left and right like it had a life of its own before wedging itself between a woman with permed hair and a man with large, thick glasses.

"Aiyah!" the woman scolded as she smacked the balloon away with her wrinkly hand.

"Watch out for people!" my mother said before disappearing into the crowd.

I was suddenly alone, smothered by the crowd, suffocated almost, but I felt a sense of relief, of safety, because I had my red balloon. But the beautiful round balloon was too far away, too out of reach as it dangled above my head. I wanted to hold it, to protect it, to make sure it was mine forever.

Through a break in the crowd, I caught sight of my mother picking through a mountain of oranges at a produce shop. She lifted one up, frowned at its imperfections, and then traded it for another. She repeated this sequence and filled the plastic bag before disappearing into the store. Fearing that she would leave me behind, I picked up my pace, taking extra measures to protect my balloon. I grabbed the string, pulled the balloon down, and wrapped my arms around its delicate round body.

I ran through the crowd to my mother with my red balloon.

It didn't take much, a quick squeeze here, a pinch there. I was four years old and I wasn't shy about wedging myself between bodies that wouldn't budge. Seconds later, my balloon—the one I had cherished, the one I wanted to take home to show my baby sister— was no more. It disappeared like it had never existed, its droopy rubbery remnants still clinging to the thin string attached to my wrist, leaving me with a deep sense of emptiness, a void, and shock as I stood there with my arms stretched out.

Where had my balloon gone? The bystanders trickled by without even noticing that a part of me had disappeared as if it had never existed.

When I was growing up, balloons were a rare commodity in my household. My parents immigrated to Canada in the early 1980s from a village in Guangdong. Their upbringing in China and their working-class status in Canada limited their access to celebratory goods like creamy cakes, wrapped presents, and birthday parties crawling with screaming classmates. Working as a seamstress and a cook, my parents alternated morning and evening shifts to take care of my sister and me—my mom working from 8:00 a.m. to 6:00 p.m. at Koret, a garment factory in Gastown, while my dad made us bologna sandwiches for lunch before heading out to do the dinner prep at Ho Tak Kee, a wonton noodle restaurant at East Broadway and Kingsway.

My parents had spent the first thirty years of their lives under the veil of Communism in China. The only evidence of their early union was a photograph of their younger selves in muted padded suits—practical, unmaterialistic, devoid of any celebratory joys like balloons, a wedding dress, or champagne. Their marriage was a secret, as my mother's immigration papers, which took six years to process during the late stages of the Cultural Revolution, had listed her as single. My mother arrived in Vancouver in 1980, single on paper and three months pregnant. My father joined us a year later.

Unlike the Chinese migrants who arrived in the 1960s and 1970s, and then the 1990s, many of whom brought immense wealth and social capital from Hong Kong and Taiwan, my parents were peasants who grew up without the luxuries of an education and access to Western knowledge. Prior to immigrating to Canada, my mother had never ventured farther from home than wherever she could pedal on her bike. The roads were unpaved and we didn't have mountain bikes, my mother often scolded. Throughout my life, she was never shy about reminding me of how privileged I am. I still can't imagine what she went through when she first arrived in Vancouver, clutching a small leather suitcase and having to field questions from immigration officials.

For immigrants like my parents, Chinatown is a lifeline. Its sights and sounds provide a sense of familiarity where newcomers could converse with others in the same dialect, access medical and financial services with relative ease, enjoy a Cantonese homestyle meal, and buy ingredients to make dumplings or noodles that smelled and tasted like home.

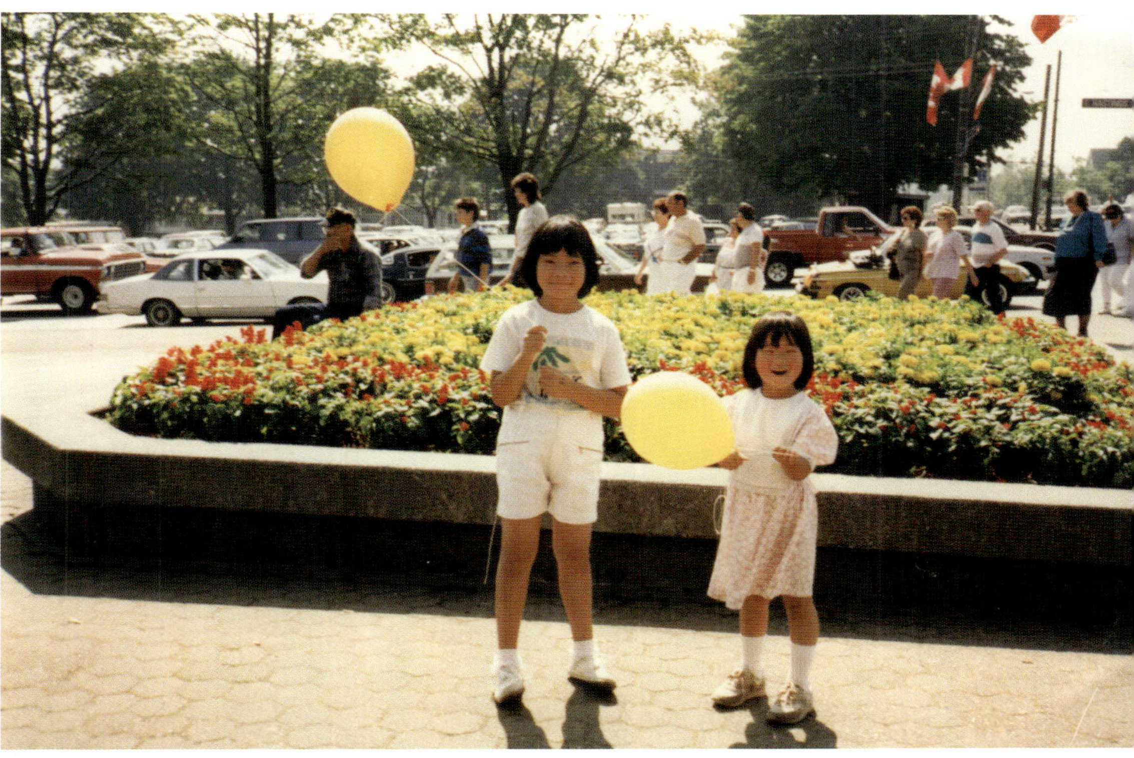

Donna and Susan at the Pacific National Exhibition in 1988

My early experiences of Chinatown were through accompanying my mother on her daily errands, socializing with my parents' friends, or visiting my grandmother. Chinatown was not only a social network and food paradise, but also a place where my mother came alive, where she shed the struggles of an immigrant, where she could be herself as she picked up crumbs of gossip from store clerks, where she flirted with the handsome butcher, and where she complained about hardships to the herbalist.

Now I wonder what happens to someone like my mother when neighbourhoods where they once belonged are displaced or disappear like my red balloon.

It's odd how you remember buried childhood memories.

The memory of the red balloon came rushing back as I was seated across from Carol Lee, philanthropist, entrepreneur, and co-founder of the Vancouver Chinatown Foundation. We were in her restaurant, Chinatown BBQ on East Pender, enjoying a cup of lychee tea. Carol's grandfather had paved the way for her family when he opened Foo Hung Curios in the 1920s. The Chinese weren't allowed to work in many professions, so they had to be entrepreneurs to survive, Carol explained. I thought back to my parents' struggles and my father's brief flirtation with owning his own restaurant, my weekends waiting tables and wrapping dumplings, the smell of the hot kitchen as the flames licked the bottom of the shiny wok. It was the only way to make money, Carol added.

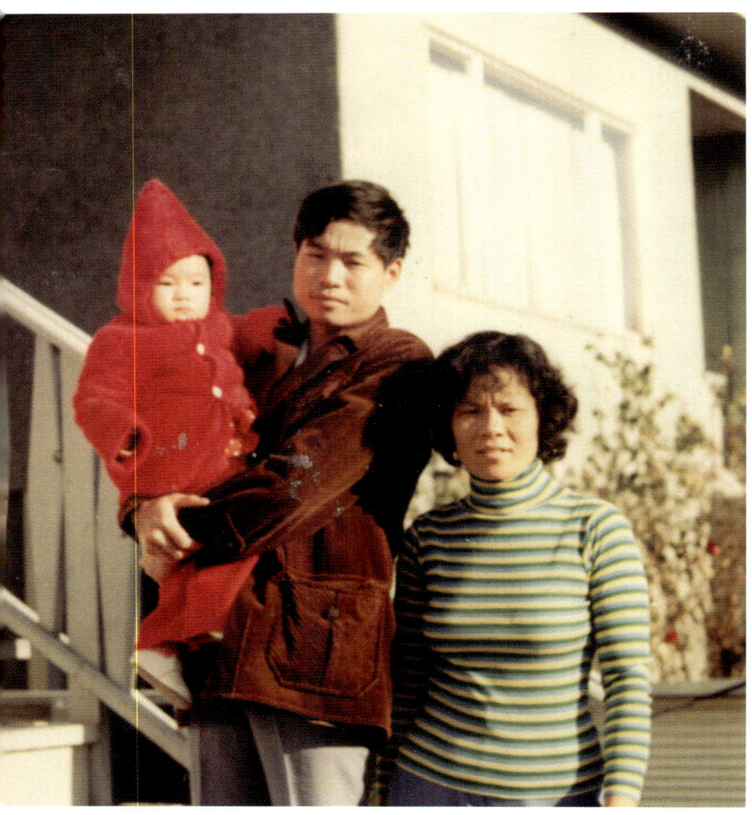

Donna, Dad, and Mom in 1981

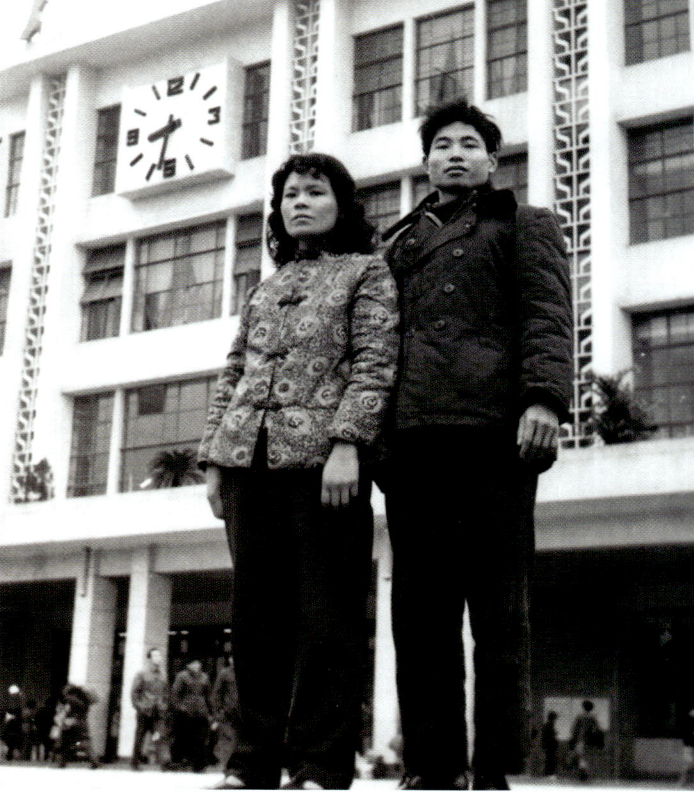

Mom and Dad in front of Guangzhou train station in 1980

In the days following our conversation, I couldn't help but question whether my memory of the red balloon was real. I started questioning my memory of Chinatown as a bustling commercial epicentre, busy enough that I could still feel the discomfort of being wedged between people, the loud bellowing vendors, the mixture of smells both good and bad, the sounds of different dialects melding together like the soundtrack of my childhood.

Was it a dream? Why did I only remember the red balloon while sitting in Chinatown, in a restaurant whose décor reminded me of a Chinatown I visited as a child? One where we spent early mornings sipping on hot tea and dining on har gow, pork siu mai, shrimp rice rolls, and sticky rice wraps. What does place mean to identity and the preservation of memory? If a place is lost, what happens to our memories and our connection to a piece of our heritage? If Chinatown is lost, what impact will it have on my own identity as a Canadian of Chinese heritage? If Chinatown disappears, what does it mean for Vancouver and Canadian history, both of which remain incomplete without the Chinese Canadian chapter? Will we brush all the struggles and triumphs of the Chinese community under the rug, sweep away the resilience and adaptability of earlier settlers?

What if Chinatown disappears into thin air like my red balloon?

Illustrating Vancouver's Chinatown

Vancouver's Chinatown was a bustling commercial hub in the 1960s and 1970s, and once a self-sufficient community for early Chinese settlers. Like many Chinatowns around the world, Vancouver's began to decline in the early 1980s, with shifting priorities among the Chinese community and evolving migration patterns that introduced a group of cosmopolitan and highly educated Chinese who didn't necessarily identify with the old Chinatown.

In Vancouver, the new generation of Chinese immigrants who arrived after 1967 contributed to the emergence of the new Chinese middle class as they began taking on professional jobs that were historically closed to the Chinese. In addition, the preference for business migrants in the 1980s and fears associated with Hong Kong's return to China in 1997 triggered new waves of Chinese immigrants to Canada, many of whom brought substantial wealth and human capital. Socioeconomic changes in Vancouver, as well as elsewhere in Canada, permitted middle-class Chinese to move into better neighbourhoods, reducing the community's dependence on Chinatown. This encouraged the beginnings of new "Chinatowns" in the suburbs, with shiny shopping malls fully equipped with barbeque meat shops, noodle restaurants, and herbalists.

Since the 1990s, the decline of commercial activity in Chinatown has been coupled with concerns regarding safety in the neighbourhood and gentrification. In 2021, Jordan Eng, director of the Vancouver Chinatown Business Improvement Association (BIA), noted that unlike other neighbourhood associations, the Chinatown BIA spends

50 percent of its budget on preventing vandalism and crime.[2] Repeat vandalism and graffiti in Chinatown has left business owners frustrated with the effort and time required to clean up the damage only for it to be repeated the following day. In addition, reports of violence in Chinatown because of its proximity to the Downtown Eastside (DTES) have dissuaded Vancouver residents and tourists from visiting the area. Chinatown's commercial activity was further exacerbated by the global pandemic, which fostered additional anxiety within the community as anti-Asian racism increased 717 percent.

In June 2021, at a time when global events forced us to look inward, I dusted off my camera and embarked on a trip to Chinatown as a local tourist. I had been a regular in Chinatown prior to the pandemic, attending family dim sum expeditions at Floata Restaurant and guiltily supporting gentrified businesses—dining at eateries like Sai Woo and Fat Mao, drinking cocktails at the Keefer Bar and Mamie Taylor's, sipping coffee at Propaganda and Musette, and gorging on pistachio vegan ice cream at Umaluma. Although criticized for diluting the character of the neighbourhood, many of these non-Chinese or fusion establishments were what brought me back to Chinatown as an adult and made me feel that this was the Chinatown of my generation. But in 2021, the deserted streets were a stark contrast to the busy Chinatown of my childhood, let alone pre-pandemic Chinatown.

As I peered from behind the camera lens, I wondered how I'd grown up in Vancouver without ever noticing the details of these beautiful buildings. They were each unique—a mixture of styles, East meets West, storeys added on later, mezzanine floors, stained-glass windows, narrow stairways. Their individual beauty and layered history ached with deterioration—chipping paint, unstable balconies, broken windows, graffiti. How did this happen? Besides the Mah Society Building, the Lim Sai Hor Building, and Wing Sang, very few of the historical buildings had been restored to their former beauty. It further saddened me to see that Ming Wo Cookware, a legacy business that had been in Chinatown for more than a hundred years, was gone.

Even prior to the pandemic, the historical buildings, many of which are owned by clan-based associations, struggled to raise money and support to maintain the structures. Populated by an older generation of Chinese who were central to building a supportive community for early immigrants, the associations have struggled to attract a new generation of supporters who can carry on their responsibilities and traditions. Although the buildings are tangible artifacts, their deterioration also affects intangible assets such as language, knowledge, and traditions passed down from ancestors.

In July 2021, I completed my first painting of a building in Vancouver's Chinatown, a three-storey brick building on East Pender where Bamboo Village currently resides. This book features a collection of illustrations inspired by a neighbourhood that has a special place in my heart. Through documenting key historical buildings such as the Chinese Benevolent Association, the Wing Sang, Ming Wo, and Chin Wing Chun, I have tried to capture what the buildings looked like at a time when Chinatown was an economic and commercial hub. In doing so, this book invites questions regarding place and memory, as well as a dialogue that unravels and reimagines a Chinatown that once was and could be, and asks:

- What lessons can we learn from the resilience and perseverance of early Chinese settlers?
- What traditions, knowledge, and memories are lost if historical buildings deteriorate?
- What is lost when local businesses, some of which are over one hundred years old, close their doors?

Illustrations provide a visual way to tell a story and offer the opportunity to discuss the meaning behind history, silence, reconciliation, and resilience. Writing and illustrating the history of a racialized group often involves piecing together a broken puzzle, one where someone has deliberately hidden the pieces. In conducting research for this book, I've had endless conversations about the inconsistencies in when these buildings were constructed, what they were used for, and who occupied them and when. The historical gaps surrounding Chinatown—from its sparse history in books to inconsistencies in government records—have left me asking more questions than there are answers for.

In saying this, this book has taught me a valuable lesson—that there is immense agency and power in silence, and often silence is the best form of protection among racialized groups. Silence, however, is uncomfortable, especially for a researcher. But it is this discomfort that has made me appreciate how sometimes the best stories are embedded in the sights, sounds, and smells of a place, where a visit to a barbeque meat shop magically transports you to a different time or unravels buried childhood memories, like my red balloon.

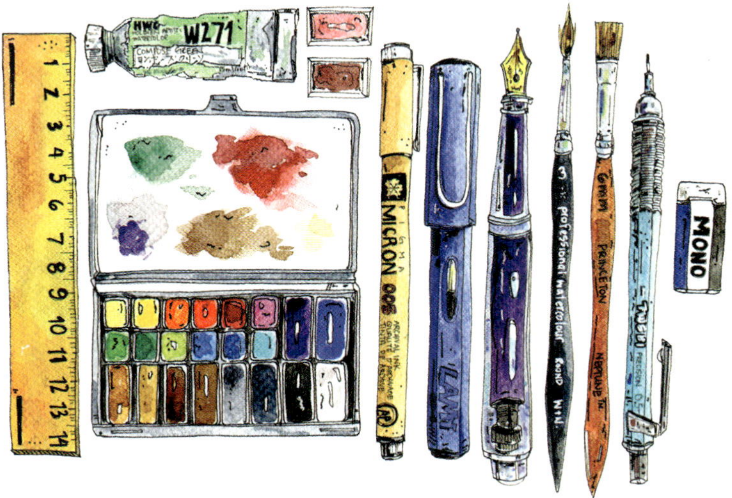

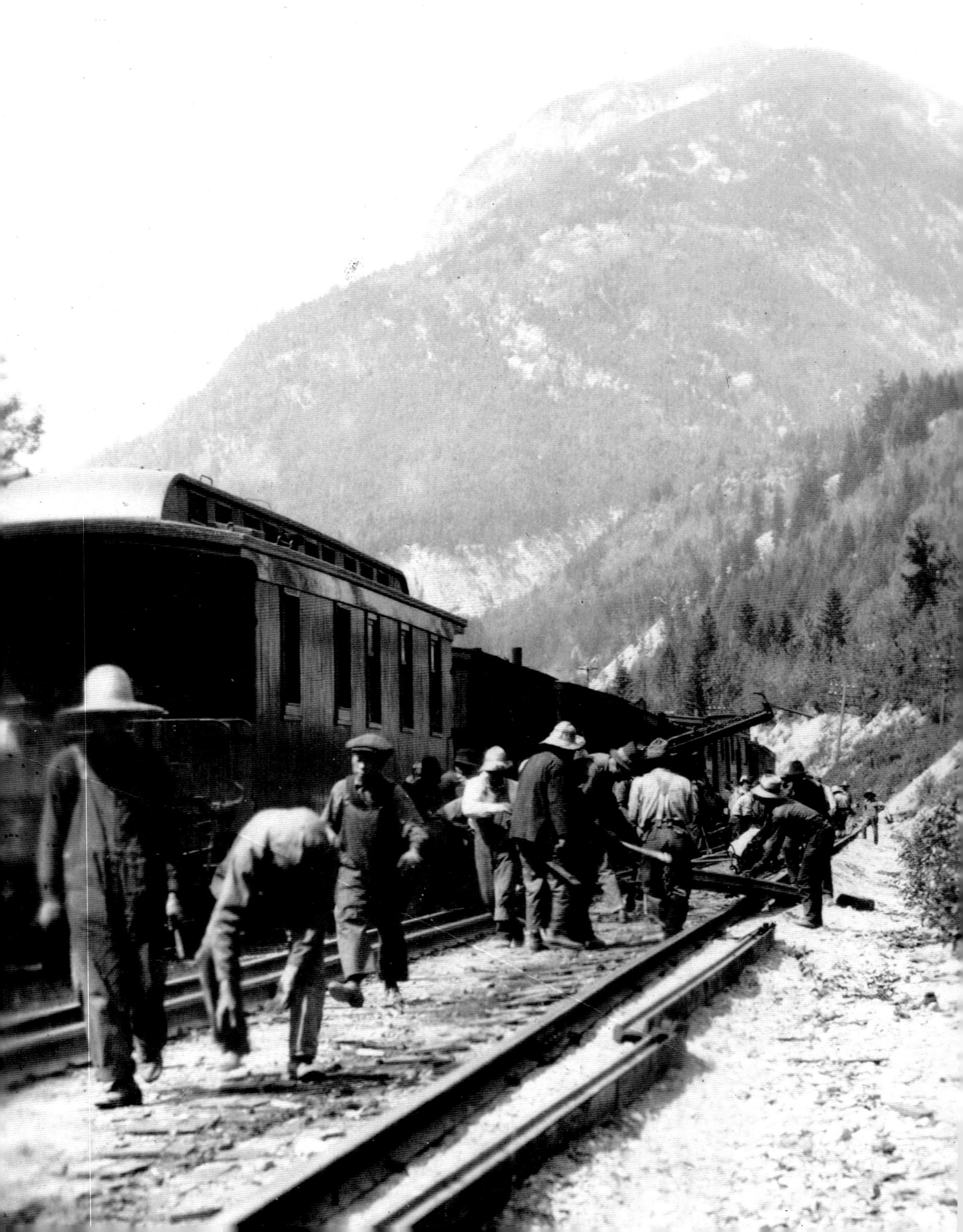

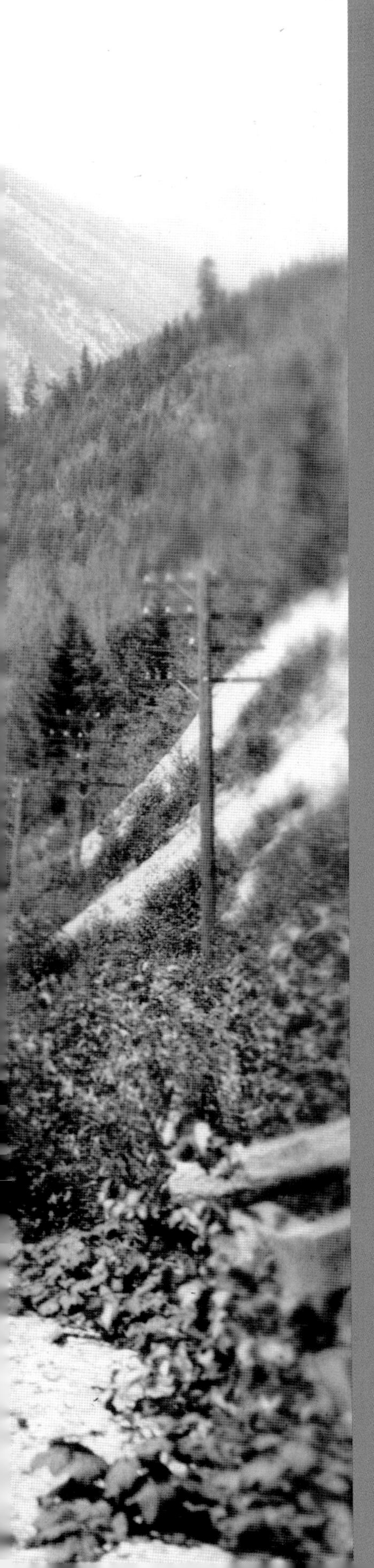

CHAPTER 1

Bachelors, Railways, and Old-World Politics

Throughout the nineteenth century, Chinese sojourners ventured overseas in response to political instability, rising crime, and socioeconomic inequalities in China. In Guangdong Province, agricultural reforms had failed to meet the demands of a growing population, leaving many vulnerable to crime and banditry as the rest of the country faced political and economic turmoil under a weakening state. For many in Guangdong, an overseas sojourn was characterized as a sacrificial journey to accumulate wealth before returning to the homeland for a better life.[1]

Migration for economic gain wasn't new to southern China. In 1757, Guangzhou was designated the main trade port to the West, leading to the transformation of the local economy and fostering the growth of trade-savvy migrants. Even before sojourners ventured overseas, residents in southern China had established intricate "pseudo-family" networks based on clan, surname, or regional affiliations that helped migrants travelling from one region to another. In 1858, when the Chinese community in California learned of the discovery of gold in British Columbia, it was this network that spread word that another "gold mountain" had been found. When an estimated seventeen thousand Chinese labourers arrived in Canada between 1881 and 1885 for the extension of the Canadian Pacific Railway (CPR), their journey was made possible through this established network.

The first Chinese in British Columbia arrived as prospective miners for the gold rush (1858–69) in the Fraser River, Kootenays, and Cariboo. Some miners had resided in California and travelled to BC by land or sea, and were followed by a chain of migration a year later when word spread throughout villages in southern China. Migrants travelling by sea mainly arrived at the fur-trading port of Victoria on what was later named Vancouver Island.[2] By the 1860s, a small Chinatown had developed in Victoria to serve sojourners from China and transient workers returning from the mines. Other Chinatowns would develop wherever the Chinese gathered and worked, such as in New Westminster and Nanaimo, as well as small communities in Cumberland and throughout BC's interior. By 1886, a small population of ninety Chinese had settled in what would become Vancouver's Chinatown.[3]

Vancouver's Chinatown started on the northern mudflats of False Creek along present-day Carrall and Pender Streets. The land the Chinese settled on was once seasonal villages frequented by the Coast Salish Peoples, whose way of life was intricately interwoven into the natural landscape. Prior to the development of a Chinese settlement along Carrall and East Pender, the area would flood during high tide, transforming it into a connecting waterway that the Coast Salish used to travel between False Creek and Burrard Inlet. As the False Creek shoreline was filled in, businesses developed along East Pender, Columbia, and Carrall Streets, in addition to Canton Alley and Shanghai Alley, consequently disrupting and displacing Indigenous Peoples and their ways of life.

Until the 1920s, the commercial activity of the Chinese was largely confined to East Pender between Carrall and Main Streets, with some businesses expanding eastward toward Gore Avenue. As the population mainly consisted of labourers, tailors, and businesses such as laundries, restaurants, public baths, grocers, social hubs, and theatres for Cantonese opera developed to accommodate their needs.

The gender ratio between men and women in early Chinatown was stark—approximately sixty women in a population of two thousand in 1901. This resulted in a "bachelor" society made up mainly of men. Even as the population grew a decade later, women were still outnumbered twenty-eight to one, with most belonging to merchant households. Some men had wives and children in China, but Confucian culture restricted women from travelling overseas and confined them at home to care for the family. Even when men wanted to bring their families to Canada, financial instability and racial legislation, such as the Head Tax and the Exclusion Act, prevented family reunification. As the Exclusion Act barred any Chinese from entering Canada between 1923 and 1947, many Chinatown "bachelors" were not able to reunite with their families until the act was lifted. Some waited until the late 1950s or 1960s to sponsor their families because of additional restrictions and requirements, such as acquiring citizenship to qualify as a sponsor.[4]

Merchants played a key role in early Chinatown, often providing housing, contracting employment, sending remittances, and spurring political activities in the homeland. Merchants such as Yip Sang

The resilience and perseverance of early Chinese migrants helped carve out a stepping stone for subsequent generations to succeed.

and Chang Toy helped build a network that initiated formal organizations such as the Chinese Benevolent Association (CBA), which would become the umbrella organization that represented all Chinese regardless of surname or background. Aware that their sojourn in Canada was temporary, many early migrants were invested in improving the situation in China so they could one day return. Some also invested their time and finances into political organizations such as the Chinese Empire Reform Association (CERA), which was created to modernize the dysfunctional Qing monarchy without overthrowing it. Merchants such as Yip Sang hoped that a reformed governing system in China would facilitate renewed stability, which

would also benefit trade opportunities between Canada and China. However, other organizations such as the Chee Kung Tong, which supported Dr. Sun Yat-sen's revolutionary efforts, felt otherwise, and went as far as to mortgage their properties to support overthrowing the Qing.

As early migrants began planting roots in Canada, government legislation increasingly restricted their movement and livelihood. Upon the completion of the CPR in 1885, the federal government passed the Head Tax to slow the entry of Chinese into Canada. Initially set at fifty dollars, the tax increased to one hundred dollars in 1901 and to five hundred dollars in 1903 before the Chinese Exclusion Act was passed in 1923. In Vancouver's Chinatown, policies and urban development perpetually challenged Chinese settlers with expropriation, redevelopment, and policing. In 1912, the expropriation of the original Sam Kee Building on Dupont (later Pender) left one of Chinatown's prominent merchants, Chang Toy, with a sliver of land that was deemed impossible to build on. Additionally, prior to being home to the Dr. Sun Yat-sen Classical Chinese Garden and the Chinese Cultural Centre, the land that was once the False Creek mudflats was home to a row of wooden false-front buildings. In 1904, the south side of Pender was purchased by the railroad, resulting in the expropriation of the wooden buildings for industrial use.

Despite exclusionary and discriminatory circumstances, the resilience and perseverance of early Chinese migrants helped carve out a stepping stone for subsequent generations to succeed. These sacrifices are further demonstrated by the buildings commissioned by early Chinese settlers that remain standing today.

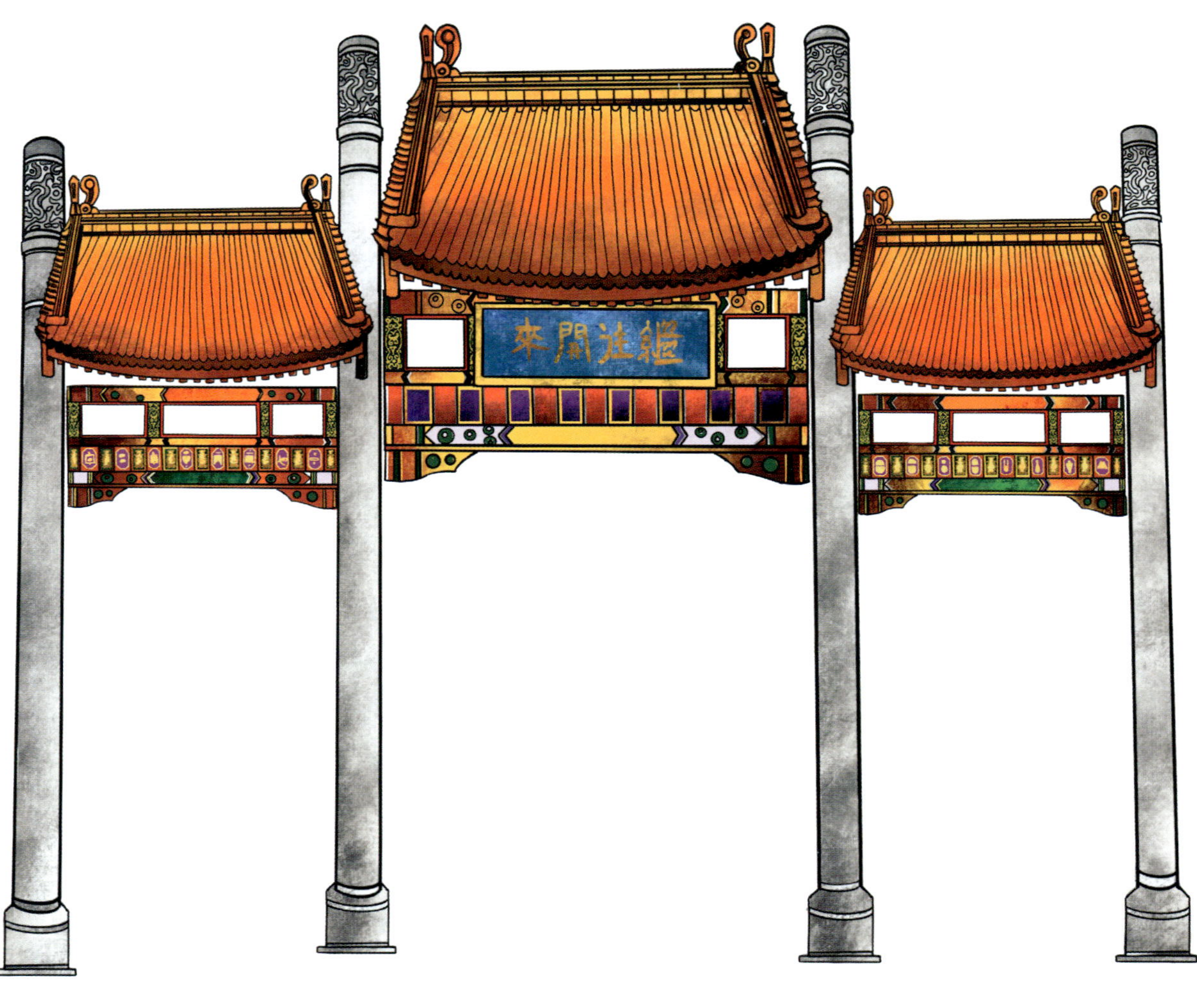
鑑進閒來

Architecture in Chinatown

Chinatown's architecture is more than just bricks and mortar; embedded within its unique mix of clan and society buildings, rooming houses, and multipurpose commercial structures is a story of perseverance that lends itself to a living history. Many of the buildings have evolved with the area's socioeconomic changes—reinvented into temporary boarding for transient workers, permanent homes for families, entertainment venues, restaurants, cafés, barber shops, grocery stores, community space, retail, offices, meeting areas, and cultural institutions. Chinatown's architecture exhibits versatility through its ability to accommodate a multitude of purposes that can be interpreted as Chinese, Western, or something in between.

The mixture of architectural styles in Chinatown demonstrates the struggle early Chinese settlers experienced in carving out a space for the community. Many of Chinatown's historical buildings were commissioned by wealthy merchants who contributed immense capital and influence by hiring some of the city's best architects, such as Thomas Ennor Julian, Bryan and Gillam, W. T. Whiteway, and R. T. Perry. Buildings such as Yip Sang's Wing Sang Company were constructed to suit both business and residential, where joining structures were added later to accommodate a growing family. Society buildings such as the Mah Society and the Cheng Wing Yeong Tong also underwent structural changes to meet the organization's evolving needs, adding storeys to the existing building. The construction of new buildings and the adjustments to existing ones show not only the versatility, layered character, and flexibility in design, but also the determination of early Chinese settlers who overcame discrimination when negotiating their right to place.

William Henry Chow, known as the first Chinese Canadian architect, contributed to the development of buildings despite legal restrictions preventing non-citizens from professions such as architecture and engineering. Born in southern China in 1874, W. H. Chow arrived in Canada in 1894 and was later listed in newspaper advertisements as a contractor and timber dealer rather than an architect. He was initially included in the BC Society of Architects, where he signed off as "architect" on his building drawings, but he was later denied admission to the profession when the Architectural Institute of British Columbia was incorporated in 1920. W. H. Chow continued to work closely with leading architects such as W. T. Whiteway and played an integral role in developing Chinatown, including altering buildings such as the Chinese Times, Chinese Empire Reform Association, Yue Shan, Ming Wo, and 141–147 East Pender.

Certain architectural characteristics stand out in Chinatown—namely, the recessed balconies, narrow stairways leading to society meeting rooms, mezzanine floors, and array of signage. Recessed balconies, characterized by an open exterior set into the building's facade, are featured on buildings like the CBA, Ming Wo, Mah Society, Chinese Freemasons, and Chin Wing Chun. Also found in southern China, Hong Kong, Macao, and other Chinese diasporic communities, recessed balconies provide temperature regulation, an open space for ceremonial functions such as ancestor worship, and a place for clothes to dry and children to play.[5]

Mezzanine floors, often constructed as an addition between the ground and second floors, are common throughout Chinatown but are not unique to the area. Characterized by their low ceiling height, mezzanines further demonstrate the versatility of space and the ingenious adjustments made to buildings to accommodate the community's needs. Often visible from the building's exterior, mezzanine floors have been transformed into versatile spaces for accommodation, dining, events, recreation, storage, and even as a workspace for typesetters for the longest-serving Chinese Canadian newspaper, the *Chinese Times.*

Chinatown also features characteristics similar to other diasporic Chinese communities such as red lanterns, ornate lampposts, tiled roofing, lion statues, and a majestic gate. Some elements, especially on boxy one- or two-storey storefronts east of Main Street, were added after Chinatown was designated a historic site in 1971, whereas other buildings were purposely built with Chinese-inspired features. The addition of cultural motifs helped to distinguish and celebrate Chinatown as a historical and cultural space that residents, organizations, and shop owners would be proud of. Motifs such as dragons and phoenixes, combined with colour schemes of red, gold, blue, and green, which are thought to symbolize luck, happiness, prosperity, and peace, appear on building columns, lampposts, and throughout the Dr. Sun Yat-sen Garden.[6] In the 1950s and 1960s, neon lights lined East Pender as the reunification of families and arrival of new migrants brought new life to Chinatown. Buildings were reinvented to accommodate families rather than single men, while commercial spaces transformed from barbershops, laundries, and gambling dens into large restaurants with entertainment areas for a new generation.

In 2002, the Millennium Gate was built to demarcate Chinatown's boundary. The three-storey structure honours the sacrifices of Chinese settlers with tall poles holding up an orange terracotta tiled roof, ornate panels inscribed with characters that say, "Remember the past and look toward the future," and lions guarding the entrance.[7] The Millennium Gate sits just west of the site of a temporary wooden gate built for a 1912 visit of the Duke of Connaught.

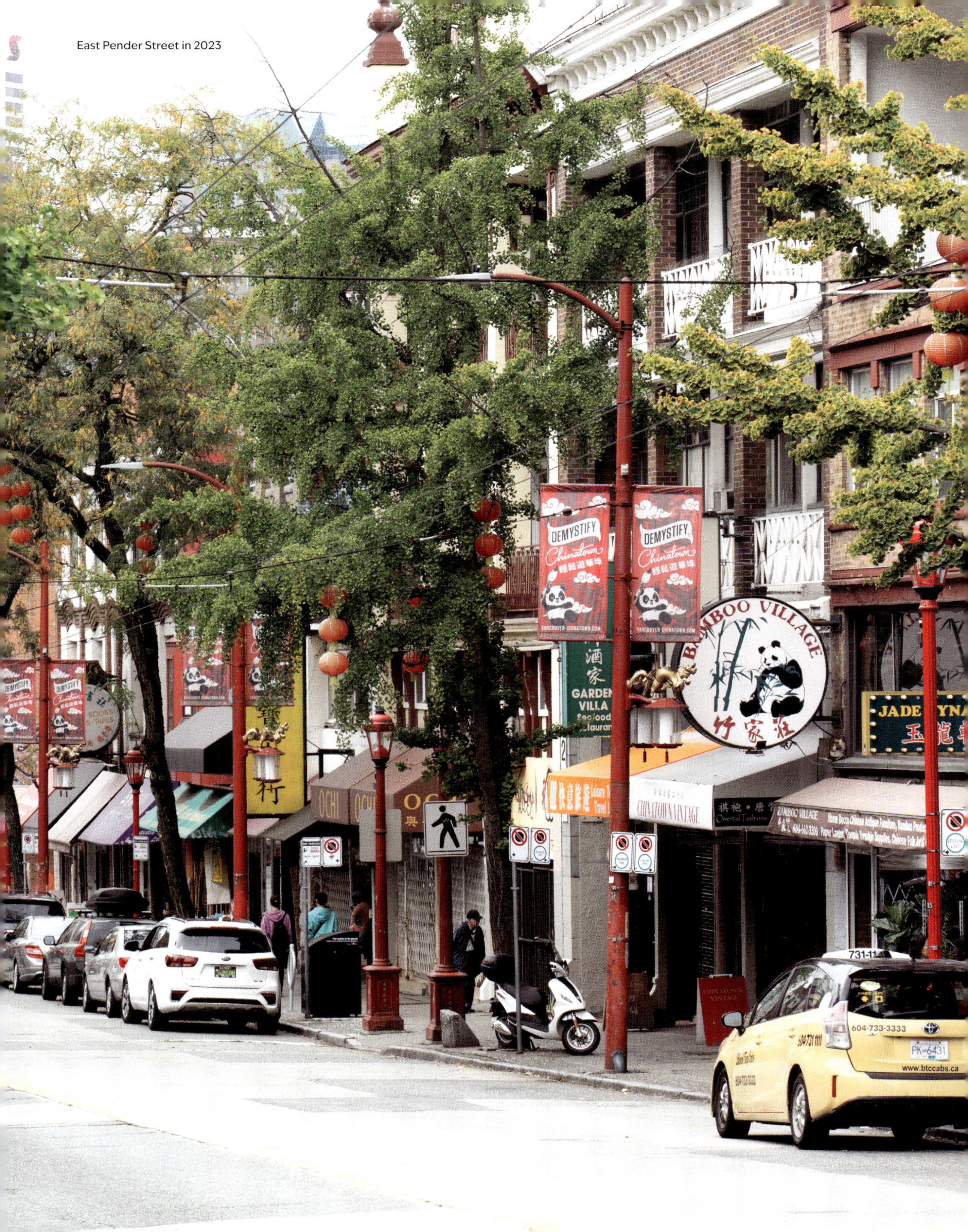

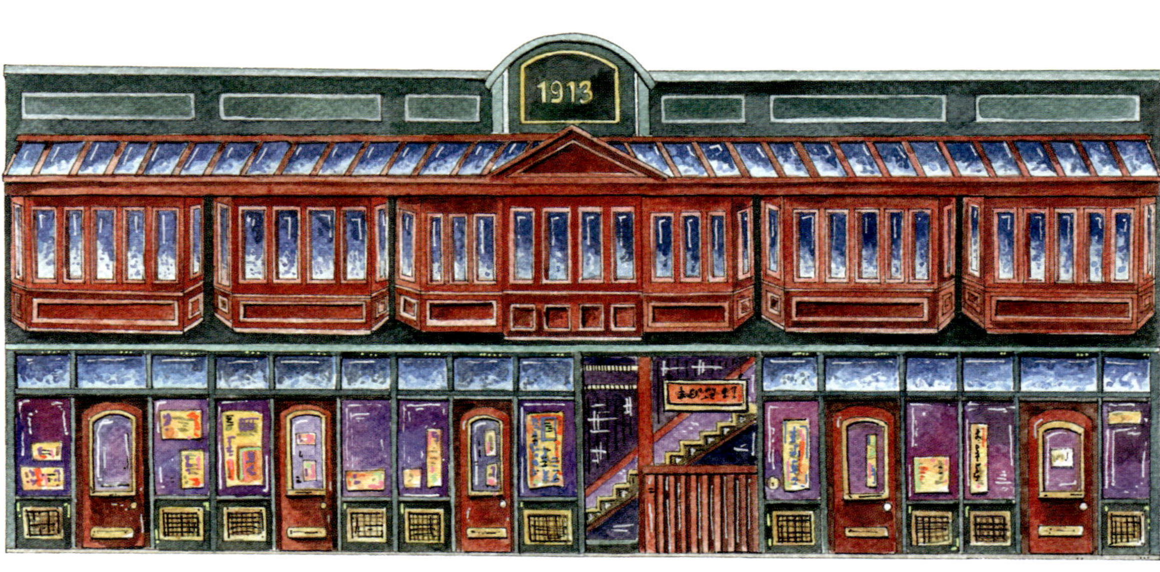

1913

Sam Kee Building
8 West Pender
Built 1913

In 1907, the Sam Kee Company was one of four businesses in Chinatown that made more than $150,000, six times more than the average income of two-thirds of Chinatown's businesses.[8] The owner, Chang Toy, operated multifaceted ventures such as import-export, retail, charcoal and fuel sales, labour contracting, fishing and sugar, steamship ticket sales, and real estate development.[9] Recognizing the importance of a "pseudo-family," Chang Toy honoured clan networks by providing shelter, a meeting space, employment connections, remittance services, and community to labourers from his hometown.

Chang Toy was born in 1857 to Hakka peasants in Poon Yue County of Guangdong Province. Despite the socioeconomic setbacks associated with his father's passing, Chang Toy acquired a basic education and an arranged marriage. In 1876, within two years of arriving in Victoria, Chang Toy was offered a business proposition by Chu Lai of Wing Chong Company, which he declined so he could pursue opportunities in New Westminster. Chang Toy would remain close acquaintances with Chu Lai, who would serve as a wholesaler to the laundry and grocery store he later opened in Vancouver.

Merchants were middlemen—often possessing the business acumen, social influence, and language ability to weave between different groups and represent the community's interests, while playing a key political role within Chinatown and the homeland. Leading merchants such as Chang Toy and Yip Sang (Wing Sang Company) supported the Chinese Empire Reform Association (CERA), organized two early chambers of commerce (1898 and 1899), and formed the Chinese Benevolent Association (CBA). After the 1907 anti-Asian riots, Chang Toy partnered with the president of the CBA to purchase weapons for other business owners. In 1900, he served as president of CERA, where he helped establish the Chinese School and provided accommodation for travelling scholars in the Sam Kee Building.

As an instrumental import-export company, the Sam Kee acted as a wholesaler of rice and other goods from China and exported fish from British Columbia to China and Japan. The company also held real estate properties, including ten lots in Chinatown, land in Gastown, property in downtown Vancouver and in Nanaimo on Vancouver Island, and water frontage along False Creek and in southeast Vancouver. Chang Toy owned five hotels and held more holdings outside of Chinatown than within.[10] The Sam

Kee Company also helped sojourners send remittances home to support their families by acting as a clearing house, receiving money and then forwarding it by personal carriers or mail to firms in southern China that would distribute funds to the appropriate recipients.

In 1912, the city informed Chang Toy that his building on the southwest corner of Dupont (later Pender) and Carrall was in the way of a road-widening project. After negotiations, Chang Toy was left with a narrow strip of land measuring six feet and two inches wide. Undeterred, he hired architects Bryan and Gillam to design a steel-framed building with bay windows extending over the street to increase the second floor and the width of the building. The two-storey building served multiple purposes, with retail on the ground floor and office space upstairs. The basement, which extends under the sidewalk and is lit by glass blocks (areaways), once housed public baths.

Known as one of the narrowest free-standing buildings in the world, this architectural masterpiece underwent renovations in 1966, 1975, and 2013.[11] In 2015, Jack Chow Insurance renamed the Sam Kee Building the World's Famous Building and installed LED lights and new windows to showcase the interior.[12] Despite never learning how to speak English and retaining traditional dress until his death in 1921, Chang Toy was a pillar of the community and a middleman between cultures, and his building at 8 West Pender continues to symbolize the ingenuity, grit, and tenacious spirit of the Chinese in early Chinatown.

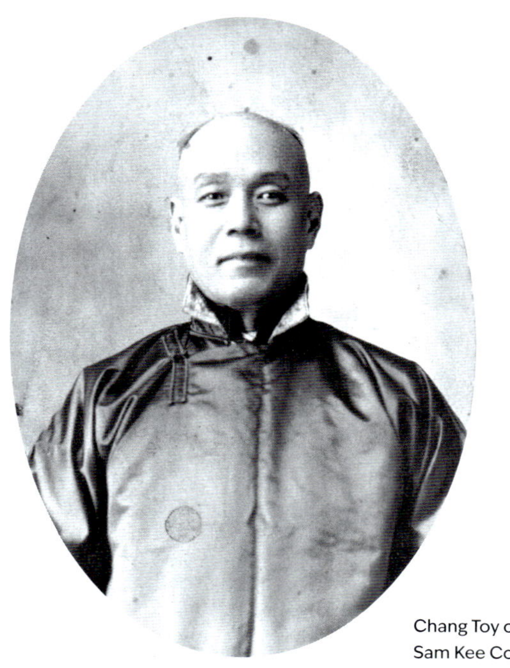

Chang Toy of the
Sam Kee Company, 1905

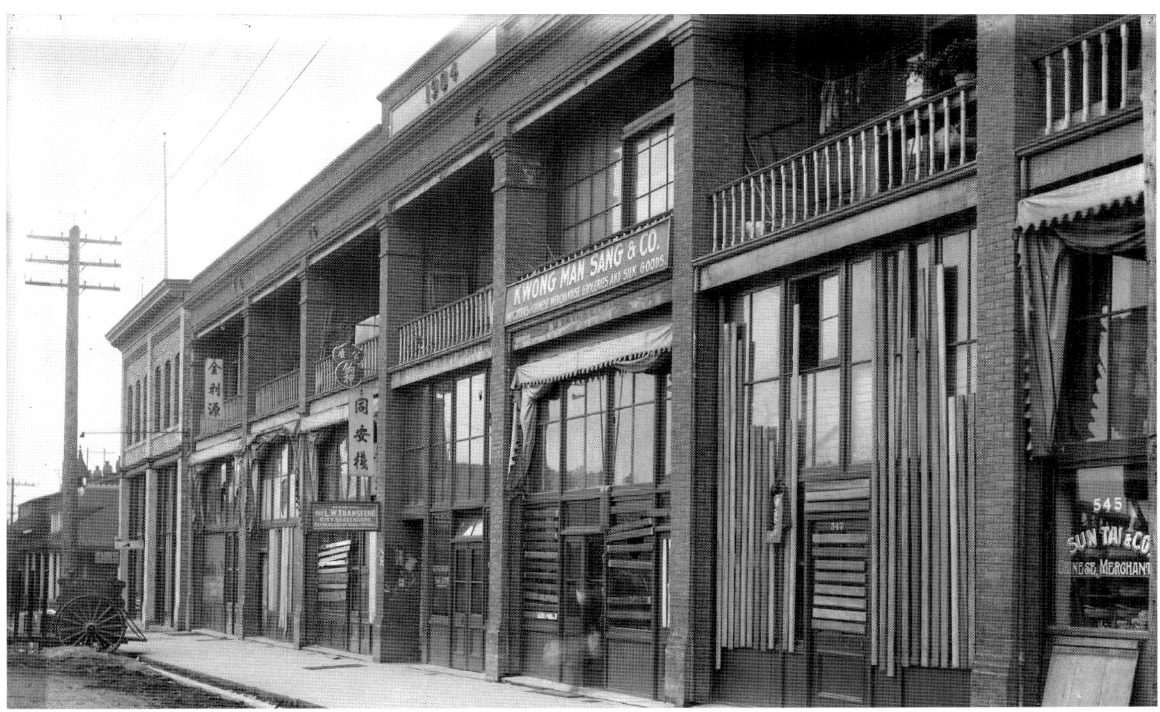

Damage to buildings on Carrall Street from anti-Asian riots, 1907

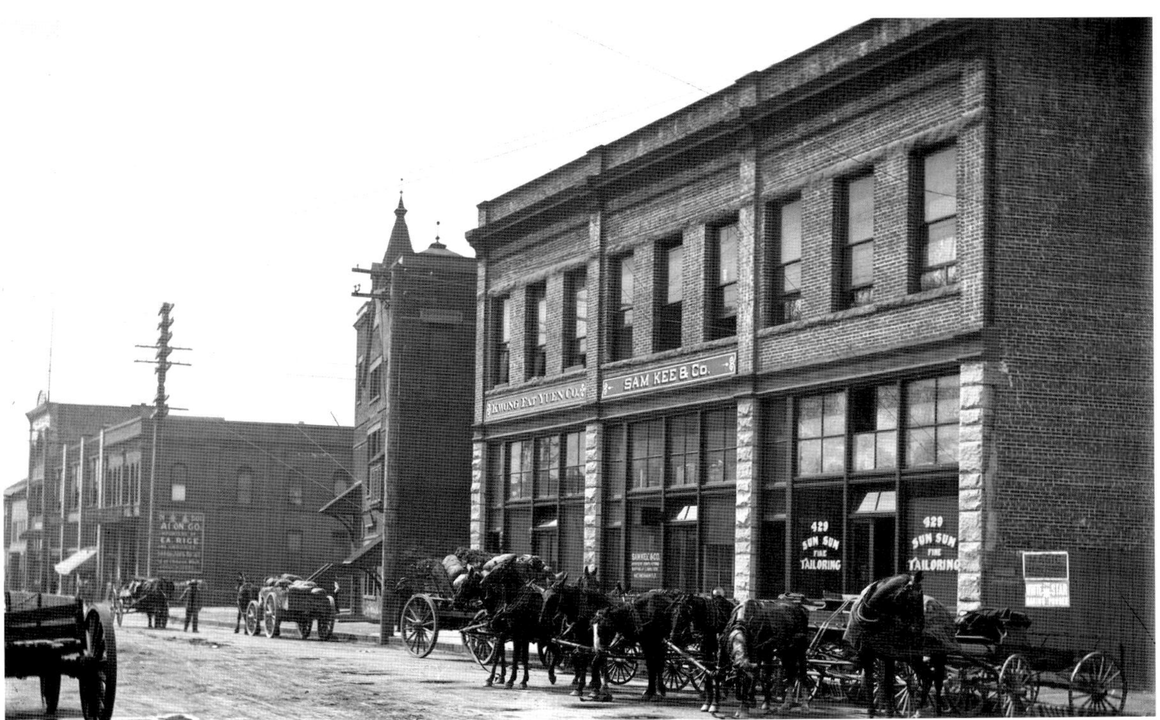

Several of Chang Toy's properties along Carrall Street, 1906

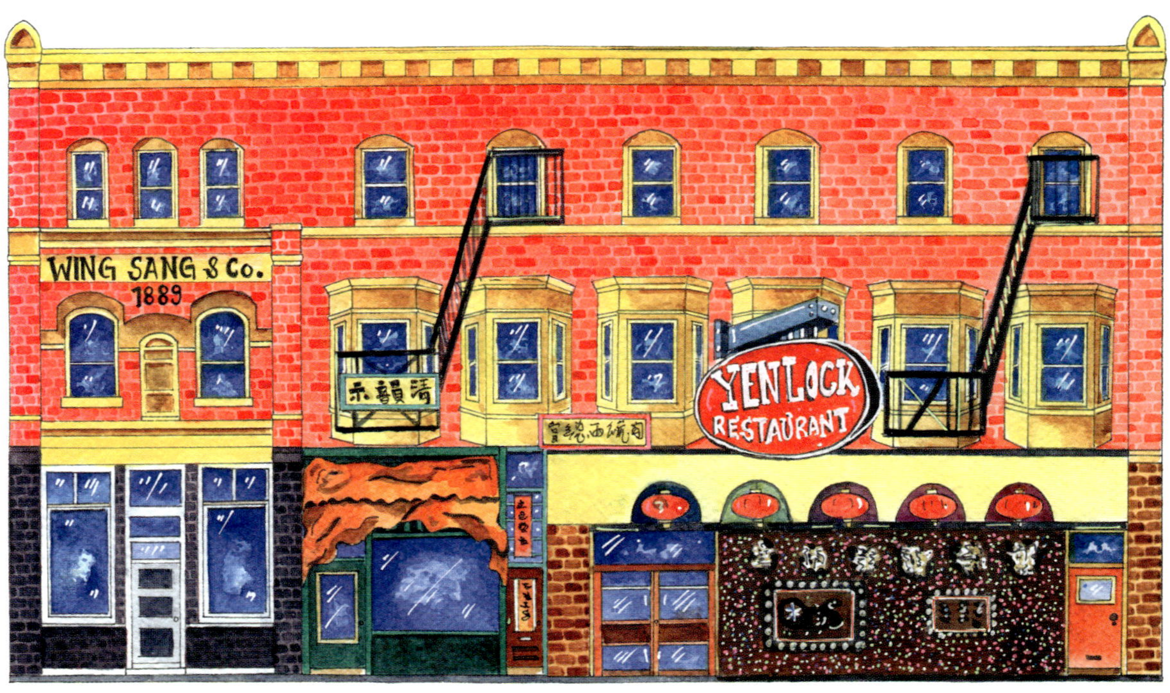

WING SANG & Co.
1889
清韻禾
司硫西鏡寶
YENLOCK
RESTAURANT

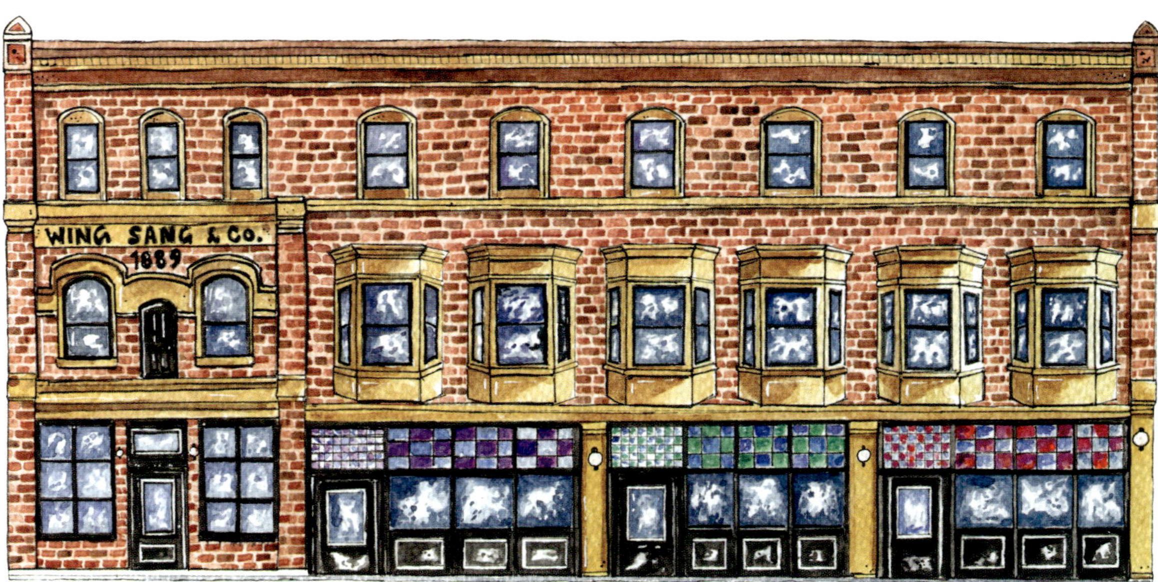

WING SANG & Co.
1889

Wing Sang Building
51–69 East Pender
Built 1889/1901/1912

The mysterious unprotected second-floor door on the Wing Sang Building has always raised curiosity. At first glance, the narrow entrance resembles something out of a fairy tale, a passageway or a trap door that could transport you to a different realm or time. But upon closer examination, your curiosity quickly turns to alarm as you realize that oblivious individuals could open the door thinking it leads to a closet but find themselves sprawled on the sidewalk.

Built in 1889, the Wing Sang Building is the oldest standing brick building in Chinatown. The small unprotected door on the second floor of the original Wing Sang at 51 East Pender provided an alternative entrance for goods without having to depend on the interior stairs. As early Chinatown was built on mudflats, Pender would flood during high tide, allowing goods to be easily unloaded from boats and hoisted up into storage on the second floor. Since then, the watery edges of False Creek have been filled in and the tide no longer infringes upon Pender as it did in the late 1880s.[13]

The expansion of the Wing Sang Building and its multiple uses reflect a period of rapid growth in Chinatown and Vancouver. The larger building that encloses the original two-storey structure was built in 1901 and designed by architect Thomas Ennor Julian (also known for Holy Rosary Cathedral at 646 Richards Street). This building includes six bay windows along the second floor, as well as additional windows on the third floor. To accommodate his growing family of three wives and twenty-three children, owner Yip Sang (1845–1927) had a six-storey addition built behind the Pender Street frontage and separated by a narrow passage.

Yip Sang arrived in San Francisco in 1864 to find his fortune in the California Gold Rush. However, by the 1860s, prospects for individual miners were poor, as remaining gold was only accessible using heavy-duty machinery.[14] Yip Sang found work washing dishes, cooking, and rolling cigars before heading north in 1881 to the goldfields in BC. Many Chinese prospective miners weren't prepared for the cold conditions in BC's interior, which exposed some to starvation and hypothermia before they even reached their destination. Of those who did arrive, thousands were unable to stake claims because of the frozen rivers and rocky terrain. Experienced Chinese miners, having learned from being cheated and looted in California, tended to work stakes that others had abandoned. Having failed to find gold in BC, Yip Sang made his way to Vancouver, where he sold coal door to door.

In 1882, at the age of thirty-seven, Yip Sang met Lee Piu of the Kwong On Wo Company, which supplied the CPR, and his luck started to change. By this time, Yip Sang had taught himself English, and he was hired to keep a record of employment and pay men in the railway camps. From 1882 to 1885, he contracted Chinese men to work on the extension of the railway from Port Moody to Shuswap. Having gained a reputation for working longer hours at lower rates of pay, the Chinese were seen as threats to work prospects. Upon the completion of the CPR in 1885, a fifty-dollar Head Tax was instituted to curb the influx of Chinese migrants.[15]

After a brief trip to China, Yip Sang returned to Vancouver in 1888 as a married man and father, and established his import-export business, the Wing Sang Company. Equipped with a ticket office, the Wing Sang sold tickets for the CPR steamship line and handled both passenger and freight traffic. Yip Sang also imported products from Hong Kong and China, while selling opium, which was legal until 1908. Similar to Chang Toy, Yip Sang dipped into multiple industries, such as labour contracting for fishing and mining. He also provided mail service and operated Wing Sang as a pseudo bank where customers could send remittances back to China.[16]

In his later years, Yip Sang was often found sitting by the front entrance of the Wing Sang Building in his hand-embroidered skullcap, conversing with the community over tea or tobacco while keeping an eye on his family. As one of the most successful early businessmen in Chinatown, with his import-export business alone bringing in fifty thousand dollars a year, Yip Sang used his influence and capital to develop Chinatown. In addition to his influential role in the Chinese Empire Reform Association (CERA), Yip Sang was also crucial to the formation of the Chinese Benevolent Association (CBA), Board of Trade, and the Chinese Hospital, and real estate development in early Chinatown. Known as a disciplinarian, he had twenty-three children and eighty-one grandchildren. He had four wives, but his first wife (Lee Shee) passed away at an early age before he married the others.

The Wing Sang Building has housed Chinatown's first doctor, Wo Fat Bakery, the BC Royal Café, Yen Lock Chop Suey, and the Rennie Museum. In 2023, the Wing Sang Building became home to the Chinese Canadian Museum.[17]

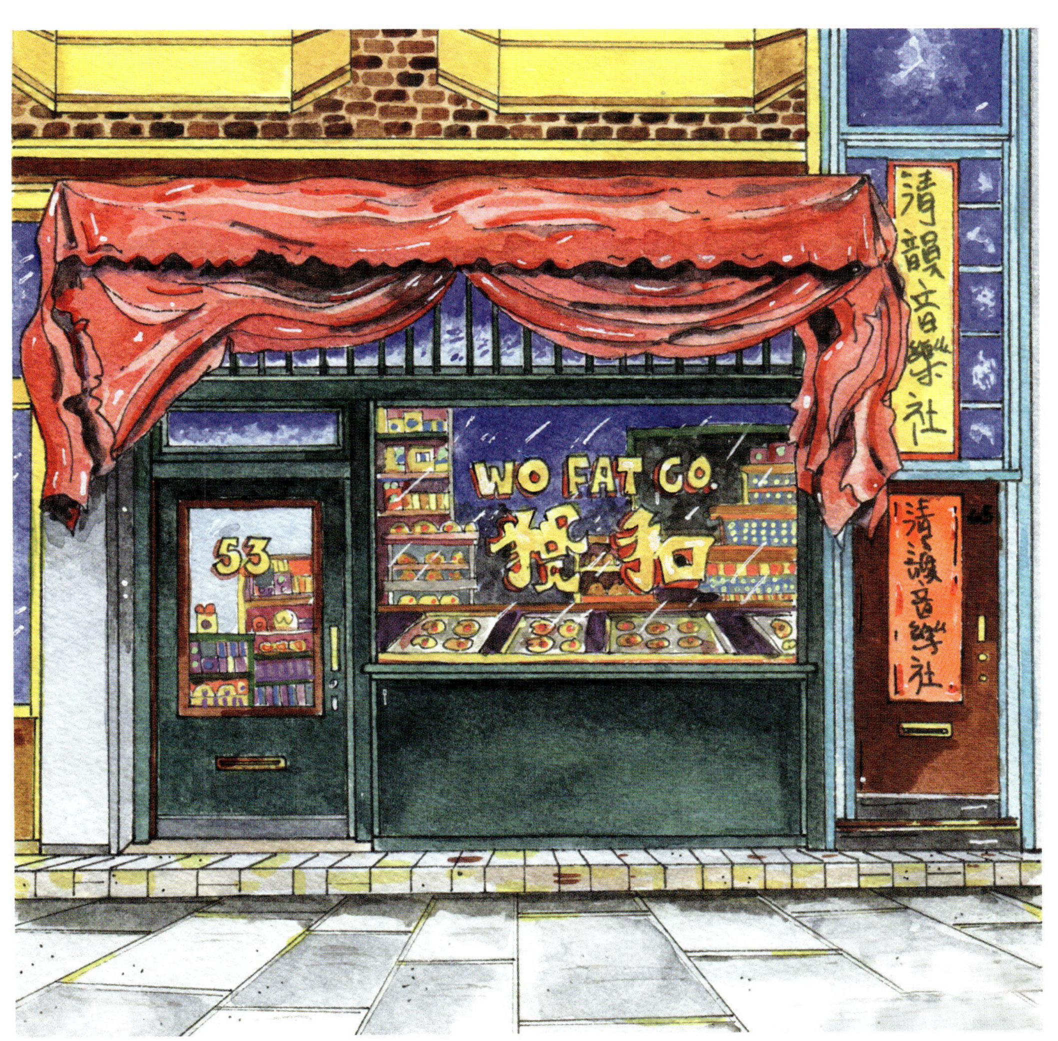

清韻女日樂社
清韻音樂社
53
WO FAT CO.
和和

Family Superstitions

Interview with Lincoln Chew,
descendant of Yip Sang's first wife, Lee Shee

Large families are complicated—even more so when you're a descendant of Yip Sang, who had twenty-three children with four wives.

Lincoln Chew, a descendant of Yip Sang's first wife, Lee Shee, recalls the chain of superstition imposed on his family line because of subsequent deaths in the family. Lee Shee passed away at an early age. Her daughter, Fung Ngor, also faced an early death when her husband passed away during the Great Depression, leaving her as the sole bread-winner and carer of five children. The deaths cast a shadow on Fung Ngor's family despite their status as offspring of Yip Sang's first wife. Fung Ngor's family became the black sheep in the Yip family because of Chinese superstitions that associated widows with bad luck. This also meant that she didn't benefit from connections afforded to other members of the Yip clan.

However, Lincoln shares how one Christmas, as the family was on the brink of starvation, they received a visit from Yip Kew Ghim—the eleventh son of Yip Sang, also known as Dr. Yip in Chinatown. As a child, Lincoln remembers Dr. Yip occasionally visiting his parents' restaurant, the Ho Inn on East Pender. Yip Kew Ghim was a tall, slim man who wore gold-rimmed glasses and reminded Lincoln of a Chinese version of the great American general Joseph Stillman.[18] Dr. Yip started the first health clinic specializing in Western medicine and later went on to manage Mount Saint Joseph Hospital. Yip Sang's son was accompanied by Dong Shee, Yip Sang's second wife, who defied the superstitions to honour the descendants of her husband's first wife by providing a turkey and gifts to celebrate the holiday.

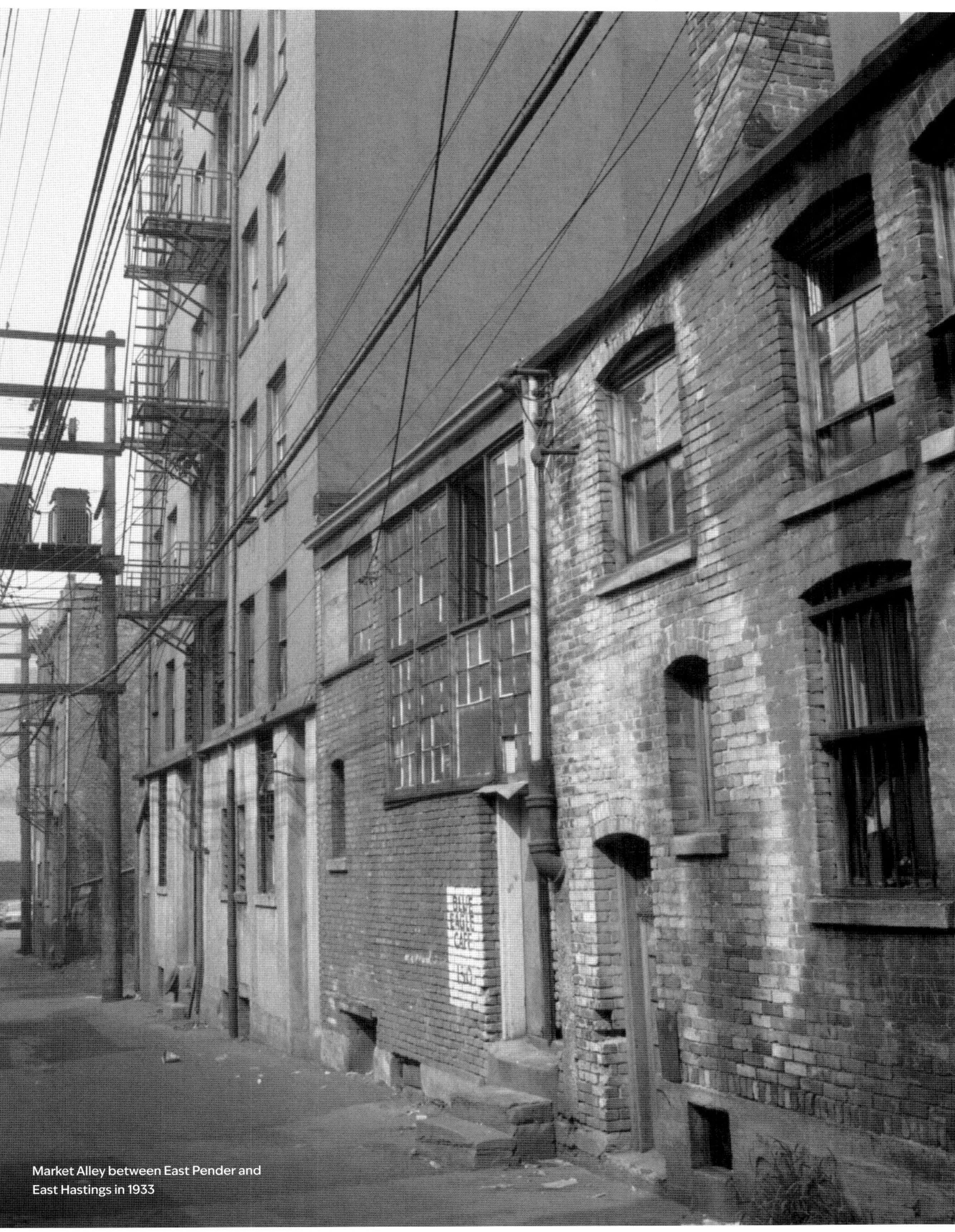

Market Alley between East Pender and
East Hastings in 1933

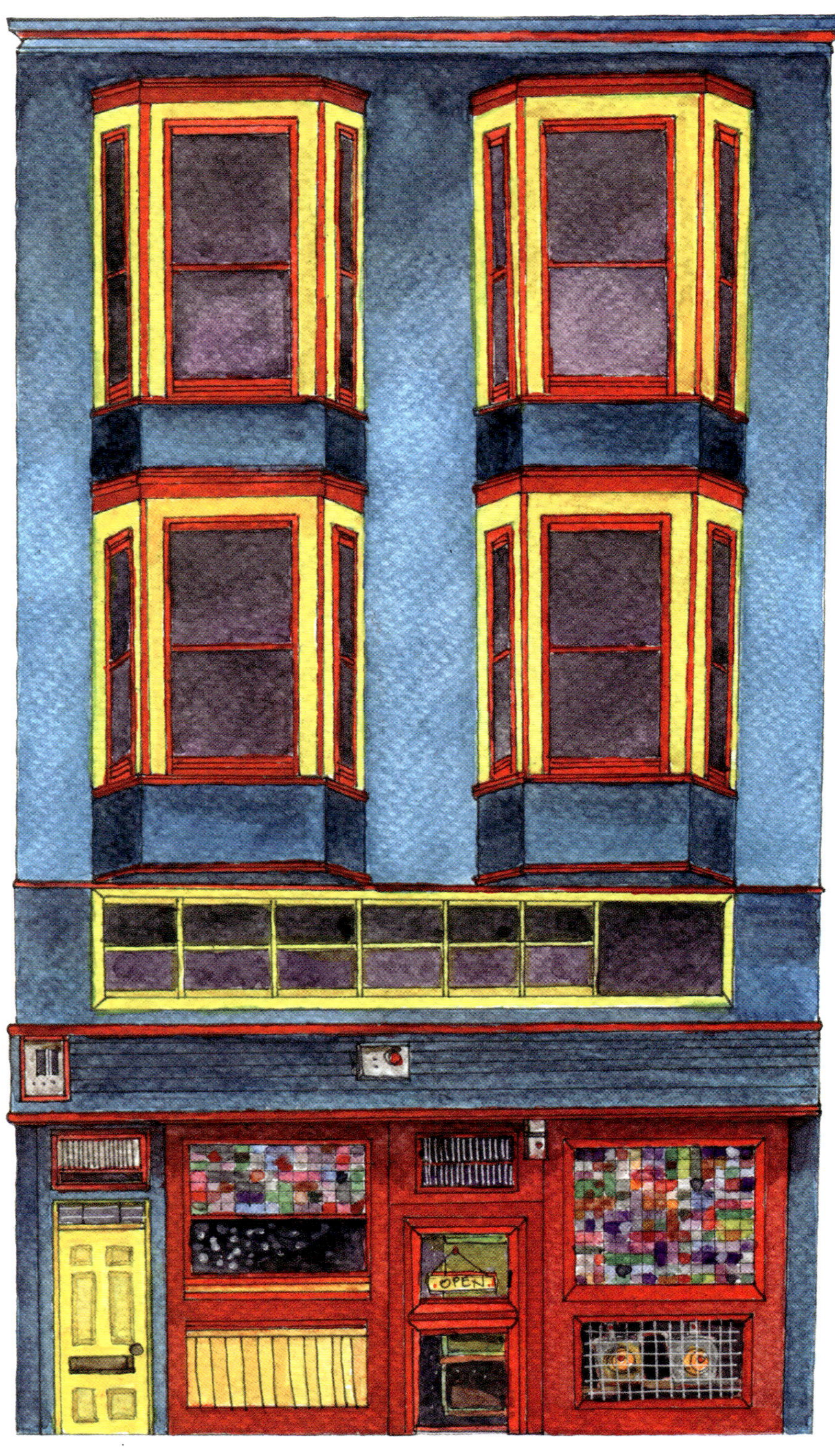

OPEN

Commercial Alleyways
Shanghai Alley and Canton Alley

In 1904, on property recently purchased from the Canadian Pacific Railway, Yip Sang of the Wing Sang Company began constructing four tenement buildings grouped around a private street known as Canton Alley. The alley's storefronts were home to wholesale fruit and vegetable dealers, among other businesses. To the east, the railroad had deeded to the city a piece of land that would become Shanghai Alley, where the Sing Kew Theatre was relocated in 1905. The two alleys contributed heavily to the development of the area's commercial activity.

In August 1944, health officials claimed that the death rate in Chinatown from tuberculosis was six or seven times higher than in other parts of Vancouver and removed three hundred Chinese tenants from their homes in these tenement buildings. In May 1945, however, a public nurse reported that the initial claims were exaggerated, as only 16 percent of those who died from tuberculosis in Vancouver were Chinese. Regardless, in 1949, claims about conditions in the tenement housing were used to justify the demolition of Canton Alley and much of Shanghai Alley.

Only two original buildings remain in Shanghai Alley: a four-storey building with mezzanine at 509 Carrall Street and the addition to CERA that housed the organization's newspaper and school. Located on the southwestern edge of Chinatown, 509 Carrall Street was built in two phases, with the eastern side in 1901 and the western-facing addition in 1914. Originally built for Kwong Man Sang, the building extends the full lane from Carrall to Shanghai Alley and served as stores, a rooming house, and meeting rooms for associations. Throughout its lifetime, the building has been altered to include space for various organizations.[19]

Market Alley, which once ran between East Pender and East Hastings from Carrall to Main Street, was also once a thriving commercial area.

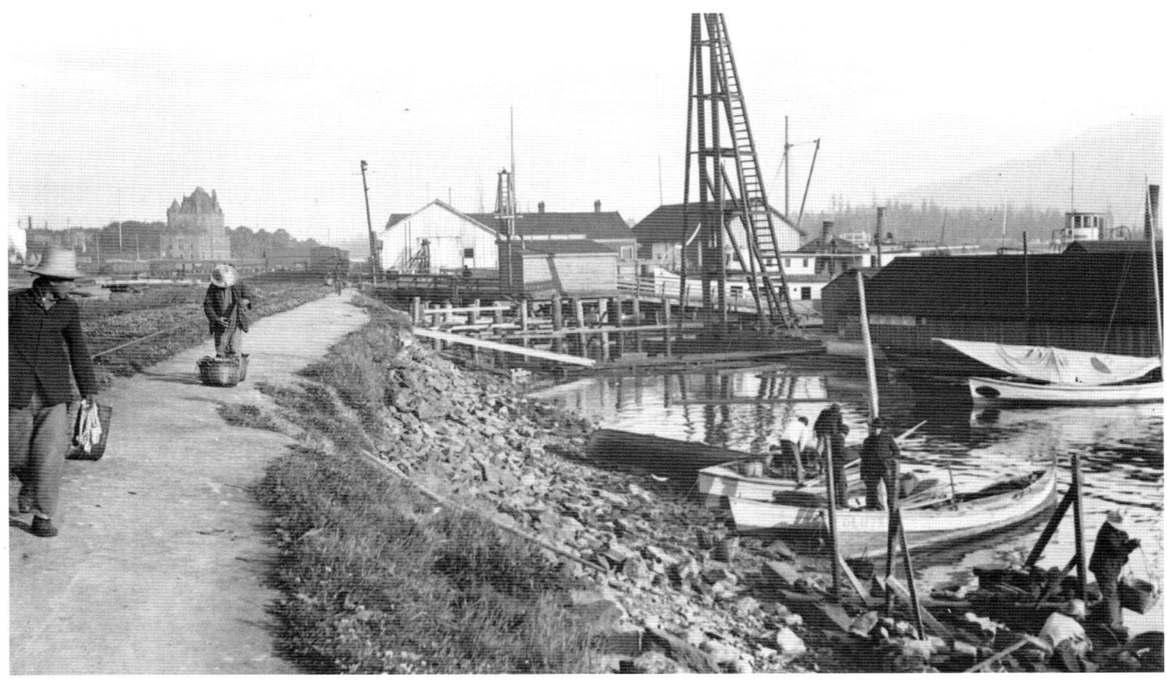

Fish peddlers on the waterfront, 1905

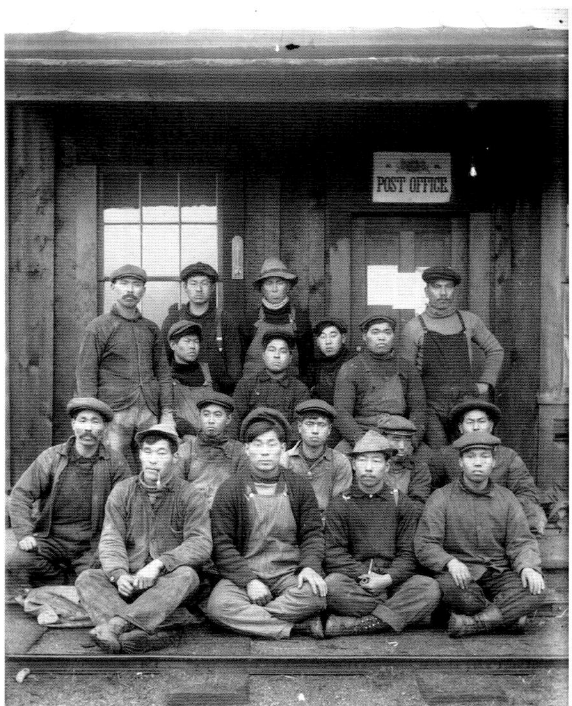

Men in front of post office, date unknown

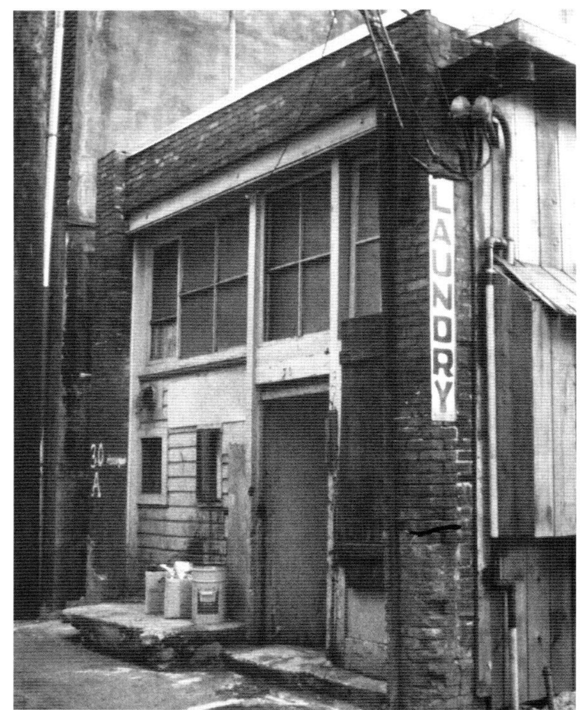

A laundry in Market Alley, 1977

Work in Early Chinatown

Early Chinese migrants faced employment restrictions that largely confined them to manual labour or housework. Male labourers were initially recruited to clear land for settlement in early Vancouver, but they also found work at the Hastings sawmill, canneries, farms, restaurants, shingle mills, laundries, and as help in households outside of Chinatown.

As there was a shortage of female help in early Vancouver, Chinese houseboys were often employed by households or by hotels and ships. In 1900, there were 260 Chinese domestics in Vancouver; they earned approximately ten to thirty dollars per month in private households, and more if they worked in hotels or on steamships. As sewing, cleaning, and cooking were seen as "feminine" work, the Chinese willingly filled the gap, as this type of work didn't compete with other men.[20] Some also worked for merchants in Chinatown, whereas those who were financially able opened small grocery stores, took jobs as vegetable peddlers, or opened tailors and laundries.

Small businesses operated by the Chinese, such as laundries and greengrocers, were not without their struggles. In 1893, the city attempted to pass a law to restrict Chinese-operated laundries to Chinatown but failed when only two out of thirty-six laundries abided. In 1900, new regulations restricted the activities of Chinese-operated laundries but expanded the laundry zone to allow non-Chinese-owned steam laundries to conduct business. Although steam laundries didn't compete with the Chinese-operated laundries, owners feared the competition presented by the Chinese, as they tended to charge less and work longer hours.

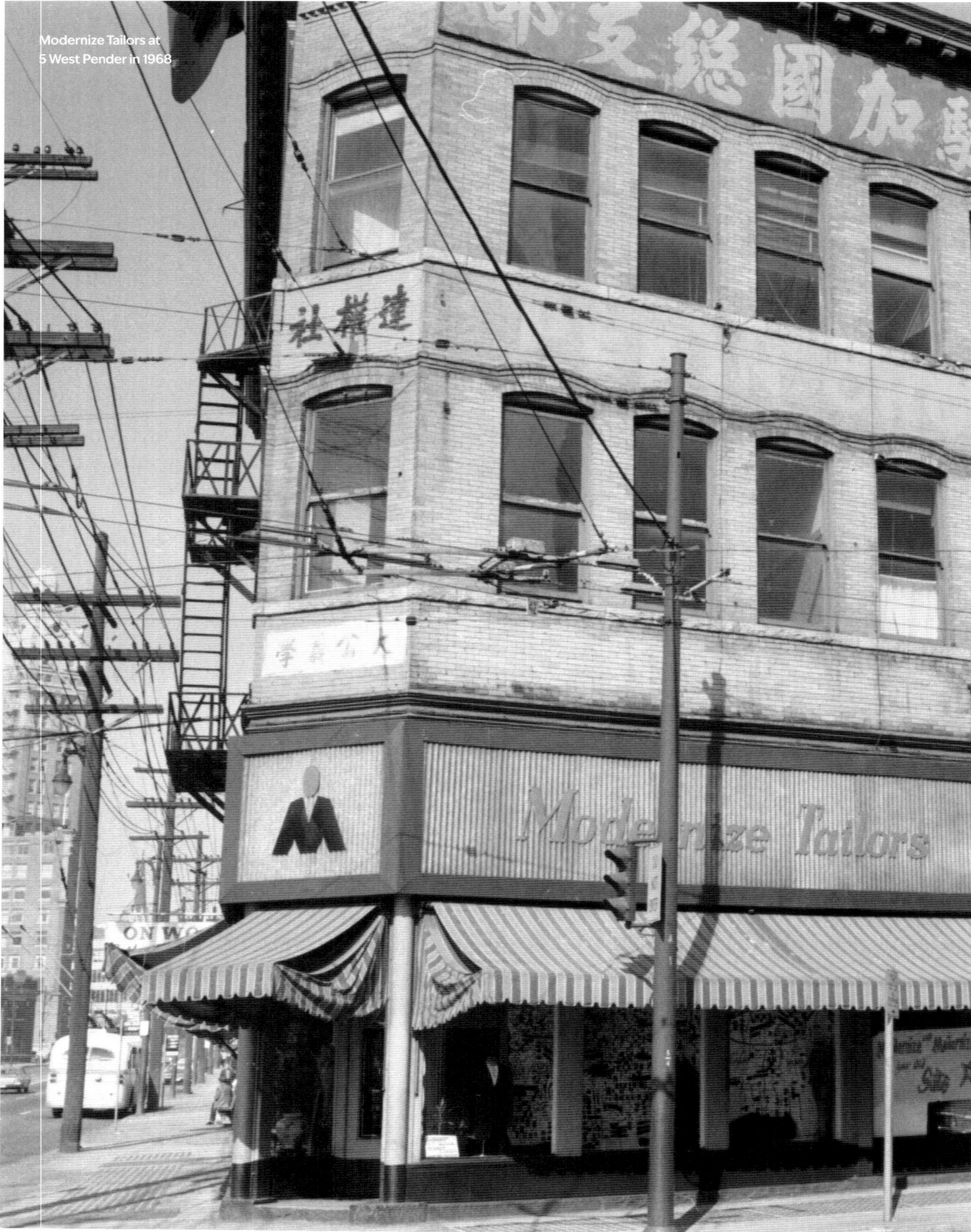

Modernize Tailors at
5 West Pender in 1968

Modernize Tailors
27 East Pender
Established 1913

Tailoring was a burgeoning trade in Chinatown, as it catered to the needs of both the Chinese and the non-Chinese populations. In 1913, there were approximately forty tailors run by either the Chinese or the Japanese.[21]

In 1911, twenty-year-old Wong Kung Lai arrived in Canada and found work as a house-boy before the Wongs' Benevolent Association connected him with an apprenticeship as a tailor. Two years later, Wong Kung Lai founded Modernize Tailors, which continues to operate in Chinatown. Growing up, Wong Kung Lai's children passed their time in the tailor shop, playing with wool and spools of thread when not attending Mon Keang Chinese school at the Wongs' Benevolent Association. The tailor shop would later employ relatives when they first arrived in Canada.

Having been denied jobs in engineering despite obtaining university degrees, Wong Kung Lai's sons, Bill and Jack, took over the tailor shop in the 1940s and continued to oversee operations until Bill's death in 2017.[22] Mia Wu, who began her career as an apprentice at Modernize Tailors in 2014, took over the business and keeps the tradition alive.

At its height in the 1940s and 1950s, Modernize Tailors had twenty employees and operated seven days a week. The small intergenerational business weathered the rise of big box stores and fast fashion by relying on a loyal customer base, including celebrities filming in Vancouver.[23] Throughout its time as one of Chinatown's legacy businesses, the tailor shop operated from several locations, including 5 West Pender and now 27 East Pender.

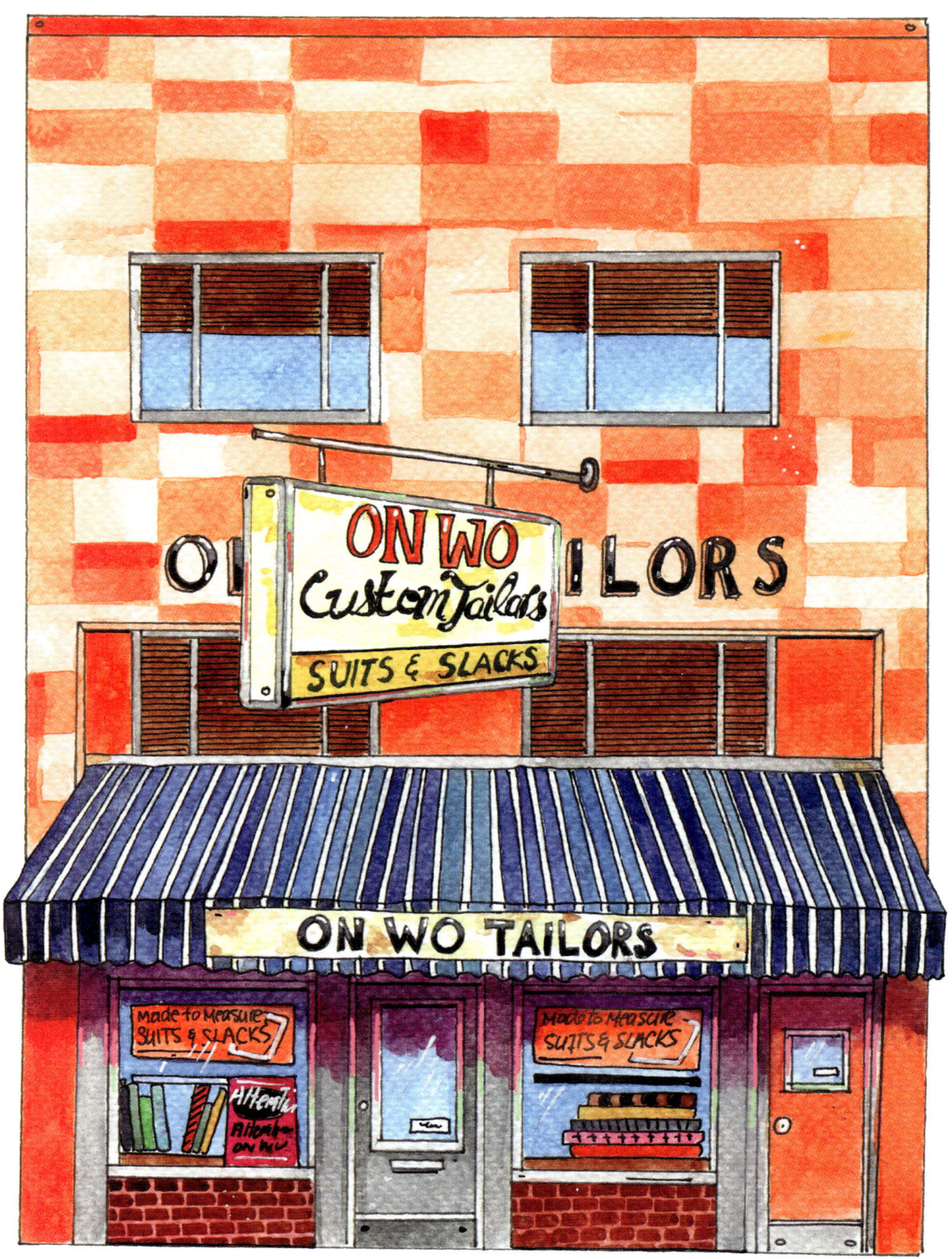
ON WO
Custom Tailors
SUITS & SLACKS
ON WO TAILORS
Made to Measure
SUITS & SLACKS
Made to Measure
SUITS & SLACKS

On Wo Tailors
11 West Pender
Built 1905

Pressed up against the original Chinese Freemasons Building (5 West Pender) is a small two-storey building that some call the Pink Panther. The commercial storefront sits empty, its blinds drawn and its metal gate rolled down, as it quietly watches the traffic trickle by under the Millennium Gate on Pender.

From 1940 to 1980, On Wo Tailors altered and made clothes under multiple labels such as Lees Garments and On Wo Shirt and Overall Company. Owned by Henry K. Lee, who served as the designer, pattern maker, and customer fitter, On Wo made suits, skirts, top hats, custom overalls, jeans, wool skirts, and made-to-measure drape trousers with pleated fronts and narrow cuffs. On Wo Tailors was also popular among non-Chinese clients, recognized by Red Robinson, long-time *Vancouver Courier* writer, who remembered it as the place he went to in high school for custom-made zoot suits. In 2010, Robinson recalled that one of the great slogans of his time was "Don't be a schmo, go to On Wo."[24]

Lifelong Lessons: Chinatown's Children

Interview with Pearl Louie, daughter of Ming Fun Louie

Ming Fun Louie was only nine years old and recently orphaned in 1919 when he boarded the SS *Monteagle* bound for Vancouver. Ming's paternal uncle paid for the child's passage and told immigration officials that Ming was sixteen.

Ming was put to work to repay his uncle's loan for his five-hundred-dollar Head Tax and passage. He worked long hours pulling a large wooden cart delivering huge sacks of rice, vegetables, and other staples to businesses and households in Strathcona and as far away as English Bay. During his excursions outside of Chinatown, Ming faced repeated threats and violence from older boys and men, which motivated his lifelong passion for boxing.

Throughout his lifetime, Ming recalled the lesson his uncle taught him. When Ming first arrived in Vancouver, he was provided with a small closet-like space to sleep in, and it was in this space where the young boy hung his freshly washed clothes to dry. One day, afraid that his only pair of socks wouldn't dry before the next morning, he washed just the upper half while leaving the bottom half dirty, as it would be hidden in his shoes. When his uncle walked by and noticed the half-washed socks, he berated Ming for a job half done. The ridiculing continued until 1921, when Ming was able to pay back his uncle and leave Vancouver. At the age of twelve, he had vowed never to do a task halfway again, no matter how small.

He found work at a sawmill but quit when he witnessed an acquaintance lose his arm in one of the gigantic saws. Ming returned to the Lower Mainland and worked as a strawberry picker before finding work laying walkways and finishing sections of the Butchart Gardens in Victoria. In Victoria, he met Mrs. Jennie, who got Ming a job as a dishwasher at the Empress Hotel. When he was sixteen, Ming was offered a chance to apprentice as a pastry chef at the King Edward Hotel in Toronto. In 1926, he assisted in making hors d'oeuvres and pastries for a dinner banquet honouring Mary Pickford and Douglas Fairbanks Jr. Ming eventually settled in Regina, Saskatchewan, and started a family.

Ming never forgot that one slip could define your reputation and undermine any achievement. He would always tell his children that practice doesn't make perfect … only perfect practice makes perfect.[25]

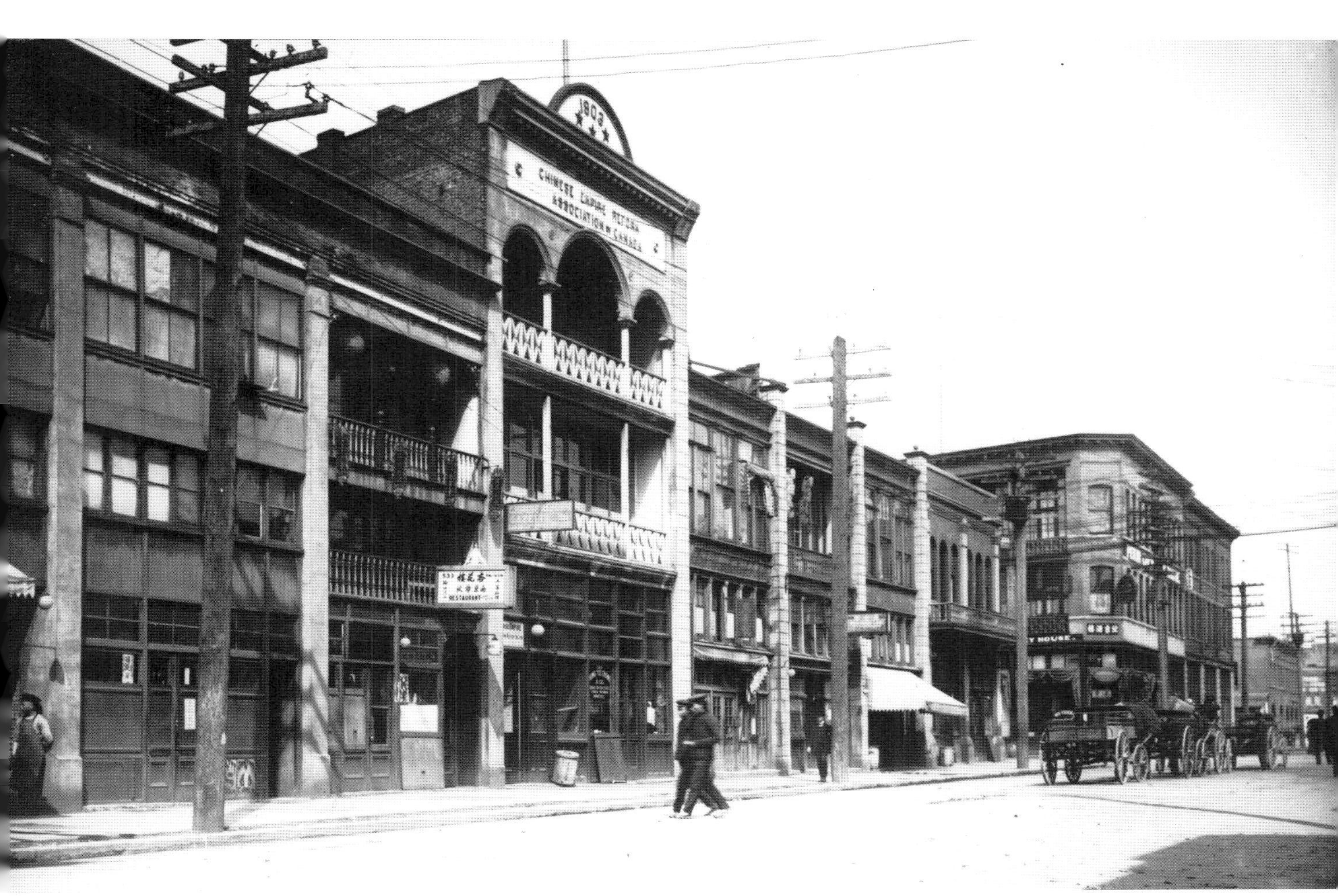

The CERA Building and others on Carrall Street in the early 1900s

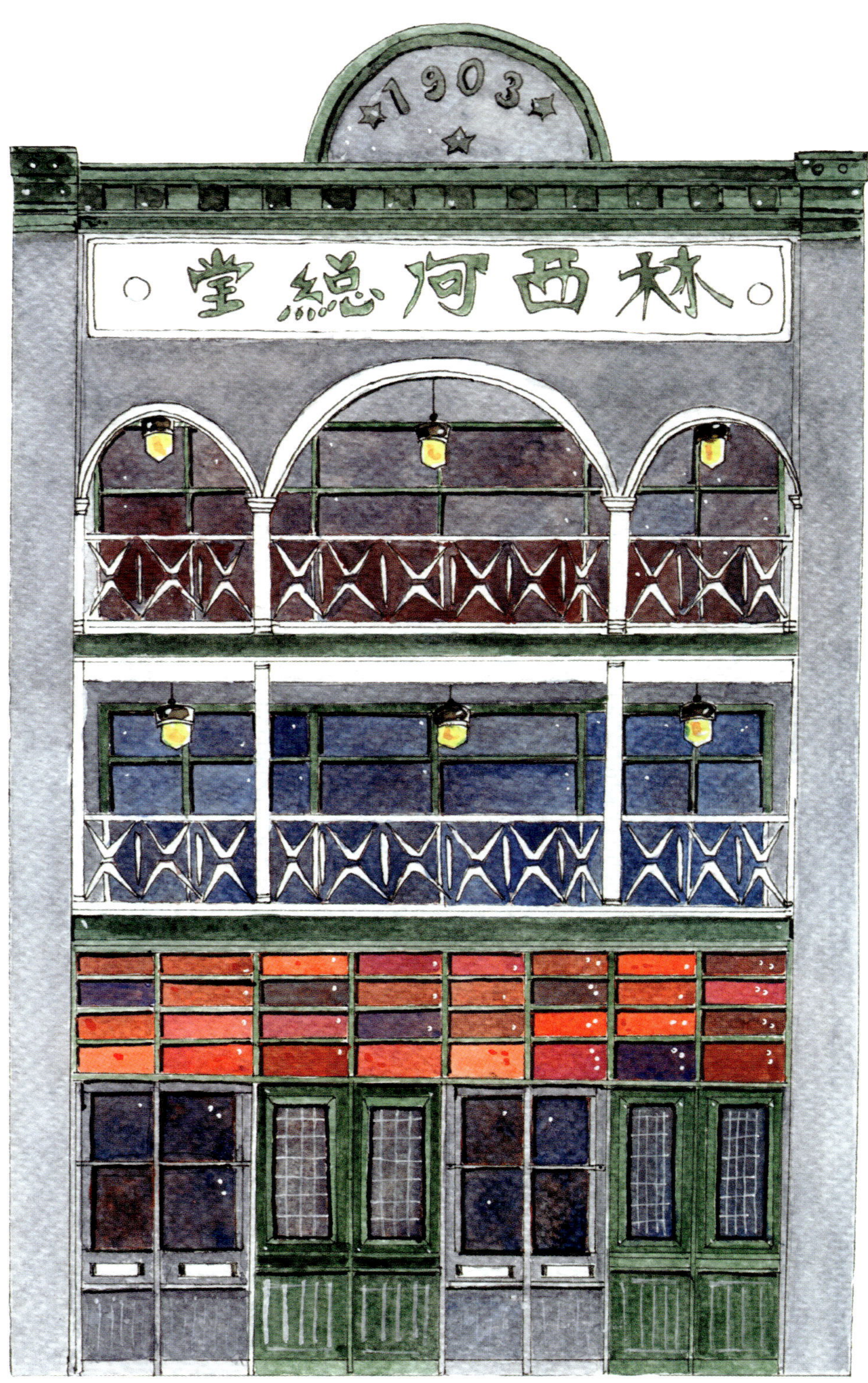

1903
林西何總堂

Chinese Empire Reform Association/Lim Sai Hor Association Building

525–531 Carrall Street
Built 1903

In a black-and-white photograph, the elegant Chinese Empire Reform Association Building at 525–531 Carrall Street commands an opulent presence. In the near background on Dupont Street (Pender) is its political rival, a three-storey brick building with mezzanine that once housed the father of modern China, Dr. Sun Yat-sen, and his supporting organization, the Chee Kung Tong (later Chinese Freemasons). But the delicate bones of the Chinese Empire Reform Association Building, with its upper two floors of recessed balconies, mezzanine floor, and half-moon crown imprinted with its date of completion in 1903, capture your attention, transporting you back to the early twentieth century.

The building was created as the Vancouver headquarters for the Chinese Empire Reform Association (CERA). CERA was formed in 1899 in Victoria by the political refugee Kang Youwei, who had escaped a death sentence in China after boldly initiating reforms to modernize the Qing Dynasty. Kang was from a distinguished class of scholars, which gained him a position as the personal adviser to Emperor Guangxu, who governed China from 1875 to 1908.

The Qing failed to increase food supply as the population grew exponentially. Economic and agricultural struggles were exacerbated by the Opium Wars (1839–42; 1856–60), the First Sino-Japanese War (1894–95), and the Taiping Rebellion (1850–64) that consequently claimed more than twenty million lives.[26] The Emperor rushed to reform institutions but was met with distain by conservative members of the Qing, including his aunt, the Empress Dowager Cixi, who staged a coup d'etat and placed the Emperor under house arrest. Kang, along with his associate Liang Qichao, fled China, but six leading reformers were executed.

Kang's first order of business upon his arrival in Victoria was to send birthday wishes to Empress Dowager Cixi brazenly requesting that she step down from power.[27] In 1900, CERA plotted an armed uprising in China, which failed, as promised funds were delayed. Some accused Kang of deliberately withholding funds because of a disagreement with radical co-conspirators such as Dr. Sun Yat-sen. In the meantime, China continued to be at the mercy of foreign powers, which led the Qing government to relax its resistance to change by adopting constitutional reform. This monumental change shifted CERA's relationship with the Qing from animosity to cooperation, while providing a platform to prevent Sun and his republican supporters from overthrowing the monarchy.

With chapters in 150 cities, CERA largely depended on the support of overseas Chinese to rectify the situation in China and rescue Emperor Guangxu. In Vancouver, CERA garnered support from wealthy and influential merchants such as Yip Sang (Wing Sang Company), Chang Toy (Sam Kee Company), and Won Alexander Cumyow, who was the first Chinese person to be born in Canada. These merchants were invested in protecting business and trade interests by ensuring a stable, strong, and prosperous homeland.

From 1903 to 1911, CERA printed a newspaper, the *Chinese Reform Gazette* (*Yat Sun Bo*), that was likely produced in-house in the attached building facing Shanghai Alley. CERA also created the Patriotic School to instill Chinese culture and language in the next generation.[28]

CERA lost its relevance after the 1911 revolution that overthrew the Qing Dynasty and the imperial system in China. A modern republican government was installed with Dr. Sun Yat-sen as president in 1912. Despite its demise, CERA held on to the building until it was sold to the Lim Sai Hor Kow Mock Association in 1945. The association initially started in Victoria in 1908 to unite members with the surname Lim, before joining forces with Kow Mock in the 1930s, when many organizations faced the impacts of a dwindling population brought on by the Exclusion Act.[29]

After 1945, the building's exterior was significantly transformed, reducing its original columns, arches, recessed balconies, and crescent crown to a box-like structure. The association turned the upper floors into a dormitory consisting of double- and single-occupancy rooms as well as shared living areas. The third floor also houses a meeting hall, office, storage, and a reading room. Tenants on the third floor often paid more rent for what were known as "premium rooms" because of the skylights that provided natural light.[30] In 1993, an intricate altar was installed on the third floor for ancestor worship during special festivities such as spring and autumn festivals and Lunar New Year.[31] In 2017, the building's exterior was rehabilitated to its 1903 appearance.

The building combines hybrid architectural features, borrowing from both European and southern Chinese influences, including a double-storey commercial space on the ground floor with full-height windows allowing room for a loft or mezzanine. The upper floors are complemented by an ornate cornice and dentils, as well as windows and skylights to admit natural light and airflow.[32] Over the century, 525–531 Carrall Street has been home to restaurants, tailors, merchants, and the Lein Nam Club. The building is joined by an additional structure that faces the once bustling Shanghai Alley (530 Shanghai Alley).

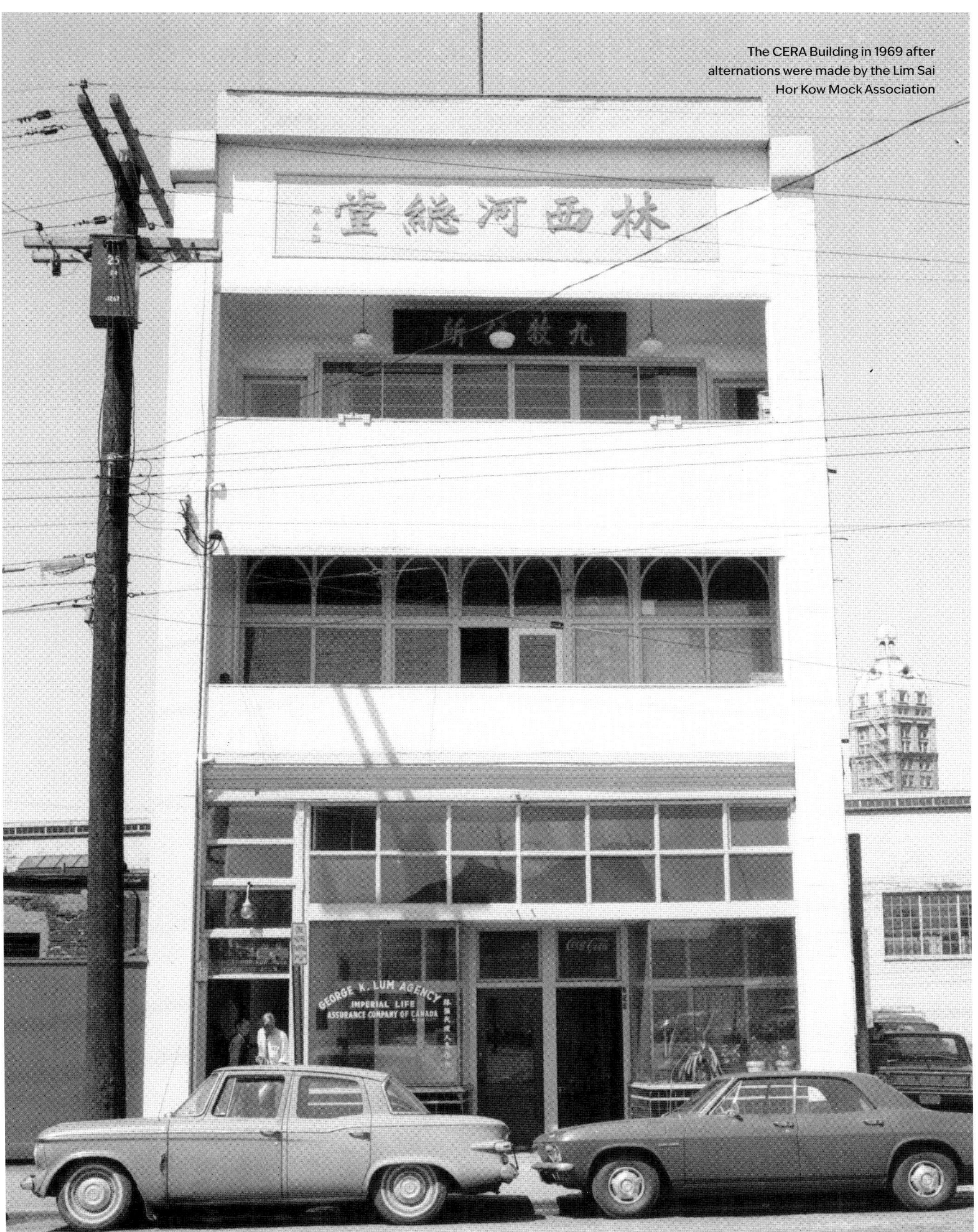

The CERA Building in 1969 after alternations were made by the Lim Sai Hor Kow Mock Association

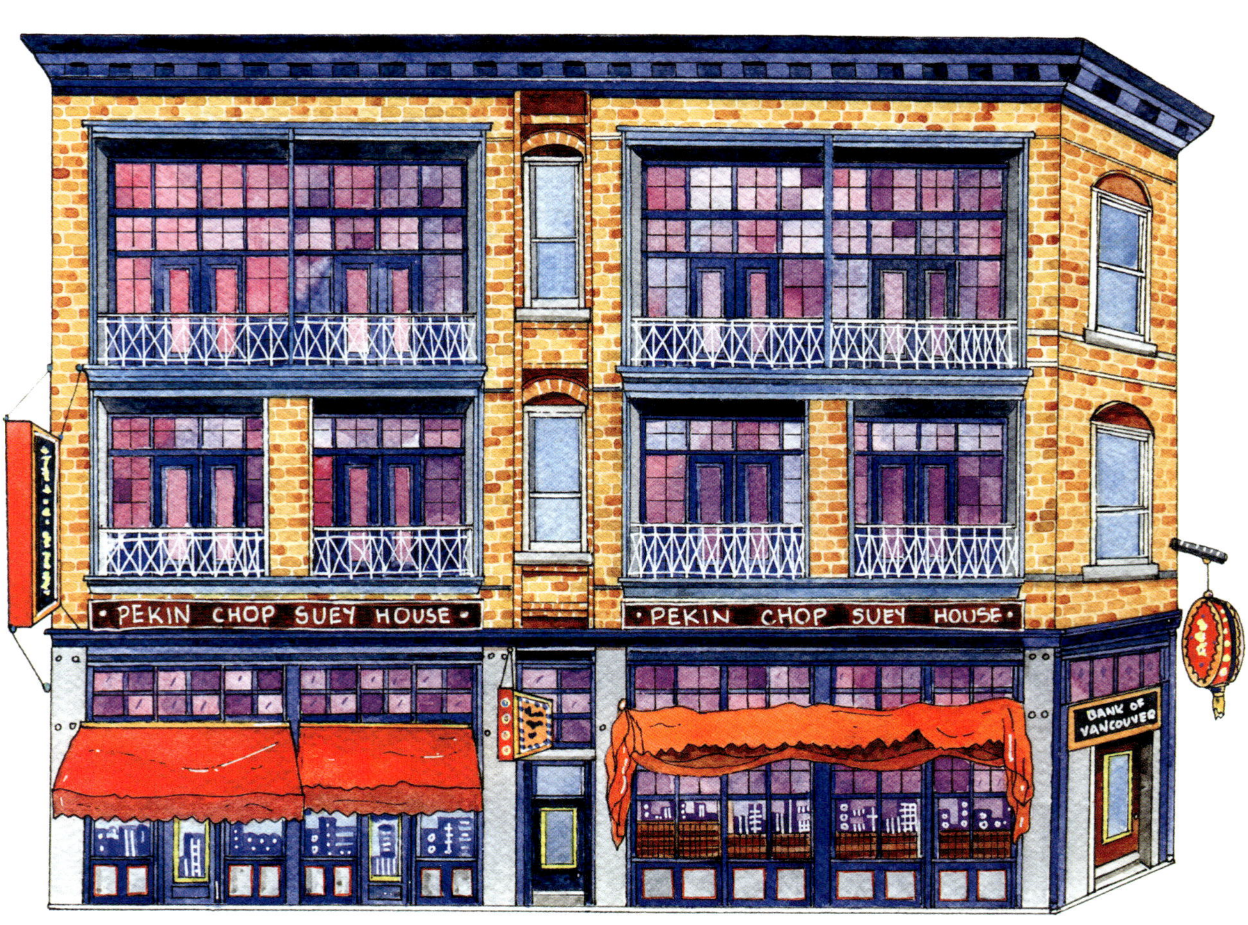

PEKIN CHOP SUEY HOUSE
PEKIN CHOP SUEY HOUSE
BANK OF VANCOUVER

Chinese Freemasons Building

5 West Pender
Built 1907
Also see *Chinese Times* newspaper and
110–116 East Pender

The eerie ghost sign of Pekin Chop Suey is etched on the second floor of the Chinese Freemasons Building at 5 West Pender. Built in 1907, the three-storey brick building fuses two cultures with its Victorian-style facade along Carrall and Chinese characteristics of recessed balconies and wrought-iron railings facing Pender. The multipurpose building was first acquired as a meeting place and dormitory by the Chee Kung Tong (later Chinese Freemasons), a fraternal organization that supported Dr. Sun Yat-sen's efforts to overthrow the Qing Dynasty.

Sun Yat-sen (1866–1925) was from a poor rural family and had none of the advantages of education and status. His identity, however, was familiar to many Chinese labourers who identified with Sun's humble origins. Like thousands of poor Chinese from southeast China, some of the Suns had immigrated to California and Hawaii as labourers. In 1879, Sun joined an older brother in Hawaii, where he received an education in mission schools that introduced him to ideas about democracy and republican government as well as Christianity. He went on to study medicine in Hong Kong.

Disappointed by having been denied the chance to practice medicine in British dominions while also being equally ignored by the Chinese, Sun became a Chee Kung Tong member and saw it as a network to carry out his revolutionary goals of overthrowing the Qing Dynasty. In 1904, Sun helped write the organization's constitution, promising to further extend the global network and influence as well as transform the group into an open revolutionary party. In support of Sun, members raised funds through gambling, brothels, people smuggling, and opium trading. The Victoria branch even mortgaged its lodge for fifteen thousand dollars to support the cause.[33]

The origins of the Chee Kung Tong are complex, but it was likely formed as a fraternal organization in Fujian Province during the eighteenth century and spread to surrounding provinces through migration. The early network provided a web of mutual aid where migrants were supported as they moved to and between towns. Early members were inducted and taught secret hand symbols, as well as legends and rituals so they could identify one another. Members were then considered part of the pseudo-familial network that offered protection and aid. Originally made of up misfits, migrants, and the lower class, the organization was naturally dedicated to fighting for greater justice in China.[34]

The Chee Kung Tong was an "open" organization that didn't restrict its membership based on surname, clan, or region. Instead, the organization admitted members based on allegiance to brotherhood and appealed to early Chinese railway workers and mining labourers. Although it didn't officially establish itself as an organization in Canada until 1863, it is believed that Chee Kung Tong members were already among the first Chinese who migrated north from California during the Fraser River Gold Rush in 1858. By the dawn of the twentieth century, its popularity resulted in the establishment of more than forty Chee Kung Tong lodges in BC alone, with its overall membership in Canada estimated to be between ten and twenty thousand, or 60 percent of the Chinese population.[35] During the early twentieth century, Chee Kung Tong membership was largely outside China, as any support for overthrowing the Qing in China was punishable by death.

In 1907, the Vancouver chapter of the Chee Kung Tong established a newspaper, the *Tai Hon Kong Bo*, or the *Chinese Times* (1907–92), to educate and politicize its members in Vancouver and around the world.

Despite its efforts, the Chee Kung Tong lost political influence in China upon the overthrow of the Qing Dynasty in 1911. Sun returned to Shanghai, where he was elected president. The Chee Kung Tong criticized Sun for reneging on his promise, especially as his attention turned to the Chinese Nationalist Party, or Kuomintang (KMT). In response, the Chee Kung Tong was criticized for being incompatible with a modern, republican China as the organization was backward, feudal, and lacked political ideology.[36]

The Chinese Freemasons Building was constructed with commercial space on the ground floor, versatile upper floors, and a mezzanine. In 1913, iron and wood posts, wood corbels, and shop doorways and metalwork for awnings were added to the ground floor for its new tenant, the Bank of Vancouver. Yucho Chow, Chinatown's photographer, had his studio on the upper floors. The building was once home to Modernize Tailors, one of the longest-running businesses in Chinatown.

During the 1907 anti-Asian riots, the Chinese Freemasons Building sustained significant damage to its exterior.

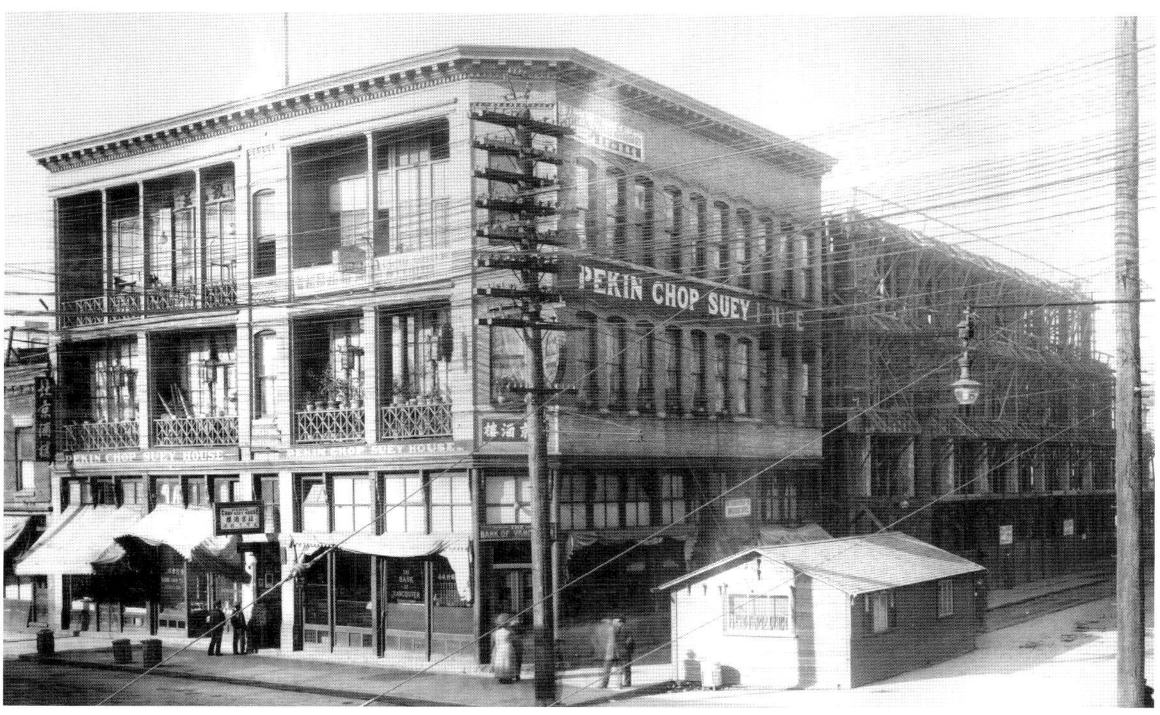

The Chinese Freemasons Building in 1911

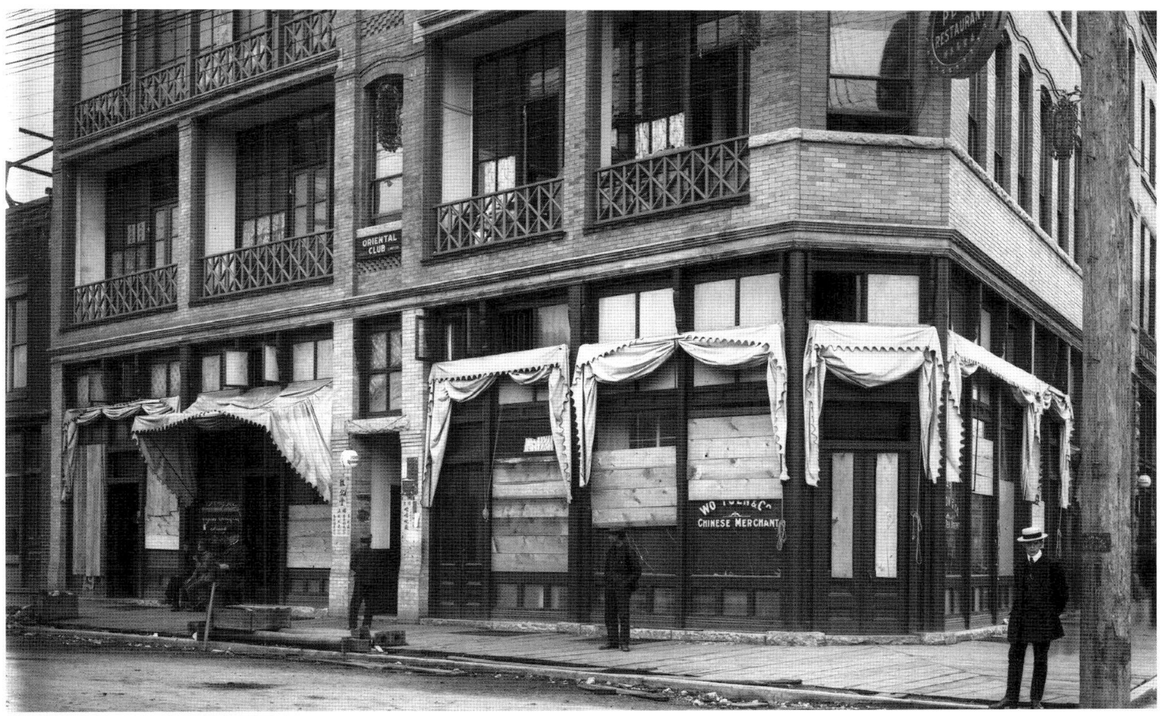

Damage to the Chinese Freemasons Building after the 1907 riots

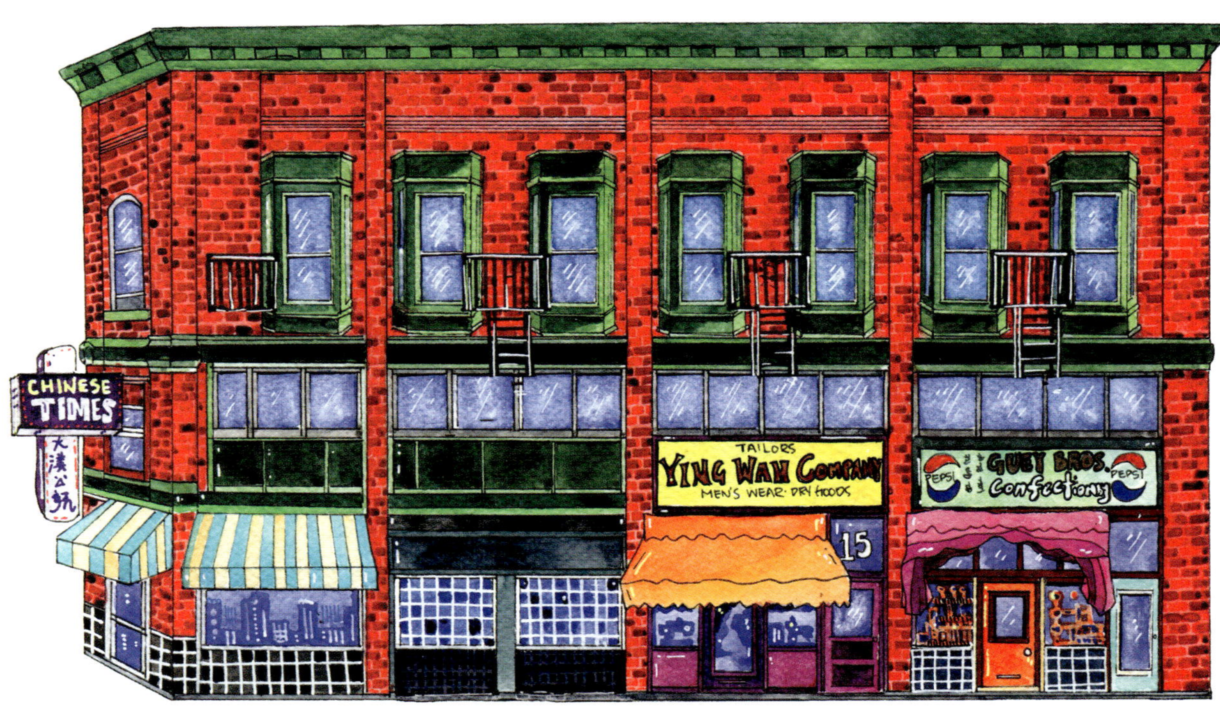

CHINESE TIMES
大漢公報
TAILORS
YING WAH COMPANY
MEN'S WEAR · DRY GOODS
15
GUEY BROS.
Confectionery
PEPSI
PEPSI

Chinese Times Building
1 East Pender
Built 1901

If you squint hard enough, you can almost see the faint remnants of the *Chinese Times* newspaper pasted on the exterior of 1 East Pender and the few fedora-clad Chinese "bachelors" huddling to get a glimpse of the events unfolding in their homeland.

Named for its longest-serving tenant, the Chinese Times Building on the northeast corner of Pender and Carrall was commissioned by one of Chinatown's leading merchants, Yip Sang of the Wing Sang Company, who hired W. T. Whiteway to design it. In contrast to the temporary wooden structures with false frontier fronts that lined Pender in the early twentieth century, the brick edifice of 1 East Pender came to symbolize the permanence of the Chinese as they set down solid roots in Canada.

Recognizing the evolving needs of the Chinese community, the building was designed for both commercial and residential use. Unlike tenement buildings, which provided dormitory-style living with shared bathrooms for single occupancy, the Chinese Times Building could accommodate families in a mixture of small residential rooms on the upper floors. Although technically two storeys, the building has a slender mezzanine floor between the first and third floors, which is visible from the exterior. The building also features a deep decorative metal cornice with dentils set against the skyline, brick corralling, and recessed panels, and the upper floor is finished with metal-clad bay windows that overlook Pender.

From the 1930s to the 1990s, the *Chinese Times* newspaper occupied the ground and mezzanine floors, with the typesetters strategically positioned on the low-ceilinged mezzanine because they sat all day long.[37] Established by the Chee Kung Tong (later Chinese Freemasons), the *Chinese Times* was the longest-running newspaper in the Chinese community, published daily from 1907 to 1992.

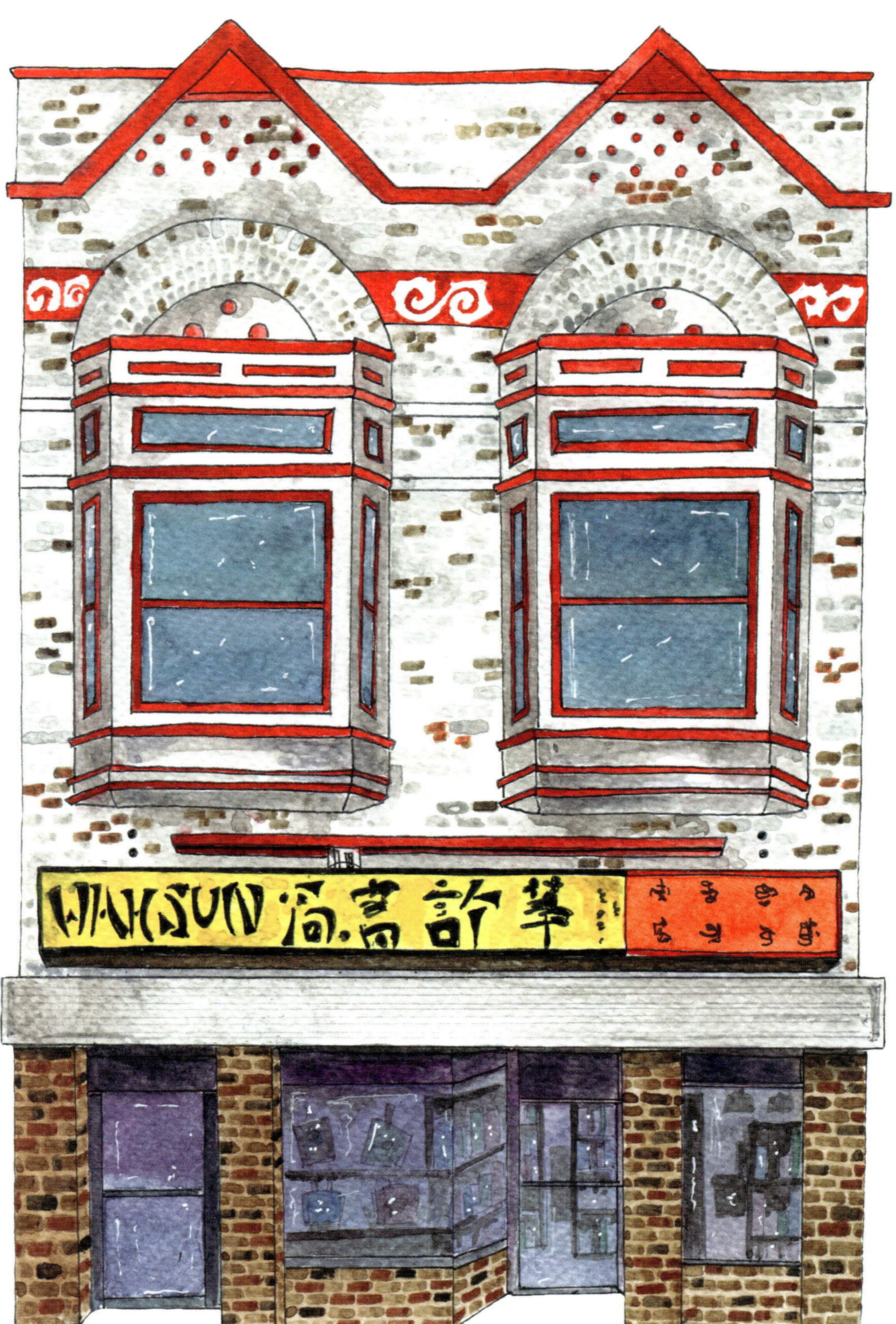

WAH SUN 華記書局

Wah Sun Stationary
78–80 East Pender
Built 1900

The two-storey brick building at 78–80 East Pender is an anomaly among its younger neighbours—the Vancouver Film School, the Chinese Cultural Centre, and the Dr. Sun Yat-sen Garden—all of which were built in the second half of the twentieth century. Built in 1900 for the Man-On Company, the Victorian Italianate building was once surrounded by frontier-style wooden buildings constructed on stilts to protect them from the high tides of False Creek. Between it and Carrall Street were labour contractors, groceries, residences, an opium manufacturer (Hip Tuck Lung Co.), and a tailor. Directly behind it, along Carrall Street, was Vancouver's red-light district, where Hart's Opera House, gambling dens, and brothels operated.

Recognized for its industrial location next to False Creek, the area surrounding 78–80 East Pender served the Great Northern Railway (GNR) during the early twentieth century. Having purchased the land on the south side of Pender between Carrall and Columbia, the GNR quickly set up their passenger and freight services with a station at 90 East Pender. Headquartered in Minnesota, the GNR was created in 1889 by Canadian-born James Hill as part of his attempt to expand the railway through Canada. Following Hill's death in 1916, the GNR scaled back its Canadian service. By the mid-1930s, many of its lines had been shut down or abandoned. The Chinatown tracks were pulled up in the 1920s after passenger service moved to Station Street in 1916. The railway was discontinued in 1964.

Before becoming offices for businesses such as the Great Northern Transfer Company, the Cloverdale Brick and Tile Company, and the Vancouver Gas Company, 78–80 East Pender was briefly used for baggage storage. Contractor W. H. Chow also had his office in the building. The ground floor has been home to Wah Sun Stationery and Sino-United Publishing.

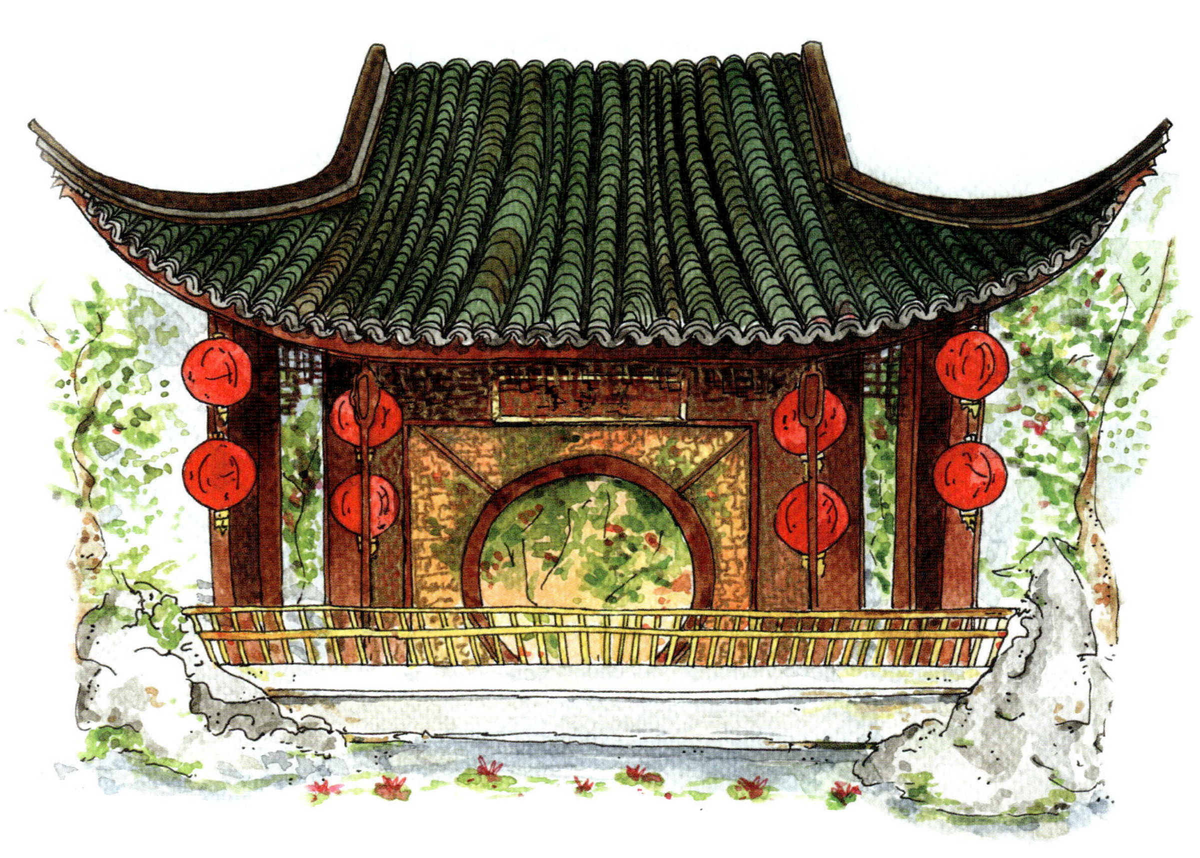

Dr. Sun Yat-sen Classical Chinese Garden
578 Carrall Street
Built 1986

Nestled along Carrall and Keefer Streets is an oasis in the middle of the urban hustle and bustle. Once you step into the garden, you almost feel as if you've entered a different dimension, one that could easily be mistaken for a wealthy household in fifteenth-century Ming Dynasty.

Built in 1986, the garden features the contributions of architects Joe Wai, Donald Vaughn, Wang Zu-Xin, and fifty-three master craftspeople from Suzhou. The garden took thirteen months to complete and consists of an intricate collection of handmade tiles, stone pebbles, Nan wood, and Ginkgo wood, while combining feng shui and Taoism in its use of craggy rocks juxtaposed against delicate foliage. Fish and turtle motifs are integrated throughout the garden, and live animals coexist as part of its larger ecosystem.

The garden and its neighbour, the Chinese Cultural Centre, were built in the aftermath of Vancouver's flirtation with freeways. The proposed freeway, which would have run along Burrard Inlet, with an exit along Carrall, would have obliterated most of historic Chinatown and its buildings.[38] Built on what was once fill-in land used for industry such as BC Electric and the GNR, the Dr. Sun Yat-sen Garden is a physical reminder of the importance of cultural and historical institutions.

Railways, the Arctic, and Gardens

Interview with Lorraine Lowe, former executive director of the Dr. Sun Yat-sen Classical Chinese Garden

The attraction of gold mountain, a term Chinese sojourners used to describe North America, often divided the traditional Chinese family unit. Families often sent their sons, like Lorraine Lowe's great-grandfather Low Yuet Wing, on a journey overseas to work. The sacrifices of early settlers undoubtedly created a foundation for subsequent generations to succeed.

Low Yuet Wing first arrived in Canada in the early 1900s and found work as a labourer on the railway. Although his Head Tax certificate indicated that he was fifteen years old, he was only eight or nine at the time and lied about his age to clear immigration. He returned to China four times during his sojourn, including in 1923, when the Chinese Exclusion Act went into effect. He returned to Canada on his own in the early 1950s, moving to Tilbury, Ontario, where he opened the Reno Grill. In 1955, Low Yuet Wing sponsored two of his "sons," Lorraine's grandfather and father, Len Lowe. Although Len Lowe was in fact Low Yuet Wing's grandson, immigration legislation during the early 1950s only permitted spouses or children under the age of eighteen to be sponsored. As a "paper son," Len arrived in Ontario and was put to work at the Reno Grill.

Unlike his grandfather, Len Lowe benefited from warmer attitudes toward the Chinese and was able to earn a degree in electronics and a job as a radio technician for the Distant Early Warning (DEW) Line. The DEW Line provided military communication during the Cold War to warn the United States and Canada of a possible missile strike from the Soviet Union. From 1960s to the early 1980s, DEW Line radar stations stretched from northwest Alaska to eastern Baffin Island. Len was stationed in the Arctic for five years but kept his work with the military a secret from his family for thirty years. In the early 1960s, Len returned to Hong Kong and married. He returned to Vancouver and worked three jobs before opening a retail television business in 1972.

From 2018 to 2024, Lorraine served as the executive director of Dr. Sun Yat-sen Classical Chinese Garden, where she has dedicated herself to revitalizing Chinatown. Her contributions have transformed the garden from a tourist site into an entertainment venue hosting a variety of performances, community days, workshops, and art exhibitions. Her love for Chinatown is something she shared with her father. Len Lowe was active in the Chinatown Lions Club, the Chinese Cultural Centre, and SUCCESS, as well as other charitable organizations.[39]

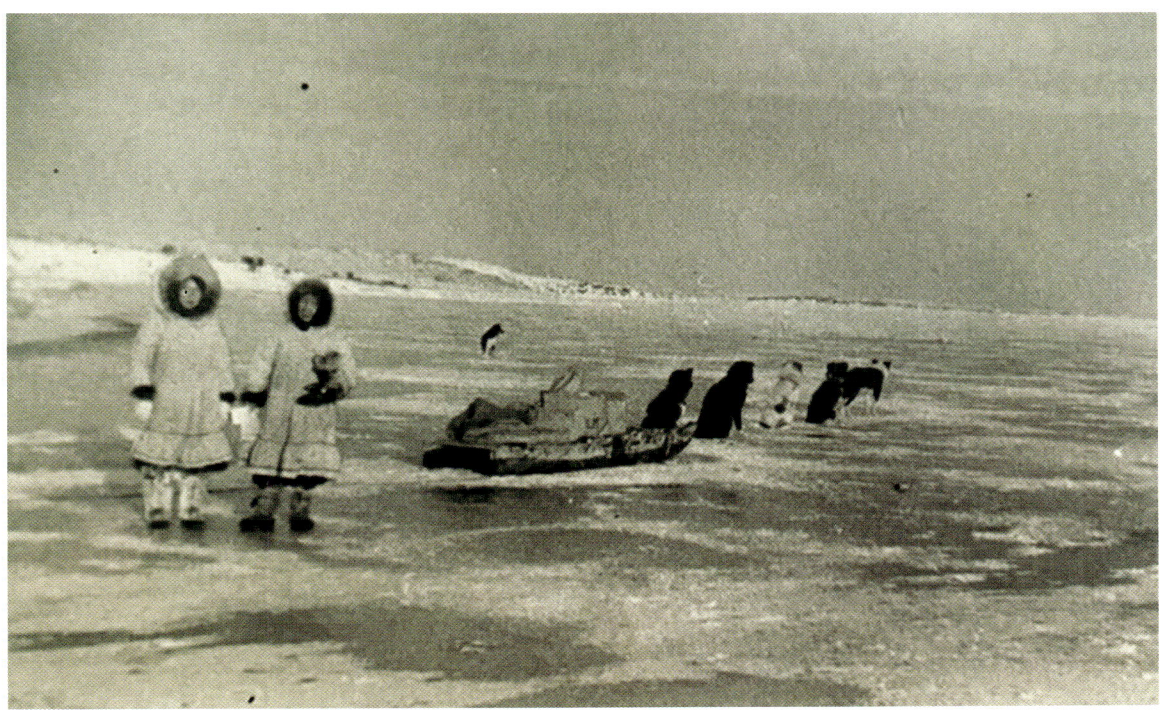

Len Lowe was stationed in the Arctic for five years

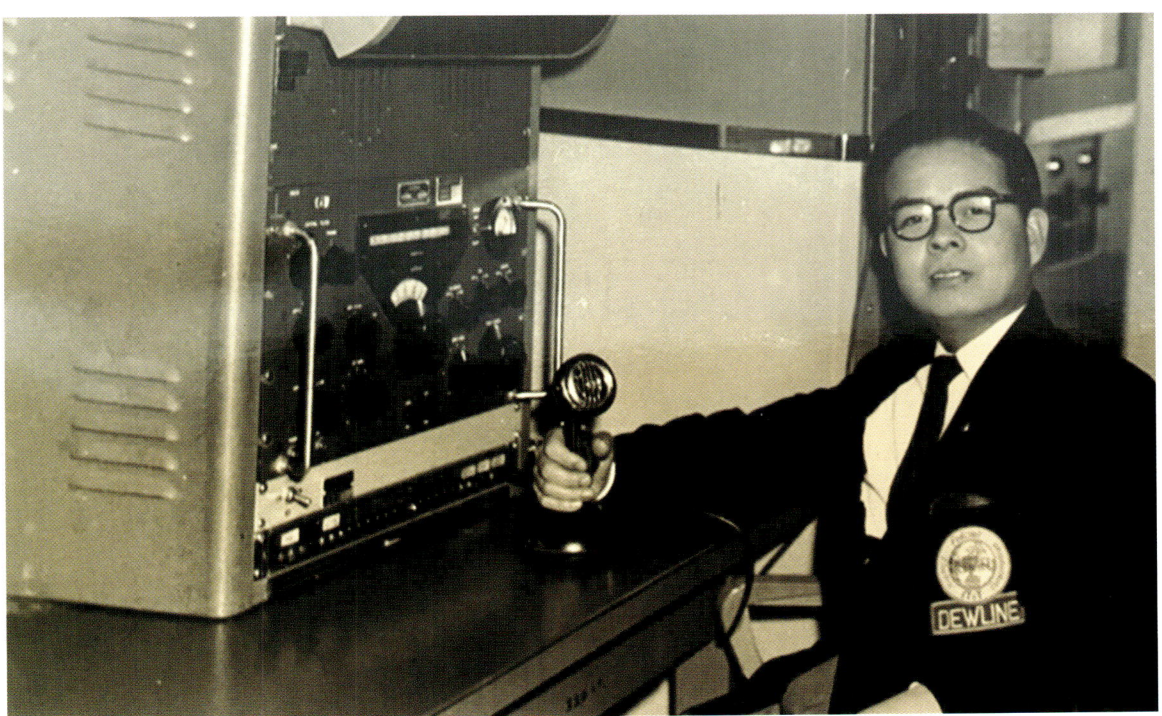

Len Lowe worked as a radio technician for the DEW Line during the Cold War

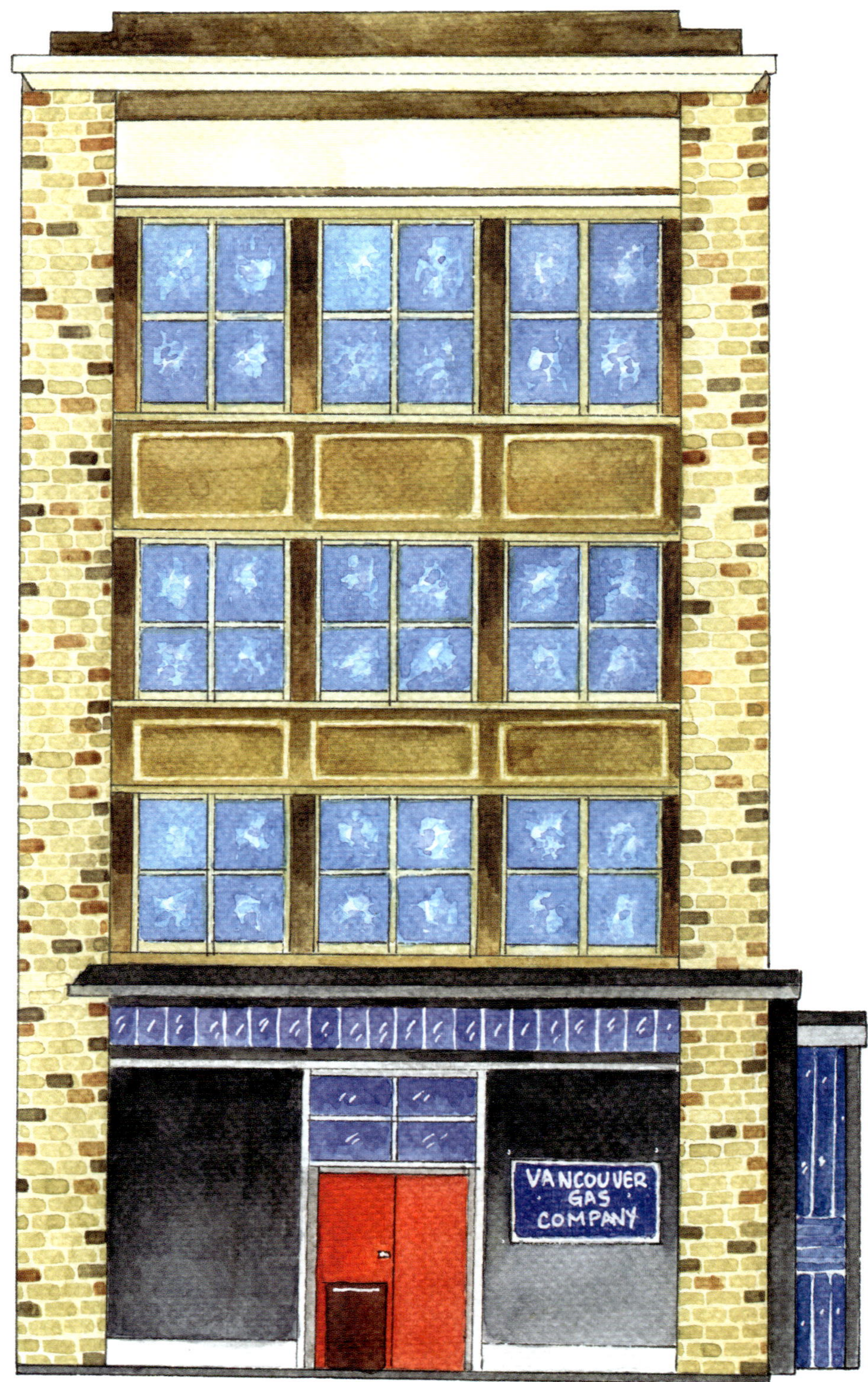
VANCOUVER
GAS
COMPANY

Vancouver Gas Company
133–135 Keefer Street
Built 1910

In the early twentieth century, False Creek was an industrial hub with ships delivering goods such as coal to the Vancouver Gas Company. Built in 1910 as a warehouse and meter repair shop for the Vancouver Gas Company (then part of BC Electric Company, subsequently BC Hydro), 133–135 Keefer Street is the only remaining building from the first coal gas manufacturing complex. The building's role in the coal industry became obsolete in 1957, when the city transitioned to natural gas.

Designed by Sharp and Thomson, the original building included glazed brick, small-paned windows, decorative spandrels, and a cornice. Unlike other warehouses, the Vancouver Gas Company requested the building's exterior be designed as a frame to accommodate different uses and eventually be transformed into office or residential space. This ingenious idea proved useful as the versatile building has evolved with the needs of the area.

In 2008, Gair Williamson Architects transformed the warehouse into a ground-floor restaurant and three full-floor luxury suites, plus a newly constructed fifth-floor suite with an enclosed courtyard and rooftop deck featuring a glass-bottom lap pool. In 2017, the penthouse suite was listed at $9.5 million.[40] On the ground floor is the apothecary-themed Keefer Bar, merging influences from Chinatown into delicious drinks served in beautiful glassware.

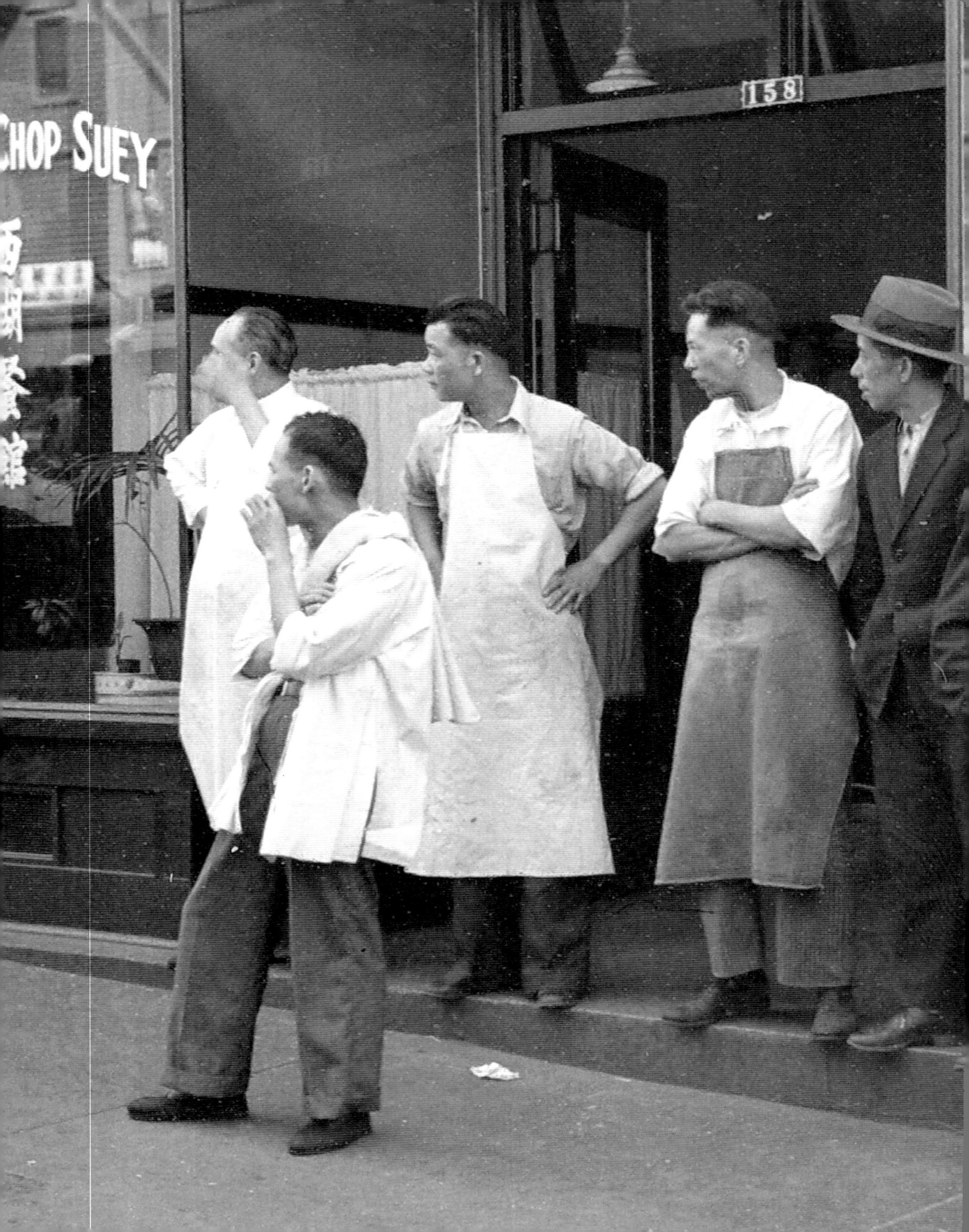

CHOP SUEY
158

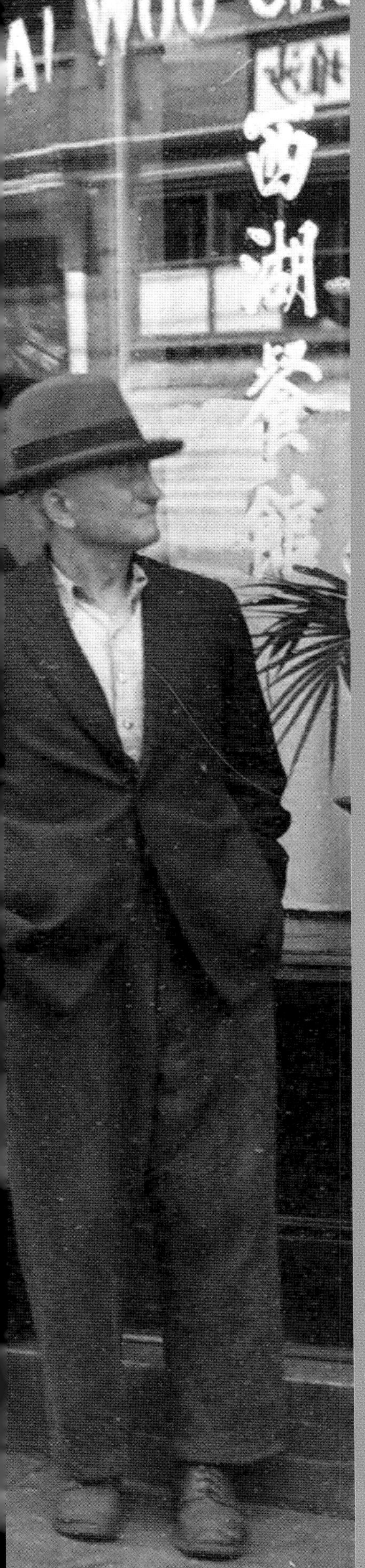

Societies, Lion Dance, and the Vanguard

With the extension of the Canadian Pacific Railway from Port Moody to Coal Harbour in 1887, Vancouver grew into an economic and industrial hub in the Pacific Northwest, and its Chinatown soon overshadowed previously larger Chinese communities in Victoria and New Westminster. By 1921, Vancouver's Chinese population of 6,500 was double what it had been a decade prior.[1] Buildings were constructed along East Pender, Canton Alley, and Shanghai Alley to provide accommodation, business, and organizational space for the growing population. This period of growth also saw Chinese businesses opening eastward to Gore Avenue and families moving into the neighbouring Strathcona area.

One of the notable phenomena from 1910 to 1920 was the growth and formalization of societies and associations in Chinatown. While merchants such as Chang Toy and Yip Sang provided services, employment, and community for early migrants, formal associations based on surname, clan, and region also formed to do the same. Some of these networks had roots in southern China, where similar connections based on identity developed to assist migrants travelling between counties and provinces. When migrants arrived in Canada and the United States, they formed similar organizations to help members of their clan. Almost forty associations were known to exist in Vancouver's Chinatown when the Chinese Exclusion Act was passed on July 1, 1923.[2]

Organizations, whether familial, regional, or political, provided a multitude of services, and many continue today. From 1911 to 1926, associations raised funds to purchase space or commissioned their own structures for reading rooms, meeting spaces, ceremonies, gatherings, and accommodation, with some organizations like the Mah assigning Vancouver as their headquarters.[3] Similar to the Chee Kung Tong, many associations advo-

cated for new migrants as well as providing basic services such as sending remittances to their families at home. Some organizations that held political interests, such as the Nationalist League, were involved in influencing the political situation in the homeland and rallied the community to support the cause.[4] During the Second Sino-Japanese War (1937–45), organizations like the Wongs' Benevolent Association, Nationalist League, Chinese Freemasons, and Chinese Benevolent Association fundraised for the war effort in China. The Wongs' Benevolent Association, for instance, founded the Hon Hsing Athletic Club in 1939 to fundraise through lion dance.

The Chinese population in Vancouver continued to grow during the initial phase of the exclusion period, reaching a high of thirteen thousand in 1931. The growth was mainly a result of the influx of transient workers from other parts of BC and Chinese relocating to Vancouver from other Chinatowns such as Victoria. In addition to the Exclusion Act, all levels of government passed discriminatory laws that further restricted business and employment opportunities. By 1941, the Chinese population in Vancouver had dwindled to seven thousand, mainly consisting of single men in their fifties.

The 1950s saw a rejuvenation of Chinatown as associations, excited about welcoming new families, revived schools and extracurricular activities such as martial arts. Although newcomers and Canadian-born children initially welcomed the organizations valued by their fathers, many began to question their relevance. For instance, many Canadian-born Chinese began criticizing the values and habits of their elders, who frequented gambling parlours and smoking dens that suited a predominantly male society. Instead, having gained the right to vote and recognition as war veterans, the new generation increasingly moved away from their parents' values and preferred organizations such as Veterans, Elks, and Lions, which embraced ideals of upward mobility and integration into broader Canadian society.

By the 1960s and 1970s, the demographic of Chinatown began to change as it saw a new generation benefiting from integration, acceptance into professions, and the opportunity to live outside Chinatown. A group of youth activists began challenging what it means to be Chinese in Canada and carved out a space for themselves through new organizations such as the Chinese Cultural Centre, Pender Guy Radio, and the Asian Canadian Writers' Workshop. As the new generation of Chinese started to move away from Chinatown, organizations struggled to maintain their membership and relevance. However, organizations continue to be active in Vancouver's Chinatown and elsewhere, providing the community with an intangible connection to history, culture, and language.

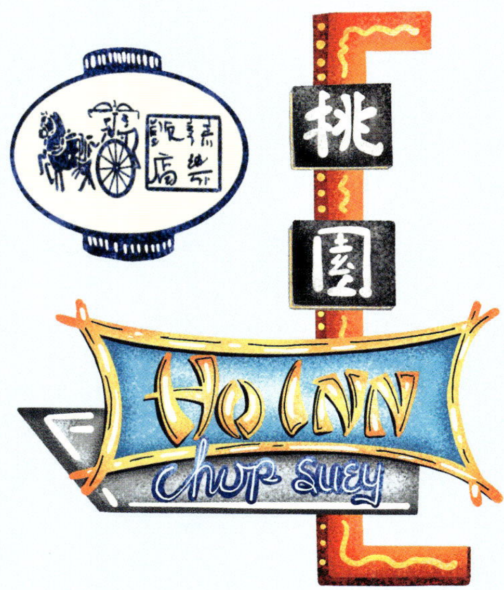

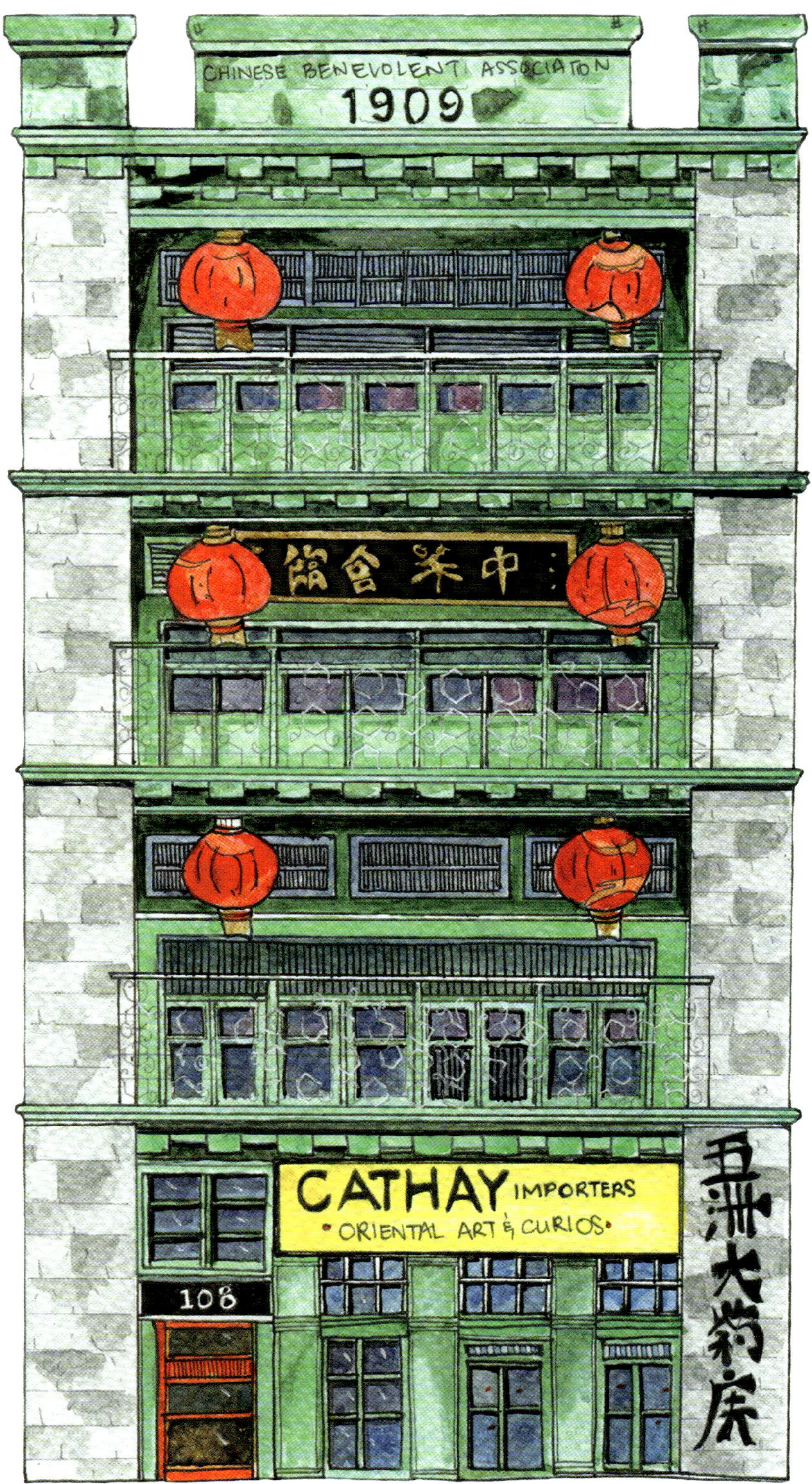

CHINESE BENEVOLENT ASSOCIATION
1909
中華會館
CATHAY IMPORTERS
• ORIENTAL ART & CURIOS •
108

Chinese Benevolent Association (CBA) Building
104–108 East Pender
Built 1909

The painted box-like shed on the roof of the Chinese Benevolent Association (CBA) Building peeks above the shadows of historic Chinatown, overlooking 100 block East Pender like a guardian. Wedged between the Sun Ah Hotel (100 East Pender) and the Chinese Freemasons (110–116 East Pender), the CBA Building, bearing majestic jade-green details with horizontal cornices on its upper floors, represents an early example of southern Chinese–influenced architecture in Vancouver. Its stoic presence and elegant grace have represented Chinatown since it was constructed in 1909.[5]

Commissioned by a group of leading merchants such as Chang Toy and Yip Sang, the CBA Building came to symbolize influence within the community. Its prominence is represented visually by its multiple recessed balconies accented with intricate wrought-iron railings, painted-box crown, and flagpole, as well as its characteristic inscription of its completion year. The high ceilings and full windows lining its balconies allow natural light and airflow throughout the building.

The building has primarily served as the meeting space for the Chinese Benevolent Association, an umbrella organization created in 1889 by leading merchants to oversee affairs in Chinatown. Although the early history of the CBA remains obscure, it was created with the intention of protecting Chinese business interests and livelihoods from discriminatory government legislation.[6] The organization, however, evolved to represent the interests of all Chinese, regardless of surname, birthplace, and political allegiance, and has acted as a mediator for the community.[7]

Despite its contributions, the CBA was not without its challenges and internal rivalries. During the 1960s and 1970s, the CBA was challenged by intergenerational conflict and a clash of values. Youth leaders in Chinatown criticized the structure of the CBA, suggesting that it was undemocratic and dominated largely by supporters of the Kuomintang (KMT), and that it failed to represent all Chinese.[8] Ultimately, the youth ousted the leadership of the CBA and established a democratic electoral process.[9]

The CBA maintains the third floor of the building as an office and meeting place, while historically renting out space to other organizations, such as the Chinese Board of Trade, the Chinese Chamber of Commerce, and the Chinese Public School. In 1910, a hospital was set up on the first and second floor of the CBA Building. The Chinese were poorly treated at Vancouver General Hospital, where the ill were either turned away or placed in the windowless basement.[10] The makeshift hospital that operated out of the CBA Building resembled a clinic, offering free medical services and beds. In 1919, the government ordered the closure of the hospital, noting its deficiencies, such as poor ventilation and lighting, as well as its damp and dirty conditions. A new makeshift hospital was set up, which housed the ill and provided a care facility for elderly and destitute Chinese men who did not have families to care for them. In 1943, the CBA raised more than thirty thousand dollars for the expansion of the hospital, which was later incorporated into Mount Saint Joseph Hospital.[11]

From 1924 until the 1970s, the first floor was home to Eng Chow Oriental Goods. From 1975, Cathay Importers, specialists in wicker and rattan furniture, rented out the first floor and used the basement for storage.

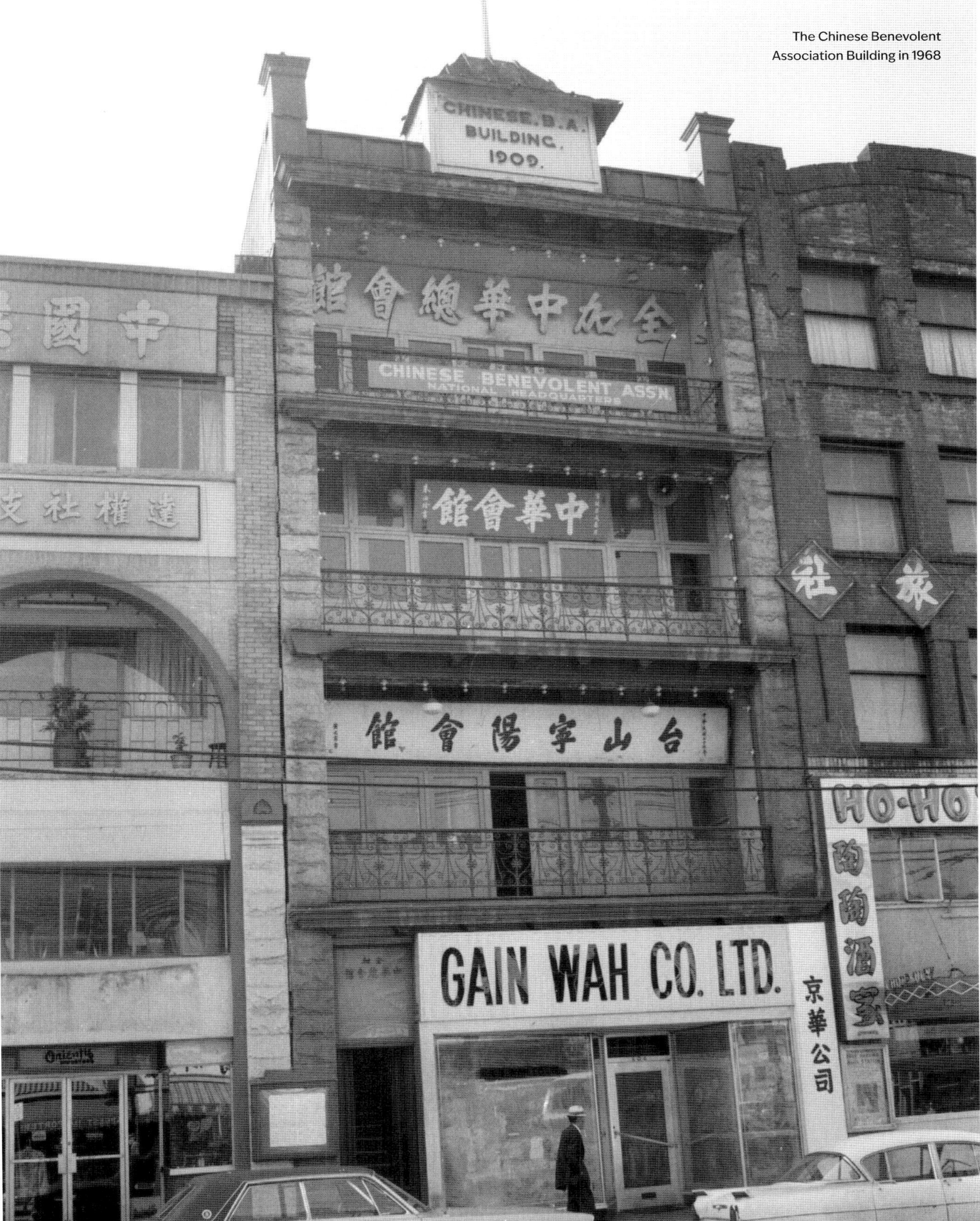

CHINESE.B.A.
BUILDING.
1909.
館會總華中加金
CHINESE BENEVOLENT ASSN
NATIONAL HEADQUARTERS
館會華中
館會陽寧山台
GAIN WAH CO. LTD.
京華公司
中國
民權社
HO-HO
陶陶酒家
社 旅

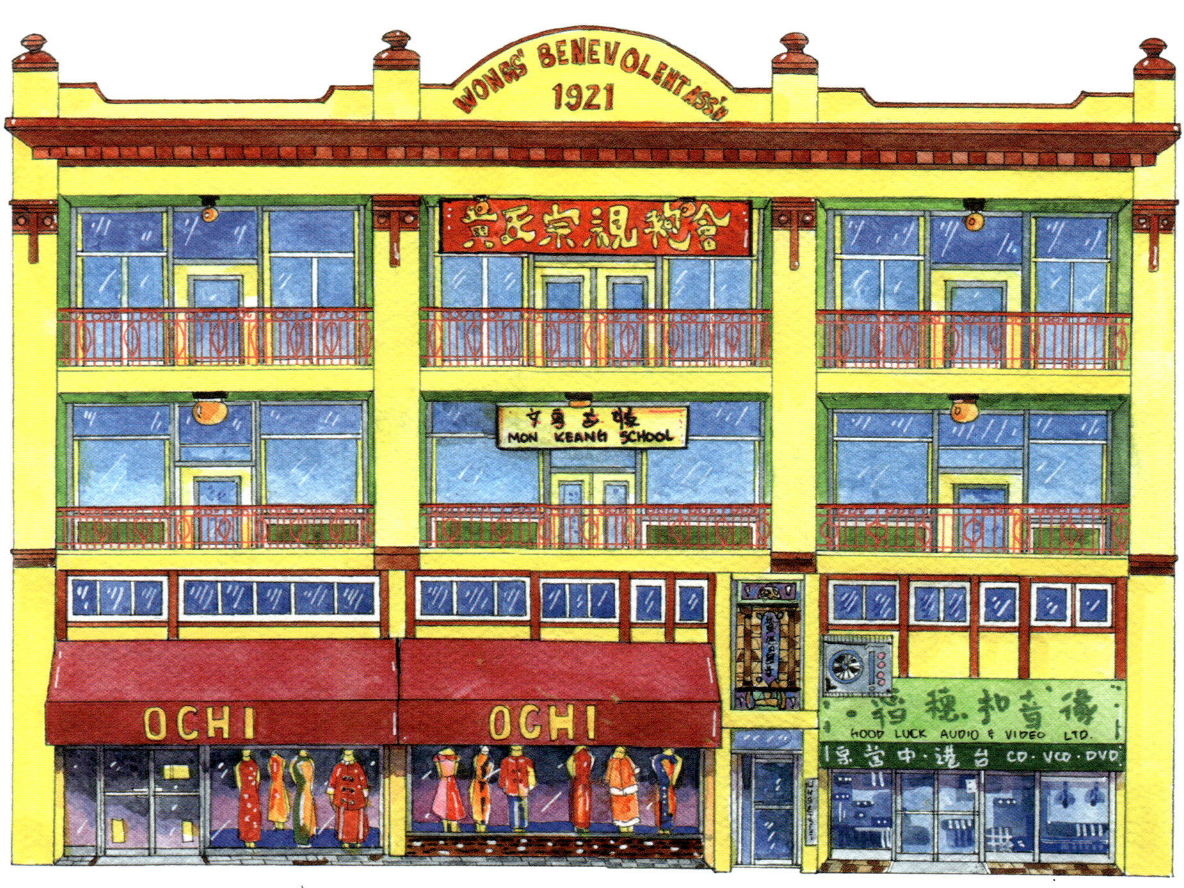

WONGS' BENEVOLENT ASS'n
1921
黃氏宗親總會
孟養義校
MON KEANG SCHOOL
OCHI
OCHI
招穗扣音像
HOOD LUCK AUDIO & VIDEO LTD.
京宮中·港台 CD·VCD·DVD

Wongs' Benevolent Association and Mon Keang Chinese School

121–125 East Pender
Built 1910/1921

I have a fond childhood memory of peeking through the entrances of the many clan society buildings on East Pender, like the Wongs' Benevolent Association. On a given day, I might catch a Chinatown "old-timer" resembling my grandmother (a fellow Wong) hobbling up the endless narrow stairs to the meeting room up top. If they were like my grandmother, they'd take their time, pausing on each floor to greet old friends and village acquaintances, their infectious laughter mixed with their village dialect echoing down the hallway adorned with martial arts paraphernalia and newspaper clippings. The hallways always smelled of incense mixed with tiger balm, while the sounds of a familiar language and crashing mahjong tiles blended with the jingle of jade and gold bangles dancing on wrinkly wrists.

The Wongs' Benevolent Association is an amalgamation of two surname organizations: Wong Wun Sun Society and Wong Kung Har Tong. Similar to other clan-based organizations, the Wongs are a community advocate that provided early settlers of the same clan with a support network for employment and accommodation. Notably, the organization played a key role in advocating for and providing a voice for the Chinese community, such as when houseboy Wong Foon Sing was wrongly accused of the 1924 murder of Janet Smith.

As one of the largest surname-based organizations in Chinatown, the Wongs' Benevolent Association has been influential in the Chinese community through its athletic and educational contributions. Known more commonly as the Chinese School Building, 121–125 East Pender is a mid-block, four-storey structure housing the association and the former Mon Keang Chinese School (1925–2011). Built in 1910, the building later gained a floor and a redesigned facade featuring recessed balconies. The building also has a mezzanine floor and an off-centre staircase lit by a large stained-glass window.[12]

In 1925, the Mon Keang School was established on the third floor, where it became an integral part of the Chinese community. With classes often taught by teachers imported from China, the school provided children with the opportunity to retain their native language, culture, and traditions. The school also served to ease fears among the older generation, who were worried their children would lose their heritage.[13]

Until the Second World War, Mon Keang School offered instruction only at the elementary school level, but it later became the only school in Canada to provide Chinese instruction at the secondary school level. Although Chinese classes were full in the 1950s and 1960s, the interest declined in the 1970s, when large numbers of Chinese started to move out of Chinatown. In 2011, the school closed because of low enrollment. Some of Mon Keang's graduates include Canada's first federally appointed Chinese judge, Justice Randall Wong, and historian and author Paul Yee.

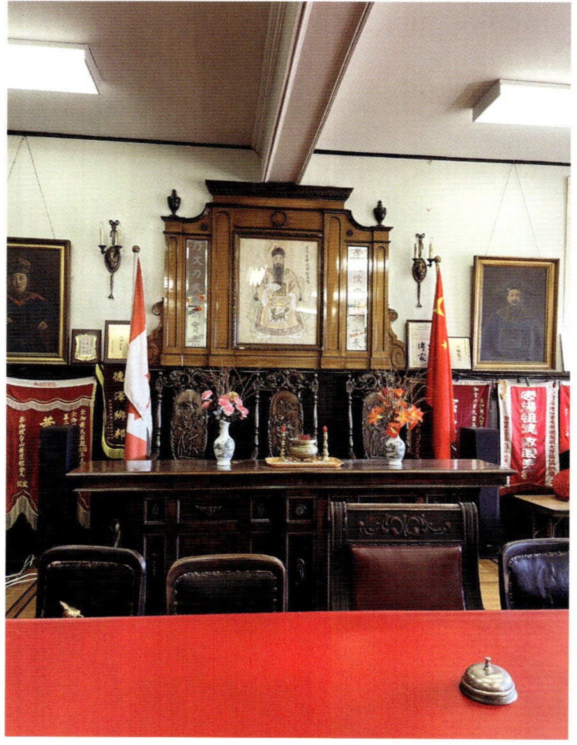

Meeting room in the Wongs' Benevolent Association, 2022

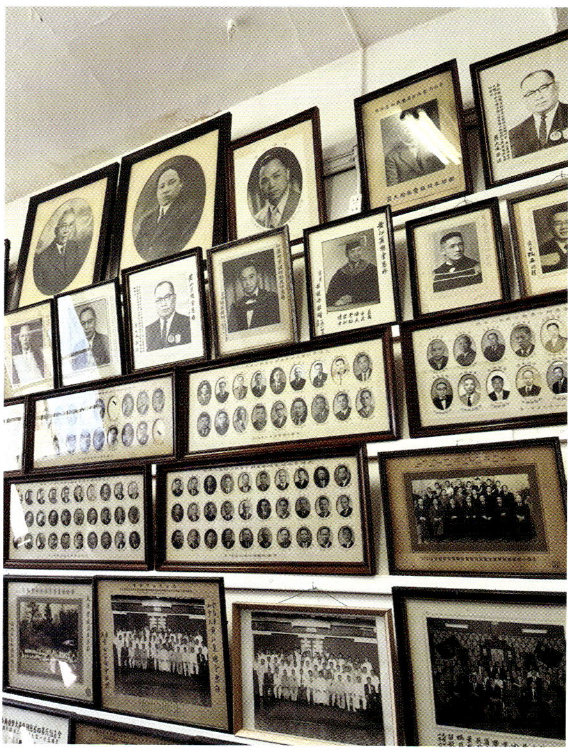

Photographs in an old Mon Keang classroom, 2022

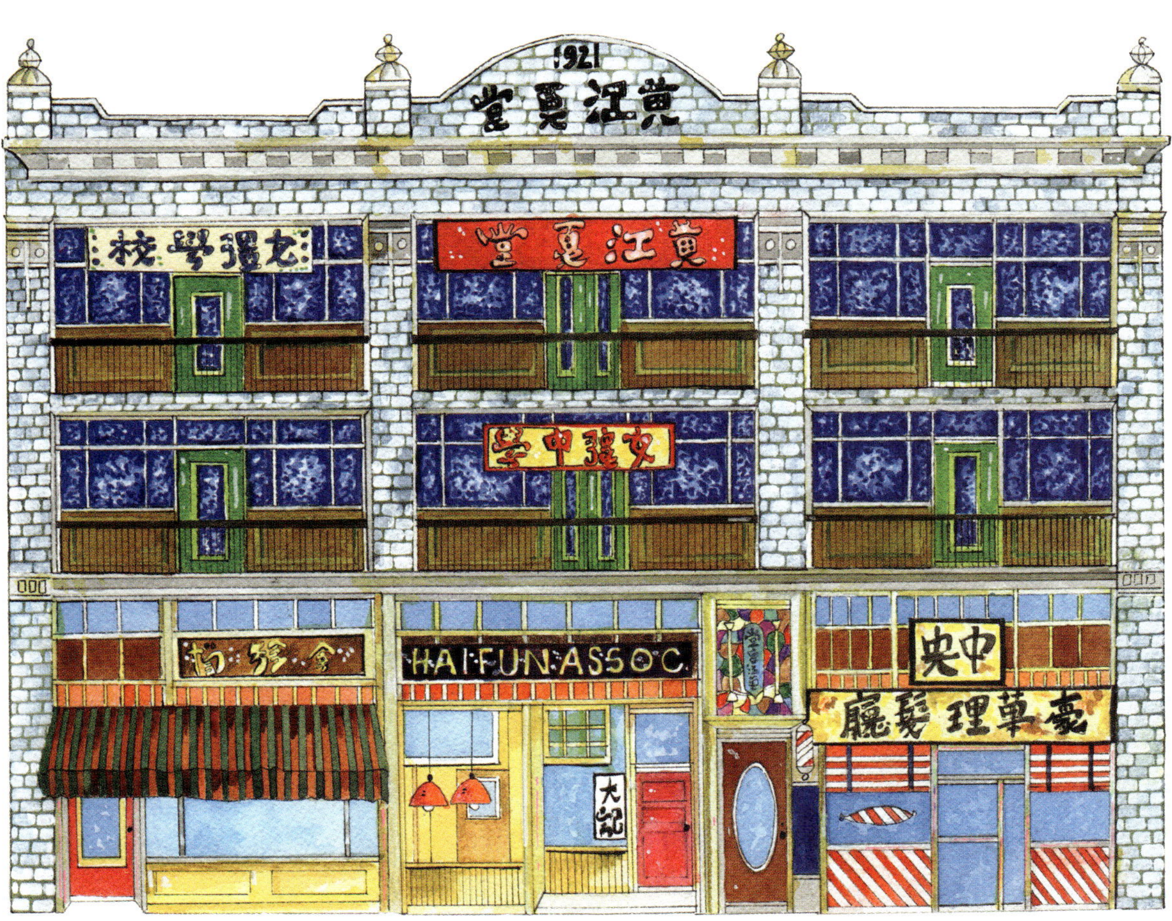

1921
黃江夏堂
九邑學校
黃江夏堂
文強中學
金發行
HAI FUN ASSOC.
大記
中央
文華理髮廳

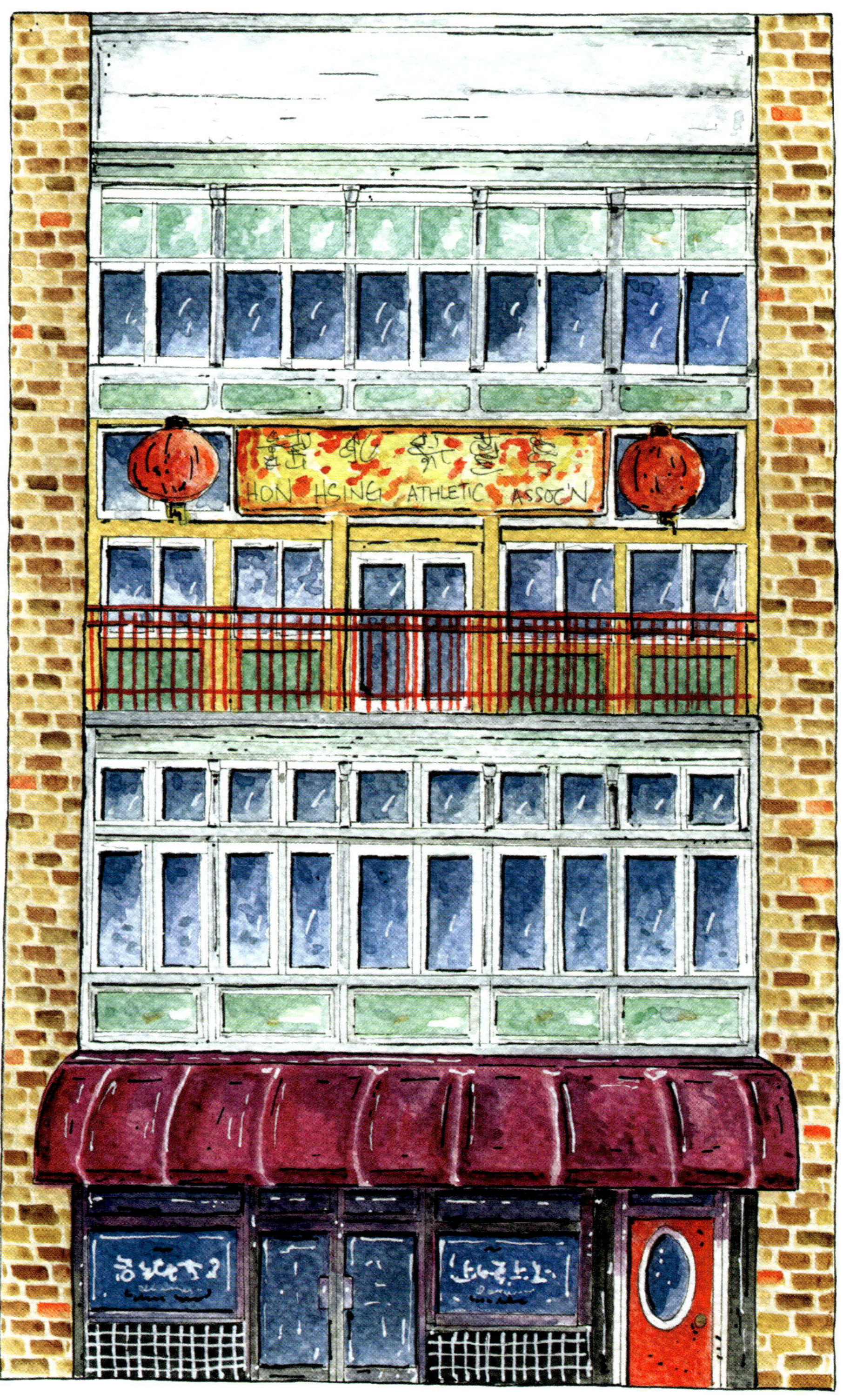

HON HSING ATHLETIC ASSOC'N

Hon Hsing Athletic Club
27 East Pender
Built 1910

Standing tall like a Lunar New Year lion perched on its hind feet, the four-storey building at 27 East Pender exudes influence, with its recessed balcony adorned with red wrought-iron railings. On warm summer days, when the windows and balcony doors are open, you can make out the shadows of Hon Hsing Athletic's martial artists moving to the rhythmic beat of drums, their steady hands balancing the decorative heads of festive lions and golden dragons. Named after a military general in the fabled Three Kingdoms who cared for his soldiers despite differences in surnames or background, the Hon Hsing also values philanthropy and passing Chinese traditions on to the next generation.

Concerned about Japan's occupation of China from 1931 to 1945, the Wongs' Benevolent Association formed the Hon Hsing Athletic Club to raise funds for China through Chinese lion dance performances. After the Second World War, fearing the loss of Chinese culture and language among their Canadian-born children, the older generation invested in athletic organizations such as the Hon Hsing to teach youth about their heritage. Athletic clubs would become pillars in preserving Chinese culture and values, as well as providing young people with the discipline and physical strength to weather adversity.

The building has been primarily mixed-use with a succession of retail businesses on the ground floor including a grocery store, a social club, the Kuo Kong Silk Company, and the Chinese Canadian Museum. Similar to the CBA building, which was completed a year earlier, 27 East Pender features recessed balconies and a side entrance to the upper floors. In 2024, Modernize Tailors moved into the ground floor.

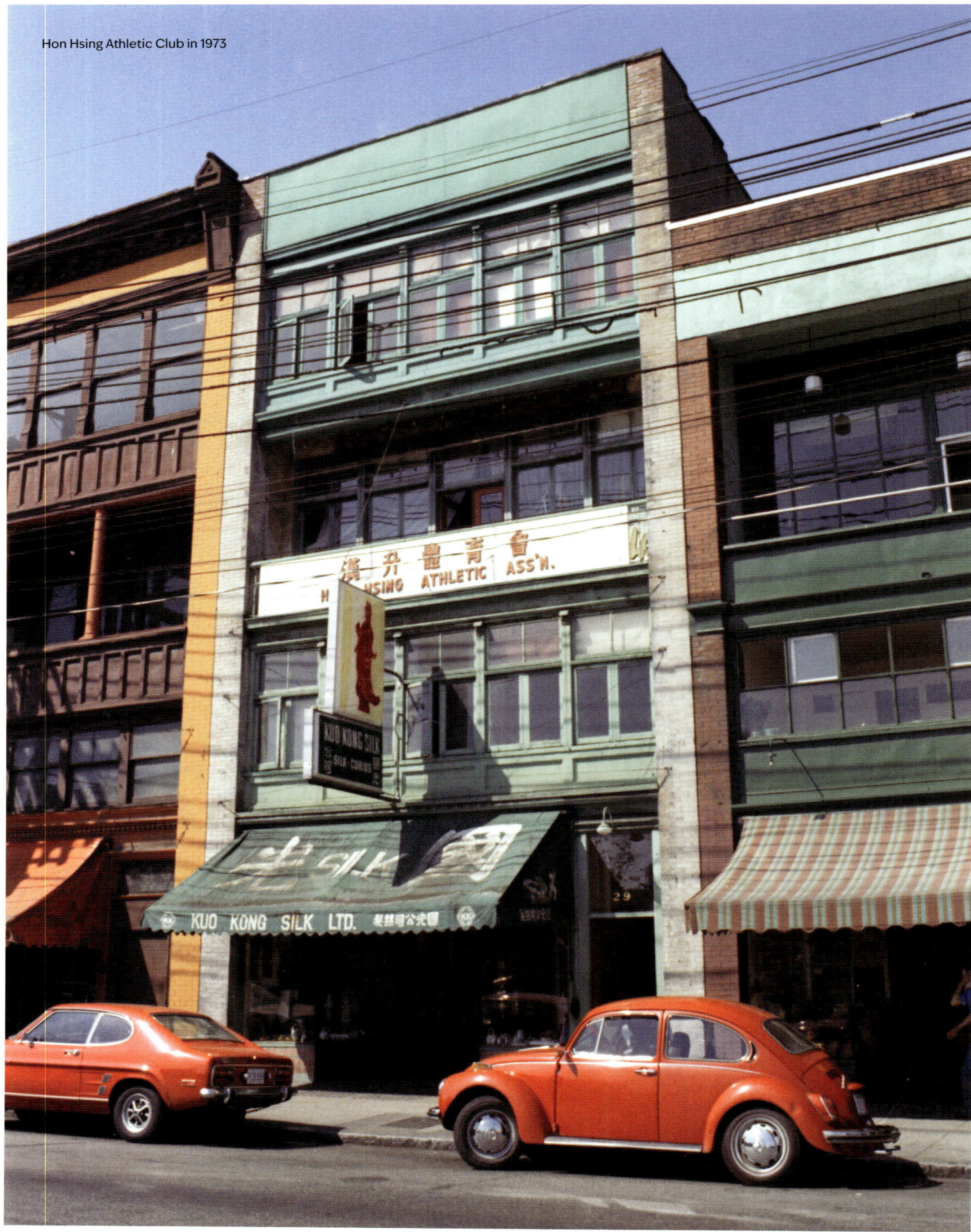

Hon Hsing Athletic Club in 1973

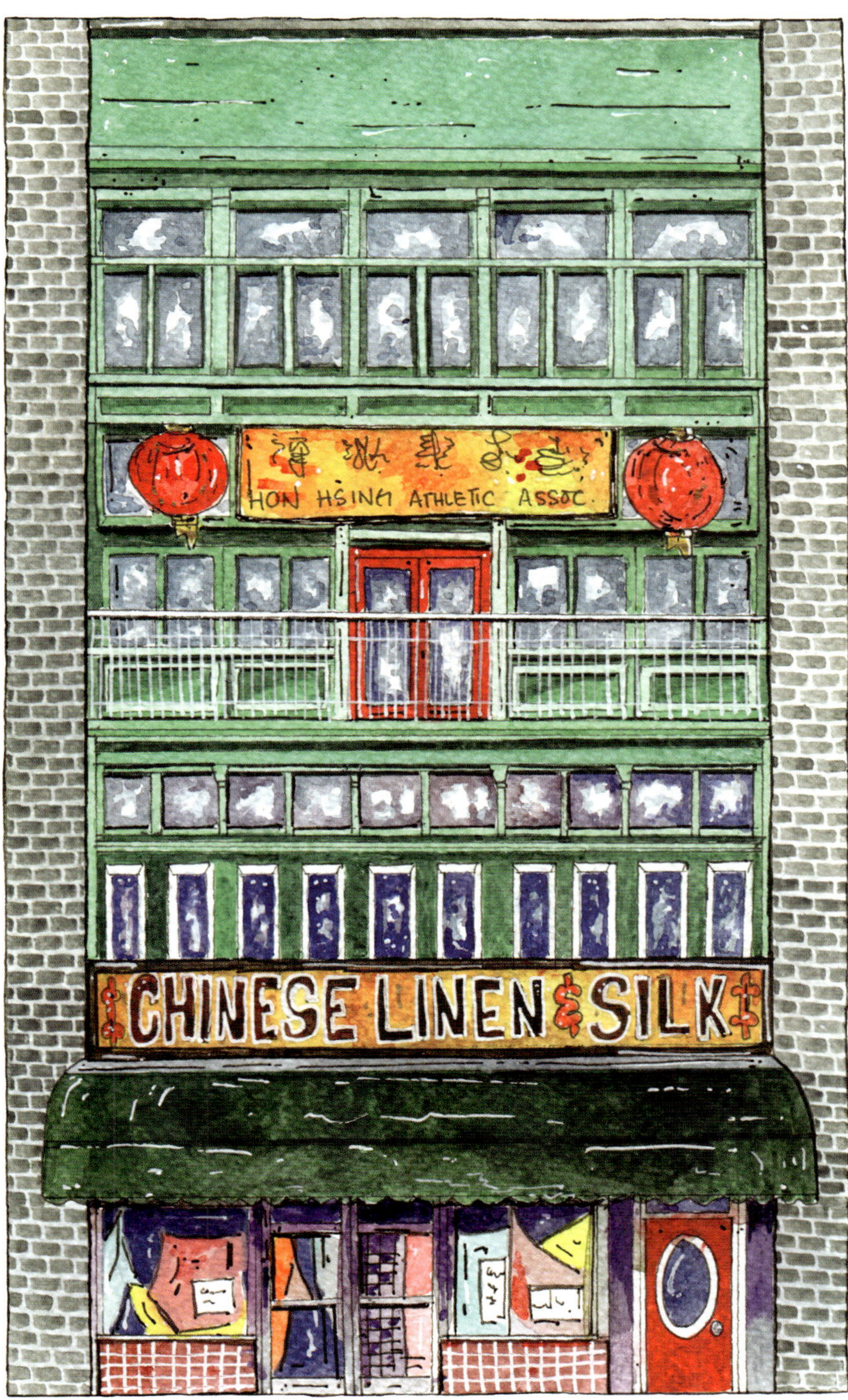

HON HSING ATHLETIC ASSOC.
CHINESE LINEN & SILK

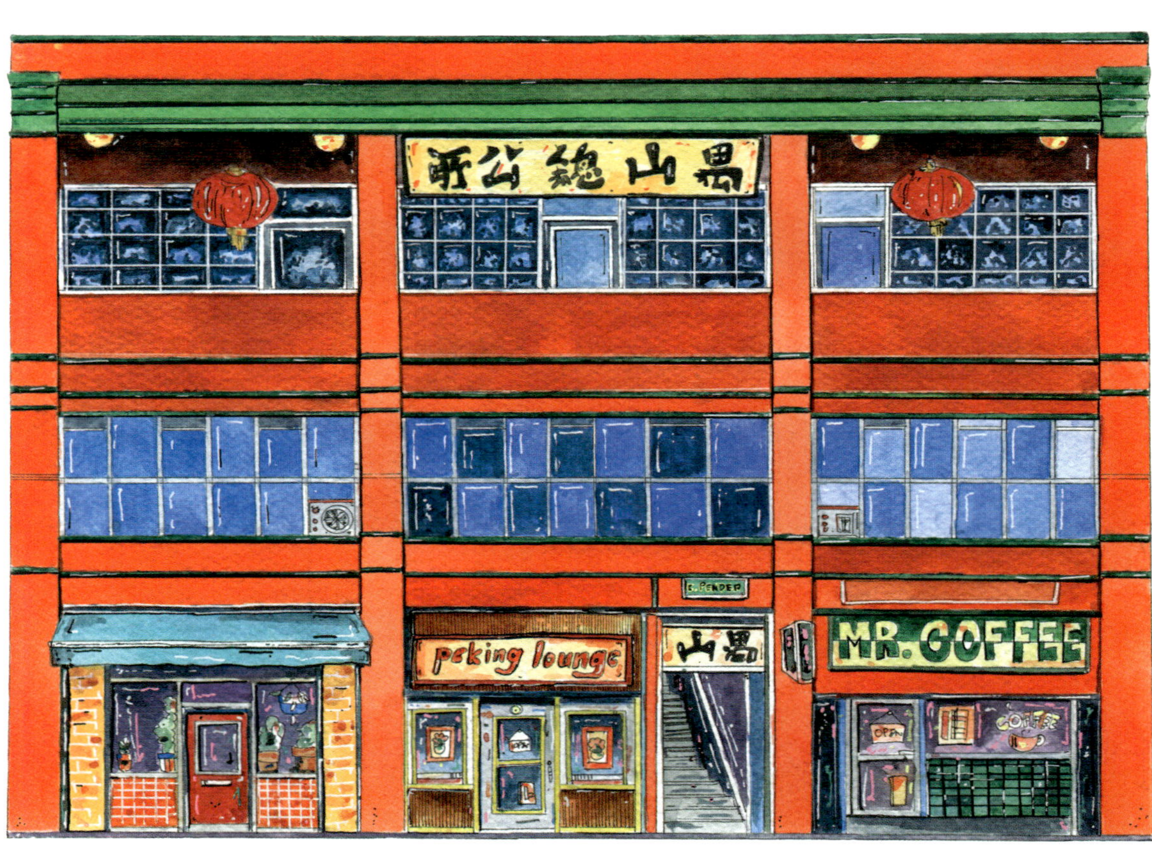
昂山總公所
6. PENDER
peking lounge
山昂
MR. COFFEE
OPEN
COFFEE

Yue Shan Association Buildings

33–39 East Pender, 30–50 Market Alley,
41–47 East Pender
Built 1890, 1912, 1920

As one of the first overseas locality-based organizations, the Yue Shan Association formed in 1858 in San Francisco to assist early settlers from Poon Yue County in Guangdong. The Vancouver branch formed in 1894 and initially gathered in merchant offices such as the Sam Kee Company until a permanent home was acquired on East Pender. Yue Shan played an important role in aiding early migrants by creating a sense of community and a home away from home, and by fulfilling obligations like shipping their bones back to China.

The ritual of returning the bones of deceased sojourners was first practised when the Chinese ventured to Malaya and Singapore as plantation labourers during the early nineteenth century. It was initially imposed by the Qing as proof that sojourners had returned home. Practised among Chinese migrants in Canada and the United States during the late nineteenth and early twentieth centuries, the ritual involved exhuming bodies after seven years, which is the minimum time needed for complete decomposition, then cleaning, drying, and packaging the bones to be shipped to China. Organizations would charter a vessel that would transport bones to Hong Kong, where they were stored at Tung Wah Hospital's mortuary until they were collected by relatives or shipped to home villages in China for burial.[14]

Yue Shan's interests have evolved since the 1940s to incorporate more social and recreational activities, such as Chinese martial arts, music, and a basketball team and sports club, as well as a scholarship fund for children of members. The Yue Shan has supported the Mount Saint Joseph Hospital (also known as the Chinese Hospital), the Chinese Public School, the Chinese Cultural Centre, and the Chinese Benevolent Association.

Built in 1890, 1912, and 1920, the Yue Shan Association buildings are a cluster of three structures surrounding a courtyard. They have been the organizational home for the Yue Shan since 1943 but also served as a dormitory and organizational space for early settlers. The ground floor has provided commercial space to a multitude of retail, including grocery stores, a drugstore, a dry goods store, a herbal medicine store, a tailor shop, a beauty salon, a furniture store, and a coffee shop.[15] The inner building, accessed via a small entrance on East Pender, once opened onto Market Alley, a small commercial district in the alley between East Pender and East Hastings that contained laundries, restaurants, and services. Today, the entrances are locked or abandoned. [16]

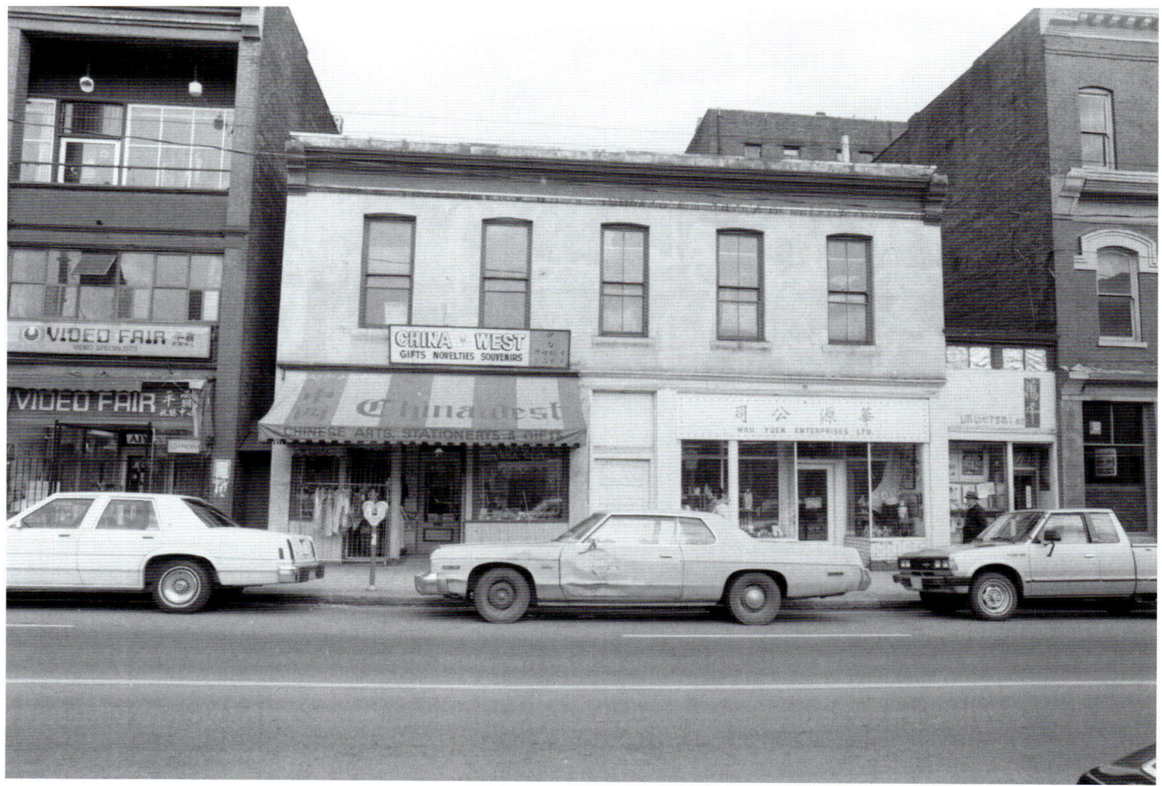

Yue Shan Building in the 1980s

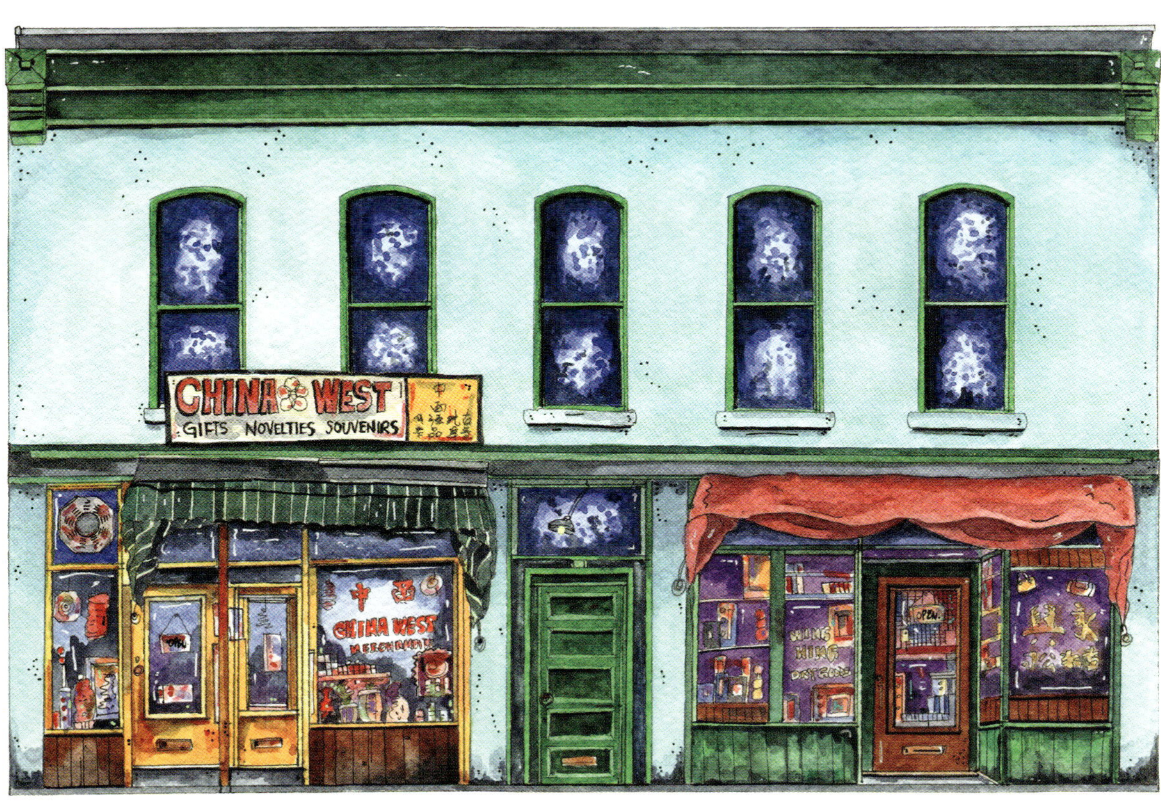

CHINA WEST
GIFTS NOVELTIES SOUVENIRS
中西
CHINA WEST
WONG HING
DRY GOODS
OPEN

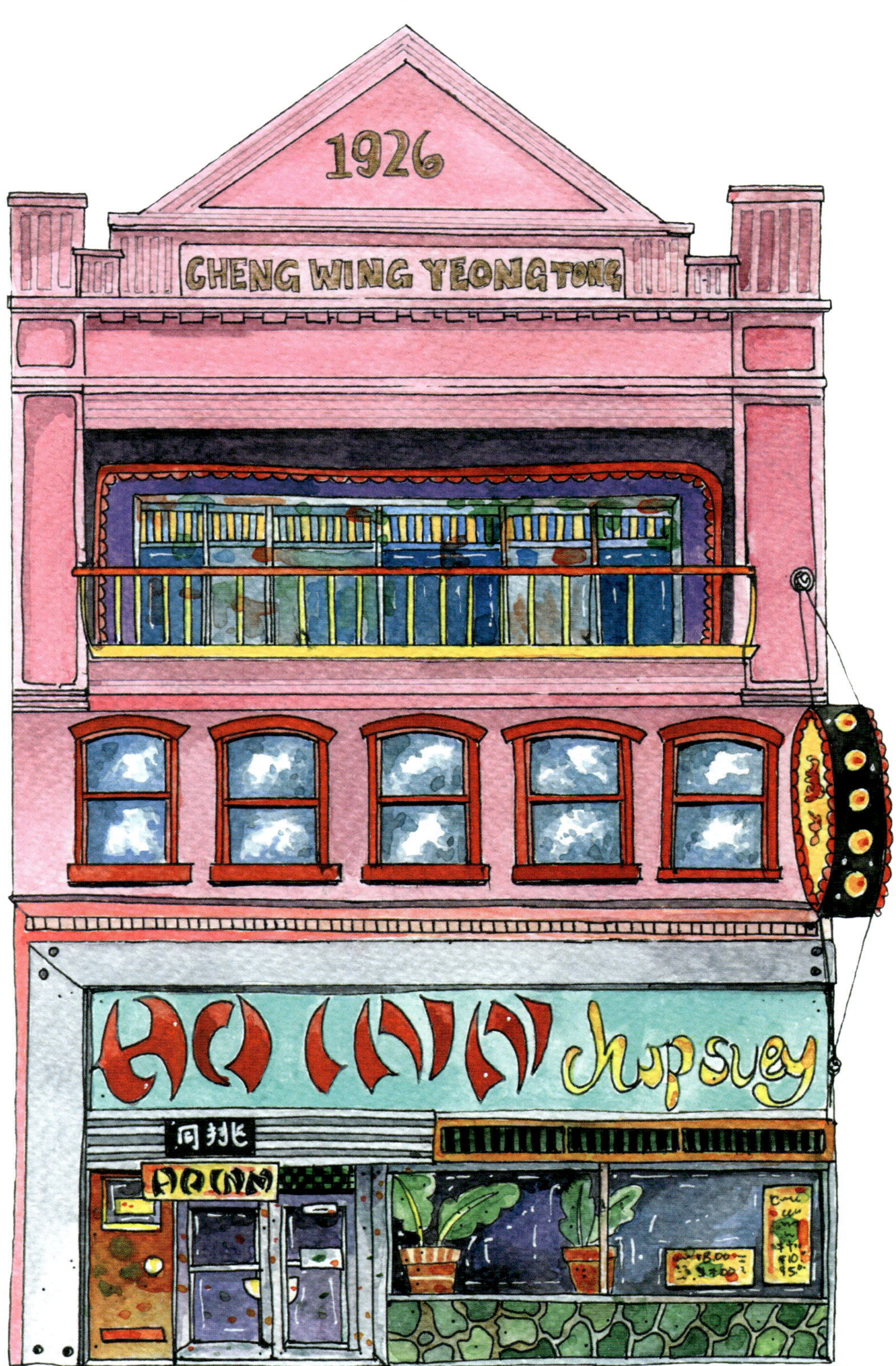

1926
CHENG WING YEONG TONG
HO LUNG chop suey
同挑
HO INN

Cheng Wing Yeong Tong Society Building

79 East Pender
Built 1911/1926

If you look carefully at the brickwork on the three-storey pink building at 79 East Pender, you might notice cuts in the brick that separate the top floor and recessed balcony from the lower floors. Built in two stages, the original building was Italianate style with commercial retail on the ground floor and contained a mezzanine along with residences on the second floor. In 1926, a third floor was added to provide meeting space and residences for the Cheng Wing Yeong Tong Society.

The layered history of 79 East Pender demonstrates how the community adjusted to the rapid growth in the 1910s and 1920s. The ground floor has been home to the Ho Inn Restaurant and Peking Lounge, and is currently occupied by Private & Co. clothing store.

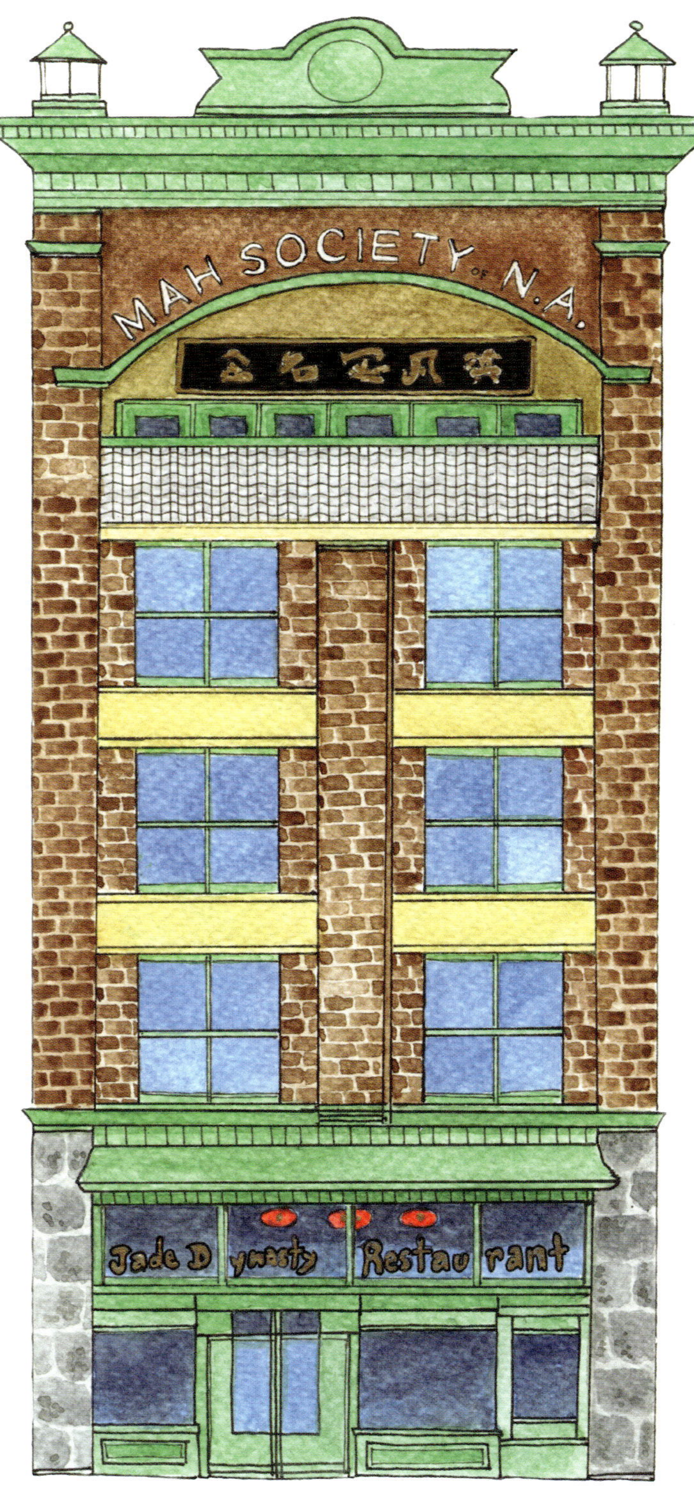

MAH SOCIETY OF N.A.
黃月巴屯石公
Jade Dynasty Restaurant

Mah Society Building
137–139 East Pender
Built 1913

In 2017, the Mah Society Building underwent major exterior and structural repairs, including the re-creation of the original 1921 roofline, making it the first of the Chinese heritage society buildings in Chinatown to be restored. The financial success of the Mah Society, a surname-based organization, is not accidental or based on luck, despite its strategic position as one of the tallest historical buildings in Chinatown. Rather, the organization's success is the result of savvy financial practices and a willingness to diversify its income by leasing space to both members and non-members.

The Mah Society started informally in 1906 as Gim Gee Tong Ba Zi Hui, a name that pays homage to the native village of the Mah clan, Gim Gee, as well as the practice known as bazi hui. Bazi hui resembles the practice of investing or buying shares, where members pool their money to meet the organization's broader needs, such as creating emergency funds or purchasing a building.[17] Unlike donations, the practice of bazi hui is more like a loan, as members are compensated for their investment and are able to buy back monetary contributions when funds are available.[18] In 1919, the Mah Society raised twenty-six thousand dollars through bazi hui and membership fees to acquire the building for forty-five thousand dollars. Two years later, members commissioned the addition of a fifth floor, which included a balcony, spacious meeting hall, office, and kitchen.

The roof on the original 1913 structure featured Chinese architectural motifs in the form of a pagoda-roof cornice and temple finials, which were replaced in 1921 with two Chinese pentagon lanterns, glazed tiled roof with flying eaves, and a horizontal cornice with dentils. However, the details were later replaced with a painted fascia band featuring the association name in Chinese and English. Society buildings in Chinatown such as the Chin Wing Chun, the Wongs' Benevolent Association, and the Cheng Wing Yeong Tong position their meeting rooms at the top as a status symbol.[19]

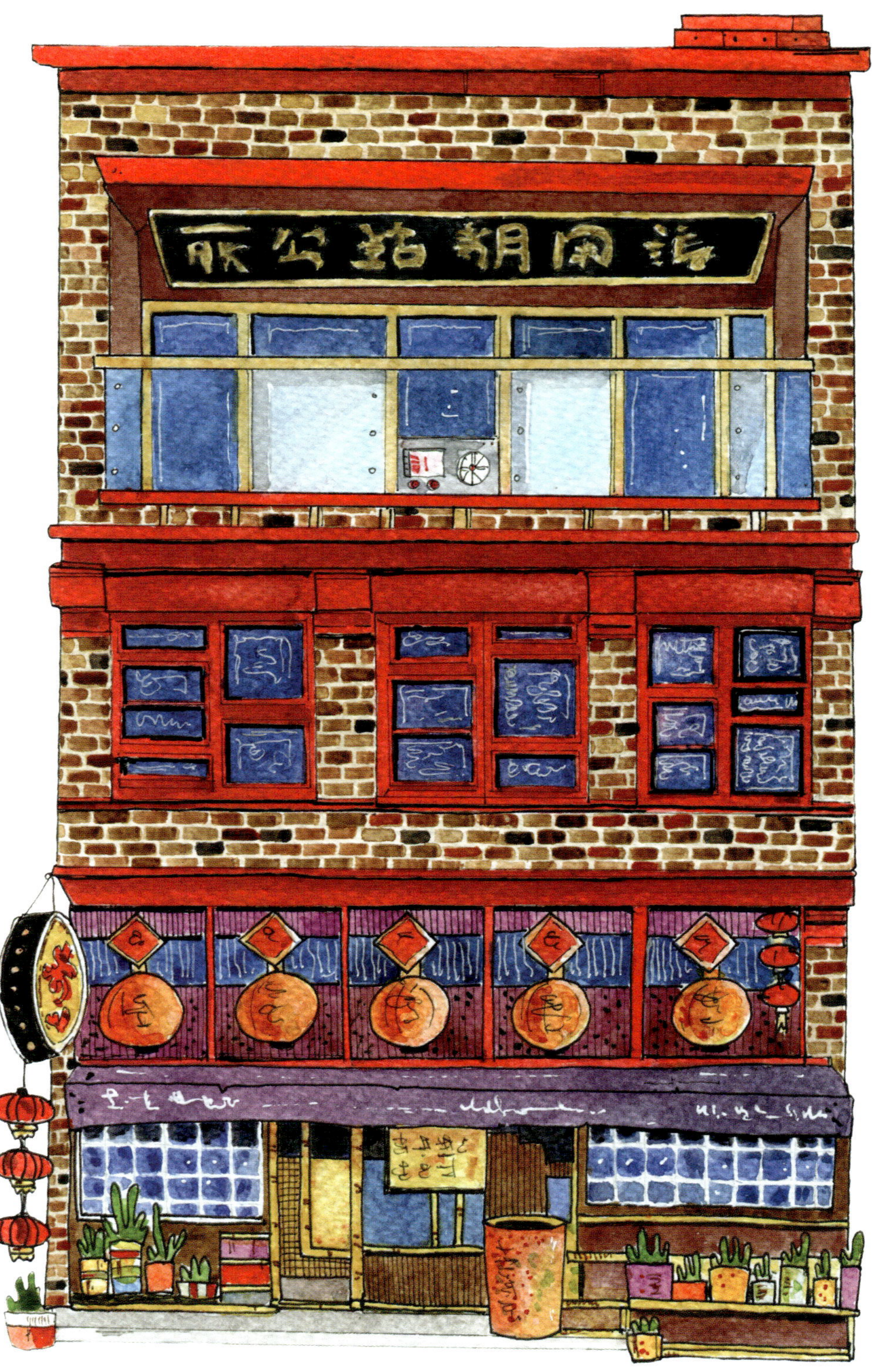
永 公 所 朝 同 海

Lung Kong Association
135 East Pender
Built 1923

Bamboo Village Trading Company, on the ground floor of 135 East Pender, offers a sensory experience as you wander through the maze of pottery interlaced with old newspapers, delicate paper lanterns, and shelves of incense sticks. Wedged into its long narrow aisles is a one-stop shop for giftware and home goods, treasures from old China, items for ancestor worship, kitchenware, bamboo goods, furniture, and plants galore.[20] The museum-like collection is like a time machine to old-school Chinatown and has been a part of the neighbourhood for forty years.

Similar to other buildings along the 100 block of East Pender, the three-storey multipurpose brick building was built to accommodate rapid growth in the 1910s to 1920s, and provided space for commercial ventures, restaurants, and association-based activities.[21] Designed by A. Ernst Henderson, the building features pale buff brick, a recessed balcony with decorative elements on its facade, the date of completion on the parapet, and a sheet metal cornice and metal frieze at mid-height. The building's storefront is arranged symmetrically, accommodating a left-hand entrance to the meeting hall above, and features a mezzanine above the ground floor that is visible from the facade.[22]

At least three native place- or surname-based associations have occupied the building, including the Hoi Ping Association, the Lung Kong Kung Shaw Association, and the Lee Kwong Kai Association. In the building since its construction, the Lung Kong Association serves the surnames Lau, Kwan, Cheung, and Chin and has historical connections dating to the Han Dynasty (206 BCE to 220 CE). According to legend, four men from four different surnames volunteered for the imperial army, where they pledged eternal friendship, brotherhood, and service to country. In 1661, their descendants built the Lung Kong Ancient Temple in the city of Hoiping in Guangdong Province. The first Lung Kong Association was formed in San Francisco in 1875.

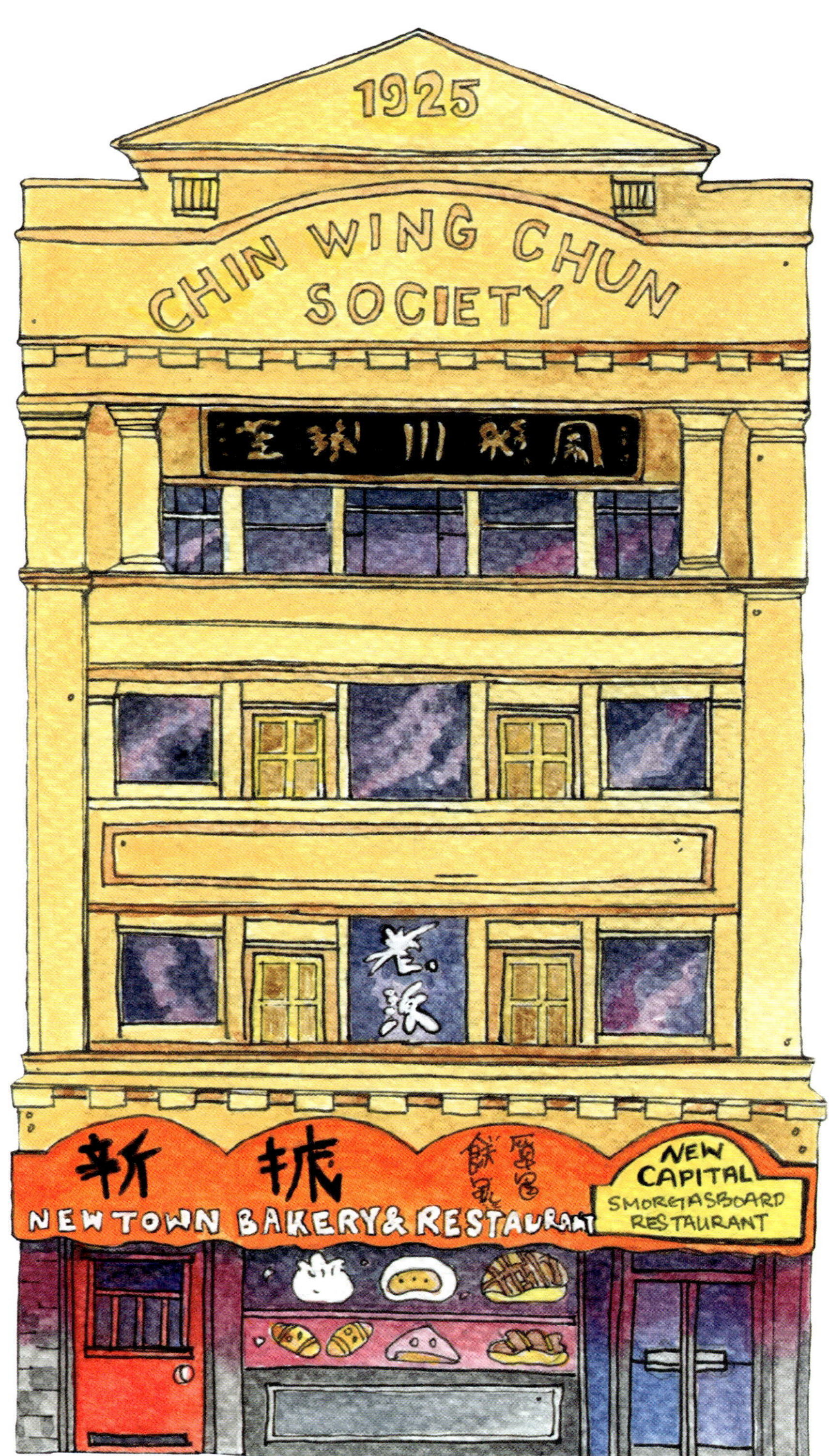

1925
CHIN WING CHUN SOCIETY
NEW CAPITAL SMORGASBOARD RESTAURANT
NEW TOWN BAKERY & RESTAURANT

Chin Wing Chun Society Building

158–160 East Pender
Built 1925

Built in 1925, the pale yellow brick-and-stucco building that is home to the Chin Wing Chun Society is a playground of activities. Behind the wooden door at 158 East Pender is a marble staircase that leads to separate floors dedicated to mahjong, martial arts, and karaoke.[23] At the very top is a large meeting room and a majestic stained-glass dome embedded in the ceiling. The building displays the date of completion and name of the society on its arched parapet. Designed by architect R. A. McKenzie, who spent five years in China, the building incorporates recessed balconies and blends Western characteristics.

Standing four storeys high with a mezzanine added after completion, the classic revival-style building has housed a series of restaurants on the ground floor. From 1925 to 1959, Sai Woo Chop Suey served homestyle Cantonese food and featured a distinctive neon sign of a green-and-yellow rooster that was lost after the restaurant closed. From the 1960s to 1990s, the building featured an imposing awning that was used by Wayen Restaurant and New Town Bakery.

Organizations outside Chinatown

Interview with Andy Yan, director of the City Program at Simon Fraser University

The designated areas where early Chinese lived and worked were more fluid than initially thought, as demonstrated by the location of the Yan Society, northeast of Chinatown in what was once the Japanese district of Paueru Gai (Powell Street). Starting in the 1920s Andy Yan's grandparents lived in the building, which functioned like other clan organizations by offering low-cost rooms, community, and services. In 2022, Andy discovered several items, including a ledger from 1929 that revealed the original location of the Yan Society at 148 Cordova near the old Woodward's department store. His discovery demonstrates that Chinatown's boundaries weren't clearly drawn, and that the city was more integrated than some believe. As well, his discovery of other documents identifying members with surnames other than Yan suggests that some clan-based societies welcomed individuals from the broader community.[24]

Andy's great-grandfather, Kwok Yam Yan (Charlie), first emigrated from southern China in the 1910s. As the history of racialized groups is often steeped in silence, it's unclear when exactly he arrived, especially as he was likely a "paper son." Although that's not clear either, Andy admits.

The system of "paper sons" or "paper daughters" involved the purchase of identity papers issued during the Head Tax and exclusion period, or later residency or citizenship documents, to circumvent Canada's restrictive immigration policies. Andy explains that in the pursuit of a better life and better outcomes for their family, many men had no choice but to live lonely and isolated existences as bachelors. The government wanted to ensure that the men had limited choices and that they were not in Canada to stay, so they restricted any opportunity for family reunification.

In the 1950s, it was estimated that eleven thousand paper relatives were living in Canada. The numbers alarmed authorities, and the RCMP recruited a contingent of police officers from Hong Kong to help conduct raids on residencies, businesses, and workplaces to check the identities of the Chinese. By 1964, the federal government was willing to forgive so-called immigration racketeers if they came forward and admitted they had entered Canada on false papers. During this time, organizations such as the Chinese Freemasons provided authorities with records of membership and donation slips that stated the name of the individual and date.[25] The records were enough for authorities to provide approximately twelve thousand Chinese "paper relatives" with residency in Canada.

Andy recalls how Chinatown once provided a network of connections, a safety net, where the sacrifices of one generation helped lay the stepping-stones for the next to succeed.[26]

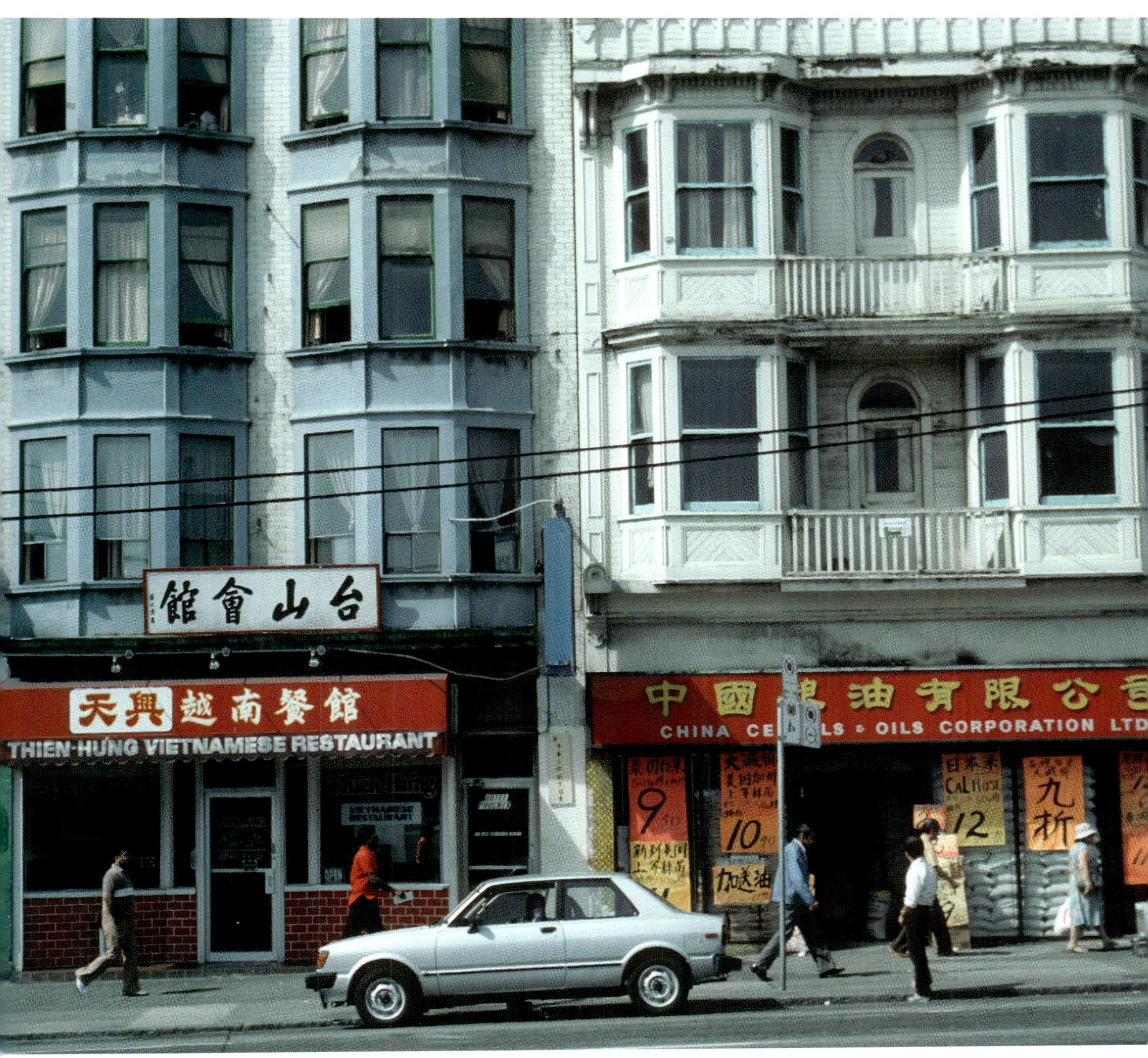

Associations and businesses on East Hastings outside of Chinatown, 1968

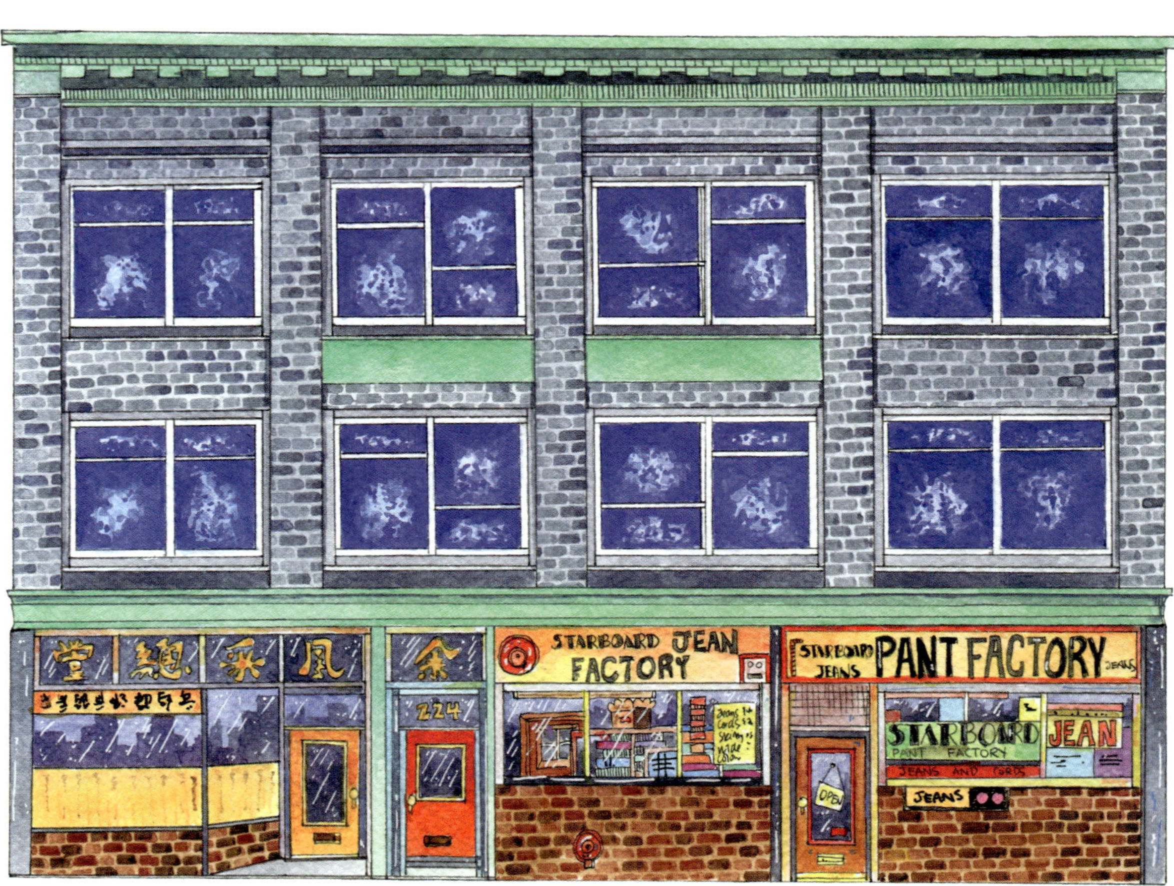

堂 聯 采 鳳 余
224
STARBOARD JEAN FACTORY
Jeans $14
Cords $2
Skinny
colors
STARBOARD JEANS PANT FACTORY Jeans
STARBOARD PANT FACTORY
JEAN
JEANS AND CORDS
JEANS
OPEN

Yee Fung Toy Society
222–226 East Georgia
Built 1911

It's easy to forget Vancouver's industrial past, when garment factories were scattered across the city. From 1972 to 1994, jeans were made and sold by Starboard Pant Factory in a three-storey brick building on the southern edge of Chinatown. Starboard once had outlets in Victoria, Surrey, and Calgary, and made five thousand sales per week, with $2 million a year in sales of casual pants. They were the first store to sell acid-wash jeans in British Columbia.[27]

Built in 1911 by Edward Evans Blackmore, the multipurpose building was also home to various businesses, such a real estate office, a grocery store (Kwong Man Sang), and the organizational meeting place for the Yee Fung Toy Society. With origins dating back to 1904 and roots in California and Victoria, the organization maintains housing units on the building's upper floors and uses the ground floor for membership and organizational services.

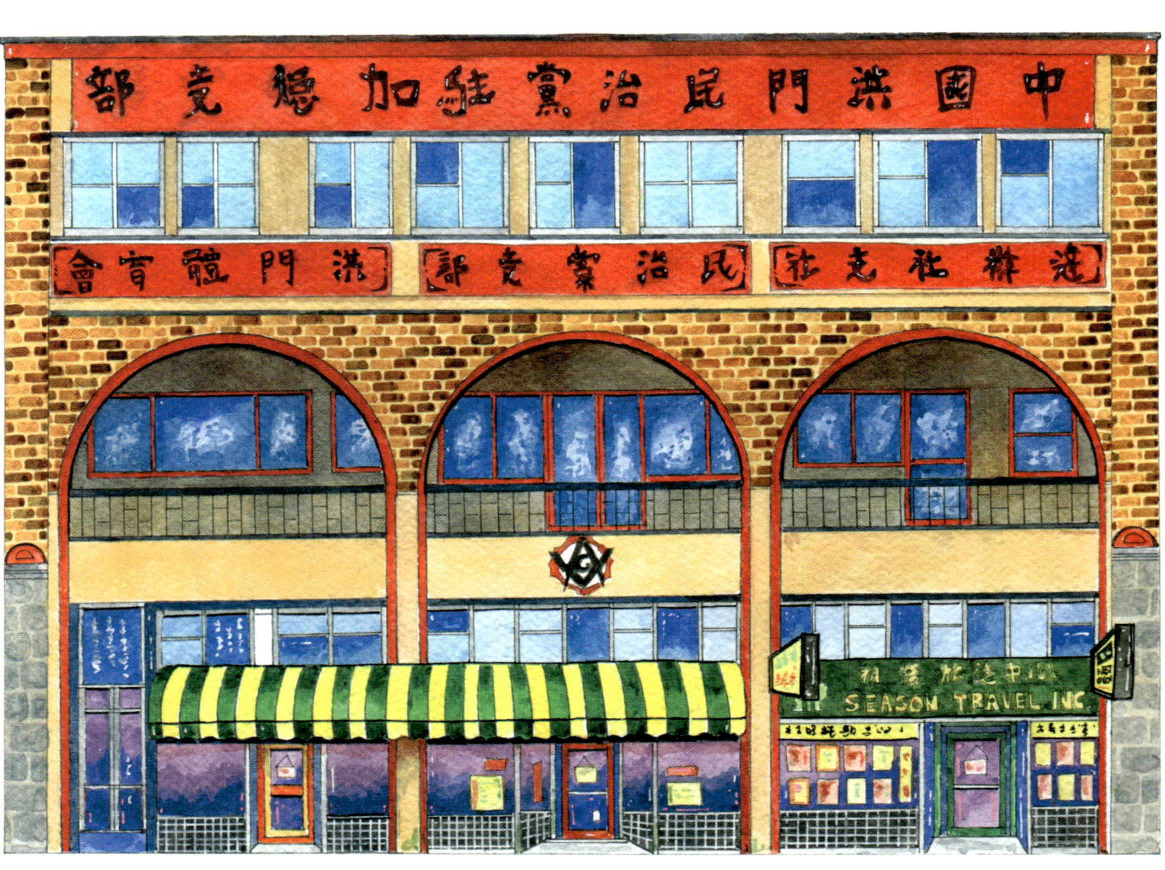
中國洪門民治黨駐加總支部
洪門體育會
民治黨支部
港僑社
中港施達旅遊
SEASON TRAVEL INC

Chinese Freemasons and Dart Coon Club
110–116 East Pender
Built 1907

The Chee Kung Tong, or Chinese Freemasons, have owned a number of buildings, including 5 West Pender, 490 Columbia, and their current headquarters at 110–116 East Pender. Originally built in 1907, the current home of the Chinese Freemasons was transformed in 1967 with the addition of three large arches and a balcony to its facade. The Victorian four-storey mixed-use building includes a large meeting hall as well as accommodation, offices, a martial arts studio, and commercial retail on the ground floor.[28]

The Chinese Freemasons were one of the first formal networks or organizations to establish themselves in Canada. The fraternal organization initially supported Dr. Sun Yat-sen's goal of overthrowing the Qing monarchy in China, even mortgaging multiple properties in Vancouver and elsewhere to raise funds. However, when Sun failed to recognize the contributions of the Chee Kung Tong, the organization lost influence in China. After establishing a republican regime in China in 1912, Sun refused to return the funds the Chee Kung Tong had helped to raise, earning him the nickname Sun, the Big Liar.[29] In 1918, the Dart Coon Club formed as an internal governing body within the Chinese Freemasons and was responsible for protecting local property and funds from Sun and Kuomintang sympathizers. Membership in the Chinese Freemasons is limited to those who are introduced by existing members and then sworn in.[30]

It is unknown why the Chee Kung Tong later changed its name to the Chinese Freemasons, as it does not have any formal affiliations with the Freemasons. The name change occurred during a period of restructuring, when members distanced themselves from Sun.[31] As the organization has historically been supported by miners, labourers, small businesses, and the working class, symbolically aligning itself with masonic values might have been an attempt to create a new identity.

The Chinese Freemasons provided membership identification to paper relatives in the 1960s and 1970s, engaged with the Strathcona Property Owners and Tenants Association (SPOTA) to stop the extension of the Georgia Viaduct in the early 1970s, and provided accommodation to seniors (490 Columbia, Chinese Hotel/Seniors Home built in 1890).[32]

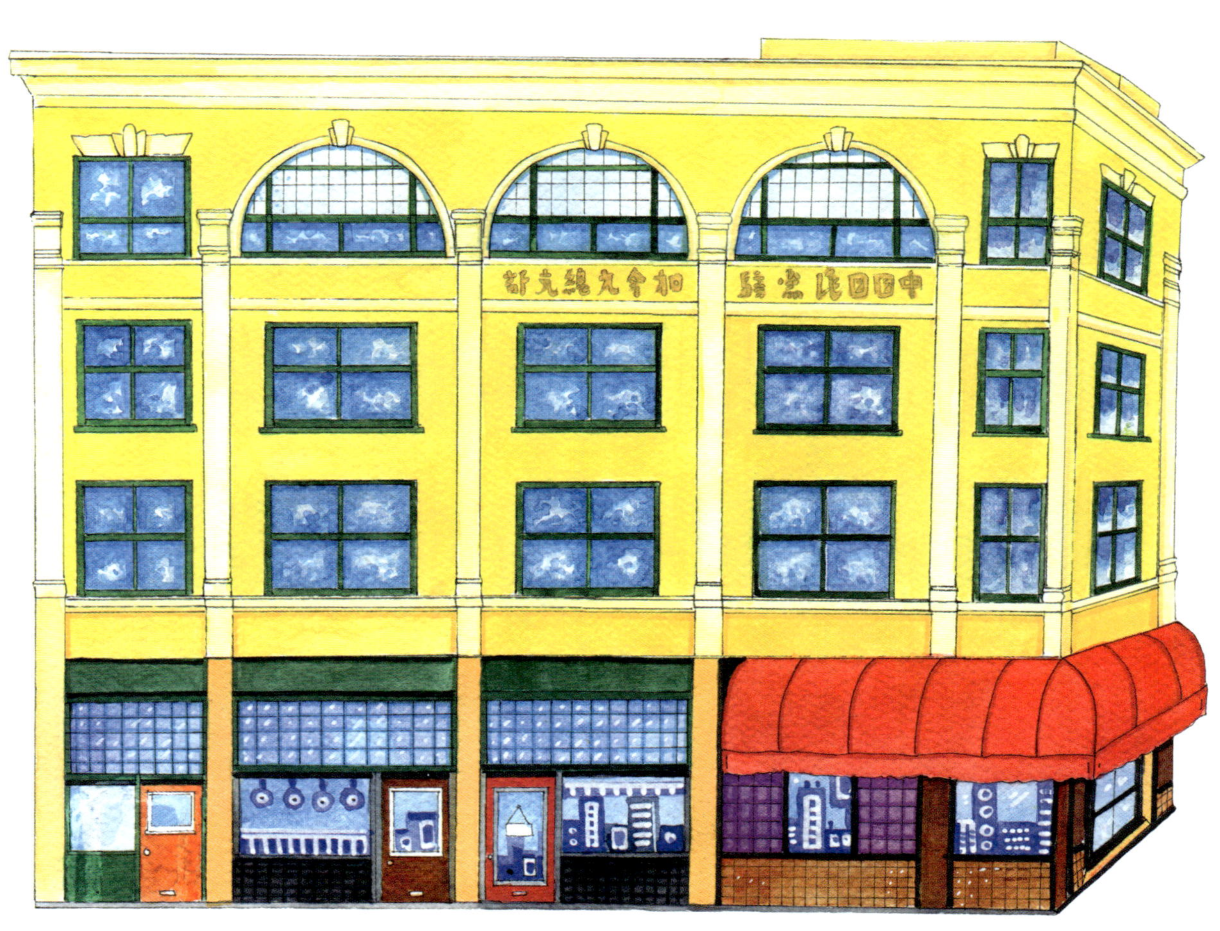

加會九總克都
中四四比他嘗駿

Nationalist League/ Kuomintang (KMT) Building
525 Gore Avenue
Built 1920

Designed in 1920 by William Edwardes Sprout, the opulent yellow four-storey brick building at the corner of East Pender and Gore Avenue was designed for the Nationalist League, or the Kuomintang (KMT). The KMT was officially formed in 1919 but had roots in Dr. Sun Yat-sen's Revive China Society, which was created in 1894 in Honolulu. Vancouver, where Sun lived for protracted periods during his exile, played an instrumental role in the overthrow of the Qing Dynasty.

When it became evident that Sun had reneged on his promise and supported the KMT instead of the Chee Kung Tong, the rift between the two organizations widened into a political feud that rippled across overseas Chinese communities. Political infighting, especially between the KMT and the Chinese Freemasons, continued in Vancouver throughout the 1920s and 1930s, with tensions subsiding during the Second Sino-Japanese War (1937–45).[33] Immediately after the end of the war in 1945, China launched into a civil war between the KMT and the Chinese Communist Party (CCP) led by Mao Zedong. In 1949, the KMT fled to Taiwan, a former Qing territory that was annexed by Japan from 1895 to 1945. In the post-1967 era of immigration, a points-based system facilitated the entrance to Canada of large numbers of immigrants from Taiwan.

Built as the most impressive and grandest of KMT buildings in North America, the large structure occupies a corner lot and was strategically crested with both English and Chinese signage. Besides the CBA and the Chinese Empire Reform Association Building, no other Chinese organizational building featured Western inscription on its facade at this time. The building was originally finished with a Chinese pagoda-style turret on its roof, which was considered more modern than the CBA Building. The building further mixes recessed balconies with Western typology. Its position on a hill adds height and prominence, which reflects its prestigious and influential position in Chinatown.[34]

Political Tensions in Chinatown and Neighbourly Barbeques

Interview with Karin Lee, daughter of Wally Wah Ling Lee, owner of China Arts and Crafts (33 East Hastings)

Death threats were a regular occurrence for Wally Wah Ying Lee. During the 1960s and 1970s, Wally owned China Arts and Crafts at 33 East Hastings, which became a regular haunt for a small group of socialists who supported the People's Republic of China (PRC). The group was involved with the Chinese Youth Association, whose members weren't shy about voicing their thoughts on how communism should be celebrated as an intrinsic part of overseas Chinese identity. Active from 1954 to the 1980s, the organization was largely supported by labour unions, left-leaning academics, and communist sympathizers. A majority of the youth were Canadian-born Chinese seeking to carve an identity for themselves and to distance themselves from the previous generation.

At China Arts and Crafts, Wally sold art, cultural, and everyday items from the PRC, as well as propaganda, pictorials, pictures, records, medicine, and acupuncture needles that would help highlight the relevance of mainland China.

As a gathering place for pro-communist China supporters, China Arts and Crafts hosted backroom political discussions that were not welcome among the older generation in Chinatown, especially Nationalist and pro-Taiwan supporters who continued to have a foothold in the community. Wally's daughter, Karin Lee, explains that it wasn't unusual for her father to receive death threats because of his controversial political views. She notes that it wasn't an accident that his store was located outside of Chinatown on East Hastings. But those threats were buffered by Wally's status as a member of the Chinese Freemasons and the head of their Athletic Club.

Karin explains that while she was growing up, her family lived on the same block as one of the key Kuomintang members. "Although our fathers were enemies in Chinatown, in south Van[couver] the kids would play with each other and see each other at neighbourhood barbeques like normal neighbours," she reminisces.[35]

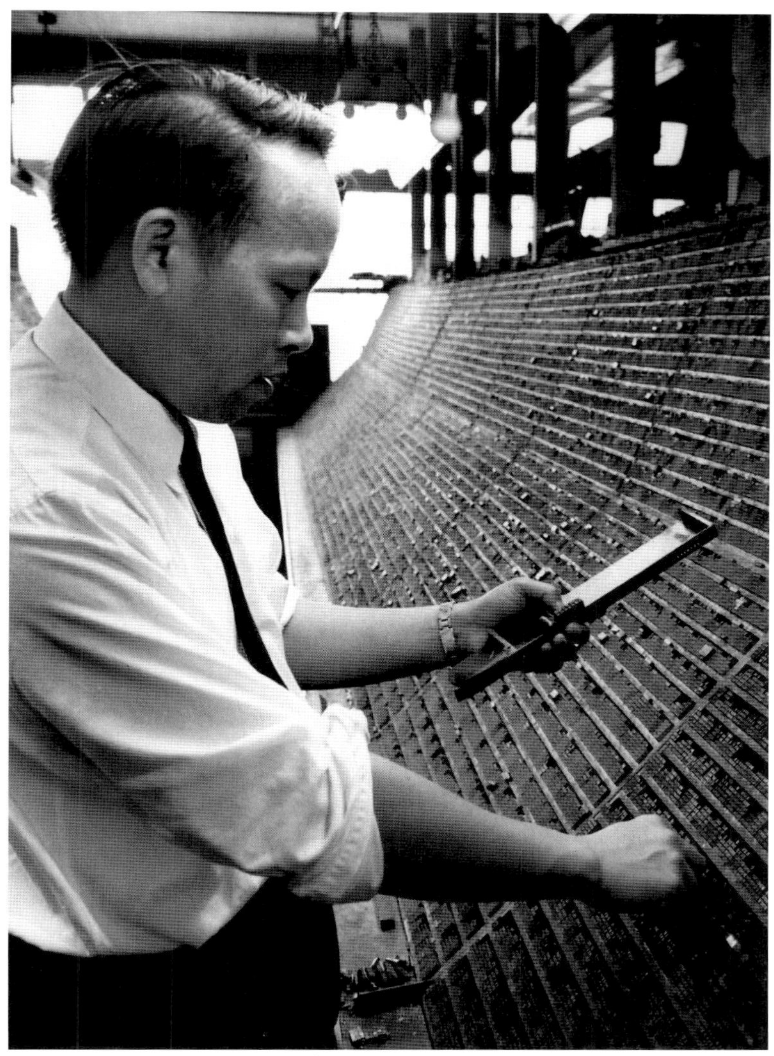

Wally Lee worked as a typesetter for the *Chinese Times* newspaper, 1964

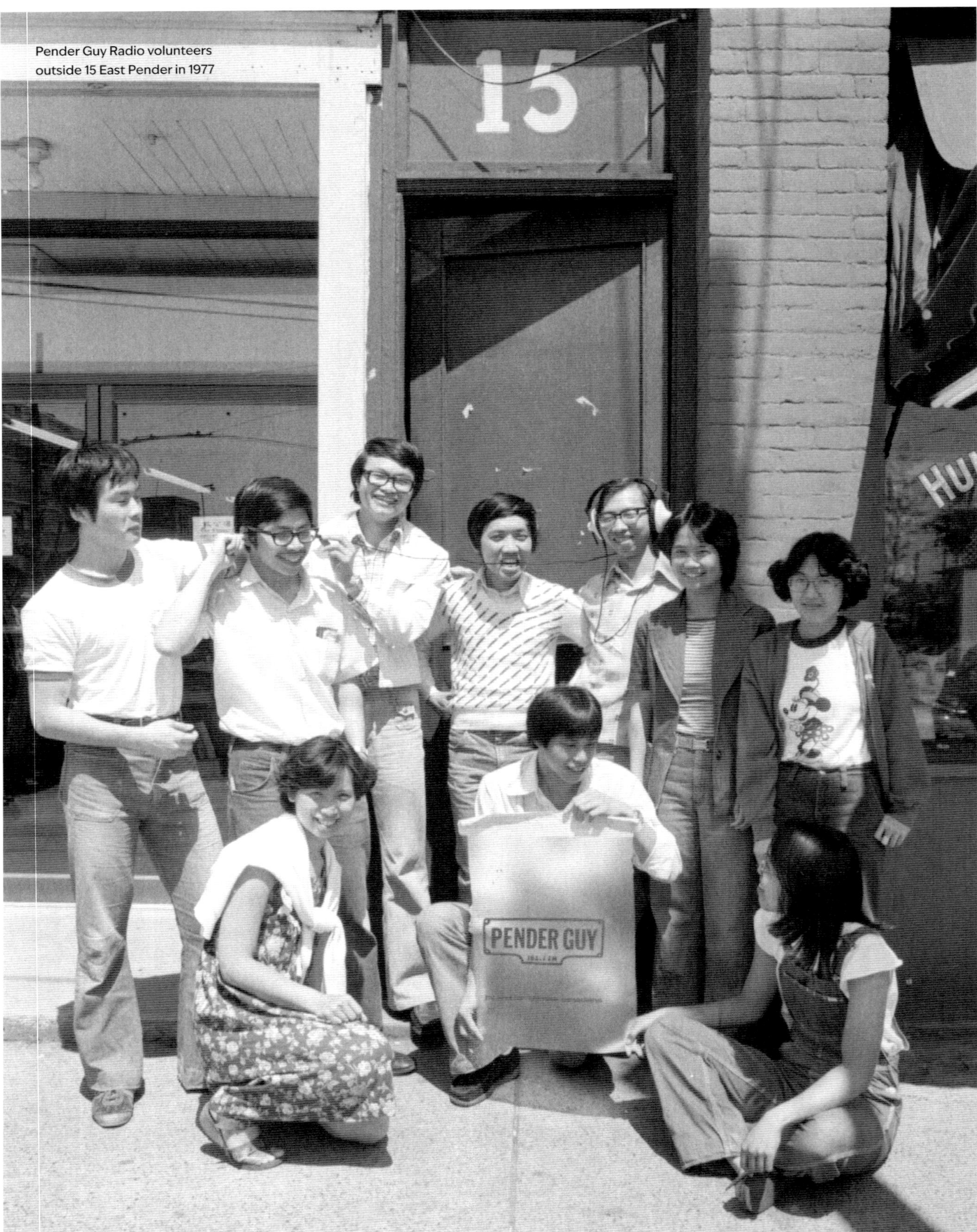

Pender Guy Radio volunteers outside 15 East Pender in 1977

Chinese Cultural Centre
50 East Pender/555 Columbia
Established 1973

Sitting on the former site of the Great Northern Railway and BC Electric Depot is a cultural institution spearheaded by a group of Canadian-born Chinese youth activists. Founded in 1973, the Chinese Cultural Centre (CCC) was the brainchild of a group of young people led by Roy Mah, a Second World War veteran who fought for the Chinese right to vote and was a champion of Canada's multiculturalism policy. Resisting traditional organizations supported by their fathers, many Canadian-born Chinese who came of age in the 1950s and 1960s embraced a hybrid life, one that combined their interpretations of what it means to be Chinese and Canadian. Moreover, having benefited from loosening geographic restrictions, the right to vote, and the ability to work in various professions, this generation tended to value upward mobility and integration into broader Canadian society.

The idea of a cultural institution that captured Chinese Canadian life gained momentum in the 1970s after Canada's diplomatic recognition of mainland China. Left-wing youth activists began challenging the previous generation's failure in addressing issues such as run-down housing, cheap labour, poor social services, and inadequate welfare. They argued that fresh leadership and unity among the Chinese was needed, and they proposed creating a community centre that would provide social programs and a sense of cultural pride that could be appreciated by subsequent generations.[36]

The radical criticisms of youth activists, however, fell on deaf ears until Roy Mah published an article on cultural preservation in *Chinatown News*. Roy noted that a record of historical events was needed to honour the contributions that the Chinese had made to Canada, and a library or exhibition would help fulfill this goal.[37] *Chinatown News*, initially called *Chinatown*, a newspaper that represented the vanguard generation of Canadian-born Chinese, operated out of 124 East Pender from 1953 to 1995. Published entirely in English and largely focused on stories associated with upward mobility and contributions of Canadian-born Chinese, the paper distanced itself from the previous generation. In 1964, for instance, *Chinatown News* noted that "our elders fear we are losing our heritage—but what they fail to realize is our heritage is North America[n], no matter how much we or they deplore it, no matter how much they try to deny it."[38]

Similar to *Chinatown News*, the youth-run radio station Pender Guy Radio further demonstrated the differences between the new generation of Canadian-born Chinese and their parents. Pender Guy, which translates to Pender Street in Cantonese, operated out of the Vancouver Co-op Radio Station from 1976 to 1981 and addressed topics like racism and sexism, generational differences, Asian American music, and civic elections and policy changes.[39] Like *Chinatown News*, Pender Guy provided a generation of young people with the tools to experiment with their identities and have a voice in the community.[40] Both *Chinatown News* and Pender Guy distanced youth from the suffering experienced by their fathers in order to carve out an identity, one that was Canadian, and that erased dependence on being Chinese and the isolation of Chinatown.[41]

Although the generational differences between Canadian-born Chinese and their parents caused divisions within the community, individuals like Roy Mah worked tirelessly to create a middle ground. Rather than criticize the previous generation, Roy drew on the strengths between youth and their parents, noting that his parents' generation was too busy working to create museums or libraries that honour culture. Instead, his generation has the ability to create institutions to remember the hard work and sacrifices of the previous generation. Roy noted that the history of Chinatown and the experiences of the Chinese in Canada are important to the younger generation, especially as they begin to carve out an identity outside of Chinatown. In his attempt to appeal to traditional organizations, Roy argued that the Chinese need a museum or a library that celebrates the Chinese and encourages those who moved out of Chinatown to return and rediscover their culture. A cultural centre would also provide educational services such as English-language instruction and citizenship classes to new immigrants, adopt open membership for Chinese and non-Chinese, and host festivities and cultural performances.[42]

Roy's idea for the CCC appealed to the older generation and gained support from traditional organizations such as the Wongs' Benevolent Association and the Chinese Freemasons. In particular, supporters appreciated the CCC's mission to preserve Chinese culture and uphold Chinese pride, especially as clan associations transitioned from traditional immigrant associations into more Canadian-oriented and progressive institutions.[43] By the 1990s, however, the broader Chinese community began questioning if the CCC actually represented the interests of a rapidly growing and increasingly diverse Chinese population, many of whom had arrived from Hong Kong, Taiwan, mainland China, South America, and elsewhere after the 1970s.[44]

Barbershop Gossip and Friendship
Interview with Sky Lee, author of *Disappearing Moon Café*

Sharon (Sky) Lee came of age in the 1960s and 1970s with a group of creative pioneers that included poet and founder of the Asian Canadian Writers' Workshop Jim Wong-Chu and author and historian Paul Yee.

Sky's family was one of a handful of Chinese Canadian families in the small town of Port Alberni on Vancouver Island. They later moved to Vancouver, where Sky's parents became staunch members of the Lee Association. Sky got her first job working for Roy Mah, who "paid us adolescents to assemble and mail out his monthly *Chinatown News*," she reminisces. "Afterwards, he kindly took us out for a meal at the Ho Ho restaurant."

Sky's novel, *Disappearing Moon Café*, weaves small-town experiences with the ghettoization of Chinatown. Sky says the novel is about community and friendship, and heavily influenced by her conversations with her dear friend the late Jim Wong-Chu, who often told her about "barbershop gossip" among Chinatown old-timers, the group of bachelors who came to symbolize life within Chinatown during the early twentieth century.

Sky adds that one of the pinnacle moments that influenced her work was a conversation with her father, who worked for the MacMillan Bloedel plywood mill, where he befriended a handful of old Chinese bachelors. During a picnic at Beacon Hill Park in Victoria, her father pointed out the rocky headland along the water's edge and said, "That was where desperately broke and lonely Chinamen went to end their lives."

In the aftermath of Vancouver's urban renewal scheme and attempts to build a freeway through Chinatown, Jim Wong-Chu and Paul Yee saved as many artifacts as they could. Paul, who worked for the Vancouver Archives, took a series of invaluable photographs of Chinatown, and Jim went on to publish a book of poetry, *Chinatown Ghosts*.[45] Sky drew murals on safety barriers as construction began on the much-anticipated Chinese Cultural Centre.[46]

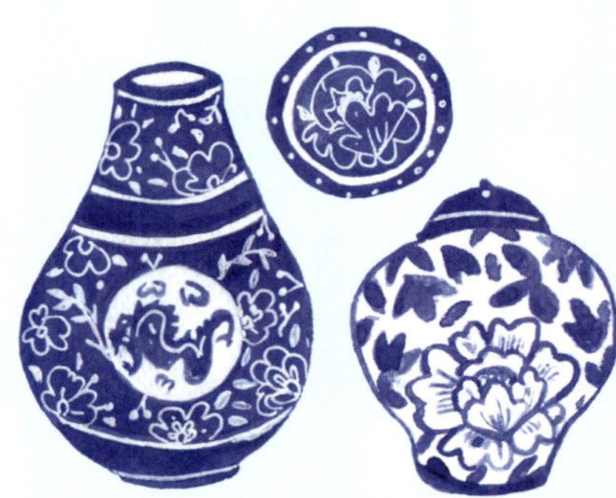

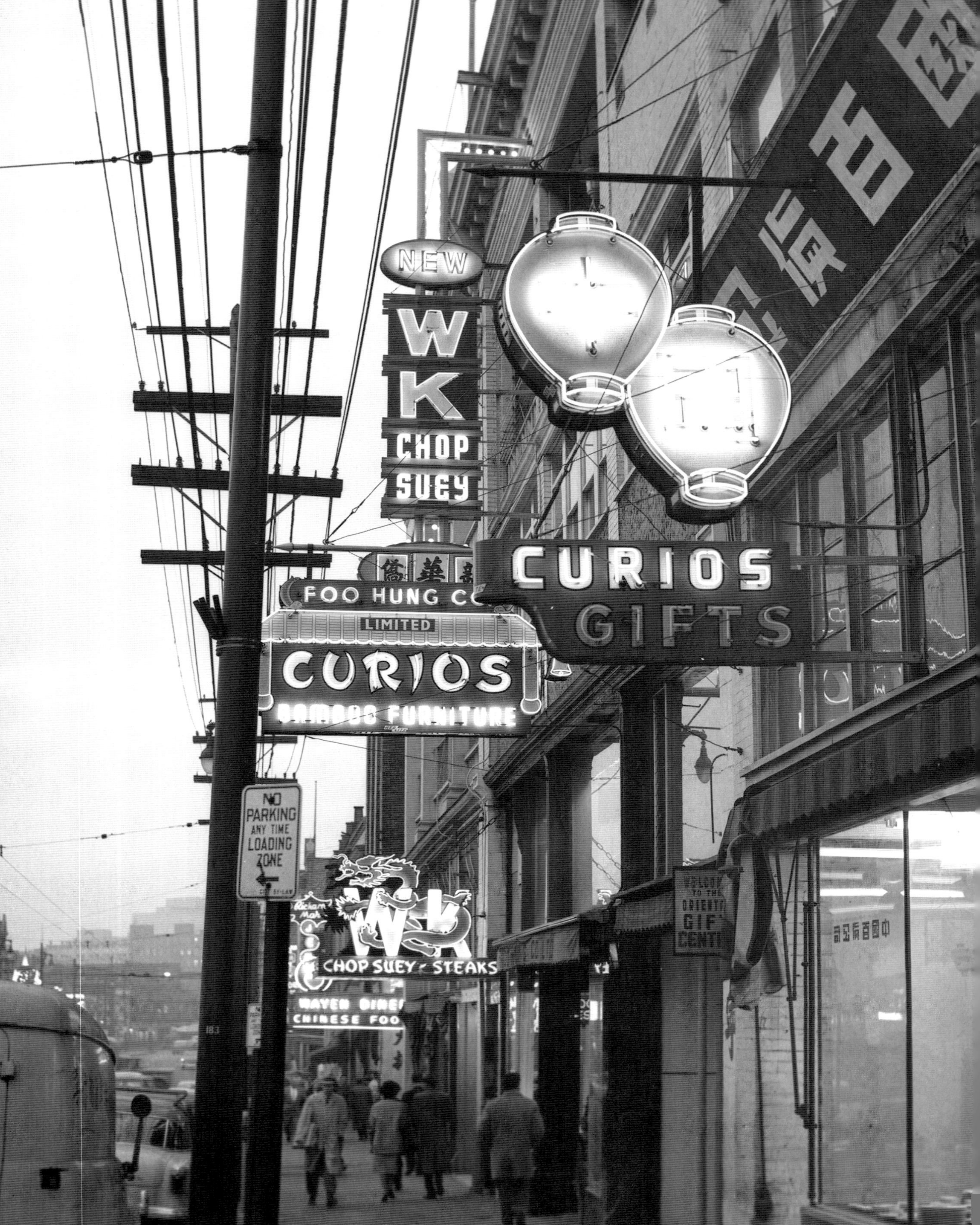
NEW
W K
CHOP
SUEY
FOO HUNG CO
LIMITED
CURIOS
BAMBOO FURNITURE
CURIOS
GIFTS
NO PARKING
ANY TIME
LOADING
ZONE
W K
CHOP SUEY - STEAKS
CHINESE FOO
WELCOME
TO THE
ORIENT
GIFT
CENT

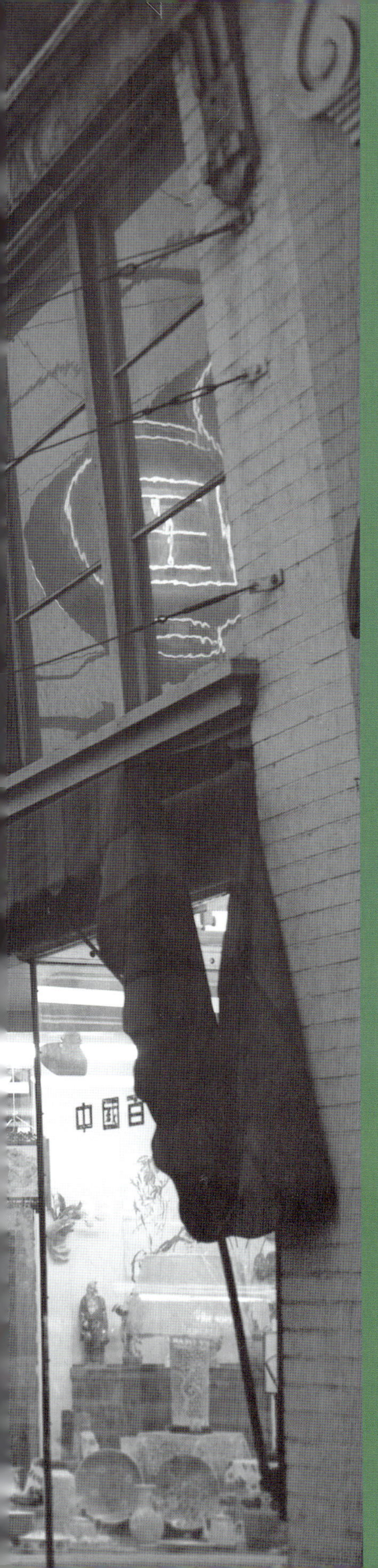

Restaurants, Entertainment, and Neon Lights

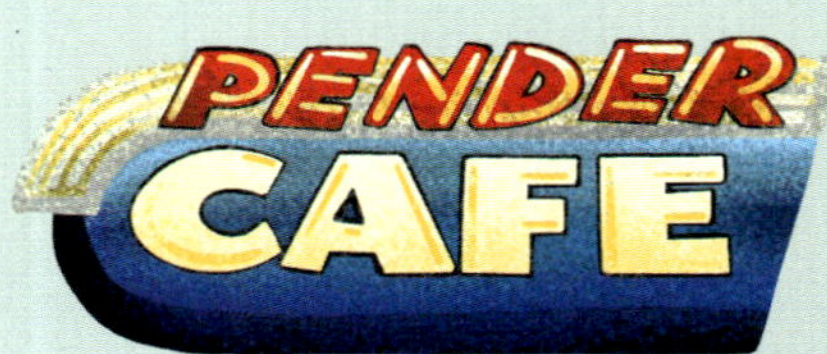

PENDER
CAFE

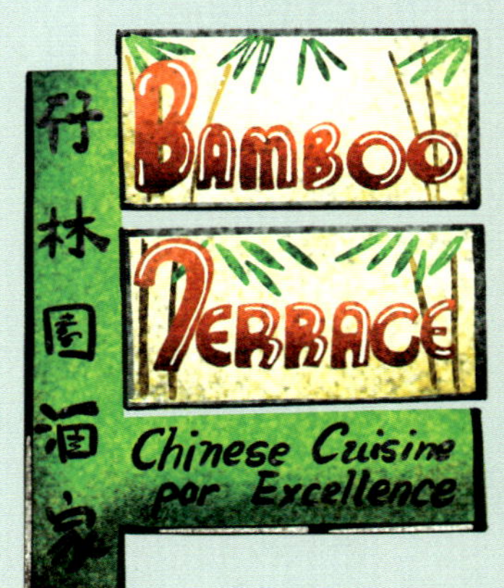

BAMBOO
TERRACE
Chinese Cuisine
por Excellence

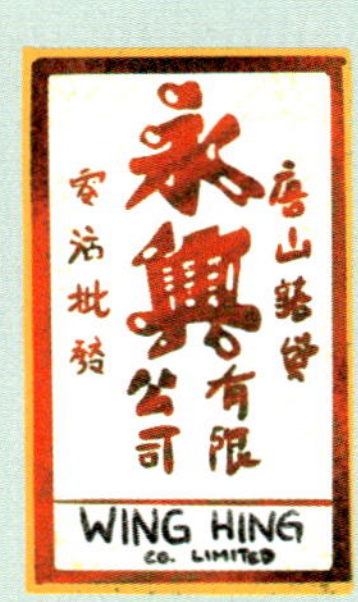

永興
公司
有限
廣山蝦母
客菇批發
WING HING
CO. LIMITED

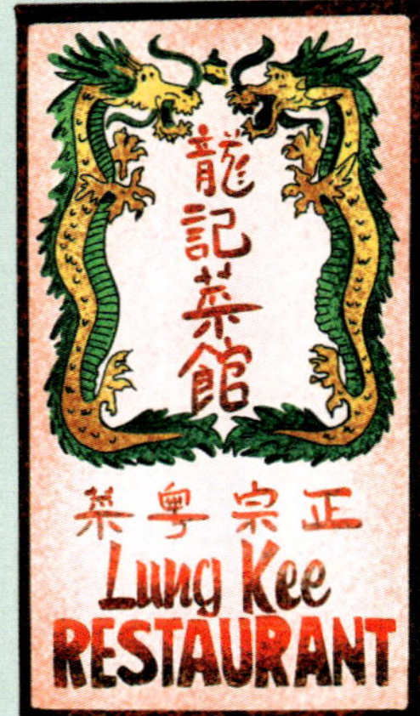

龍記茶館
正宗粵菜
Lung Kee
RESTAURANT

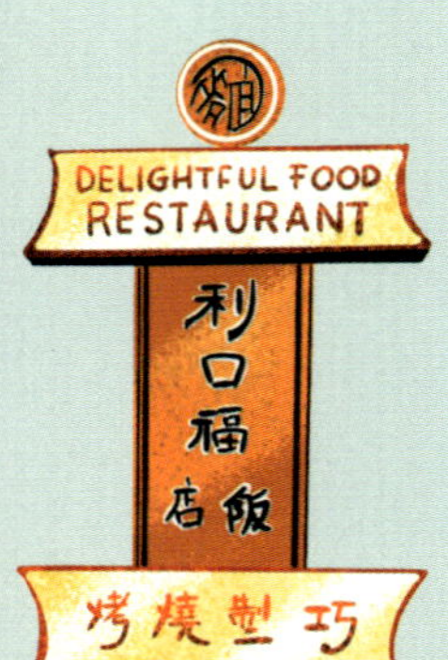

DELIGHTFUL FOOD
RESTAURANT
利口福
飯店
巧製燒烤

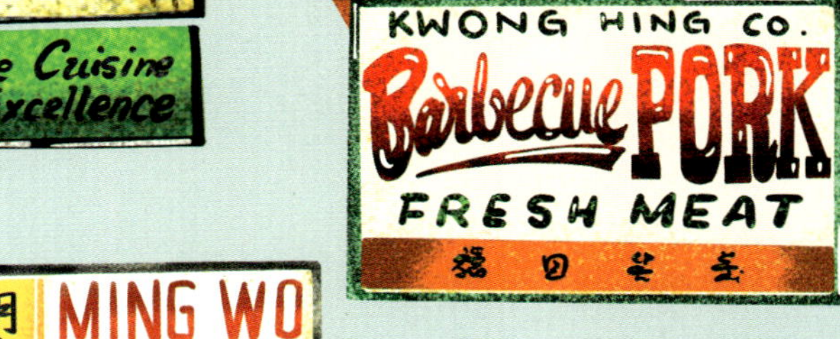

KWONG HING CO.
Barbecue PORK
FRESH MEAT

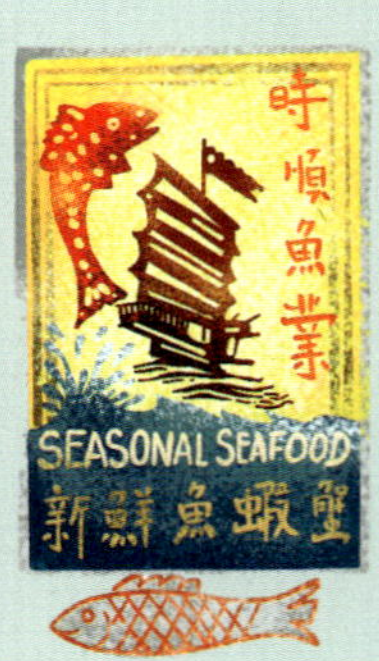

時順魚業
SEASONAL SEAFOOD
新鮮魚蝦蟹

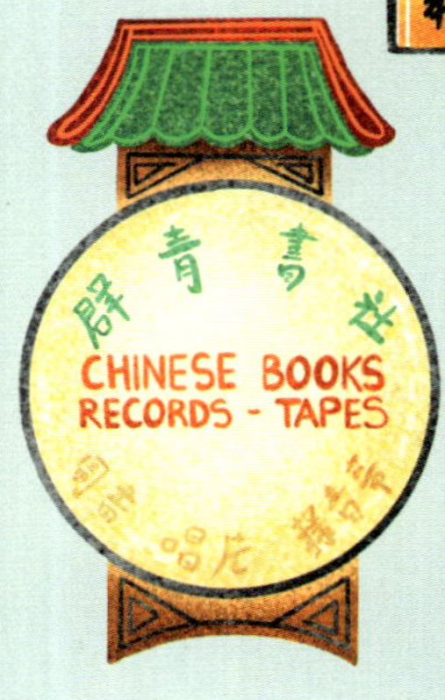

CHINESE BOOKS
RECORDS - TAPES

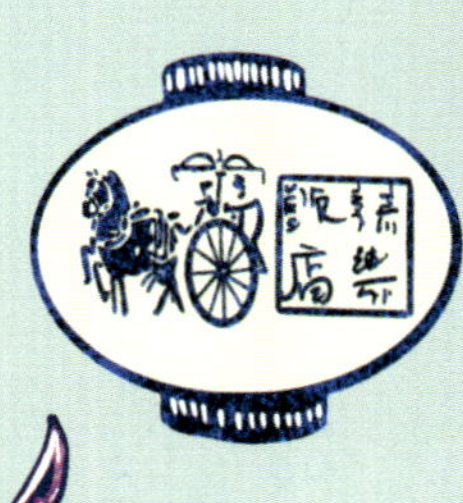

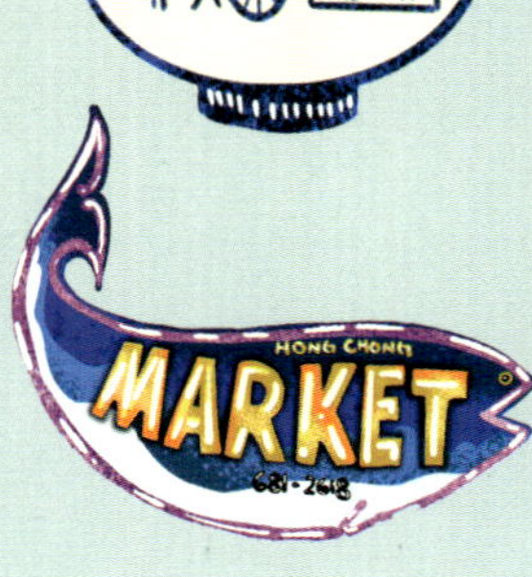

HONG CHONG
MARKET

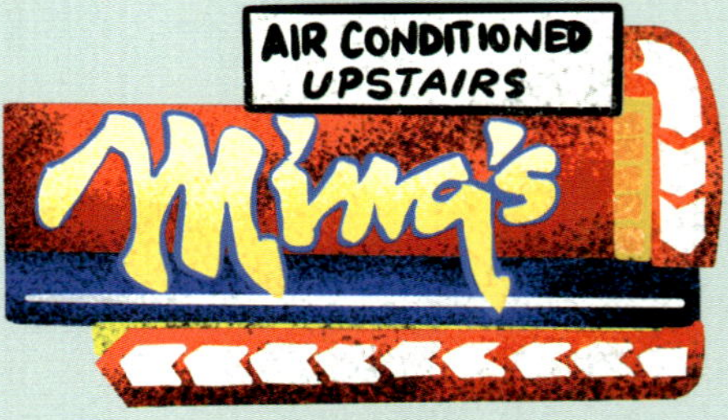

AIR CONDITIONED
UPSTAIRS
Ming's

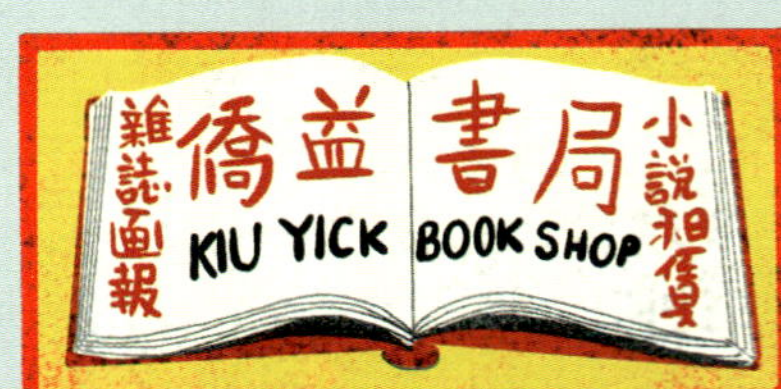

僑益書局
雜誌畫報
KIU YICK BOOK SHOP
小說租賃

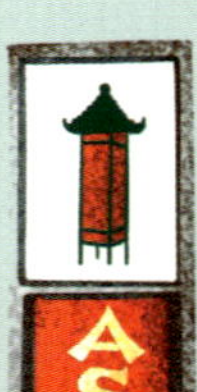

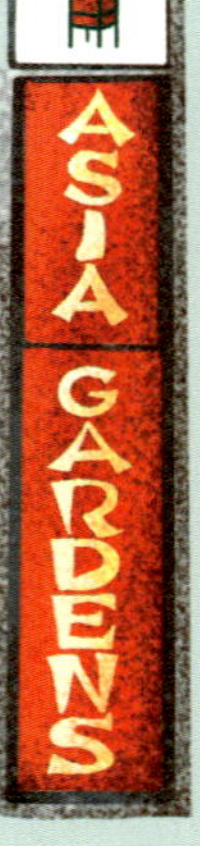

ASIA
GARDENS

FROM THE 1950S TO 1970S, Pender Street was lit with neon lights from the facades of restaurants such as Ho Ho Chop Suey, Ho Inn, Ming's, and Bamboo Terrace, turning daytime eateries and dim sum restaurants into bustling nighttime entertainment destinations. Restaurants have always been cultural beacons, using food to tantalize a diversity of diners.

Chinatown's once lively restaurant and entertainment scene emerged after the lifting of the Exclusion Act in 1947, when loosening immigration restrictions and attitudes toward the Chinese brought new people and energy to the community. Establishments like Ho Ho's and Ho Inn echoed the "chop suey craze" in San Francisco and New York, where Chinese restaurants ingeniously created palatable dishes, remodelled interiors with red lanterns and gold buddhas, and donned neon signage in "chop suey" or "wonton" font to offer an "exotic" or "foreign" dining experience.[1] The origins of chop suey are contested, but they probably date back to a southern Chinese dish of leftovers known as tsap seui, which was likely adapted by Chinese cooks for miners in the California Gold Rush. The simple dish of stir-fried vegetables and meat was once served in Chinese restaurants throughout Chinatown, along with other "hybrid" specialties like chow mein, ginger beef, lemon chicken, kung pao chicken, and egg foo young.[2]

The post-exclusion period allowed for a generation of Canadian-born Chinese who began experimenting with food and identity, creating venues such as the Marco Polo Supper Club and Bamboo Terrace. Featuring a fourteen-page menu, the Marco Polo Supper Club invited a diversity of diners to explore Chinese cuisine in a theatre restaurant that paralleled non-Chinese supper clubs like the Cave and Isy's. At its height, Chinatown was home to seven nightclubs, more than any other area in Vancouver,[3] with the Marco Polo and its predecessor, Forbidden City, as well as W. K. Gardens, Ming's, and others featuring live shows, dancing, and extensive dinner menus that attracted locals, politicians, and celebrities like Frank Sinatra and Nina Simone.

Throughout the 1950s and 1960s, family reunification facilitated the blossoming of restaurants and commercial ventures in Chinatown as new arrivals from Hong Kong and Taiwan brought more "authentic" Chinese culinary ideas. The opening of new restaurants altered the local economy in Chinatown, encouraging businesses like Ming Wo Hardware to adjust their inventory from everyday goods to cookware for restaurants like the Ho Inn, Ho Ho's, Yen Lock, and W. K. Gardens. Butchers, fishmongers, and greengrocers also boomed in Chinatown, providing a vibrant local economy that catered to the growth of the restaurant and entertainment industries. The influx of human and financial capital in the postwar era rejuvenated the area, bringing with it commercial and social development that it hadn't seen since the early 1920s.

However, by the late 1960s, Vancouver started turning off the lights, insisting that neon diminished the natural beauty of the city. As the neon signs disappeared, so did establishments such as the Marco Polo, Bamboo Terrace, W. K. Gardens, and Ho Inn Chop Suey. In 1997, Ho Ho Chop Suey's iconic three-storey neon sign was permanently removed, darkening Chinatown's once-bright nightlife.

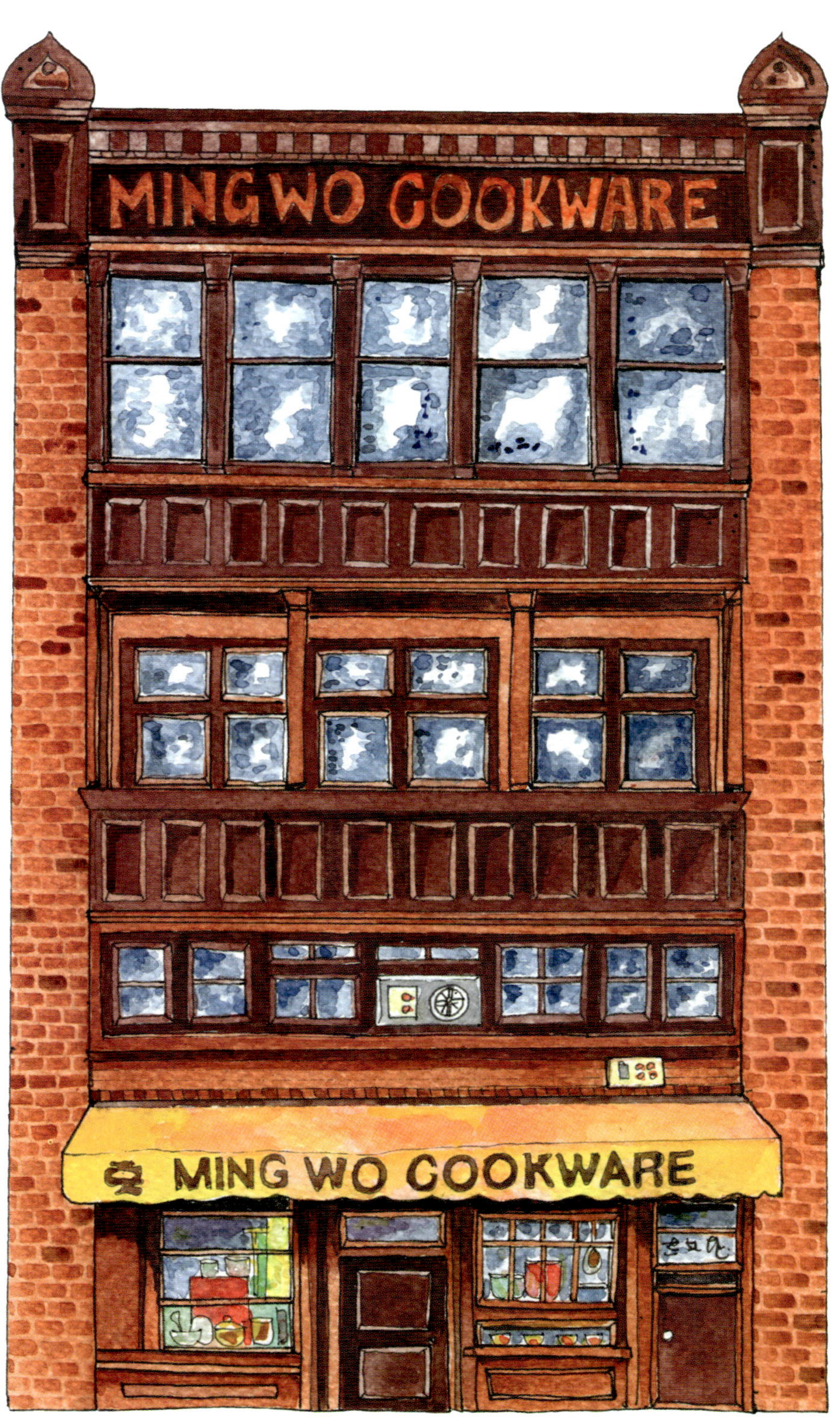

MING WO COOKWARE
MING WO COOKWARE

Ming Wo Cookware
23 East Pender
Built 1913

When Ming Wo Cookware closed its flagship store in Chinatown in February 2020, it took a piece of history with it. Having served the community since 1917, the century-old multigenerational family business was the oldest retail store in Chinatown, as well as one of the oldest in Vancouver.[4]

Founded by Wong Chew Lip, who moved to Canada from southern China in 1908, the store initially operated as a hardware store selling general household items, such as nails, hammers, stationery, light bulbs, and even guns. In the 1960s, when Chinatown reinvented itself with new restaurants, neon lights, and entertainment venues, Wong Chew Lip's son, Norman Wong, transformed Ming Wo from a general hardware store into a shop specializing in cookware. At its height, Ming Wo Cookware supplied restaurants like the Marco Polo Supper Club, Yen Lock, Bamboo Terrace, and the Ho Inn.

Constructed in 1913, 23 East Pender is a four-storey multipurpose brick building with retail on the ground floor and residential dwellings and meeting spaces on the upper floors. Similar to the Chinese Times Building (1 East Pender), the Ming Wo building provided residential space on its upper floors to accommodate families rather than dorm rooms as in other historical buildings in Chinatown. Built during an era when Chinese merchants invested heavily in real estate development, the building borrows from Chinese shophouse architecture and includes recessed balconies, slender classical pilasters and columns, a right-hand side entry to a staircase causing asymmetry to the storefront, and a mezzanine above the main floor. The mezzanine, characterized by its low ceiling height, is rumoured to have been a gathering place where Chinatown ladies played mahjong.[5]

The original owner of the building, Wong Soon King, belonged to a network of wealthy Chinatown merchants. He owned Hip Tuck Lung, an opium processor, and his was among one of the four firms in Chinatown with gross incomes of $150,000 to $180,000 in 1907.[6] Wong Soon King invested heavily in real estate, co-founded the Chinese Board of Trade, and campaigned tirelessly for improvements to Chinatown, such as the installation of sidewalks.

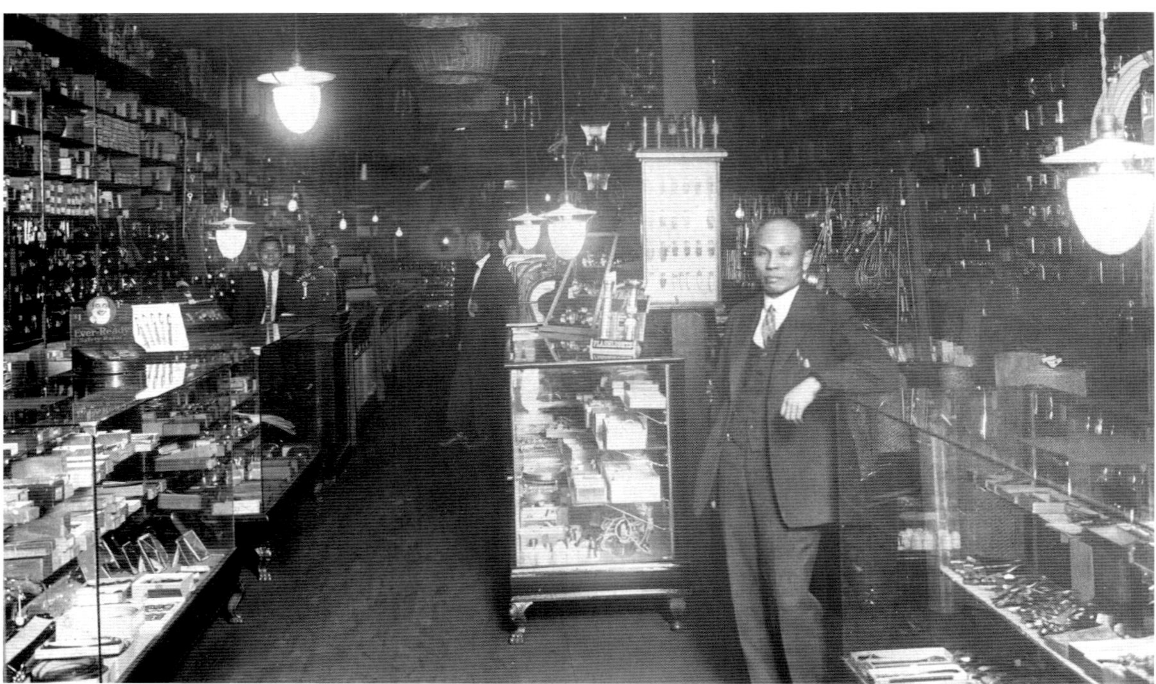

Interior of Ming Wo Hardware in 1924

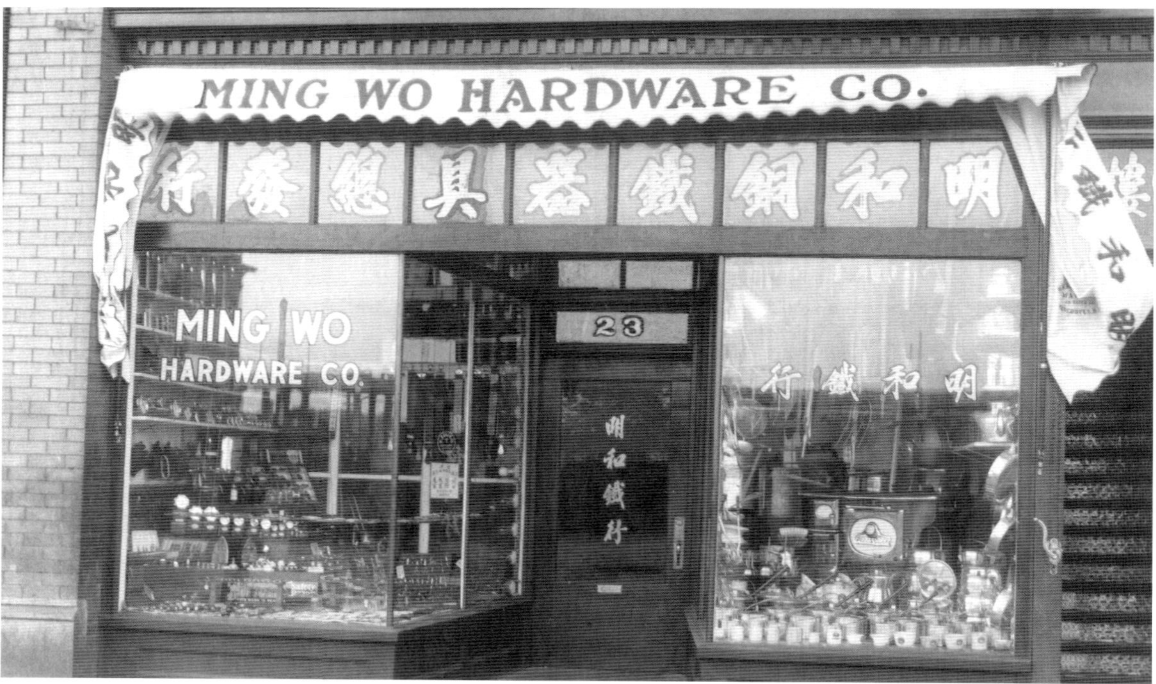

Exterior of Ming Wo Hardware in 1924

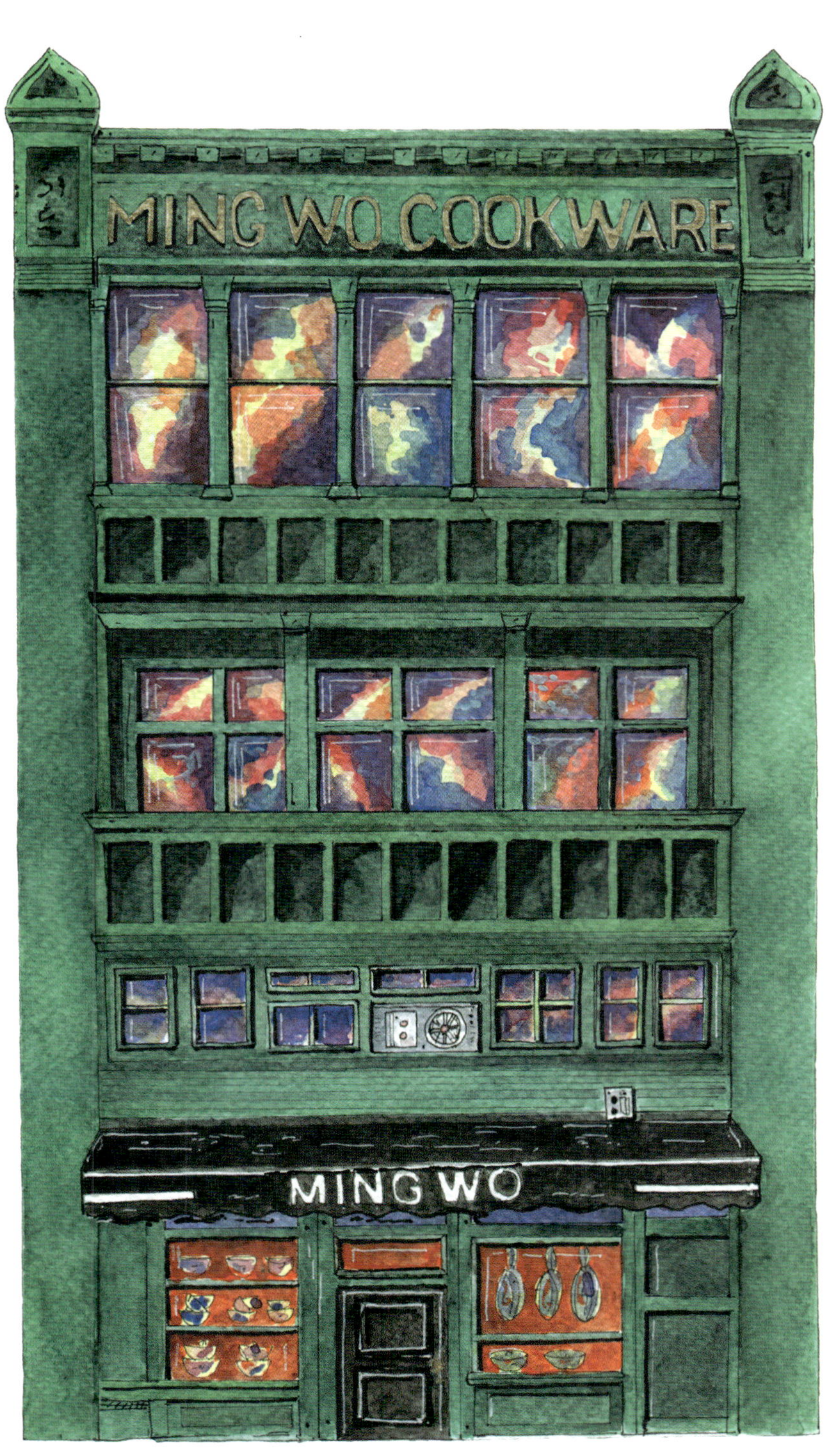

MING WO COOKWARE
MING WO

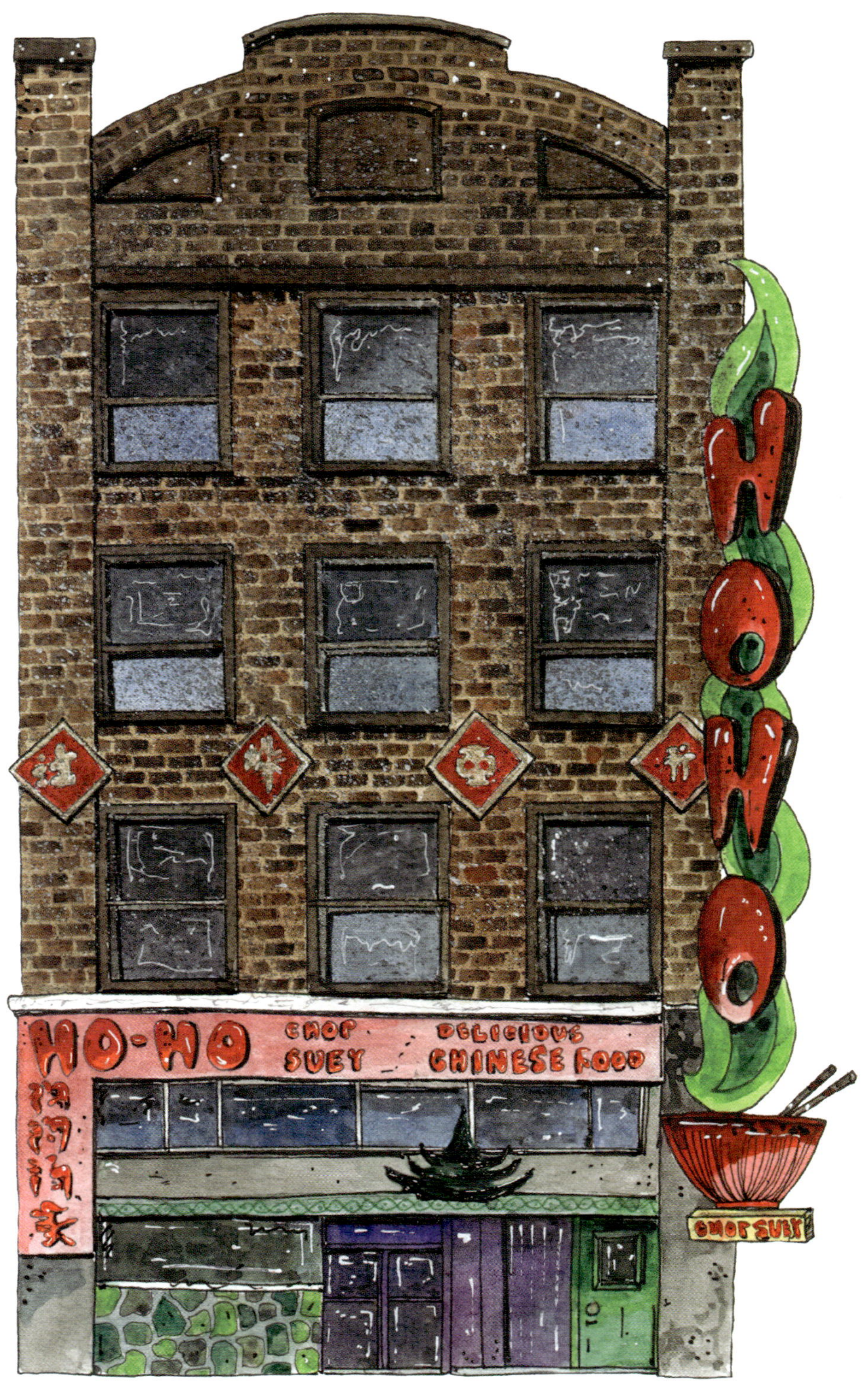
HO-HO
CHOP SUEY
DELICIOUS CHINESE FOOD
HO HO
CHOP SUEY
福 河 河 家

Ho Ho Chop Suey/
Foo's Ho Ho Restaurant
100–102 East Pender
Built 1911–12

A mysterious well-dressed man sits in the upper gallery of the theatre soaking in the array of costumes, the echo of crashing cymbals, and the emotions depicted on the actors' faces. His wealth paid for the travel of the Cantonese opera troupe, their accommodation, and the theatre they're performing in. This is his contribution to his fellow countrymen, so they can enjoy a few moments of entertainment and a brief reprieve from daily life.

Unlike merchants such as Yip Sang (Wing Sang) and Chang Toy (Sam Kee), not much is known about Loo Gee Wing other than his connections with the gold rush and his fondness for the theatre. Loo Gee Wing exists in fragments, a ghostlike figure in records, a name appearing in court registries or comments in newspapers that describe him as "dressed like a tailor's model in a suit of a prosperous English man down to his patent leathers."[7]

Regardless, Loo Gee Wing played an important role in the development of real estate in and around Chinatown. He was best known for the construction of five buildings that still stand today, several of which are in Chinatown, including the Ko Sing Opera House, or Chinese Theatre (124 East Pender), and 100 East Pender.

Built in 1911–12, the five-storey coarse brick building was heavily influenced by the Arts and Crafts movement. The coarseness and variation in the bricks is significantly different from the delicate details on its neighbour, the CBA Building. Compared to the CBA's recessed balconies and large windows, 100 East Pender's windows are set in deep intervals along the front with smaller windows along its length. The front facade includes curbed parapets, a large front entrance at street level, and a mezzanine above the ground floor. There is also evidence of a basement seen through ground-floor windows partially hidden and decorated with metal grilles.

The landmark restaurant Ho Ho Chop Suey once operated out of the ground floor of 100 East Pender. During the 1960s and 1970s, folks would stop at Ho Ho's for a comforting meal of egg foo young or beef chow fun before venturing down East Pender to one of the many nightclubs or to catch a live show. It was also a venue for large events such as birthday celebrations and marking a baby's first month.

The Quon family opened the restaurant in 1954, and it quickly became one of the pinnacle postwar "hybrid-culture" restaurants, mixing Chinese cooking techniques with local ingredients to create palatable dishes that appealed to a diverse group of diners. Like many chop suey restaurants, Ho Ho's adapted to an environment where traditional Chinese ingredients and cookware were not readily available by creating innovative dishes like chow fun, hot and sour soup, curry chicken, lemon chicken, egg foo young, garlic ribs, and fried rice. The Cantonese eatery was just one of the numerous innovative restaurants and curio shops that opened in Chinatown after the Second World War and attracted non-Chinese customers who wanted to taste something "exotic." Often restaurants like Ho Ho's became sites of cultural exchange, where non-Chinese patrons suspended prejudices and opened themselves to a diverse culinary and cultural experience.[8]

Ho Ho's signature multi-storey neon sign with a steaming bowl and chopsticks that extended along the side of the building like a beacon in the neighbourhood was taken down in 1997. Recent efforts by entrepreneur Carol Lee to reopen Ho Ho's involve recreating the iconic neon sign.[9]

The building has been owned by the Lung Kong Tien Yee Society since 1926 and contains forty-eight rooms that are the Sun Ah Hotel (or formally Queen Anne Rooms).[10]

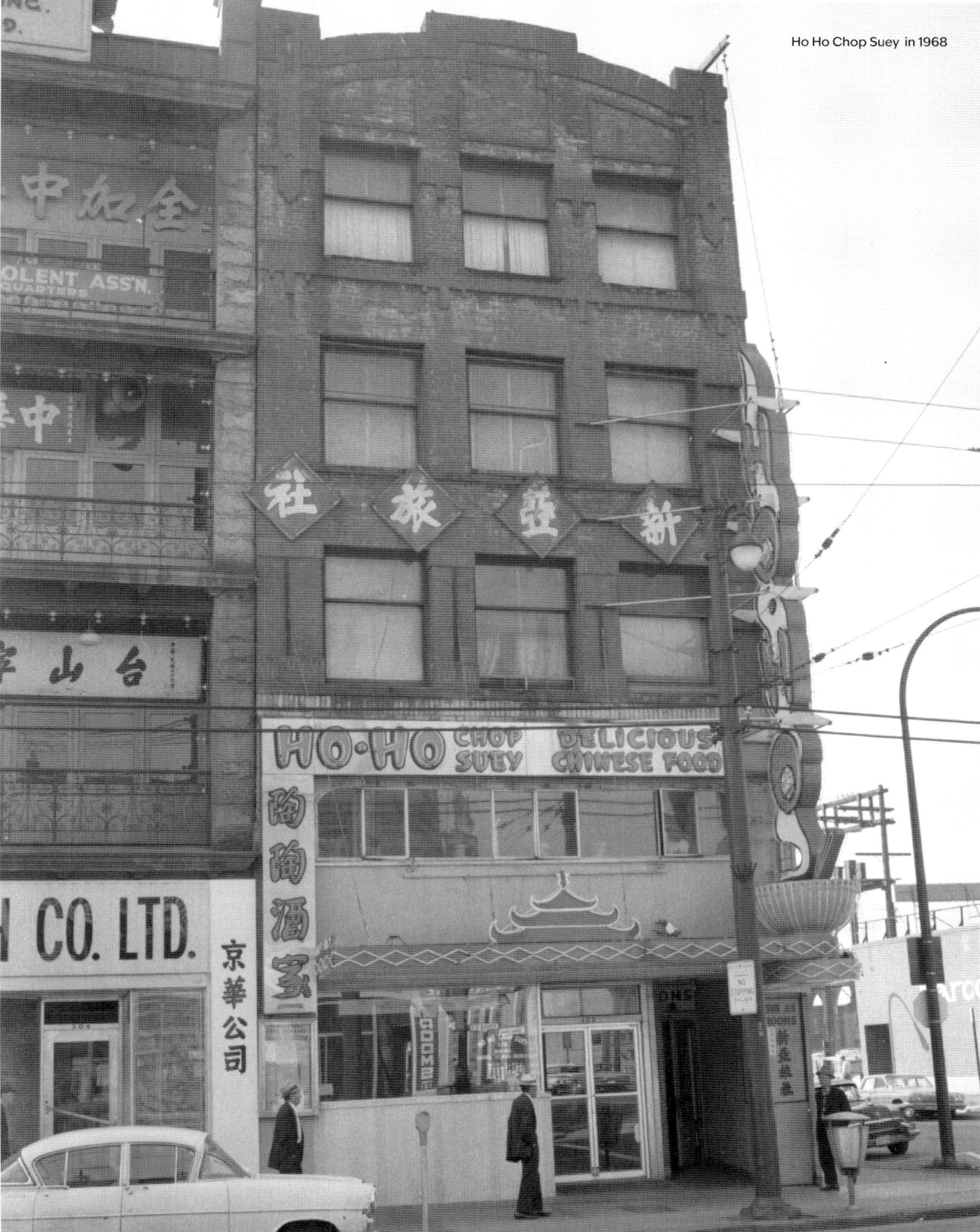

Ho Ho Chop Suey in 1968

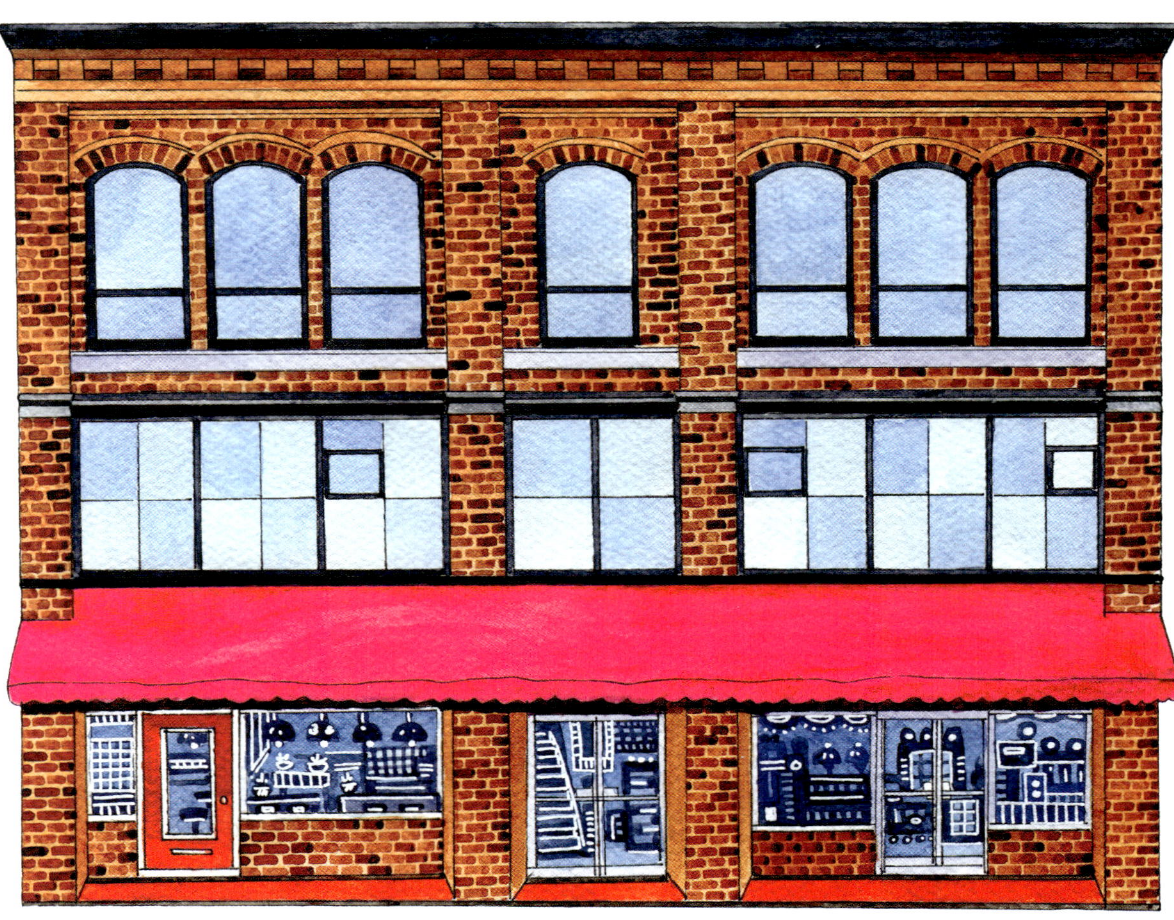

Chinese Theatre
124 East Pender
Built 1909

The three-storey brick building that once housed the Ko Sing Theatre isn't as archi-tecturally imposing as its clan-association neighbours. Appearances, however, can be deceiving, as its unimposing boxy facade and symmetrical bays surrounding a central entryway mask its rowdy history. Originally constructed as a theatre in 1909, 124 East Pender was later converted into a dormitory with commercial space on the ground floor. Over the years, it has housed several notable tenants, including the Hong Kong Café and *Chinatown News*.

Known as the Chinese Theatre, 124 East Pender was commissioned by Loo Gee Wing, a merchant who earned his fortune in the Cariboo Gold Rush. As an industrious entrepre-neur with a love of theatre, he hired architect Samuel Buttrey Birds to design a mixed-use building to house a theatre and other businesses that would support his entertainment enterprise.[11] Early theatres in Chinatown were informal, such as one in Shanghai Alley and the Sing Kew Theatre owned by Chang Toy, with general seating on one or two levels, allowing the audience to come and go as they pleased. But the entertainment business was risky. Having learned from the failure of the Wing Hong Lin Company in the Sing Ping Theatre, Loo Gee Wing designed a self-contained system within 124 East Pender that would be sustained by the income generated from multiple businesses. Theatre patrons could dine at the restaurant before seeing a show, ensuring that money was spent on the premises.[12]

Merchant capital from individuals such as Loo Gee Wing contributed to the entertain-ment scene in early Chinatown, both in constructing theatres and in paying for travelling Cantonese opera troupes.[13] Initially, actors who travelled to Vancouver and elsewhere were not highly regarded in traditional Chinese society. As the top-rated actors were retained in China, those willing to travel were considered inferior second-tier perform-ers. However, production of Cantonese opera performances began to slow down in the 1920s, making it more appealing for actors to find alternative venues in North America. Merchants like Loo Gee Wing succeeded in attracting superstars, who in turn demanded lucrative contracts and conditions that their predecessors weren't offered. Theatres in Chinatown also started to accommodate an emerging class system, where wealthier patrons could purchase better seats in the mezzanine. In 1921, Buttrey Birds was hired to install dressing rooms, a ticket office, and box seats.[14]

The Chinese Theatre was eventually converted into a dormitory but maintained its commercial space on the ground floor. In 1976, all the windows were switched from wood to aluminum, making 124 East Pender one of the first buildings in historic Chinatown to be renovated.

Hong Kong Café and the White Waitress Scandal

The Hong Kong Café occupied the ground floor of 124 East Pender from the 1930s to the 1950s. The Chinese considered establishments like the Hong Kong Café, BC Royal Café, and Pender Café to be "Western-style" restaurants that were different from traditional teahouses or chop suey restaurants. These cafés were often open twenty-four hours a day, catering to male labourers who could drop in for a hot cup of coffee and comfort food like a greasy breakfast, warm apple turnover, or sausage and mash. More importantly, during the exclusion years, cafés in Chinatown provided the bachelor population with a reprieve from daily life. Many of these men worked menial jobs as cooks, houseboys, and laundry workers, which were traditionally looked down on as women's work. These men could relax at these cafés, where they could be served rather than serving, and chat with a waitress.

As there were few Chinese women in Chinatown during the exclusion years, café owners such as Charlie Ting of Hong Kong Café hired white women as waitresses with the assumption that female staff attracted more patrons. In 1937, approximately thirty white women worked in cafés in Chinatown, many from working-class backgrounds who needed to support their families as work was scarce during the Great Depression. These women were often seen as belonging at the bottom of the social hierarchy in Vancouver, but in Chinatown their gender and race gave them status.

Until 1931, cafés in Chinatown that employed white waitresses were largely overlooked by the authorities, considered "out of sight, out of mind" compared to spaces such as beer parlours outside Chinatown that refused to serve mixed-race clientele, especially Asian men with white women. It wasn't until December 20, 1931, when Dick Lee murdered his Pender Café acquaintance Mary Shaw, that cafés in Chinatown that employed white waitresses began to be heavily policed and regulated.[15]

In 1937, responding to fears that Chinese men were corrupting white women and luring them into prostitution, the city threatened to revoke the business licences of cafés if they did not fire their waitresses. In response, café owners sought assistance from the Chinese Benevolent Association (CBA). Charlie Ting argued that he was a restaurant owner and family man who had worked hard since arriving in Canada at seventeen. He further pointed out that waitresses were allowed to work elsewhere in Vancouver, but those cafés were not policed like the ones in Chinatown.

When negotiations between the city and the CBA failed, fifteen waitresses marched to city hall and proclaimed that the city had no right to meddle in their private affairs, calling officials "a bunch of fussy old-bridge playing gossips who are self-appointed directors of morals for girls in Chinatown—we must live, and heaven knows if a girl is inclined to go wrong, she can do it just as readily on Granville Street as she can down here."[16] The waitresses also defended their employers, saying they were treated well, provided with standard work hours, paid adequately, and given flexible hours if they had children.

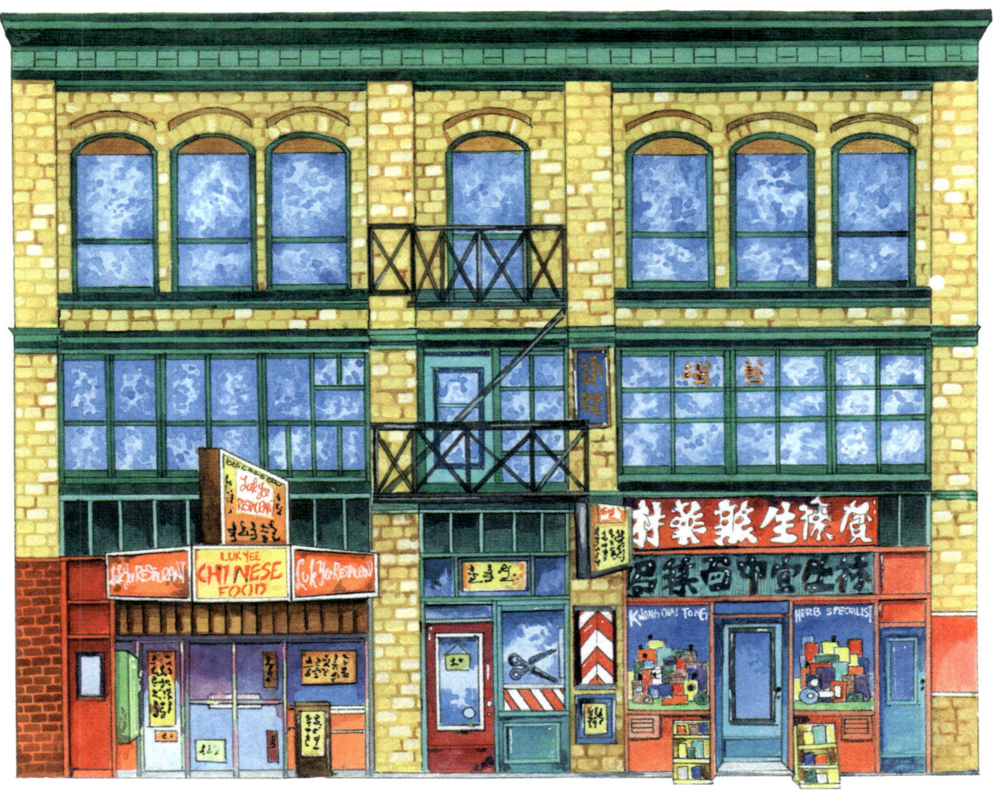

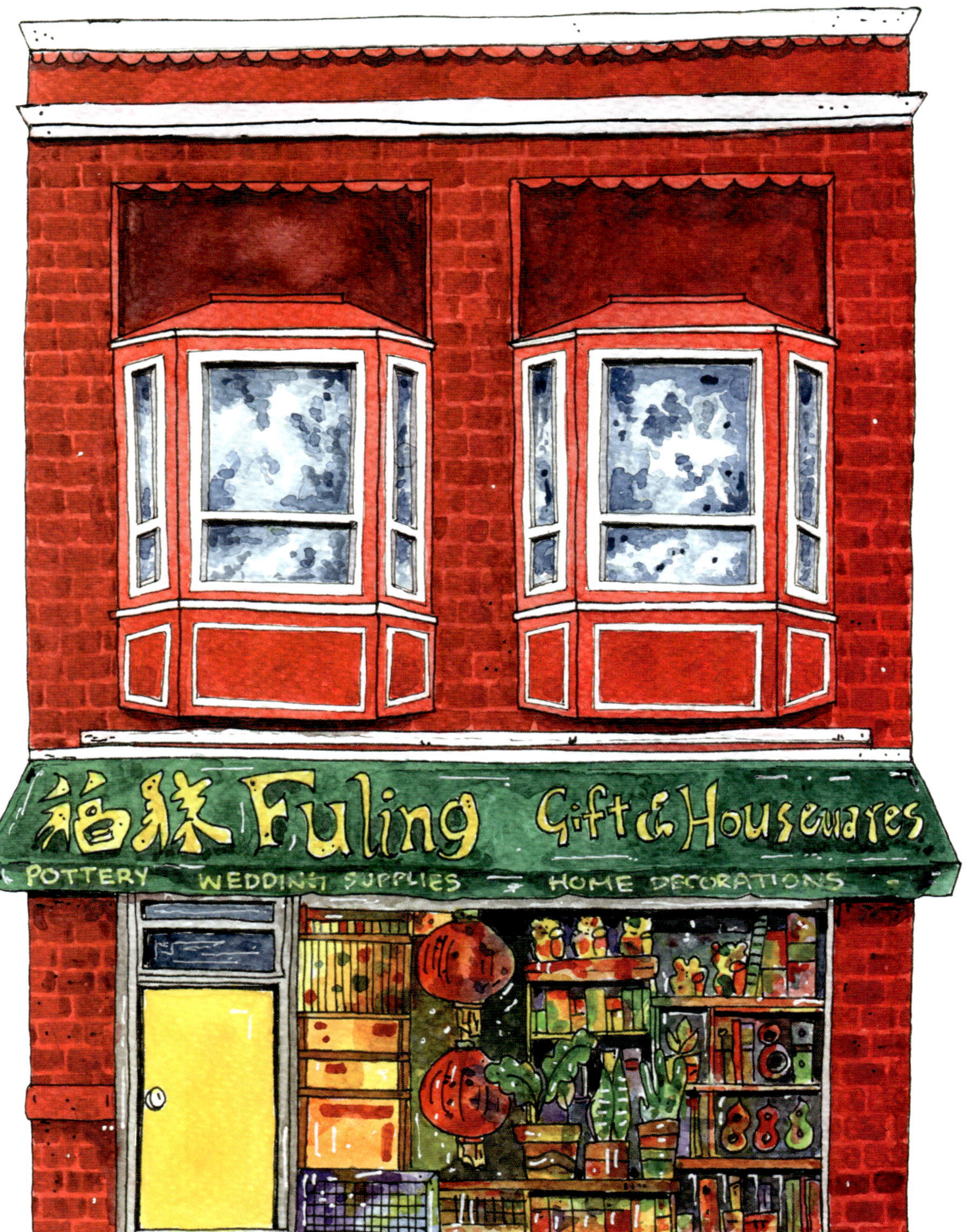

福狳 Fuling Gift & Housewares
POTTERY   WEDDING SUPPLIES   HOME DECORATIONS

Green Door Restaurant and Fuling Gifts
111 East Pender
Built 1903

The two-storey brick building at 111 East Pender exudes serendipity, and it has nothing to do with the fact that its exterior is coated in a thick layer of deep cadmium red paint. Red is considered a lucky colour in Chinese culture, and you'll find it in abundance among the Chinese décor and knickknacks that line the shelves of the building's current commercial tenant, Fuling Gifts. But before Fuling Gifts started stocking its shelves with paper lanterns and umbrellas, Chinese porcelain with dragon motifs, and replicas from the Ming Dynasty, 111 East Pender was home to the Green Door restaurant and the satellite headquarters of a revolutionary.

Customers entered the restaurant through a discreet green door in the alley between East Hastings and East Pender, which was once an extension of Market Alley. From the 1930s to 1990s, the legendary restaurant served affordable Chinese food to a diverse clientele of gamblers (1930s) and Vancouver's counterculture literati (1960s and 1970s), which makes it no coincidence that the man who commissioned its construction in 1903 was a rebel.

Chu Lai (1847–1906) made his fortune during the Cariboo Gold Rush and used his riches to open the Wing Chong Company in Victoria, a general store that imported and exported goods, manufactured clothing, and served as a headquarters for labour contracting. The Wing Chong also helped settle new migrants by providing accomodaton assistance and operating as a pseudo bank where labourers could send remittances to relatives in China.

Coming from the Hakka community, an ethnic and linguistic minority in southern China, Chu Lai made his store the base of operations for the Hakka in BC. One such connection was Chang Toy, who stayed at the Wing Chong Company until he moved to New Westminster. Chu Lai also acted as the initial wholesaler for the Sam Kee Company.

Although Chu Lai didn't live in Vancouver, he hired architect W. T. Whiteway (architect of the Sun Tower) to design a building on East Pender. The once pale blue building features key architectural details, such as a pair of bay windows, brickwork, sheet metal windows, and a cornice.

In 1885, Chu Lai defied the Chinese Regulation Act, which imposed an annual tax of ten dollars on all Chinese over the age of fourteen. He was charged and convicted of failing to pay the annual tax. Rather than pay the twenty-dollar fine, Chu Lai posted a bond of two hundred and fifty dollars to the BC Supreme Court, where the act was challenged and later dropped. Chu Lai's unprecedented challenge to the discriminatory law was recognized widely throughout the Chinese community.

At the time of his death in 1906, Chu Lai was serving as the vice-president of the Chinese Empire Reform Association (CERA). CERA organized Chu's funeral, which included a military marching band accompanied by a group of sack-clothed professional mourners, and commissioned every carriage in the city. The respect Chu Lai received from the Chinese community even attracted attention from Victoria's English-language press.[17]

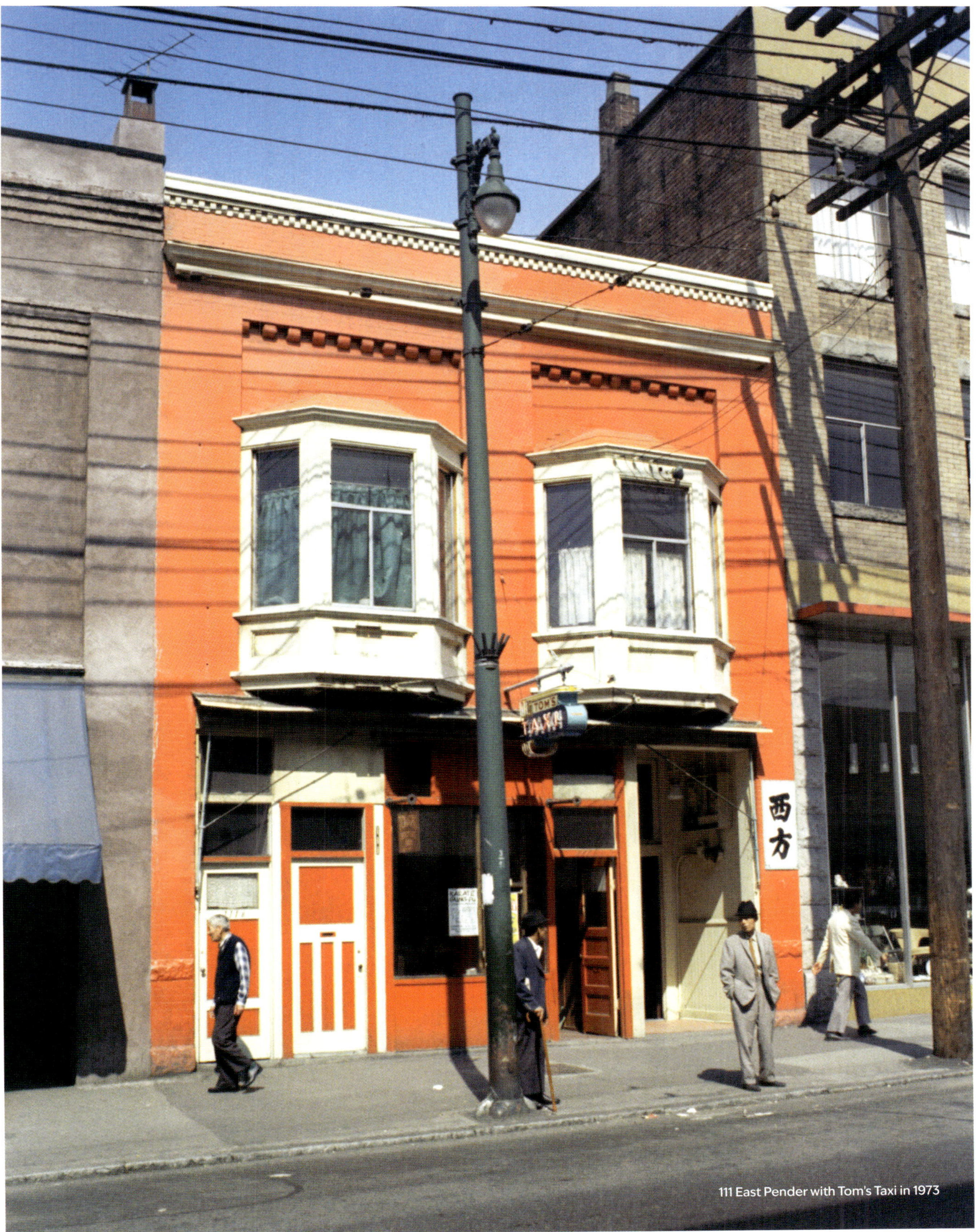

111 East Pender with Tom's Taxi in 1973

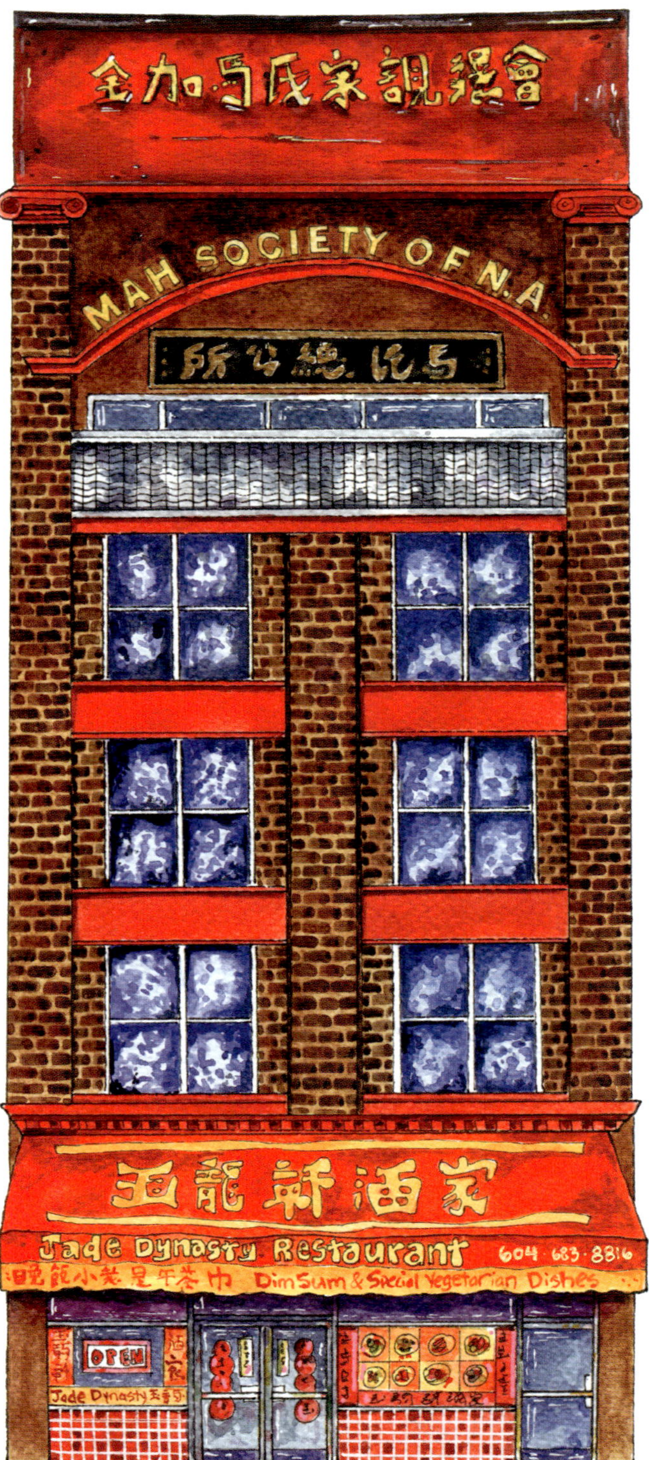
金加馬氏家親聯誼會
MAH SOCIETY OF N.A.
所公總氏馬
龍新酒家
Jade Dynasty Restaurant
604 683·8816
飲館小點見午茶巾 Dim Sum & Special Vegetarian Dishes
OPEN
Jade Dynasty

Jade Dynasty Restaurant
135 East Pender
Established 2005

Since 2005, the family-owned Jade Dynasty Restaurant has been nestled on the ground floor of the Mah Society Building at 135–137 East Pender. Over the past two decades, the restaurant has served simple Cantonese cuisine mixed with North American Chinese classics such as ginger beef and General Tso's chicken—as well as dim sum.

The delicious culinary appetizer-like tradition of dim sum, or yum cha, which associates it with drinking tea, can be traced back more than twenty-five hundred years. In Guangdong Province, teahouses were established along the Silk Road to entice travellers with sweet or savoury morsels that would keep them satisfied during their long journeys. The culinary tradition evolved into its modern version in restaurants during the nineteenth century.

Dim sum, which translates to "touching heart" or "so close to the heart," consists of a variety of flavours, textures, and cooking techniques (steamed, pan-fried, deep-fried, and stir-fried). The meal is normally served for breakfast or lunch and is always accompanied by tea, such as jasmine, black, chrysanthemum, or oolong.[18]

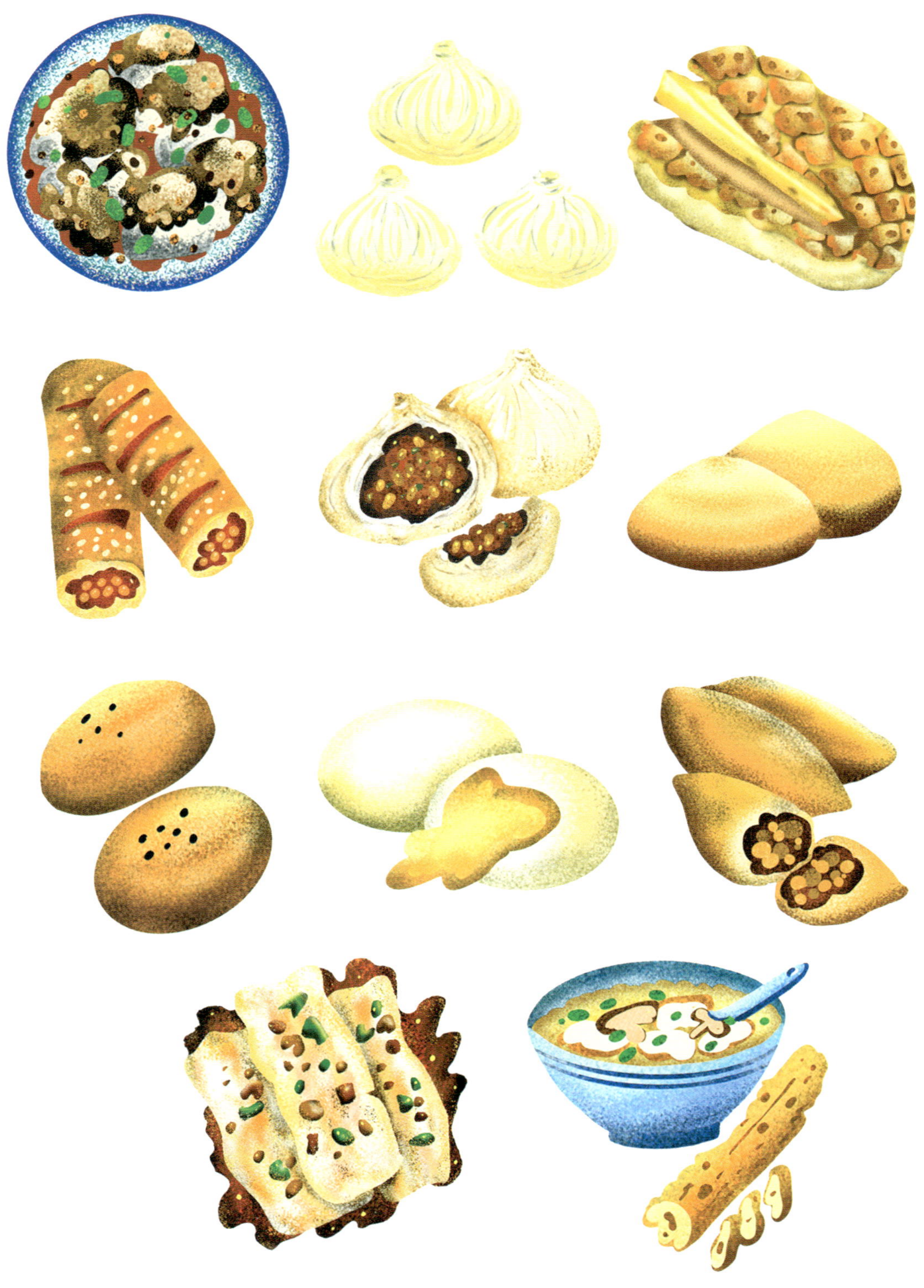

A Guide to Dim Sum

If you're fortunate, you've picked a restaurant that still serves dim sum from carts wheeled around by servers who will entice you at your table with bite-sized morsels. As the dim sum carts phase out, most restaurants will ask you to choose from the menu or order sheet, which is presented once you're seated at your table. Although this modern change avoids spontaneous splurges and falling for the marketing tactics of the tenacious dim sum cart ladies, you don't have to wait for the cart to circle the entire restaurant before it gets to you, which means your food generally arrives piping hot and directly from the kitchen.[19]

Dim Sum Etiquette

TEA LOGISTICS

When you're seated, a server will ask what kind of tea you want. You'll generally be provided with two teapots (one with steeped tea and one with hot water). Wait until the tea is fully steeped before serving. The pot of hot water is there to replenish the teapot. When your hot water is low, simply flip the lid over to signal for a refill.

POURING TEA

Serve tea to others before you serve yourself, and always serve the oldest person first because this is highly respectful in Chinese culture. If you're the youngest at the table, it's generally your responsibility to pour tea for everyone else. If someone else pours tea for you, show your appreciation by tapping your index and middle finger on the table twice if you're married, and just your index finger if you're single. Or you can mimic this gesture by bowing.

CHOPSTICK PROTOCOL

Although dim sum is meant for sharing, this doesn't mean that you need to spread your germs. A pair of communal chopsticks, often a different colour, is used for transferring the morsels from the steamer basket to your plate. Use your own chopsticks when eating. When you're done, place them on the right side of your plate or on the chopstick rest. Never stand your chopsticks upright! Also, never eat dim sum directly from the communal plate or basket.

TAKE SMALL BITES

To fully enjoy the food—and to prevent injury—take small bites of the morsels rather than eating them whole. Some of the steamed dumplings can be extremely hot or may burst (e.g., xiao long bao, or soup dumplings). Dishes such as spareribs may have loose bones. Discard bones on your plate; you can request a new plate when it's full.

DON'T BE GREEDY

Don't take the last piece, even if you really want to. Offer it to others.

BE GENEROUS

Offer to pay for the meal. This is a gesture that will often result in a wrestling match, as others will also offer to pay. Watch out for the sneaky grannies at the table; they tend to suddenly gain superhuman strength when fighting to pay for the meal.

Popular Dim Sum Dishes

HAR GOW (SHRIMP DUMPLING)

An all-time favourite. These delicate steamed dumplings encase marinated shrimp filling in a pleated, translucent wrapper.

XIAO LONG BAO (SOUP DUMPLING)

Translates as "little baskets" because of their plump sack-like shape, which holds juicy minced pork and melted jelly stock. This dumpling has a delicate skin, so be careful when you dip it into the vinegar-ginger sauce. Let it cool slightly or use your chopsticks to create a small hole to release some of the hot soup before popping it in your mouth.

CHAR SIU BAO (BARBEQUE PORK BUN, STEAMED)

These soft and fluffy buns are made from flour, starch, sugar, and sometimes milk, with a sweet and savoury pork filling called char siu.

STICKY LOTUS WRAP

Sticky rice filled with meat, savoury seasonings (soy sauce and oyster sauce), ginger, green onions, and more, all wrapped in dried lotus leaves and steamed.

CONGEE

Rice porridge that can be customized with a variety of toppings, such as scallions, salted duck egg slices, sliced crueller, and proteins. The rice protein is cooked in large amounts of vegetable or meat stock or water.

SIU MAI (PORK DUMPLING)

Another all-time favourite. This open-faced shrimp and pork dumpling is enclosed in a thin flour wrapper to give it a flower-like shape. Topped with a garnish of fish roe or minced carrot.

RICE NOODLES

Thin rice noodles that come in a variety of fillings such as mushrooms, barbeque pork, minced beef, or shrimp. Drizzled with a sweet soy-based sauce before serving. These are slippery! Slice the noodles in half and pick them up with chopsticks or a spoon.

GAI LAN

You'll want to add some vegetables to all the starchy buns and dumplings. Also known as Chinese broccoli, gai lan is steamed or blanched very quickly and drizzled with oyster sauce.

BLACK BEAN SPARERIBS

Juicy morsels of chopped ribs steamed until ultra tender in fermented black beans, garlic, ginger, wine, and other seasonings. Watch out for bone fragments!

CHICKEN FEET

Juicy chicken feet fried and braised whole in a garlicky fermented black bean sauce. Highly recommended for the extra adventurous.

SPRING ROLLS

Deep-fried wrapper filled with minced meat and vegetables. Served with plum or sweet and sour sauce for dipping.

PAN-FRIED BUNS

Buns filled with minced pork and vegetables and cooked in a pan instead of a steamer, giving them a golden crust on the bottom and smooth top. Served with soy sauce, chili oil, and sesame-based sauce drizzled on top.

TARO DUMPLING

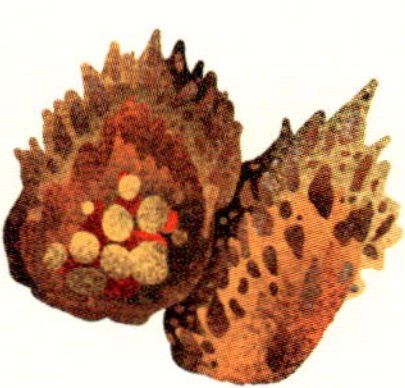

Mashed taro root dough wrapped over minced pork, mushroom, and scallion filling. Deep-fried for a crisp, honeycomb-like outer crust.

BARBEQUE PORK PASTRY

Flaky and buttery pastry shell filled with sweet and savoury minced char siu. Topped with egg wash and sesame seeds for a crispy top and nutty flavour.

FRIED SESAME BALLS

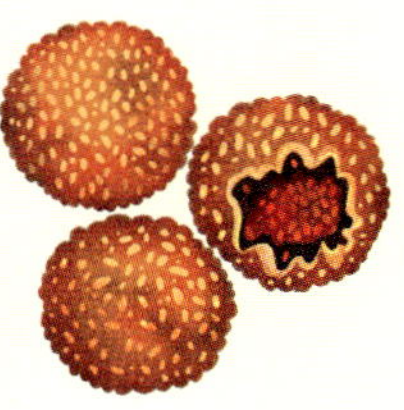

Deep fried sticky-rice flour dough balls filled with sweet bean paste and rolled in sesame seeds.

EGG YOLK CUSTARD BUN

Silky, sweet, and savoury filling of salted egg yolk custard. Recognizable by its smooth bright white dough that's sometimes marked with red dots on top.

DEEP-FRIED FOOTBALLS

Deep-fried dumplings with a crunchy yet springy texture, filled with a mixture of meat, shrimp, and vegetables.

PAN-FRIED TURNIP CAKE

Simple radish and rice flour mixed with meat, mushrooms, shrimp, and other ingredients. Cooked on hot steaming griddles that render a golden crust with a tender centre. Served with oyster sauce or plain.

CHAR SIU BAO (BARBEQUE PORK BUN, BAKED)

Similar to steamed char siu buns but made with traditional flour dough that's baked golden brown and has a slightly sweet and tacky coating.

EGG TARTS

Sweet and savoury dessert with egg custard filling and super flaky, shortbread-like crust. Portuguese egg tarts are another variety that are much sweeter and have a burnt topping.

PINEAPPLE BUN

Thick and crispy crust topping made to resemble pineapple skin over sweet egg dough filled with silky custard.

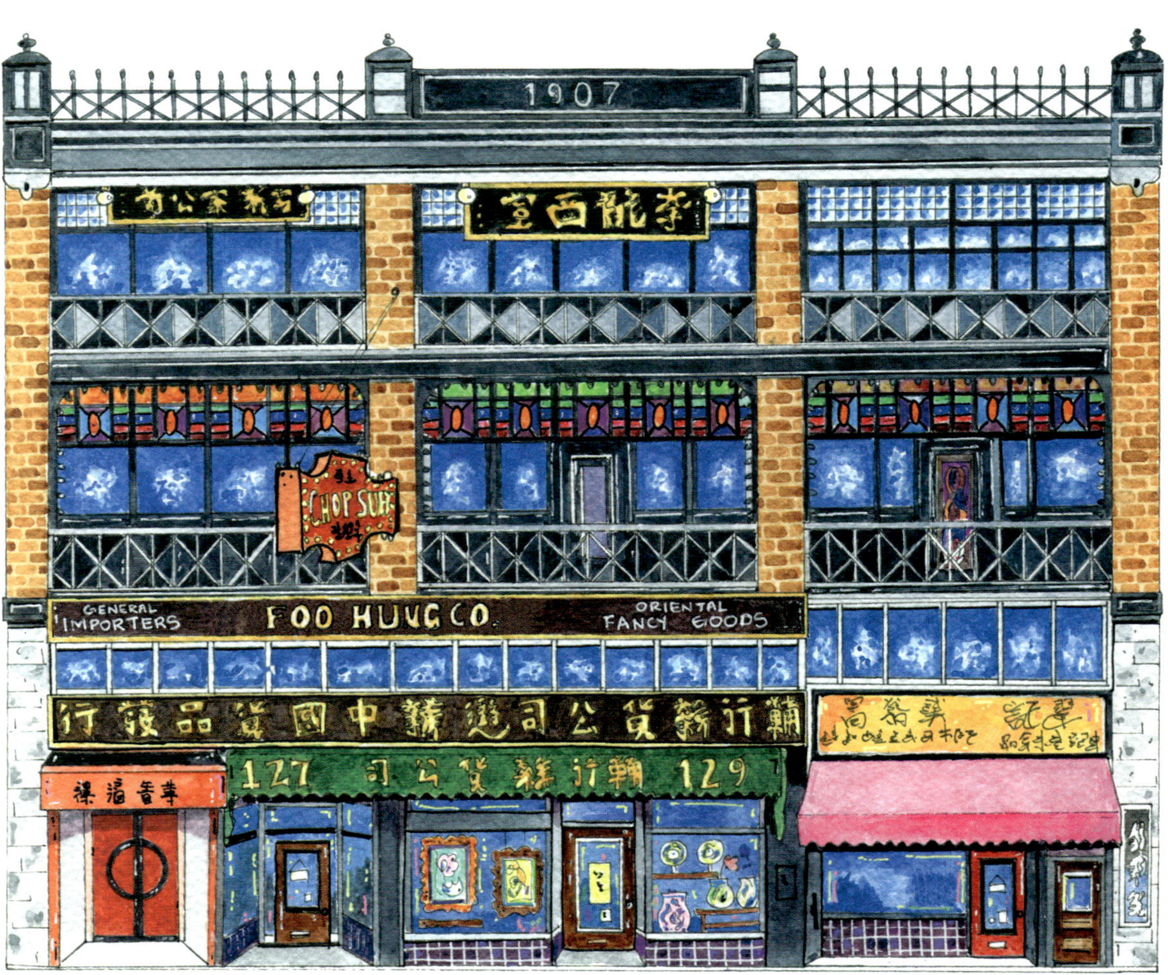

1907
CHOP SUEY
GENERAL IMPORTERS
FOO HUNG CO.
ORIENTAL FANCY GOODS
127
129

Lee Building
127–133 East Pender
Built 1907/1973

Although 1907 is inscribed on the delicate brick facade of the Lee Building at 127–133 East Pender, the building was rebuilt in 1973 after it was damaged by a fire the year prior, making it one of the first buildings to be rebuilt after Chinatown was declared a heritage area in 1971. The heritage designation limited reconstruction proposals, which required consideration of the building's socioeconomic and cultural value, its heritage, and building code requirements, all of which were further complicated by the fire damage. Under the direction of Robert H. Lee, real estate businessman and son of the building's original owner, Ron Bick Lee, architects Henriquez and Todd adopted a flexible approach in the restoration of the original facade as a free-standing frame separate from the modern building and open courtyard.

In 1910, at the age of eighteen, Ron Bick Lee arrived in Victoria, where he found work at a Chinese restaurant as a dishwasher before moving to Vancouver in 1916. Prior to founding his import-export store, Foo Hung Curios at 127 East Pender, he worked in restaurants, hotels, and import stores.[20] The store became one of the leading import-export companies in early Chinatown, importing Asian goods while exporting Canadian products such as flour and paper products, and served as a money transfer institution through a branch in Hong Kong. Foo Hung Curios, which is now the name of the gift shop in the Chinatown Storytelling Centre, an initiative of Lee's granddaughter, Carol Lee, refers to the phrase "walking side by side together."

Ron Bick Lee eventually expanded into the greenhouse business, operating Grandview Greenhouse on fifty acres in East Vancouver during the Great Depression. His son, Robert, later went on to become one of the wealthiest people in BC. Having spent his early years watching his father work days in the greenhouse and nights at a restaurant before owning his own store, Robert describes not having received a proper haircut until the age of eighteen because his father used to cut their hair using a bowl.[21] His interest in real estate started in his early teenage years and motivated him to work hard and get into university. Robert graduated from the University of British Columbia with a business degree in 1956 and immediately started working in real estate. His network grew through his father's connections in and around Chinatown, which included Tong Louie, who owned IGA and London Drugs in BC.[22]

Robert's big break came in the late 1960s, when fear spread in Hong Kong that communist China was going to try to take over the British colony, resulting in an exodus of wealthy Hong Kong residents to Vancouver. The local banks advised newcomers to consult with Robert because he knew how to speak Cantonese. Despite initial resistance, Ron Bick Lee, like many of the older generation in Chinatown, had ensured his children maintained their language and culture, believing it would come in handy one day.[23] Robert's fluency in Cantonese resulted in his first big real estate deal: selling the Imperial Towers in the West End, which was the city's largest apartment block with 263 suites.[24]

Robert notes that the "two core values that my father passed on to me are caring for family and community."[25] His eldest daughter, Carol, has carried this on through her work with the Vancouver Chinatown Foundation. Founded in 2011, the Chinatown Foundation is headquartered in the Lee Building and is dedicated to "building a more resilient and inclusive community while promoting the wellbeing of those in need," in addition to preserving Chinatown's irreplaceable cultural heritage.[26] Recognizing that the neighbourhood is struggling, Carol and her business partner, Henry Fung, adopted a three-pillar approach to revitalization: economic, cultural, and physical and social housing. Their goal is simple: to support Chinatown's revival and ensure its cultural and community spirit endures for generations to come.[27]

Throughout its history, the Lee Building was largely mixed-use, providing room for surname organizations such as the Lee Association and various businesses on the ground and upper floors, including Chinatown icon W. K. Gardens Restaurant.

W. K. Gardens occupied several locations between 1917 and 1985; however, its most enduring home was at 127 East Pender, where its three dining rooms accommodated more than seven hundred people. W. K. was a popular Chinese restaurant that hosted special dinners for notable figures like former prime minister Lester B. Pearson and was visited by celebrities like Gary Cooper and Frank Sinatra. For non-Chinese customers, a night out at W. K. provided a taste of something "exotic" and "foreign," while for the Chinese, it represented a place to celebrate big events and traditional festivals with family and friends. A 1948 advertisement noted that one could "Dine and Dance" and eat "Deep fried local Oysters" at W. K. Gardens. Patrons could dance the night away on the large dance floor, often to the sounds of Joe Tyler's Orchestra, until the rising sun drowned out the glow of Chinatown's neon lights.[28]

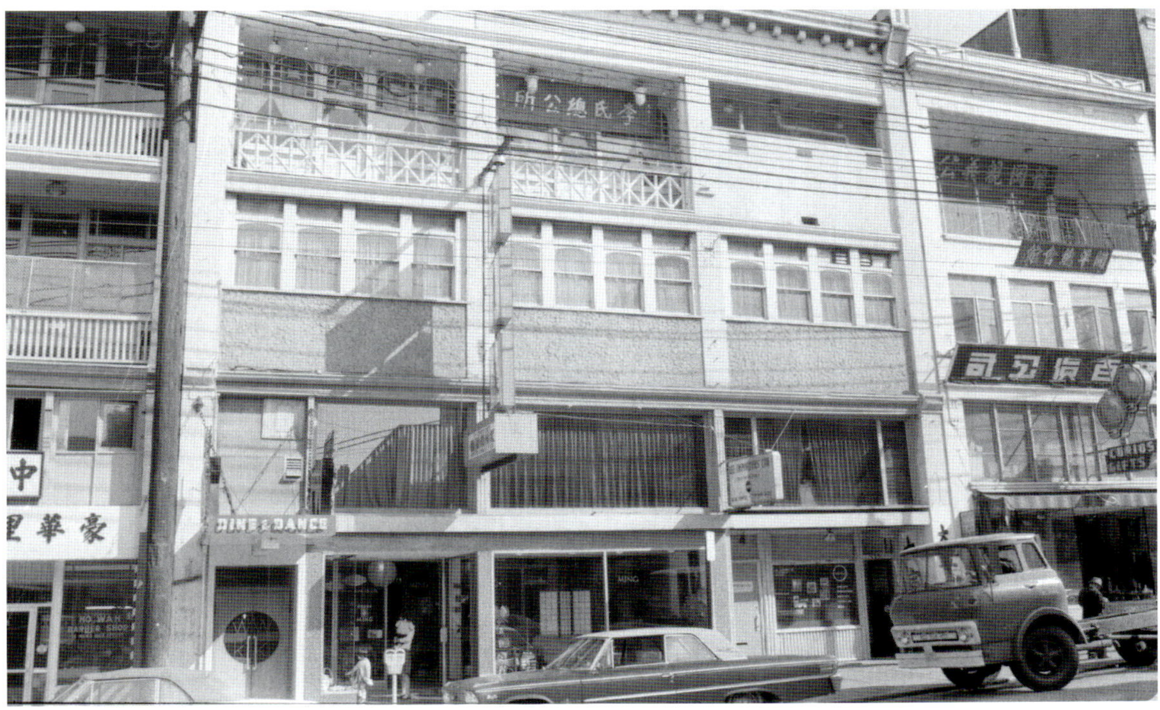

The Lee Building in 1968

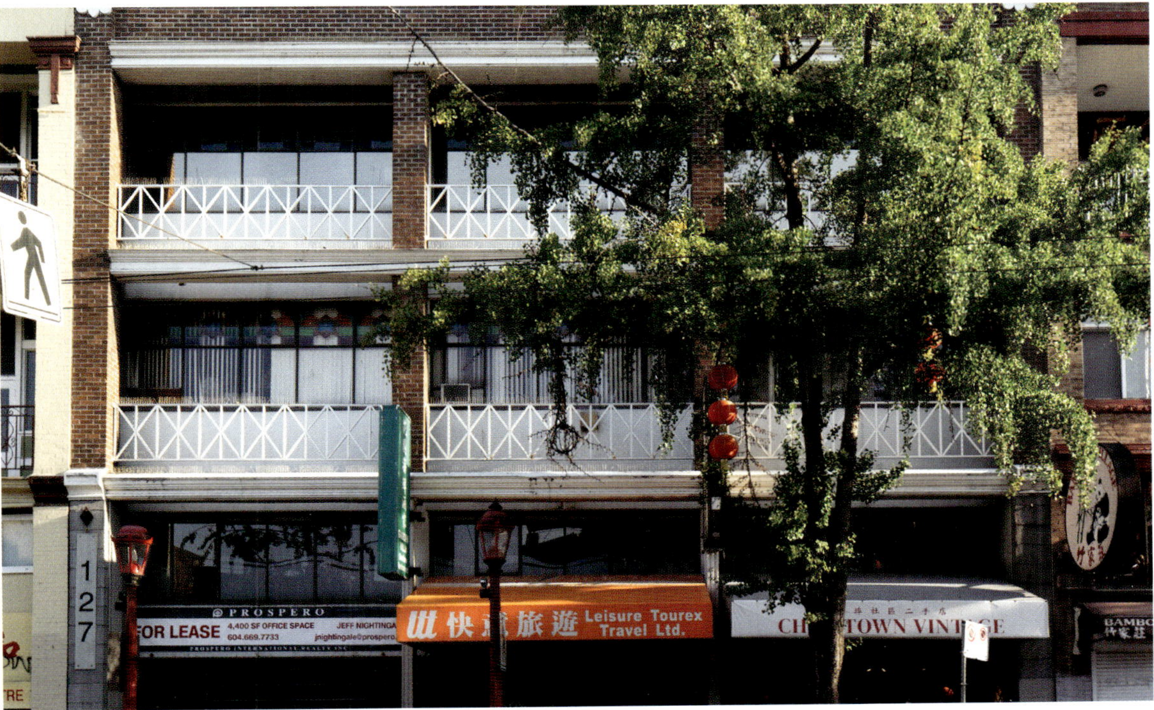

The Lee Building in 2023

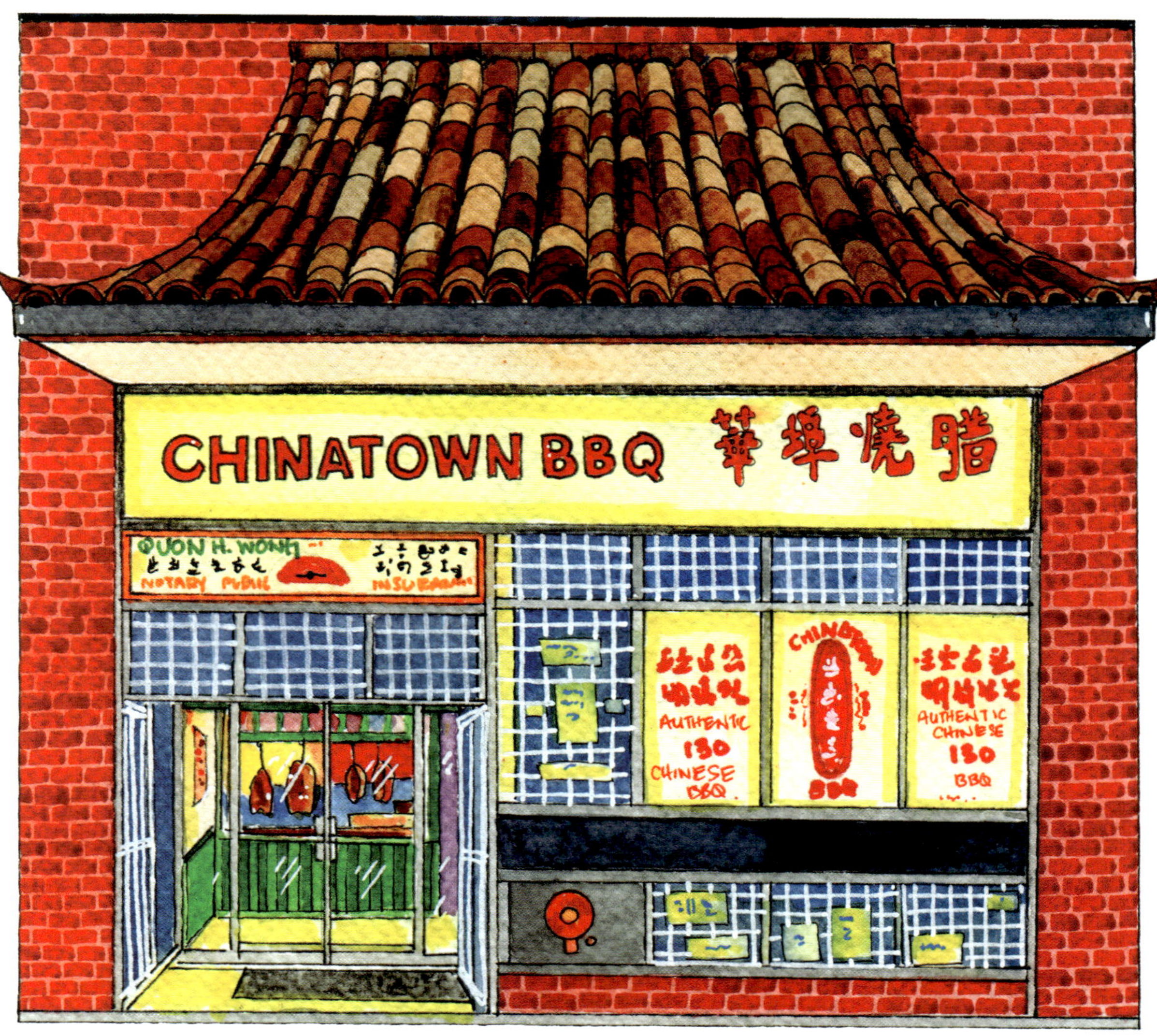

CHINATOWN BBQ 華埠燒臘
QUON H. WONG
NOTARY PUBLIC
INSURANCE
AUTHENTIC CHINESE BBQ
CHINATOWN BBQ
AUTHENTIC CHINESE BBQ

Restaurants and Revitalization
Interview with Carol Lee,
owner of Chinatown BBQ (136 East Pender)

Carol Lee, co-founder of the Vancouver Chinatown Foundation and owner of Chinatown BBQ, has fond memories of walking to Chinese school hand in hand with her grandfather, Ron Bick Lee.[29] Chinatown has always been a significant part of her life, and its revitalization is the inspiration behind her restaurant, Chinatown BBQ, known for its delicious barbeque meats and beef brisket curry and display of roast meats.

Recognizing that restaurants are central to the revitalization of Chinatown, Carol created a restaurant that is about more than just food. Chinatown BBQ, located at 136 East Pender, is a sensory experience, transporting you through time with its décor, black-and-white photographs of Chinatown, vinyl seating, and stylish diner-like menus. There is something nostalgic about the food—the way the light dances off the barbeque pork and the sweet scent of star anise, soy sauce, and lap cheong. Everything about the restaurant, from the glistening ducks in the entrance display to the font on the menus, is a cultural artifact that celebrates Chinatown and Chinese culture.

Carol's restaurant venture is part of a bigger goal to revitalize Chinatown and was inspired by the entrepreneurial spirit of early Chinese immigrants. She notes that the "Chinese Canadian experience is marked by resilience and determination, centred around creating a better life in Canada. This same determination drives the ongoing efforts to revitalize Vancouver's Chinatown." Similar to restaurants that once lined East Pender in the 1950s to 1980s, Chinatown BBQ demonstrates how food is central to Chinatown and its socioeconomic activity. As cultural beacons, restaurants have historically been institutions of cultural exchange, as well as places where families, friends, and acquaintances can get together for a meal. Despite its small size, Chinatown BBQ resembles some of Chinatown's larger restaurants, like W. K. Gardens and Marco Polo, in that it has attracted celebrities, politicians, and locals with its culinary excellence.

"It's incredibly rewarding to see customers appreciating our food," says Carol. "I'm also delighted to see more young people visiting and enjoying the restaurant. Ultimately, my goal is to increase foot traffic in Chinatown, helping to energize the area and draw a vibrant mix of visitors and locals alike."[30]

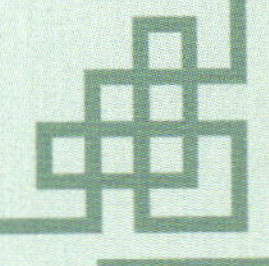

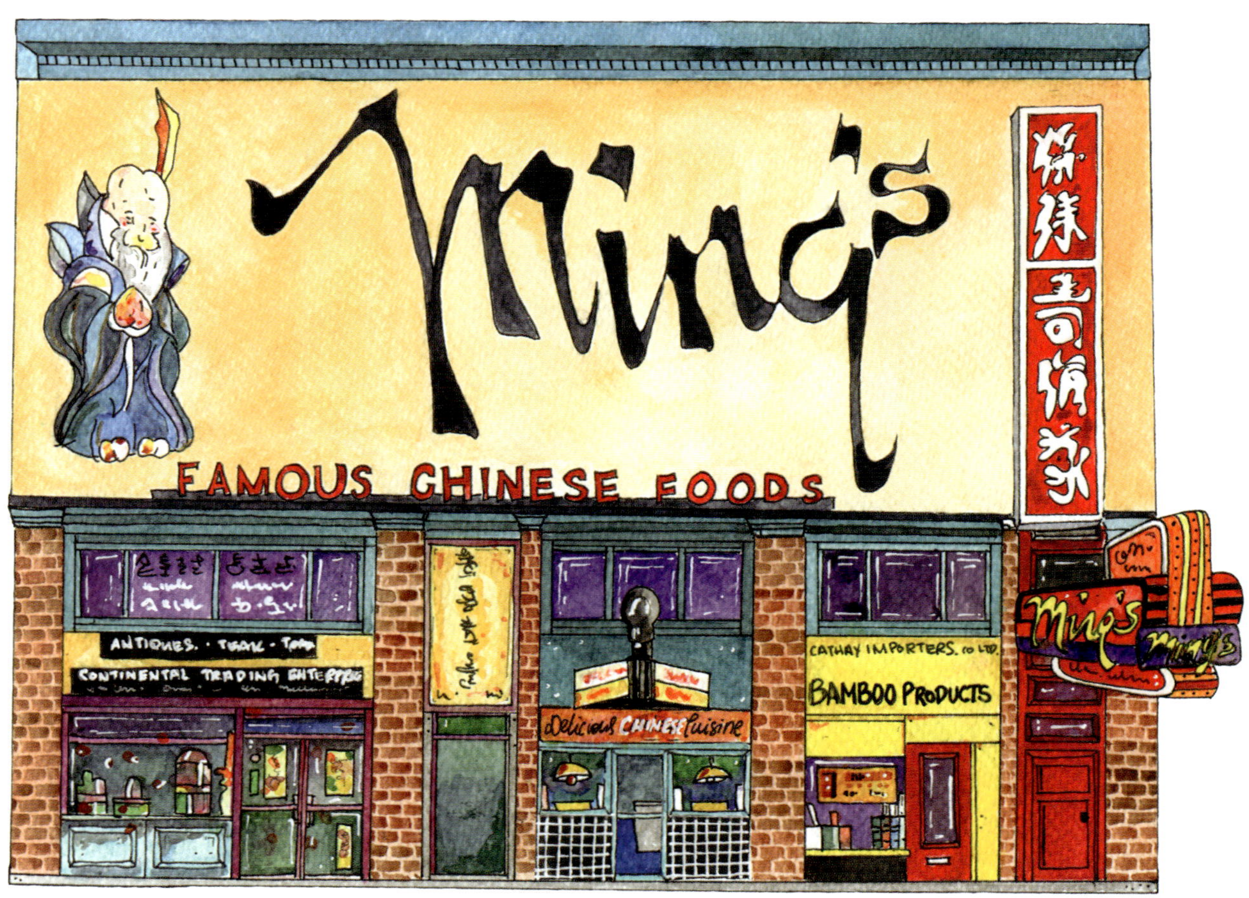
Ming's
FAMOUS CHINESE FOODS
ANTIQUES · TEAK · TOYS
CONTINENTAL TRADING ENTERPRISE
Delicious CHINESE Cuisine
CATHAY IMPORTERS. CO LTD.
BAMBOO PRODUCTS
Ming's
Ming's

Ming's Restaurant and the Anglican Chinese Mission
141–147 East Pender
Built 1921

In a 1960s photograph of 141–147 East Pender, the boxy brick building is almost unrecognizable. Instead of its recessed balconies, the muted photograph features a full frontage banner with a larger-than-life neon sign advertising Ming's Restaurant. Ming's is written in calligraphy that blends Western and Chinese penmanship, and at night the warmth of its red glowing script is reflected on the damp Vancouver streets along with other neon relics like Bamboo Terrace, Ho Ho's, and W. K. Gardens.

Built in 1921, the three-storey building with a mezzanine floor is mixed-use with retail on the ground floor and space for a large restaurant like Ming's or its current tenant, the Fortune Sound Club on the second and third floors. The building was designed by W. H. Chow, who made significant contributions to the architecture of Chinatown, such as designs for the Ming Wo Building as well as alterations to the Yue Shan and the Chinese Empire Reform Association Building.

The building shares architectural elements with others in Chinatown. In particular, it has a mezzanine that is visible from the street and a full-length recessed balcony on the upper floor. The original facade has classical pilasters, capitals, and a deep cornice that was made more "Chinese" in 1977 with the addition of Chinese (and English) characters on the frieze and decorative panels and balcony railings. The transformation represents a period of transition after Chinatown received its historical designation in 1971.

During its early days, the building accommodated the Ching Won Musical Society, which sponsored Cantonese Opera and music; the Hon Sing Club; the Chinese Social and Athletic Association; and the Anglican Church Relief Depot. In 1944, Ron Bick Lee purchased the building.

In 1931, merchants and associations were initially able to assist the unemployed; however, as the unemployment rate in Chinatown grew to 80 percent, resources dwindled and many were left destitute.[31] As part of the province's relief program, the Anglican Chinese Mission set up a soup kitchen in the building to provide two daily meals, clothes, and shoes. Under the province's relief program, Chinese men were provided with only half the relief on the assumption that they could live on less.[32]

Eventually, governments preferred to send Chinese back to China because transport was cheaper (passage was fifty-five dollars in 1935) than maintaining relief over an extended period. In order to qualify for the travel subsidy, they had to declare they would never return to Canada. By the end of 1935, approximately four hundred Chinese had returned to China under the government subsidy.[33]

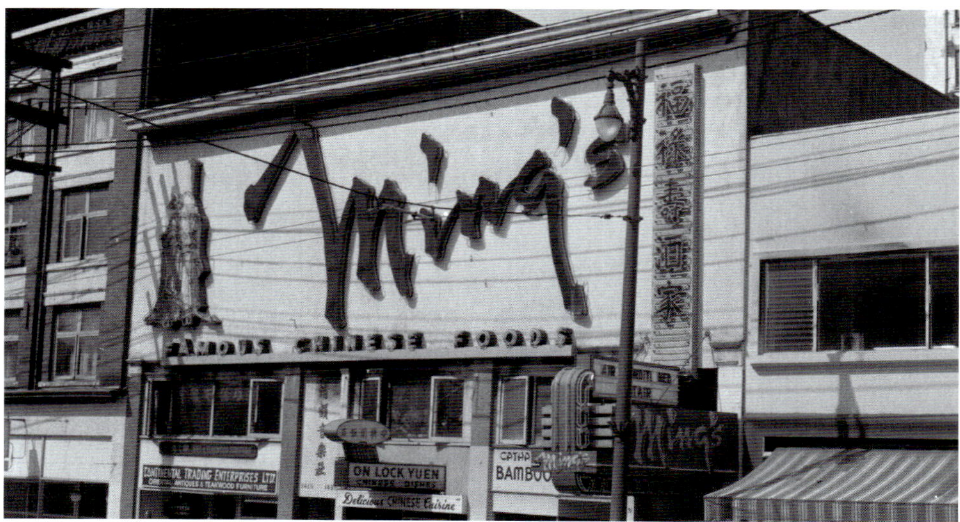

Ming's Restaurant with Cathay Importers and On Lock Yuen Restaurant in the late 1960s

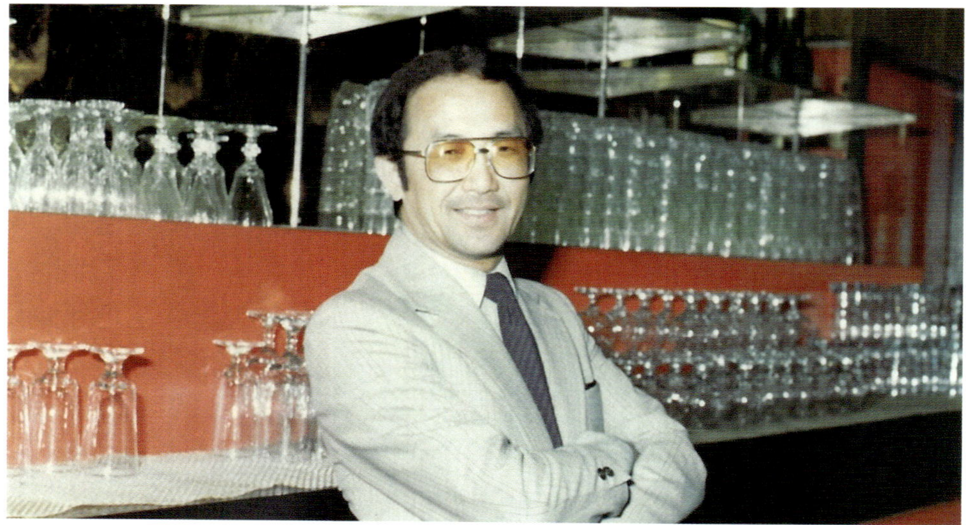

Owner of Ming's Restaurant, Wai Hon Wong, in front of the bar in 1981

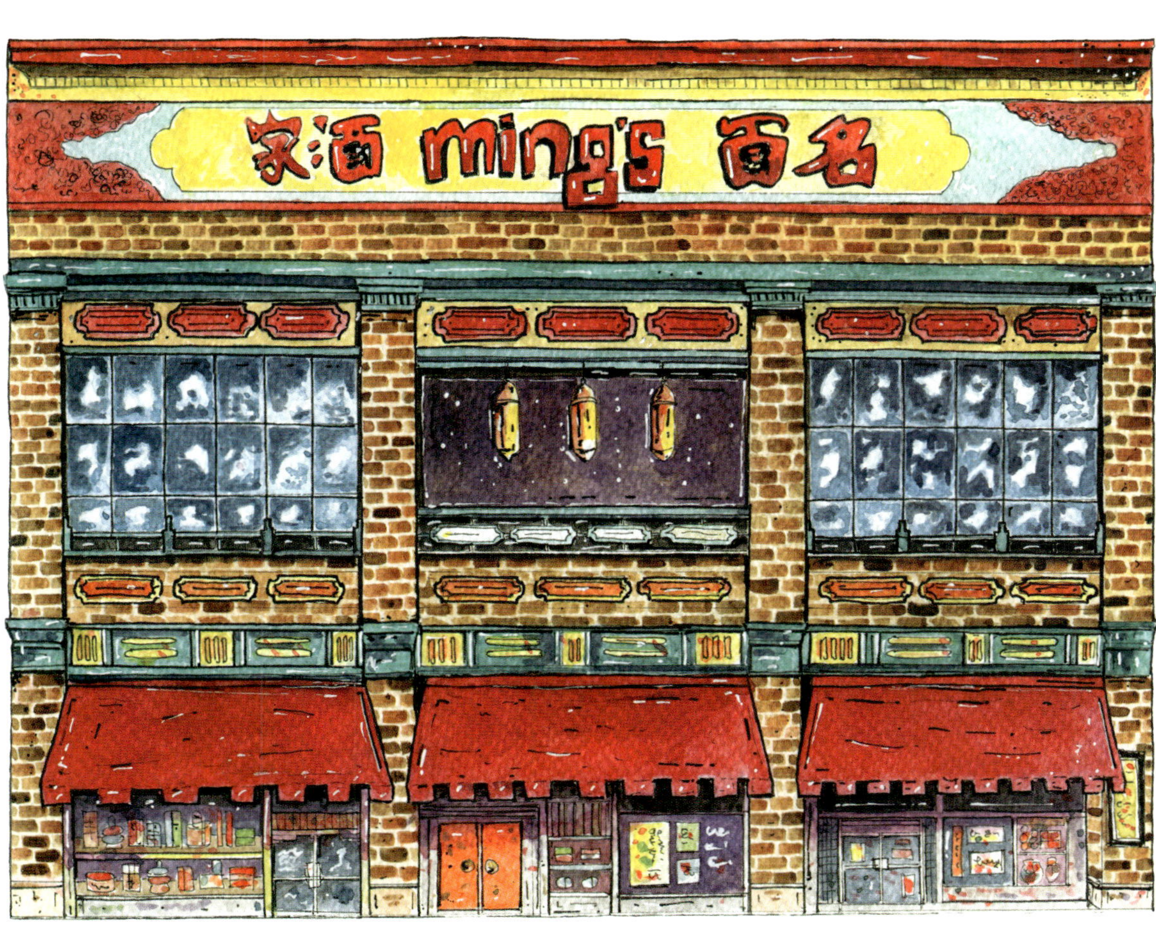

家酒 ming's 百名

Dim Sum Carts and Nightclubs

Interview with Melinda Wong and Keeman Wong

Advertising "authentic Chinese dishes at moderate prices," Ming's was a dim sum restaurant during the day that transitioned into a banquet hall and entertainment venue at night. Operating on three floors, including a low-ceilinged mezzanine, the restaurant offered Hong Kong–style cuisine by chefs recruited directly from Hong Kong. Considered the go-to restaurant for large banquets and famous for its traditional ten-course meals, it provided the perfect setting for weddings, large birthdays, and association gatherings.

In 1949, Wai Hon Wong joined his father, Shee Jing Wong, in Canada. He took over the original Ming's Restaurant, in addition to the Wayen and South Seas Dining Lounge, in 1968. Wai Hon's daughter, Melinda Wong, worked at Ming's Restaurant as a lunch hostess and at Ming's nightclub on weekends. She recalls that weekend lunches were exceptionally popular, with a lineup down the staircase. As a dim sum waitress, Melinda would serve the delicacies from a cart that she wheeled around the dining room, inspiring customers to order har gow, siu mai, and barbeque pork buns. Some of the waitresses would call out their offerings and then be summoned to a table.

Ming's nightclub was open six nights a week from 9:30 p.m. to 2:00 a.m. and joined the ranks of other Chinatown entertainment venues such as the Falcon, the Mandarin, the Kublai Khan, and the Marco Polo. Wai Hon designed a special stage that retracted after a performance and opened up into a dance floor. The club's opening night featured Cornel Chan and his Asian Trio, as well as Amy Ying, a well-known singer. The in-house band played a mixture of chart-topping rock and pop tunes with Cantopop. Some popular hits included the Eagles' "One of These Nights," Santana's "Evil Ways," and the Hollies' "The Air That I Breathe."

For Melinda and her siblings, Chinatown was a place where they experimented with their cultural identities. Her younger brother, Keeman Wong, volunteered for Pender Guy Radio and recalls spending his childhood playing in Chinatown's alleys and at his grandparents' restaurant, the Wayen.

Melinda notes that restaurants like Ming's provided a community gathering place where different generations as well as newcomers and Canadian-born Chinese intermingled like an extended family, where regulars were referred to as "uncles" or by nicknames such as Uncle Barkerville Don, Uncle Communist Pui, and Uncle Sloppy.[34]

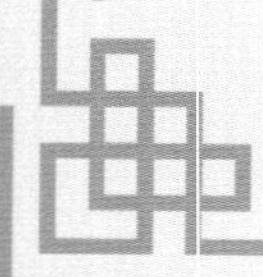

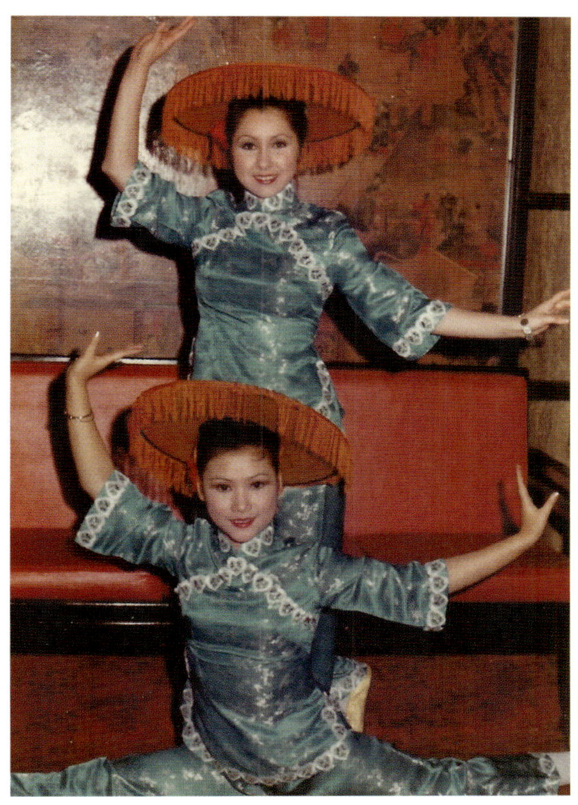

Singing sisters act at Ming's Restaurant from the 1980s

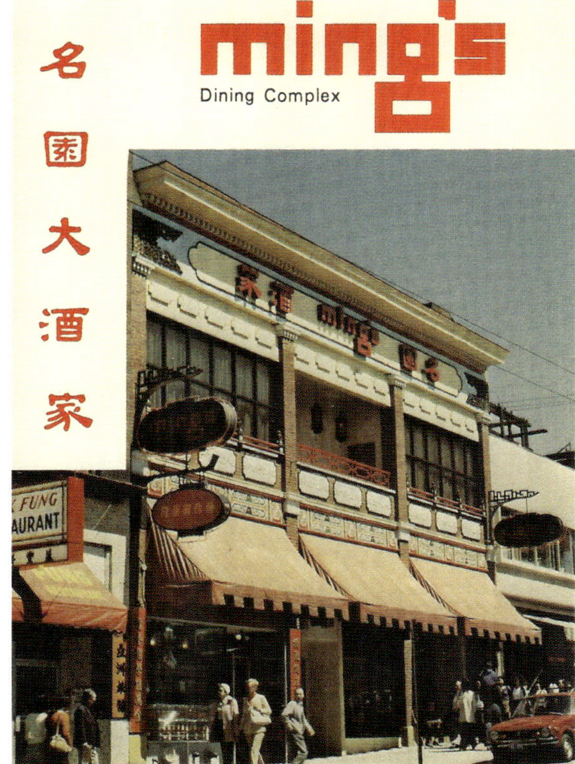

Postcard advertising Ming's Restaurant from the 1980s

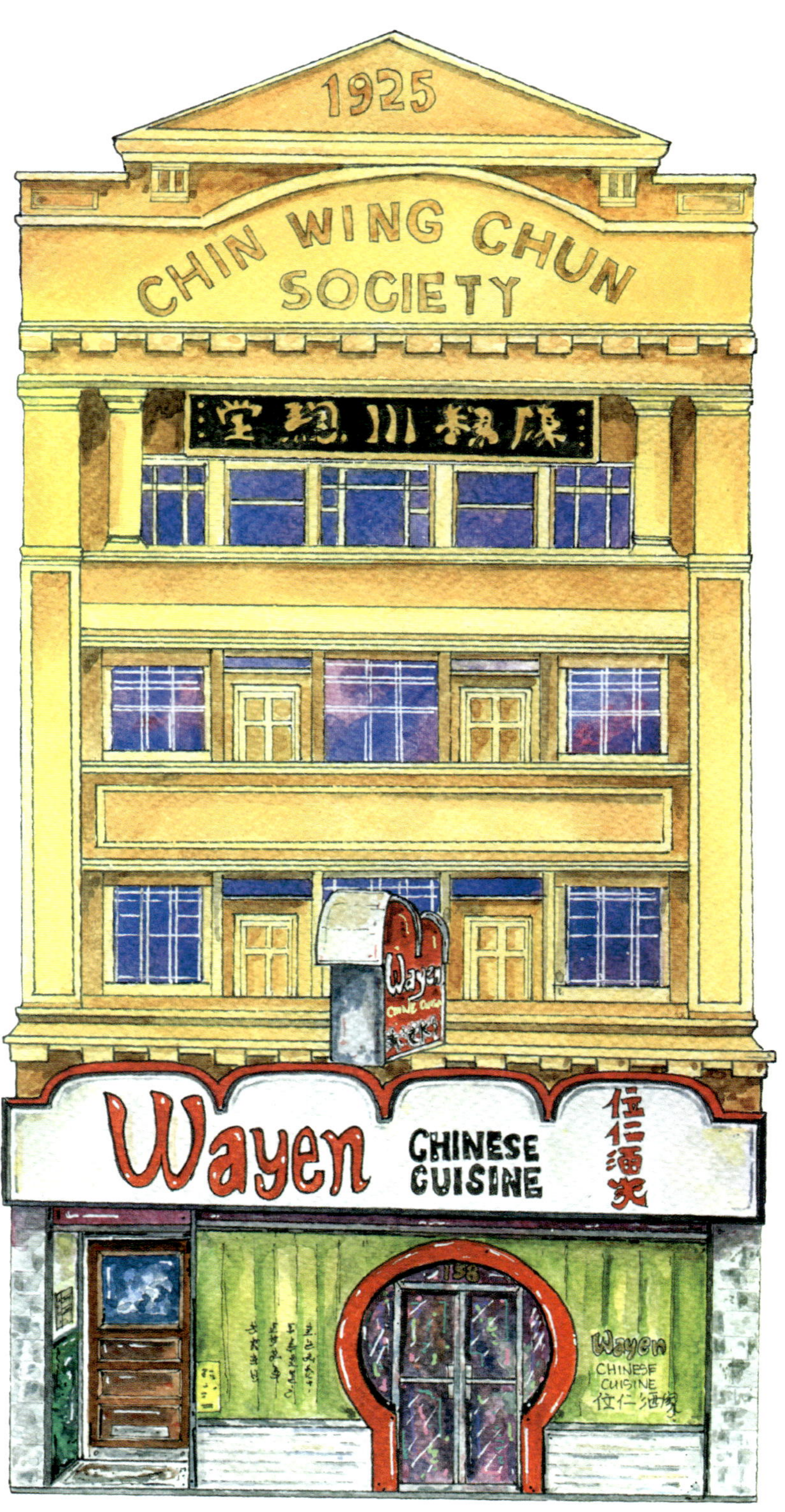

1925
CHIN WING CHUN
SOCIETY
陳穎川總堂
Wayen CHINESE CUISINE 位仁酒家
Wayen CHINESE CUISINE 位仁酒家

Old-Country Eats and Overstuffed Wontons

Interview with Melinda Wong and Keeman Wong

The Wayen is remembered for its distinctive decorative red moon gate entrance and its homestyle Cantonese cooking. Welcoming diners into its expansive dining room on the ground floor of 158 East Pender, the restaurant served quintessential Cantonese dishes like steamed minced pork with Chinese sausage and Chinese mushrooms, whole steamed chicken, and barbeque meats roasted onsite.

The Wayen was owned by Shee Jing Wong, who first arrived in Canada in the 1930s as a "paper son" and had a small tailoring business called Kwong Duck Loong on the 200 block of East Pender. Separated from his family, he was eventually able to sponsor his son, Wai Hon Wong, and wife, Wai Lin Wong, after the Exclusion Act was lifted.

Shee Jing initially set up the Wayen Café on Keefer Street where his wife, Wai Lin, dazzled customers with old-country eats, such as homemade shrimp dumplings, pork dumplings, barbeque pork buns, and other delicacies, which were often served with a cup of Dickson's coffee. The success of the café encouraged the Wong family to scout out a larger location. The café reopened at 119B East Pender, expanding its offerings to include Cantonese village-style home cooking in the 1960s, before moving to 158 East Pender, where it operated until the early 1980s.

The Wayen was a family-operated enterprise, where family meals were interrupted to serve customers and chopping vegetables became a form of childcare. Shee Jing's granddaughter, Melinda Wong, remembers she would often take the bus to Chinatown with her grandmother and spend the day at the Wayen. Melinda and her siblings would help their grandparents wrap wontons, hang out in the back room where their grandfather kept his abacus, or watch the elderly woman who worked in the kitchen tirelessly roasting meat at the large barbeque pit.

Melinda recalls that her grandmother would remind her not to overstuff the wontons and not to waste food such as broccoli stems. When the restaurant slowed down, the children would wander down East Pender to the bookstore to pick up newspapers for their grandparents. If they were well behaved, they were allowed to buy a toy, comic book, or some stationery.

After taking a bartender's course, Melinda's father, Wai Hon Wong, opened the South Sea Dining Lounge below the Wayen. Unlike the homestyle setting of the Wayen, South Sea offered a themed dining experience featuring fish shadow boxes, fishing nets, and models of Chinese junks lining the walls. A large aquarium filled with tropical fish welcomed customers into the dining room. South Sea was more upscale than the Wayen, with tablecloths, soft lighting, and carpeted floors. It offered Cantonese food in a relaxed and more intimate atmosphere with space for private dining.[35]

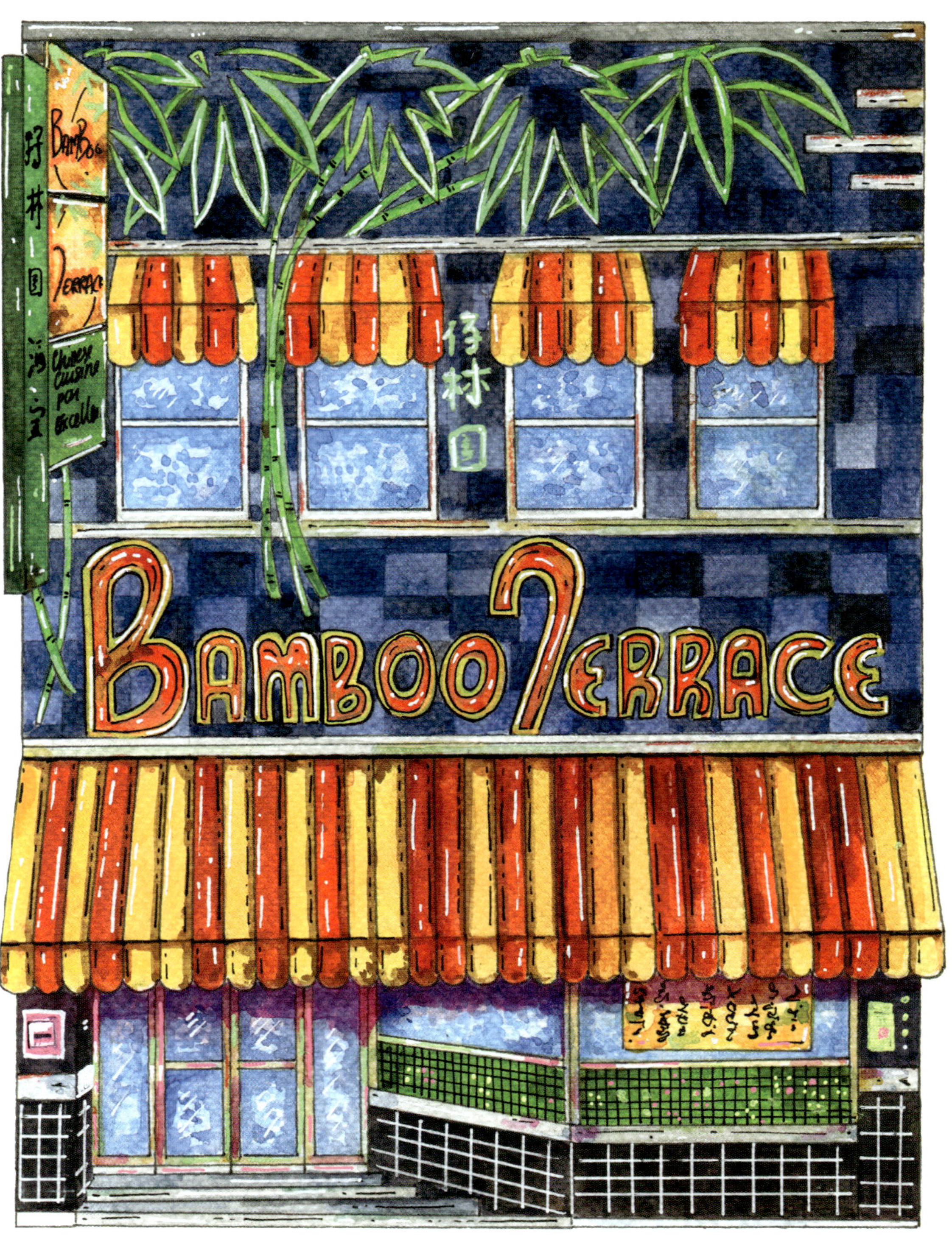
好
竹
園
海鮮菜
Bamboo
Terrace
Chinese
Cuisine
par
excellence
竹林園
BAMBOO TERRACE
回

Bamboo Terrace and Smilin' Buddha Cabaret
155 East Pender and 109 East Hastings

At 155 East Pender is a two-storey building with a facade that once glowed with neon-green bamboo leaves. Once home to the Bamboo Terrace, the restaurant advertised a "distinctive modern Oriental atmosphere" and "Chinese cuisine at its best." The restaurant is connected to yo-yo champion Harvey Lowe, who contributed significantly to Chinatown's nightlife.

Born in Victoria in 1918, Harvey Lowe gained success at a young age through international yo-yo competitions that allowed him to travel across North America and Europe to compete. His parents, who owned a tailor shop, maintained traditional Chinese values. For example, his father wore braids as a sign of allegiance to the Qing Dynasty and kept a concubine who bound her feet despite being born in Canada. Unfortunately, his father died when Harvey was three, but his mother supported the family with income generated through sewing. In grade six, Harvey purchased a thirty-five-cent tournament yo-yo, a Duncan 77, and started entering competitions in Victoria and Vancouver. In 2005, Harvey Lowe was inducted into the American Yo-Yo Association Hall of Fame.

In 1952, Harvey, with his peers Albert Kwan and Wong Kwong Gim, acquired 109 East Hastings, where they opened the Smilin' Buddha Cabaret. The establishment catered to a working-class clientele who dined, danced, and enjoyed cabaret-style shows. There were rumours that famous musicians such as Ike and Tina Turner and actors like Dennis Hopper frequented the Smilin' Buddha. In the 1970s, the Smilin' Buddha became ground zero for Vancouver's new independent punk and alternative music scene. After the club closed in 1992, the original neon sign was recovered from the scrapyard by the band 54-40, who later took it on tour. The band then donated the sign to the Museum of Vancouver.

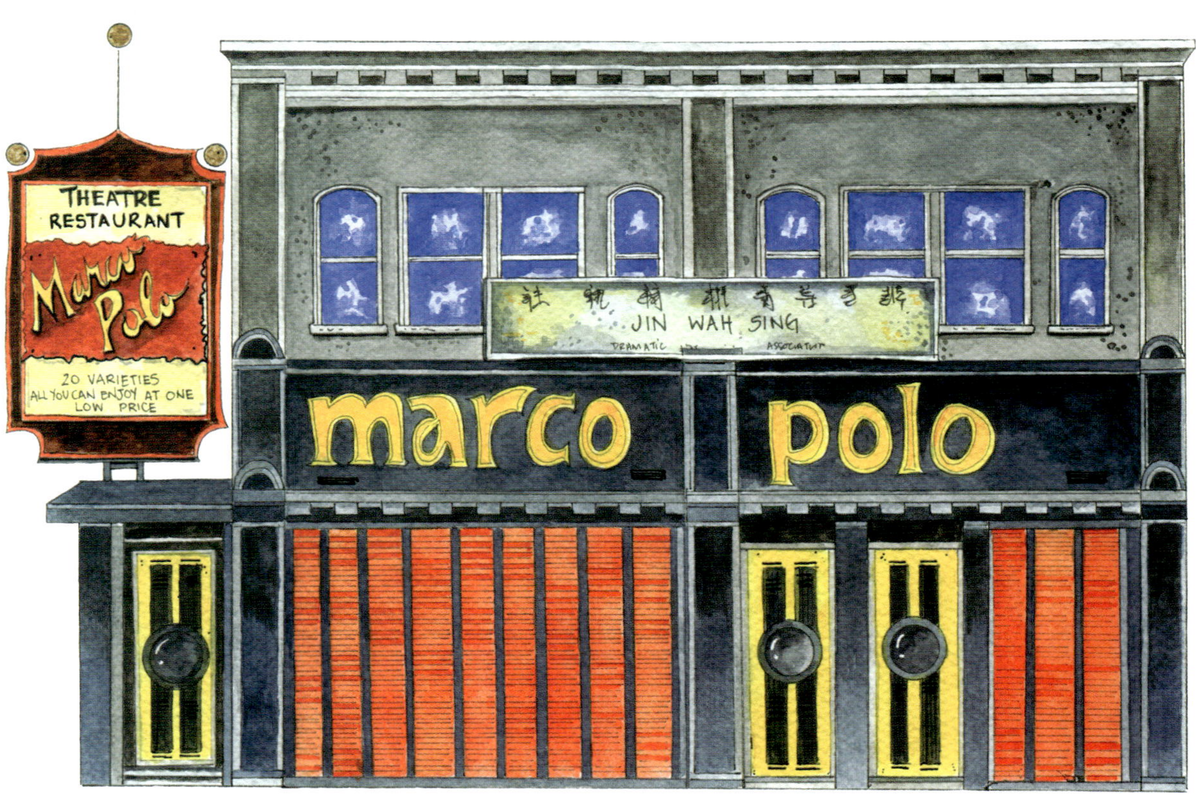
THEATRE
RESTAURANT
Marco
Polo
20 VARIETIES
ALL YOU CAN ENJOY AT ONE
LOW PRICE
JIN WAH SING
DRAMATIC ASSOCIATION
marco polo

Forbidden City and Marco Polo Supper Club
86–90 East Pender
Built 1904

When 90 East Pender was torn down in 1983, it marked the end of the magical era of Chinatown's buzzing restaurant scene and vibrant nightlife. From 1904 to 1907, 90 East Pender housed the terminus station for the Vancouver, Westminster, and Yukon Railway (VW&Y), a subsidiary of the Great Northern Railway (GNR) run by James Hill. The station linked Vancouver with Seattle from 1905 to 1917. By 1919, the GNR needed more space and acquired rights for a new location at the end of False Creek. When 90 East Pender was demolished, the side of the building still bore the original VW&Y sign.

After the train station was decommissioned, the building sat empty for years before it was repurposed as a restaurant. Opened in 1954, the Forbidden City Cabaret was the first of its kind, catering largely to a non-Chinese crowd with Chinese food, live shows, and cigarette table service. The Forbidden City once featured a statue of a rotating lion advertising exquisite cuisine, dining, and dancing.

Owner Jimmy Lee was born in Victoria in 1904. His family returned to China during the Great Depression, but Jimmy and his brother came back to Canada to earn money to support their family back home. Like other restaurants that emerged during a period of family reunification, such as the Ho Inn and Ho Ho's Chop Suey, the Forbidden City used Chinese techniques but local ingredients to create unique palatable dishes that appealed to both Chinese and Western tastebuds.[36]

Postwar restaurants in Chinatown only offered limited service, especially when it came to alcohol. Until 1947, the Chinese faced discrimination and restrictions in their commercial activities. As one needed to be on the provincial voters' list to qualify for a liquor licence, many Chinese-owned establishments could not sell liquor because the Chinese did not gain the right to vote until 1947.[37]

Jimmy's children, David and Janis Lee, recall how their father had to get creative when customers requested alcohol. Often, he had to rely on personal stashes, which were a phone call away or a dash down the street to one of the many boarding houses that the Chinatown bachelors lived in.[38]

In 1948, Jimmy Lee also opened the May-Ling Restaurant at 442 Main Street (now 450 Main Street). It quickly became one of Vancouver's most notorious "bottle clubs," raided constantly for selling or allowing liquor on its premises. Unlike the Forbidden City, which catered to an upscale crowd, the May-Ling, with its affordable eats and entertainment, was a more working-class venue, where veterans often went for a night out with their girlfriends.[39]

On March 23, 1957, at 1:50 a.m., twenty-one-year-old Joe McKenna shot and killed twenty-five-year-old John Donaldson at the May-Ling. The infamous case initially saw McKenna sentenced to hang, but his sentence was commuted to life. A year after, Jimmy Lee saw a fortune teller who said his businesses would bring bad luck. In 1959, he sold both the May-Ling and the Forbidden City.[40]

In the 1960s and 1970s, the Marco Polo Supper Club took over where the Forbidden City left off at 90 East Pender and became one of Vancouver's legendary entertainment venues. The theatre restaurant was the brainchild of Victor Louie and his brothers of the H. Y. Louie family. Its grand opening gala in 1964 featured a roast pig, live music, and emcee Harvey Lowe, yo-yo champion and owner of the Smilin' Buddha Cabaret.

Similar to the Forbidden City, the Marco Polo welcomed non-Asian diners to explore Chinese cuisine. With a fourteen-page menu, the club offered an endless variety of dishes at a time when food selections were less diverse than they are today. The Marco Polo hosted comedians Richard Pryor and Redd Foxx, as well as comedy nightclub mainstays like Pete Barbutti. It also featured groups such as 5th Dimension and Sly and the Family Stone, as well as the Platters and Bill Haley and His Comets. In 1968, Nina Simone appeared in what was probably the venue's most notable show.

In the mid-1970s, as other supper clubs in Vancouver such as the Cave, Isy's, and the Palomar started winding down, the Marco Polo also reduced the number of shows it offered. The establishment continued to operate until it moved to North Vancouver in 1982, taking with it a special era in Chinatown's vibrancy.

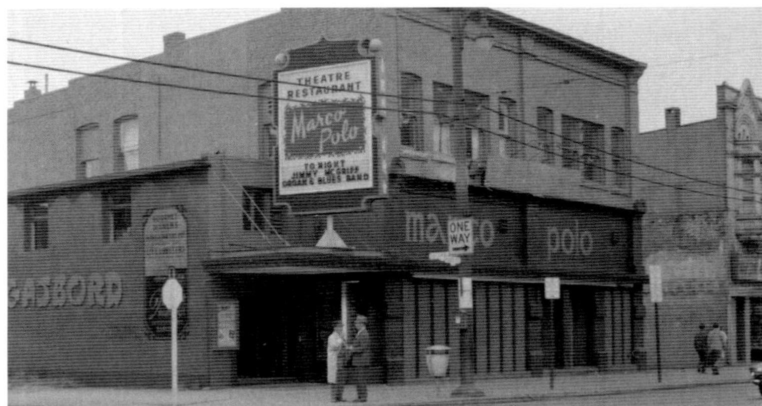

The Marco Polo Supper Club in 1973

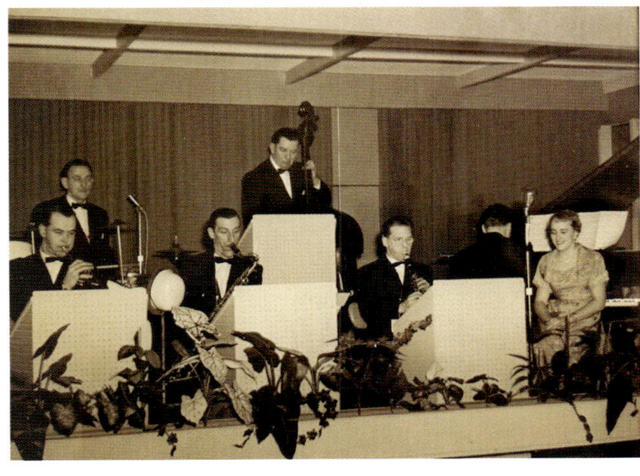

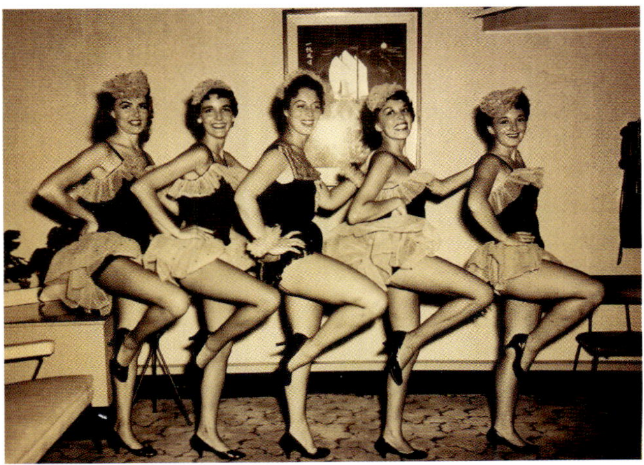

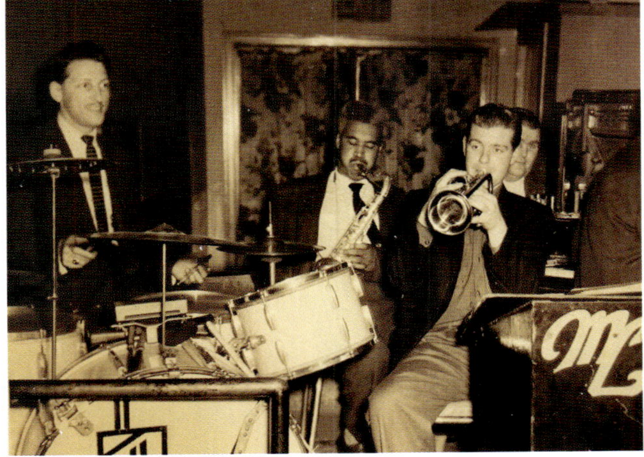

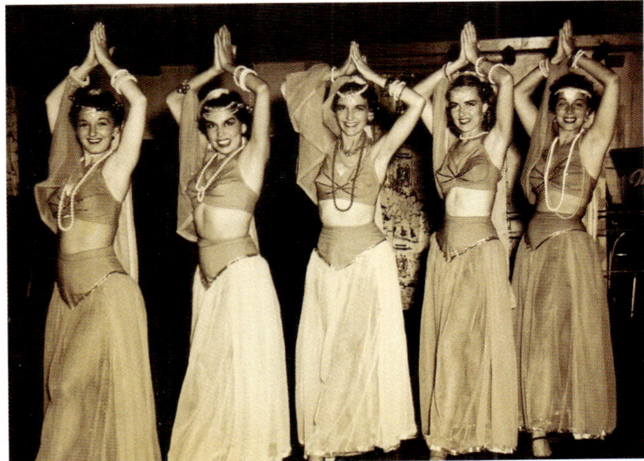

Entertainment at the Forbidden City

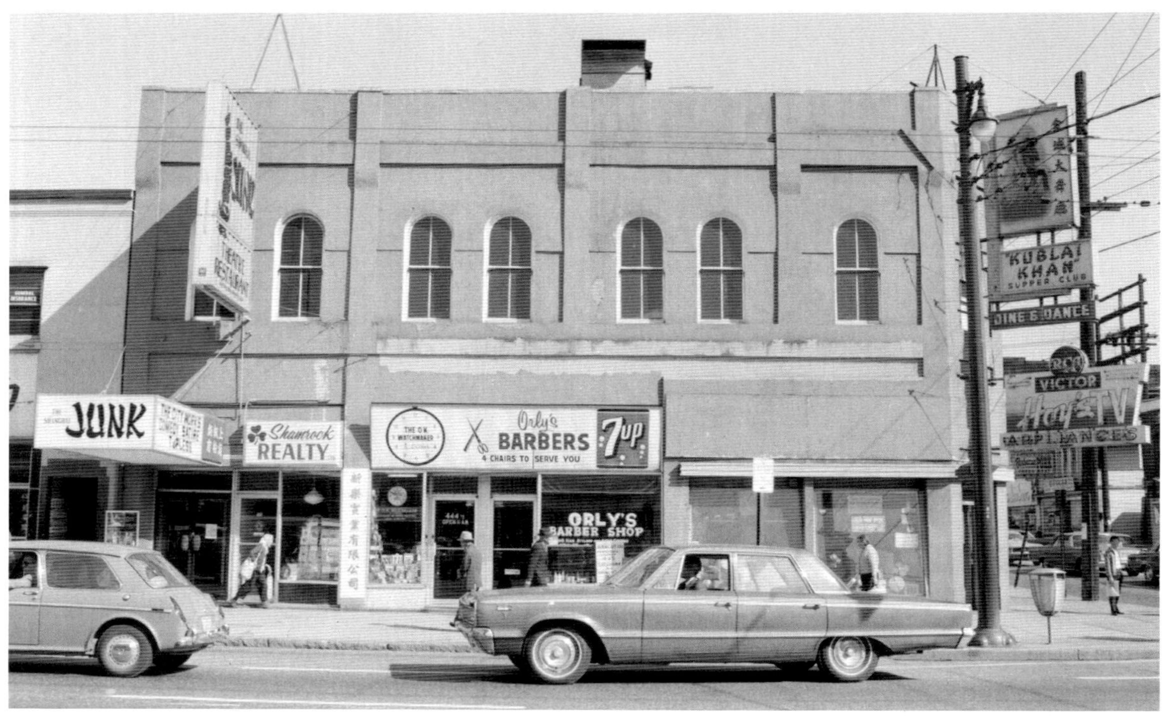

The Shanghai Junk Cabaret on the corner of Main and East Pender in 1973

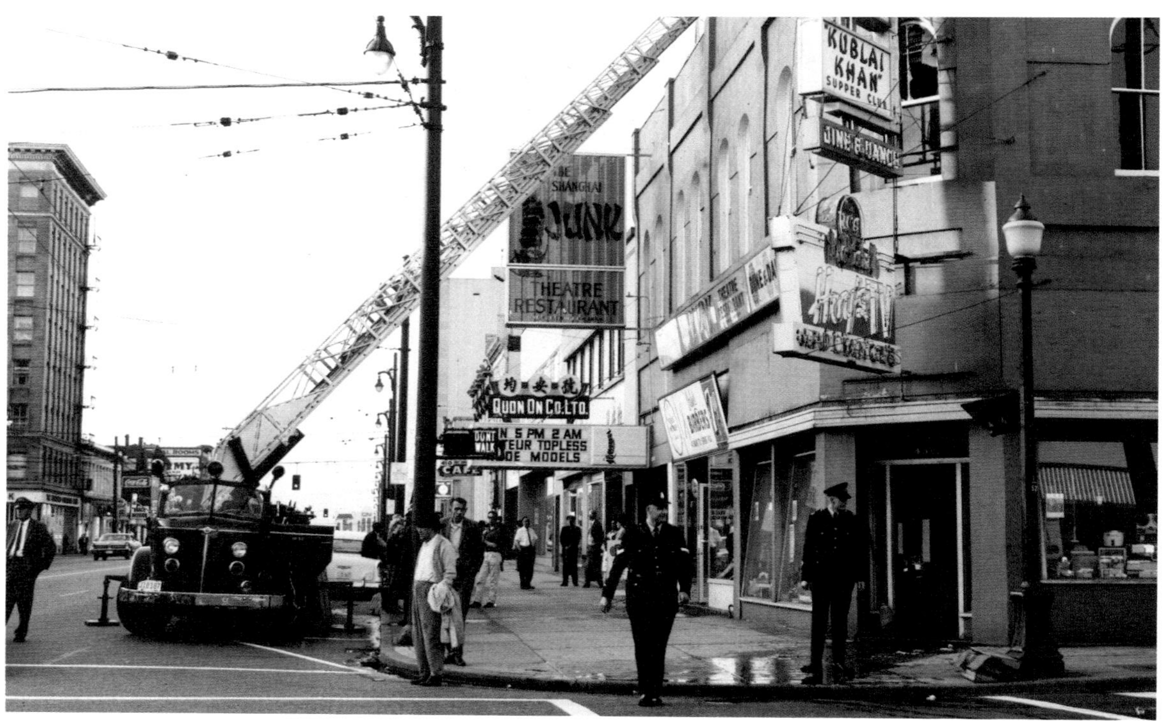

The Shanghai Junk and the Kublai Khan in 1967

From Supper Club to Strip Club to Financial Institution

450 Main Street

In the 1960s, the two-storey brick building on the northeast corner of Pender and Main housed a venue that was a far cry from the staid financial institution it is today.

First, Steven Yuen established the Kublai Khan Supper Club by investing $40,000 into refurbishing the space to attract an upscale crowd like the Marco Polo Supper Club and Forbidden City did. And then in 1966, Tommy Chong (of the comedy duo Cheech and Chong) and his brother, Stan, opened the Shanghai Junk Cabaret. Its inauguration invited scensters to "Vancouver's smartest and most sophisticated nightclub."[41] The Shanghai Junk boasted a "new era of nightclub entertaining" with its daring live strip shows alongside "exquisite Oriental and Occidental foods."[42]

At the Shanghai Junk, the Chongs defied strip club regulations that required dancing girls to wear nipple pasties. This infuriated the licencing board, which suspended the club's liquor licence.[43] In 1967, the club featured a psychedelic nude paint dance by Sandi and Lawrence that invited patrons to apply paint to a naked dancing woman. As a guitarist for one of Vancouver's top 1960s musical acts, Bobby Taylor and the Vancouvers, Tommy Chong often backed up topless dancers and strippers in performances that would transform into a "hippie vaudeville" act where he played a long-haired stoner.[44]

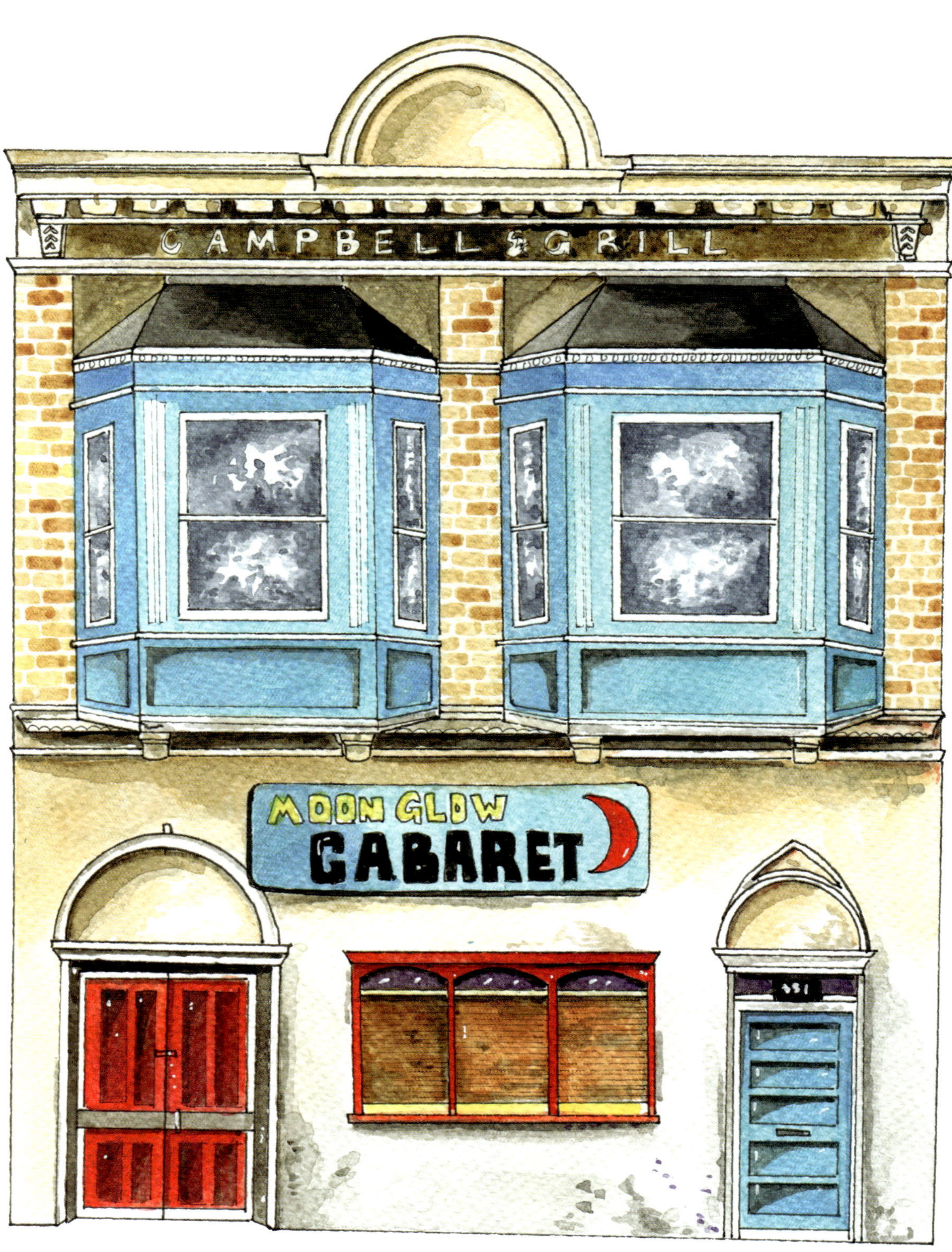
CAMPBELL & GRILL
MOON GLOW
CABARET

Moon Glow Cabaret
331 East Georgia
Built 1911

The Moon Glow Cabaret hosted the music group the Calgary Shades, featuring Tommy Chong. The band was later named Little Daddy and the Bachelors, before it became Bobby Taylor & the Vancouvers and signed with Motown's Gordy Records in 1965. The Moon Glow was on the ground floor of a two-storey brick building that was built in 1911 by Campbell & Grill, and then demolished when the city redeveloped an area of Strathcona for MacLean Park Housing.

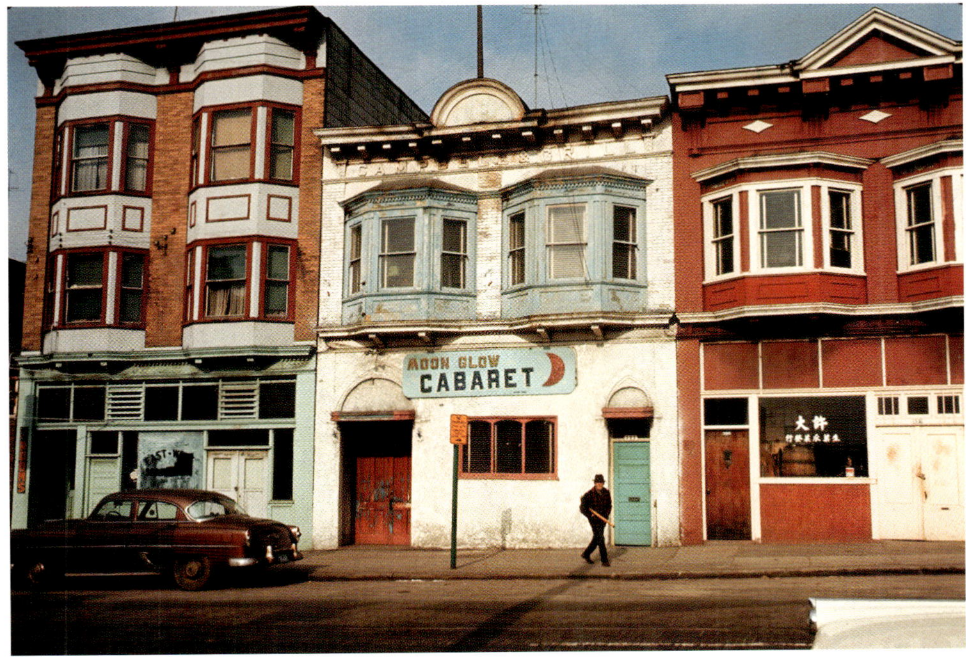

Moon Glow Cabaret and surrounding buildings on the 300 block of East Georgia in 1966

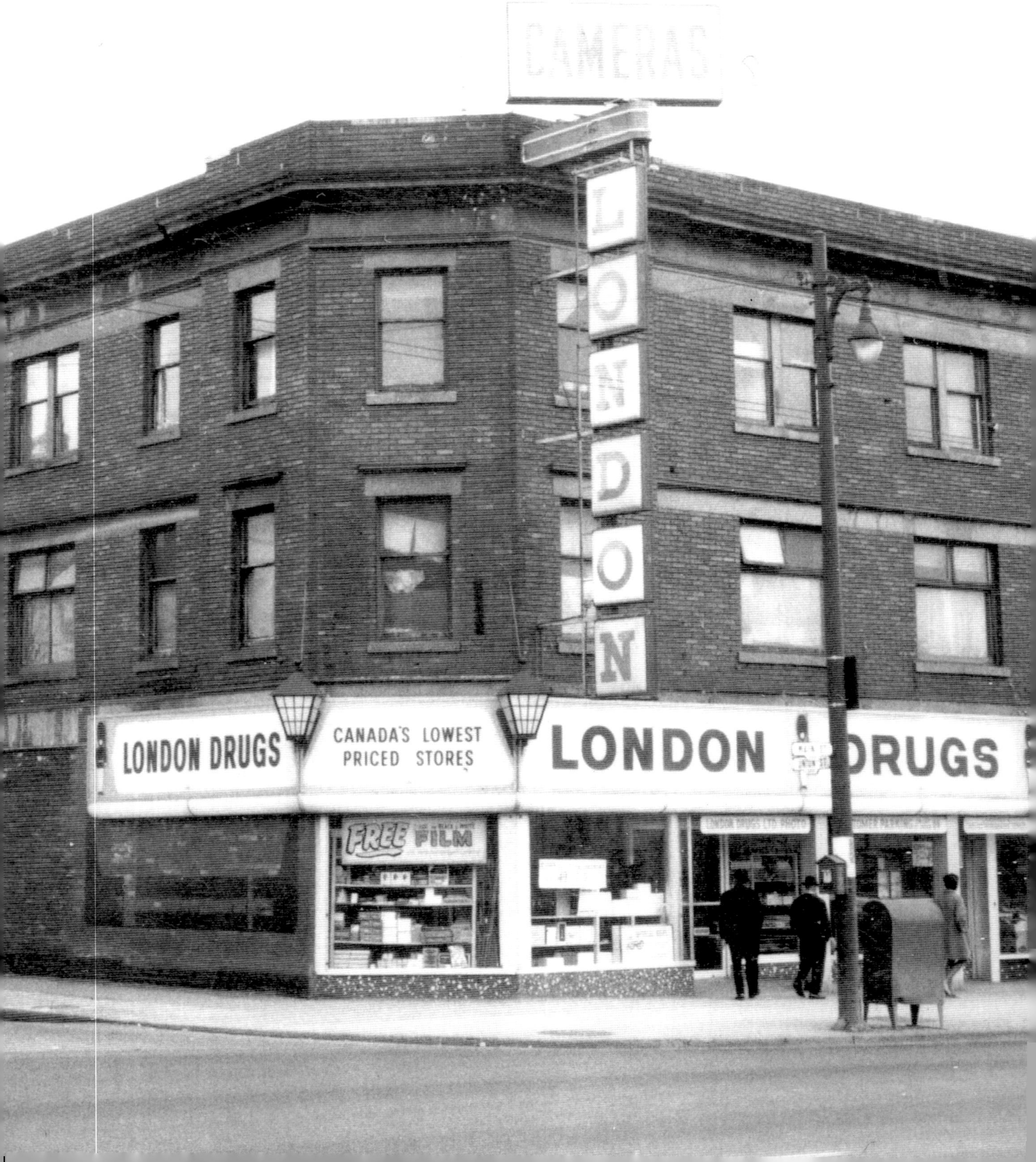

LONDON DRUGS
FREE FILM

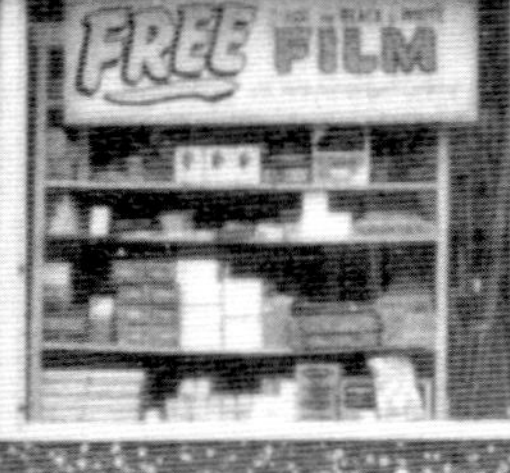

CANADA'S LOWEST
PRICED STORES

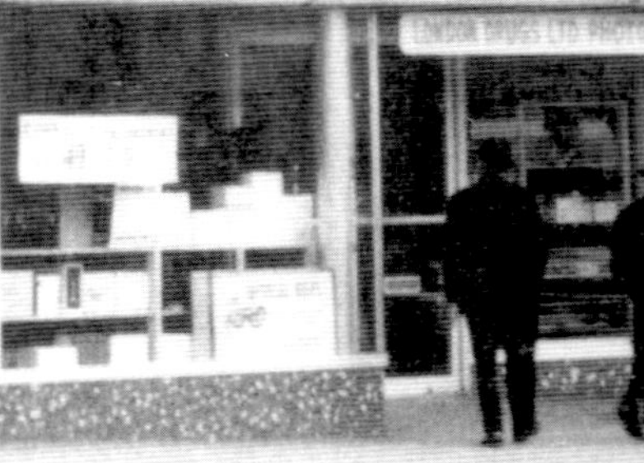

LONDON
LONDON DRUGS LTD. PHOTO

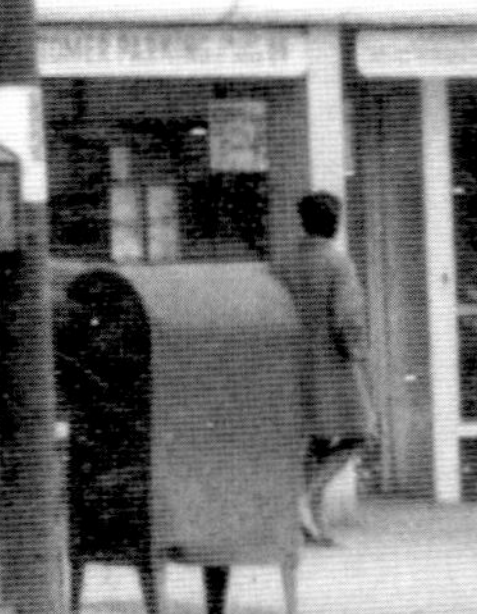

DRUGS

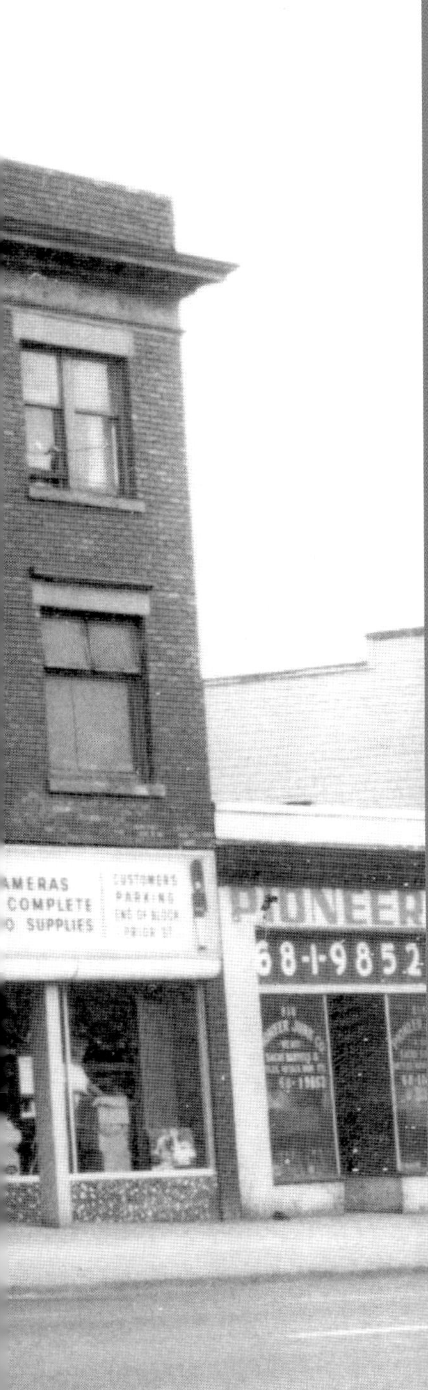

Grocers, Peddlers, and the Food Ecosystem

CHINESE GROCERY STORES, BUTCHER shops, and dry goods stores were an intricate part of the sights and sounds in the Chinatown of my childhood. I would weave in between Chinatown's crowded streets with my mother, soaking in the smells of sticky barbeque pork mixed with the comforting sweet aroma of freshly baked pineapple buns. These stores, each with their mix of fresh vegetables, dried medicinal herbs, and endless selection of instant noodles, were like a mini-amusement park. Instead of rollercoasters and cotton candy, the stores provided a labyrinth of goods, from live seafood and speckled quail eggs to cartons of Vitasoy soy beverage and creamy White Rabbit candy.

Chinatown's food ecosystem, which provides affordable food options and a cultural connection to the community, is in a precarious situation. In 2017, the Hua foundation, a non-profit youth initiative working with the community in Chinatown, published a food security report detailing the changes in the area. The report outlines that between 2009 and 2016, Chinatown lost 50 percent of its fresh food stores (e.g., greengrocers, fishmongers, barbeque meat shops, and butchers), 32 percent of its Chinese dry goods stores (e.g., herbalists), and 56 percent of its food service retailers (e.g., restaurants and takeout joints).[1] Although this period also saw the opening of new stores, including restaurants, a majority cater to mid- or high-income earners and have minimal to no links to Chinese culture, nor do they serve the fragile community of Chinese seniors.

Food insecurity in Chinatown isn't new. Chinese vegetable peddlers were once an integral part of early Vancouver, delivering fresh fruits and veggies directly to households in their horse-drawn carts and trucks. Shopkeepers in and around Vancouver, however, complained that the Chinese peddlers were a threat to their business. The city passed a bylaw in 1894 that restricted the sale of fresh food to places of business such as shops and fined Chinese peddlers who continued the delivery service. In 1914, the city imposed a one-hundred-dollar fee and a limit on working hours for peddlers, which spurred the peddlers to join forces with the Vegetable Sellers' Association.[2] The union resulted in a reduction of the fee to fifty dollars, which was still higher than the ten-dollar licencing fee that shopkeepers paid. In 1919, when thirty peddlers were arrested for not paying the fine, others went on strike, but the city refused to budge.[3]

Stores provided a labyrinth of goods, from live seafood and speckled quail eggs to cartons of Vitasoy soy beverage and creamy White Rabbit candy.

Chinese greengrocers were also subject to discriminatory legislation. By 1923, 52 Chinese greengrocers were in operation; that increased to 125 by 1935. These stores were increasingly seen as a threat, as their prices were lower, their hours were more convenient, and their merchandise was fresher, as it was supplied by farms and peddlers.[4] In 1928, calls were made to segregate Chinese stores from non-Chinese areas and to enforce strict sanitation controls as well as restrict opening hours. W. H. Malkin, a leading wholesaler who became mayor of Vancouver in 1919, started a campaign that "Oriental shops should be confined to fixed Oriental areas."[5] The Trade Licence Board Act also permitted boards to refuse licences deemed to be against public interest. In 1929, several Chinese businesses closed on Sundays to avoid anti-Chinese agitation.[6]

Chinese farmers were also affected by increasing government controls. In 1927, the province restricted produce sales from Chinese farms and gave the BC Coast Vegetable Marketing Board the power to set the conditions for the sale of farmed produce. Tensions between Chinese farmers and the marketing board intensified in 1934 when police barricaded bridges to stop farmers from delivering produce to wholesalers. In retaliation, fourteen Chinese potato trucks crashed the barricades at Marpole Bridge in August 1935. The fiasco continued into 1936, as the marketing board began seizing shipments of potatoes stored in Vancouver warehouses. The so-called potato wars between Chinese farmers and the BC Coast Vegetable Marketing Board carried on to 1937 when farmers mounted twenty-four pickets on all four bridges leading into Vancouver to stop the Chinese "bootleggers."[7]

The recent exodus of grocers, restaurants, and cookware stores from Chinatown echoes historical examples of discrimination experienced by peddlers, greengrocers, and farmers. Along with systemic forms of discrimination, the recent closure of many businesses in Chinatown is related to the neighbourhood's location next to the Downtown Eastside (DTES), the epicentre of the region's homelessness and drug crises. Nevertheless, Chinatown's affordable rent and strategic location on the doorstep of downtown make it attractive to real estate developers and new ventures, such as upscale restaurants and bars, gyms, and art galleries. Although new food establishments have moved into the neighbourhood, many have little to no connection with Chinatown's history and community. More importantly, Chinatown is home to a population of low-income Chinese seniors because of its affordability, cultural and linguistic connection, and walkability to services. Although Gain Wah and Kent's Kitchen, as well as greengrocers, provide affordable options, it also helps to retain a population of heritage keepers. With the exodus of businesses from the neighbourhood, some of whom have been in business for decades, we risk losing a valuable piece of our identities.

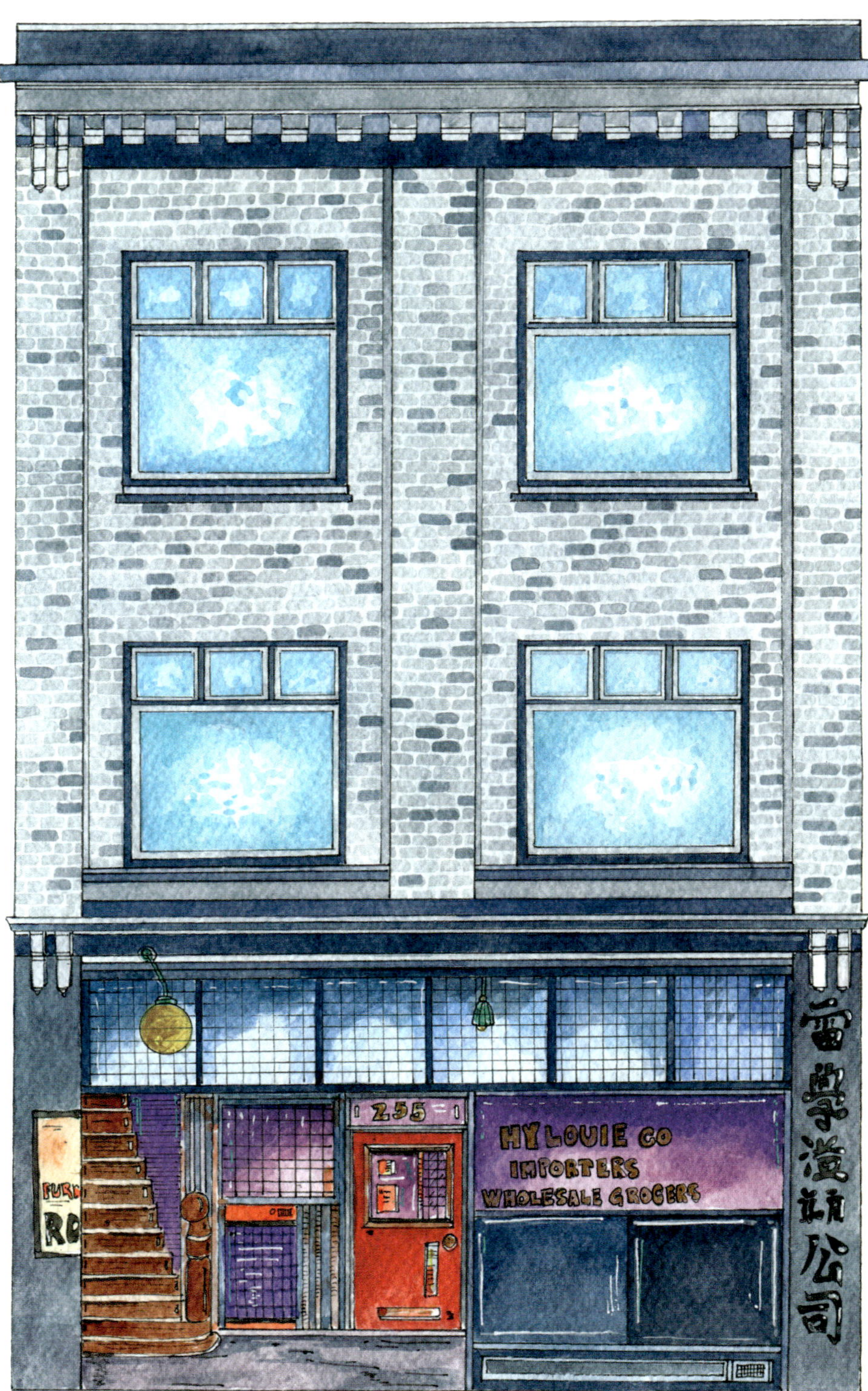

FURN
RO
255
HY LOUIE CO
IMPORTERS
WHOLESALE GROCERS
雷學澄號公司

H. Y. Louie, London Drugs, and IGA

252–260 East Georgia and 255 East Georgia

Tucked away in the southeast corner of Chinatown are the beginnings of what would become the second-largest food wholesale chain in Western Canada. Along East Georgia near Gore are two buildings (252–260 East Georgia and 255 East Georgia) where the multigenerational H. Y. Louie Company started and succeeded under the discipline of Hok Yat Louie and the tenacity of his second son, Tong Louie.

In 1896, Hok Yat Louie (1875–1934) left his wife and children in Guangdong and migrated to Canada, where he set up a farm on land he leased with others. Among Hok Yat's duties was delivering produce, which he did by getting up at 3:00 a.m. to make the four- to five-hour trip to the market.

In 1903, Hok Yat opened the Kwong Chong Company, where he sold seed, fertilizer, and wholesale groceries before moving into 255 East Georgia. The three-storey brick building would become the initial site of his shop and was where he started his Canadian family after returning to China to marry a second wife, Young Shee. They had eleven children, including Tong Louie, while his first wife and children maintained the family home in the village in China.

Hok Yat's wholesale business was not without its hurdles. During the Great Depression, W. H. Malkin, a rival wholesaler who would later become mayor, prevented three large food distribution companies from buying from major Chinese suppliers such as H. Y. Louie. This embargo, in addition to the passing of minimum wage legislation, severely impacted Hok Yat's business. As many businesses in Chinatown relied on paying workers at a lower rate, the minimum wage legislation meant businesses like Hok Yat's had to lay off employees. Layoffs during this time meant that people could not afford to purchase goods, which further impacted food sales. In 1931, it was estimated that 80 percent of Chinatown's residents were unemployed.[8]

Throughout the 1930s and 1940s, Hok Yat's eldest son, Tim, and second son, Tong, worked diligently to maintain the business. Tong recalls the discrimination he faced in the industry. When he tried to deliver goods through the front door of a café, the owner said that "if I was going to do business with him, I should come through the alley entrance, and that was that. My pride was hurt, but business was business. From then on, I used the alley entrance."[9]

Before the 1940s, it was difficult for the Chinese to move into better residential neighbourhoods. When Tong and his wife bought a house in the upscale West Point Grey neighbourhood, residents complained that their property values had dropped 20 percent and petitioned to prevent Chinese from owning or occupying homes in their area. City council recommended bylaw changes to restrict the Chinese from owning and occupying homes in stipulated localities.[10]

Tong took over the company from his brother after the Second World War. Under Tong's leadership, the company became a regional giant in the food distribution industry. The H. Y. Louie Company bought forty-seven IGA grocery stores in 1965, nine large supermarkets from Dominion Stores in 1968, and the London Drugs chain in 1976. The company now owns some of the most recognized businesses in British Columbia.

The two-storey brick building at 252–260 East Georgia was occupied by the H. Y. Louie family from the 1930s to 1950s. H. Y. Louie hired W. H. Chow to design the addition at 255 East Georgia as his home and warehouse.[11] The building continues its grocery roots and is home to Tin Lee Market and Garlock Seafood.

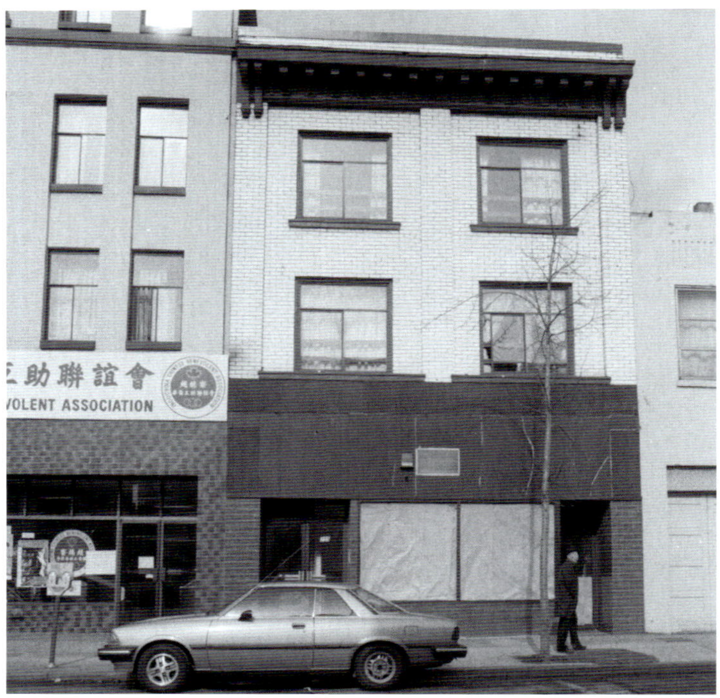

The original home and warehouse of H. Y. Louie at 255 East Georgia, 1985

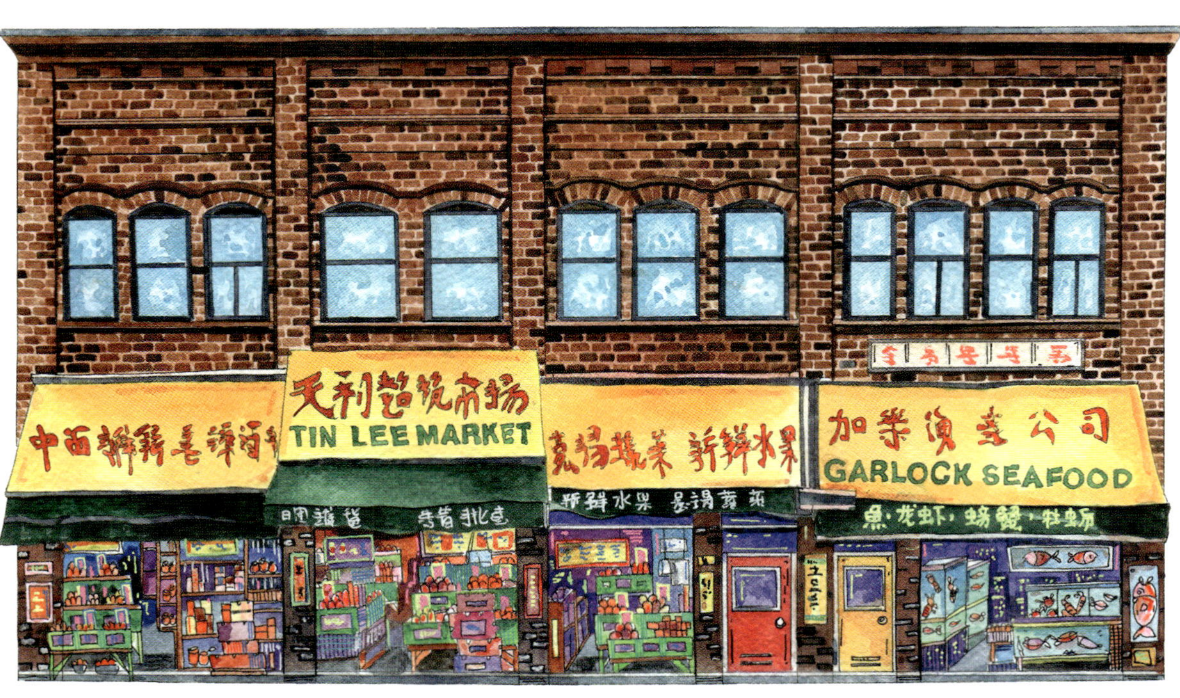
中西辦館喜慶用車
天利超級市場
TIN LEE MARKET
烹調蔬菜 新鮮水果
加樂海產公司
GARLOCK SEAFOOD
魚·龍蝦·蟹蟹·牡蠣

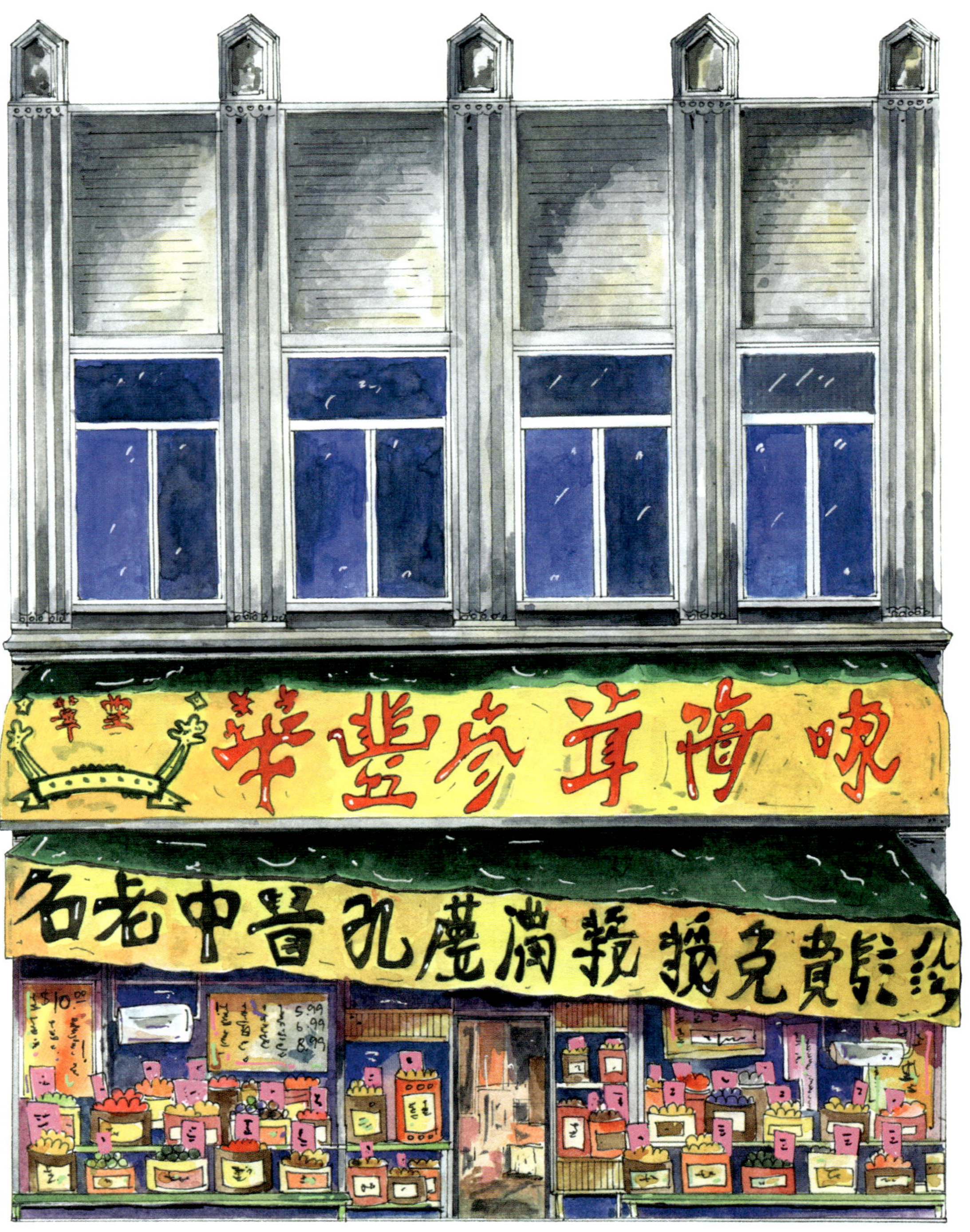

華豐參茸海味
名老中醫
5.99
6.99
8.99
$10.

Kwong Man Sang
236 East Pender
Built 1932

The gothic-looking two-storey building at 236 East Pender was home to long-term grocer Kwong Man Sang, where fresh fruit and packaged goods once extended well into the sidewalk out front. In a colour photograph from the 1970s, bok choy, gai lan, yellow onions, and prickly Chinese melons are propped up on wooden crates outside the store's entrance. Just above it, a red-and-white sign advertises the store's name and its role as an importer, retailer, and wholesaler. Built in 1932, the building is now occupied by non-profit artist organizations.[12]

The 200 block of East Pender, which was once considered a general commercial zone rather than part of Chinatown, was lined with greengrocers, fishmongers, butchers, and even a florist. Each shop provided residents and restaurants in Chinatown with a ready supply of affordable goods and added to the distinctive Pender landscape with eclectic neon signs and overhanging awnings that extended well into the street. Their convenient location within steps of bustling restaurants such as Kwangchow, Nanking, Jimmy Wong's Yung Kee, and Sam Lock contributed to the intricate food ecosystem in Chinatown, where it's not uncommon to see a cook in his apron zigzagging between stores to pick up items for the dinner rush.

A Guide to Asian Grocery Stores and Staples

Whether it's to pick up childhood favourites like shrimp crackers and soy beverage or to have access to an endless selection of soy sauce and chili oil, I love shopping at Asian grocery stores. Most of all, I love marvelling at the variety of mouth-watering red bean or matcha-flavoured desserts, from sponge cakes to mochi filled with ice cream, and picking up my current obsession: tteokbokki (Korean rice cakes).

But shopping at Asian grocers can be daunting. Smaller stores require patience, ingenuity, and creativity to navigate, as their narrow aisles tend to be crowded and items are often scattered among unmarked shelves. Larger Asian chain grocery stores like T&T and H-Mart offer a modern one-stop-shop experience. With brightly lit, wide aisles and multiple floors, these supermarkets generally feature neatly lined shelves stocked with an endless selection of sauces, instant noodles, rice, and sweets, as well as a beauty section where you can pick up the latest Korean facemasks. When shopping at an Asian grocer, take your time and be adventurous—try the durian ice cream!

Here are some staples to help stock your kitchen:

VEGETABLES AND FRUIT

I tend to stop first at the produce section, as it usually lines the exterior of smaller grocers or is conveniently situated at the entrance of large supermarkets. Next to the basics such as broccoli and garlic, you'll find shiitake mushrooms, red chilis, sweet potatoes, taro root, lotus root, stalks of lemongrass, bok choy, gai lan, yu choy, green onions, and mustard greens. In the fruit section, you'll find displays of oranges, mangos, dragon fruit, perfectly round and crisp Asian pears, spiky rambutan, bundles of lychee, and even durian.

RICE AND NOODLES

Rice is a staple in any Asian household, from jasmine and basmati to sweet glutinous rice used for sticky rice wraps. All flavours and side dishes, from meat to fermented vegetables to soy sauce, are meant to enhance the rice. So don't drench your rice in soy sauce; instead enjoy its delicate taste. Rice is ground down to make other foods, from desserts to noodles. Noodles come in a variety of shapes and sizes, from thin vermicelli to thick udon. You'll find fresh noodles in the refrigerated section and dried noodles in the aisles. You can also find different varieties of noodles, such as yellow egg noodles, which can be used in soups and stir-fries. And don't forget instant noodles if you're up for a quick processed-food binge.

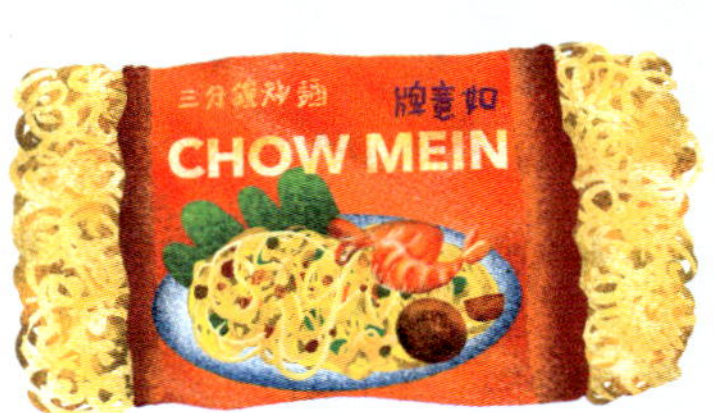

MEAT AND SEAFOOD

A visit to an Asian grocery store or to Chinatown isn't complete without a stroll by the live seafood aisle or fishmongers like Hung Win Seafood and Garlock Seafood, where you'll find live crab, lobster, fish, and more. Be careful of those claws! You can also find the non-moving variety in packages or on ice. Both seafood and meat are generally sold by weight. At a store's meat section or specialty butchers like Dollar Meats in Chinatown, you'll find pre-packaged regular cuts of pork, beef, and chicken, or you can ask the butcher for a specific cut. You'll also find a variety of pieces that suit the nose-to-tail cooking style in many Chinese households, such as ox tongue and pig snout.

CONDIMENTS

The real party is in the sauce aisle, where you'll find a range of tastes like sweet, salty, sour, bitter, and umami to tantalize your tastebuds. The essentials include light and dark soy sauce, oyster sauce, sriracha hot sauce, fish sauce, hoisin sauce, chili sauce, spicy bean paste, rice vinegar, and sesame oil. When I was a kid, I would create my own fusion dish by lacing white rice with fermented shrimp paste and ketchup. Be adventurous!

STARCHES AND FLOUR

Starches such as wheat starch, tapioca starch, and sweet potato starch are a key ingredient in noodles, dumpling wrappers, and sauces. There are also different types of flour beyond wheat flour, such as rice flour, glutinous rice flour, mung bean flour, mugwort powder, and soybean flour. These are used to make noodles, baked goods, and steamed desserts.

DRIED FOODS AND CURED MEATS

The art of preserving and drying food is an intricate part of Chinese culture. If you visit my mother's house, you'll often find a string of homegrown green beans hanging from the ceiling of her sunroom, where they're dried and replanted the next year. In Asian grocery stores, you'll find dried beans, seeds, nuts, vegetables, meats, and medicinal herbs. In more modern grocery stores, these dried goods will be stored in vacuum-sealed bags with professional-looking labels, but if you visit an herbalist or greengrocer in Chinatown, you can customize the amount of the dried goods you need. Adzuki beans, white and black sesame seeds, and white lotus seeds can be used in baked goods and desserts. Cured and salted meats and seafood can be used as toppings on noodles, rice, baked goods, or a steaming bowl of congee. Packaged pork floss, dried shrimp and scallops, and lap cheong (dried sausage) are found in the aisles, but you can also find fresher varieties of cured and salted meats in the cold cases. Use these meats in soups, on top of rice or noodles, as a side dish, in stir fries or congee, or as a snack. Keep opened and unused portions in the refrigerator.

SWEETS, BEVERAGES, AND SNACKS

A visit to the Asian grocery store isn't complete without a stroll through the sweets and dessert aisle, or the chip aisle for shrimp crackers and sweet bean chips. You'll find mini Kit Kat bars in flavours such as strawberry, matcha, and even apple, along with the famous White Rabbit candy with its edible inner rice wrapper. Not far from the packaged sweets, you'll find the beverage section with cartons of soy beverage and chrysanthemum tea, as well as packaged tea such as green, matcha, and hojicha. Don't forget the frozen desserts! Behind the freezer doors are delicacies like red bean, mango, black sesame, and matcha mochi ice cream, as well as red bean popsicles, Swiss rolls, frozen custard buns, and ice cream. Larger grocery stores will have fresh baked goods, so pick up a loaf of bread, Swiss roll, fruit tart, slice or two of sponge cake, or pineapple bun. During seasonal holidays, such as the Mid-Autumn Festival, you can find beautiful tins of mooncakes.

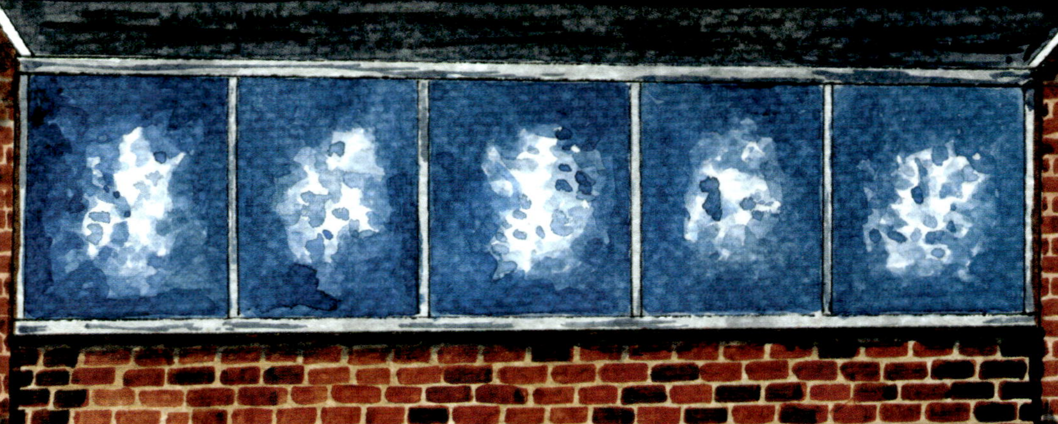

營企際國譽區
INFINITY International Enterprises
www.infinityproducts.ca
器電屍榮城豐
FORUM Home Appliances
www.ForumAppliances.com

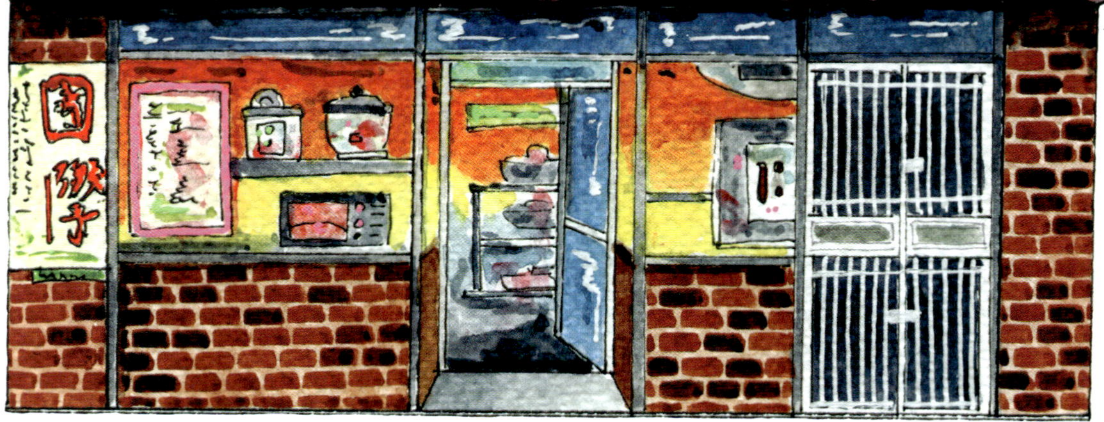

INTERNATIONAL
Plumbing & Electrical Supplies Inc.
國際潔具水電器林中心
FORUM
HOME APPLIANCES INC.
豐林家庭電器中心
PLUMBING ELECTRICAL HEATING AIR CON HARDWARE HOUSEWARES
國際

Forum Home Appliances
245 East Pender
Built 1948

Kitchen tools and small appliances line the tidy metal shelves of Forum Home Appliances, where you can pick up a state-of-the-art rice cooker along with an espresso machine. Forum Home Appliances started in 1988 as a plumbing store. After the fiftieth customer requested a rice cooker, owner Tony Lam decided it was time to switch gears and stock appliances in addition to plumbing supplies. In 1995, the family opened a second store in the new Chinatown Plaza on Keefer Street. By the early 2000s, with more Chinese moving to the suburbs, Forum Home Appliances opened additional stores in Richmond and Burnaby.[13]

The Lam family immigrated to Vancouver in 1975 from Hong Kong, where Tony had worked in the stock market and his wife, Avis, had been a teacher. Like many immigrants, they found that migrating to a new country meant a new start and a career change. When Tony arrived in Vancouver, he took whatever job he could find—first as a delivery driver for a wholesaler before he found work with Max Goldberg Plumbing. Avis worked at the food court at Pacific Centre Mall downtown before finding a job at the Four Seasons Hotel.

With Tony and Avis entering retirement, their children, Tracy To and Ross Lam, have taken over.[14] Businesses like Forum depend on mutually beneficial relationships and resource sharing with complementary businesses within Chinatown, such as restaurants and small kitchenware stores. Tony's daughter, Tracy, explains, "When we don't have something, we send people over to Tinland, and they do the same. We complement each other." Tinland Cookware, once located across the street on the ground floor of the May Wah Hotel, closed its Chinatown branch in 2022.

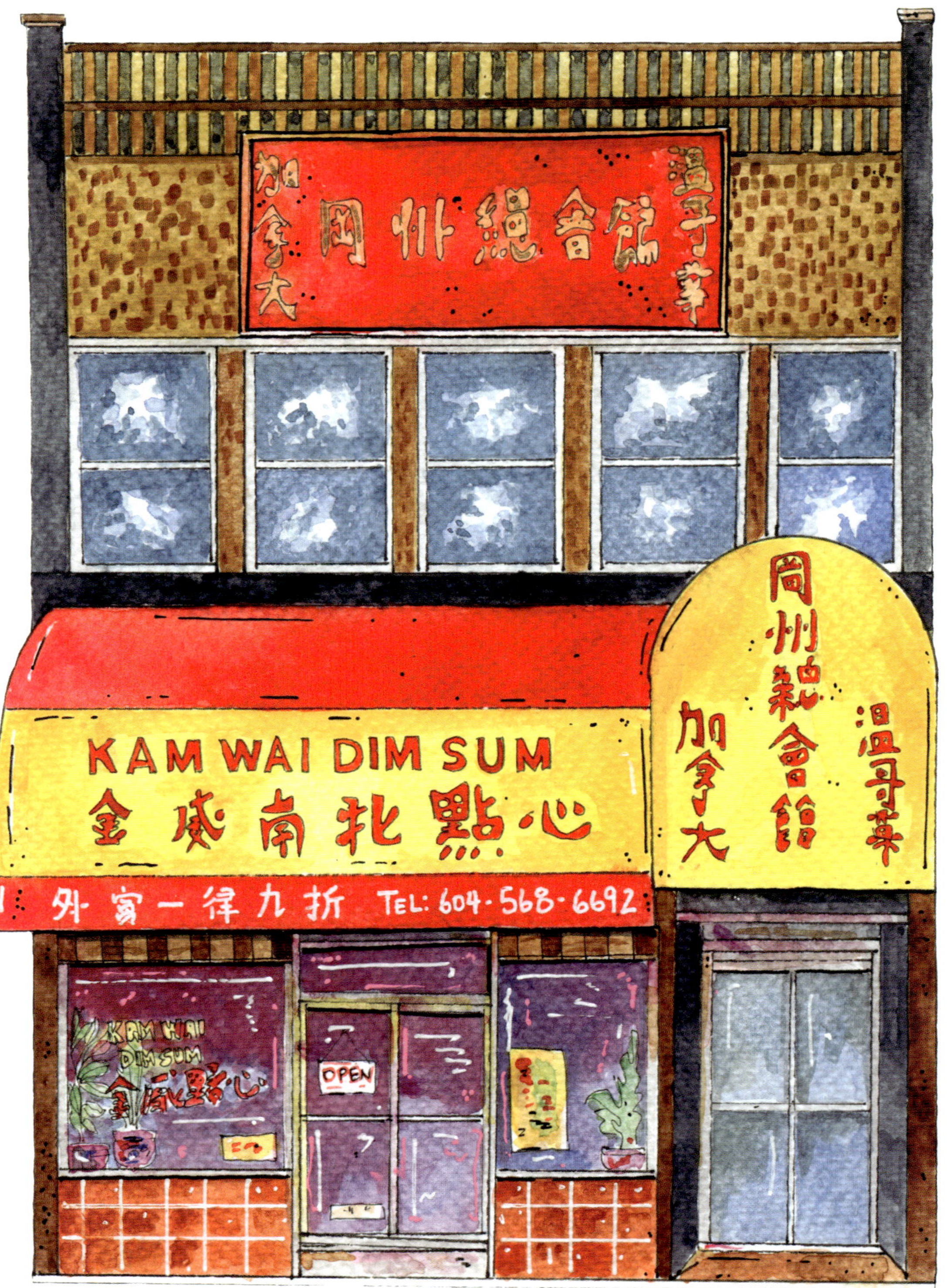
加拿大 岡州總會館 溫哥華
KAM WAI DIM SUM
金威南北點心
外賣一律九折 TEL: 604·568·6692
岡州新會館 溫哥華 加拿大
KAM WAI DIM SUM
金威點心
OPEN

Kam Wai Dim Sum
249–251 East Pender
Built 1928

It took William Liu, co-owner of Kam Wai Dim Sum, a year to learn how to properly wrap a har gow (shrimp dumpling). I'm not surprised, as I've spent a lifetime watching my mother make the dough from scratch, roll it out so it's nearly paper thin, and perform a folding-and-tucking magic act that results in a pleated pocket for the shrimp filling. The iconic dumpling with a delicate translucent skin is one of my favourite dim sum treats. Served with a bit of chili sauce, it's a juicy flavour explosion.

When you walk into Kam Wai, you're immediately greeted with the comforting smell of freshly steamed buns, followed by a line of fridges stocked with frozen packs of steam-it-yourself dim sum. Just behind the fridges is the production house, where all the items sold at Kam Wai are made by dumpling specialists like William's mom.[15]

Kam Wai is an all-hands-on-deck family business. William's father and grandfather opened Kam Wai in 1991 on the ground floor of the Nationalist League Building at 525 Gore Avenue. The family was involved in several businesses, including an antique store. When they opened Kam Wai, they hired chefs from overseas who taught them the ins and outs of making dim sum. Kam Wai was initially a wholesale business, selling to restaurants and stores, but in recent years, it has expanded to include takeaway and eat-in options.

The two-storey building that houses Kam Wai was built in 1928 and renovated in the 1970s, which is likely when the faux tiles were added to its facade like other buildings along the 200 block of East Pender to align with Chinatown's heritage designation. William explains that during a recent renovation they found the roof tiles hidden under the giant yellow-and-red awning. Prior to Kam Wai, the building housed Wah Shuen, Chong F. Fruit and Produce, and Kwangchow Restaurant. The building is owned by Kong Chow Benevolent Association of Canada, which uses the upper floor for organizational purposes.[16] Kam Wai moved into 249 East Pender just before the 2010 Winter Olympics.

As an important pillar in Chinatown's food ecosystem, Kam Wai Dim Sum also provides affordable meals for seniors. For six dollars, seniors at the May Wah Hotel across the way can enjoy a bowl of congee and a steamed bun.[17]

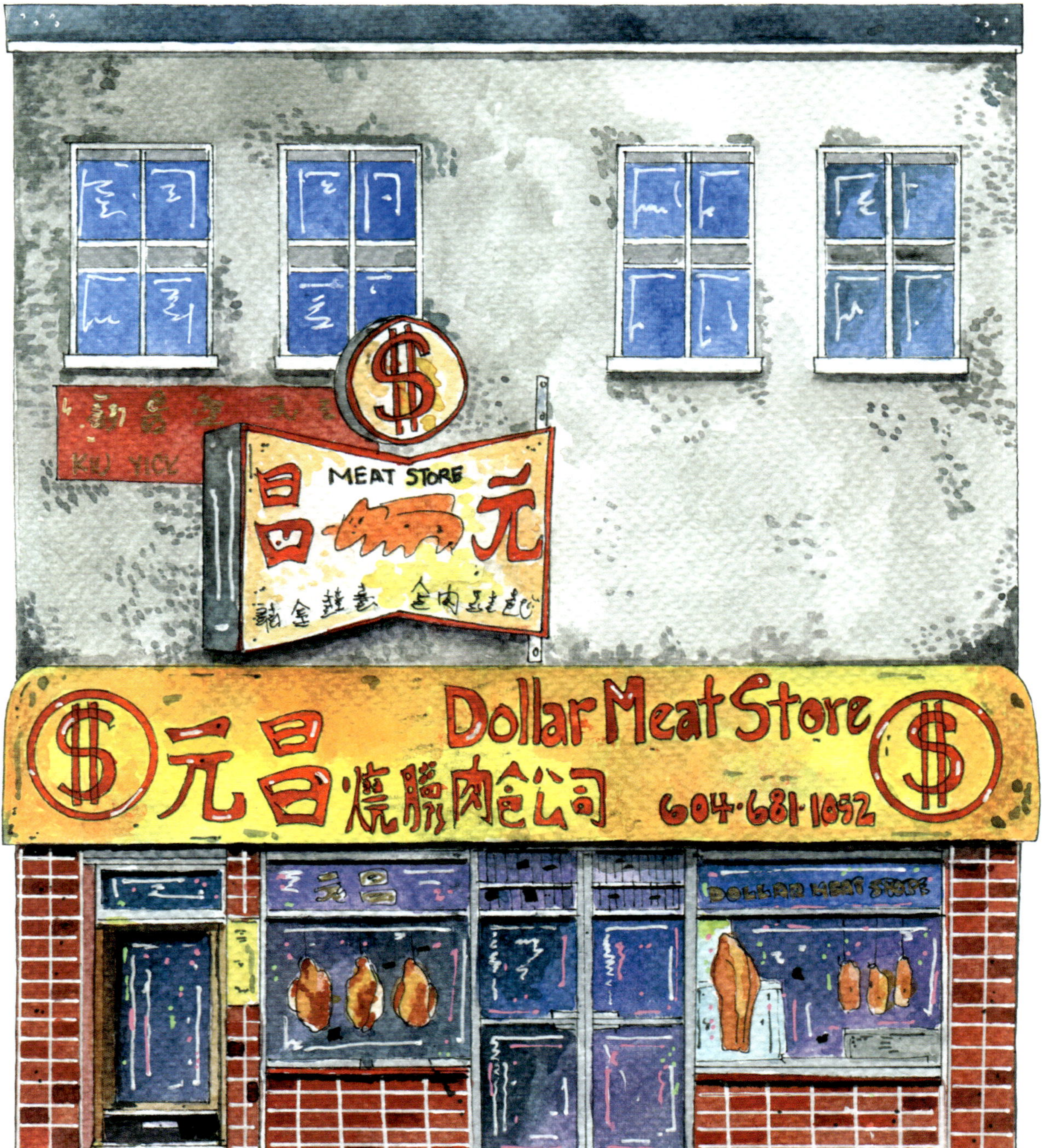

$
MEAT STORE
昌 元
KIU YICK
Dollar Meat Store
$
元昌 燒臘肉食公司
604·681·1052

Dollar Meat Store
266–272 East Pender
Built 1954

Dollar Meat Store is a one-stop-shop for carnivores, providing raw cuts and cooked meats. Its décor consists of large cabinets lined with pre-packaged cuts of meat, while its greasy front window displays roast pork, barbeque cutlets, and golden ducks dripping with fat. Dollar Meats offers affordable and accessible meal options, providing patrons with ready-to-eat packed containers of soy chicken, roast pork, or a half or whole roast duck served with plum sauce.

Along the ceiling hangs an assortment of lap cheong, a favourite in my household. My mother would steam the dried pork sausages (featuring a perfect ratio of fat to meat and seasonings) in the rice cooker, either adding them directly to the rice or placing a small bowl with the sausages on top. The salty, savoury flavour of the lap cheong and its pockets of fat brought the rice to life, transforming it into a treat with a simple meal of steamed vegetables.

Similar to a number of stores along the 200 block of East Pender, the simple yet versatile two-storey boxy building was built after the Second World War and likely replaced turn-of-the-century houses that had once lined East Pender. From the 1960s to 1980s, BC Lower Mainland Farmers' Cooperative Association occupied the top floor of 266–272 East Pender. From 1990 until their recent closure, Kiu Yick Trading Company, a bookstore and travel agency, used the space.

Other businesses that have occupied this location include Quong Kee Produce (1916), Kwong Wing Laundry (1920), and Yuen Lee Company (1928). By 1940, two butchers, Shing Chong Company Poultry and Fook Lee Meats, had moved in. They were accompanied by a third butcher, Shang Lee Company Meats, a few doors down, making the upper stretch of East Pender near the Nationalist League Building a meat lover's paradise.[18]

Throughout the 1970s, barbeque meat shops in Chinatown were on the brink of closure. Claiming that the shops failed to comply with a bylaw that required perishable meat be kept above sixty degrees Celsius or below four degrees Celsius, health inspectors temporarily shut down five barbeque meat shops in 1975. To justify the closure, health inspectors used a 1965 incident in Tacoma, Washington, where two people died of food poisoning from barbeque meat that was thought to have been improperly prepared and stored. The cases in Tacoma, however, were caused by chicken purchased from a super-market, not a Chinese meat store.[19]

Merchants in Chinatown demonstrated against the discriminatory bylaw by protesting in the streets and waving banners that said "Save Chinatown, Support Chinatown BBQ Products." The dispute grew into a national campaign to support Chinese barbeque shops across Canada. In 1978, Vancouver East MP Art Lee took a roast pig for a taste and safety test at Parliament Hill in Ottawa, where he won over Jean Chrétien, who was a cabinet minister at the time.[20] Eventually, in the 1980s, the government accepted barbeque meat in Chinatown.

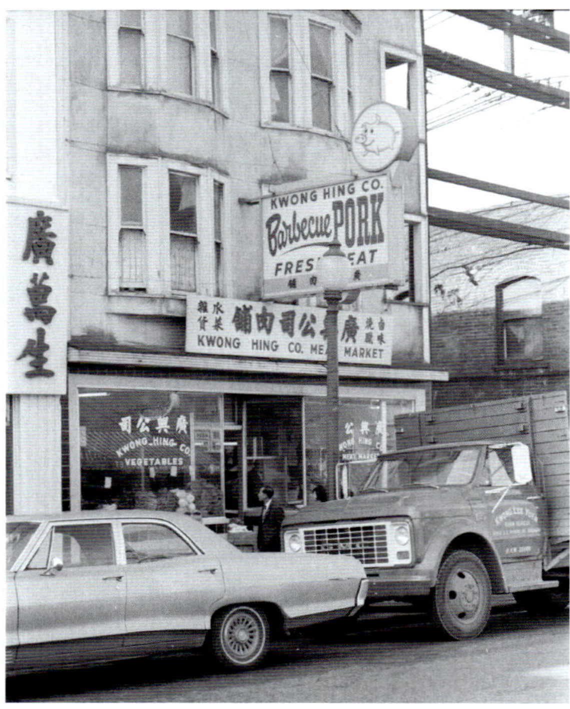

Kwong Hing Barbecue Pork at 224 East Pender in 1969

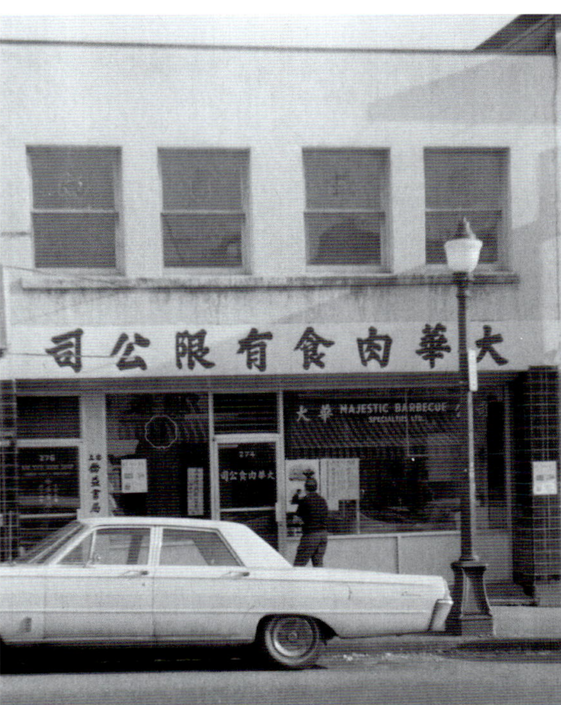

Majestic Barbecue at 274 East Pender Street in 1969

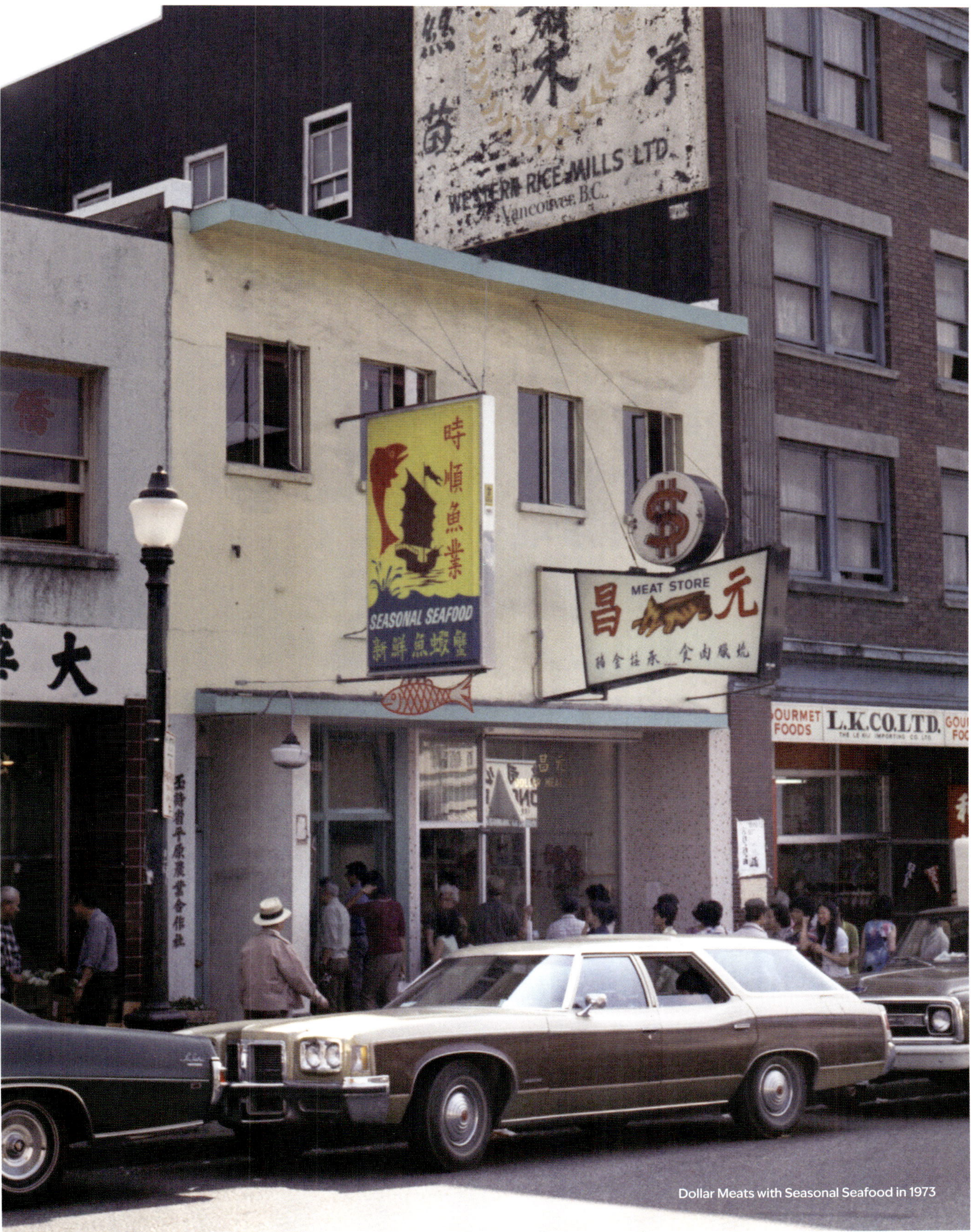

Dollar Meats with Seasonal Seafood in 1973

A Guide to Chinese Barbeque Meats

Unlike American barbeque, Cantonese barbeque doesn't rely on smoke and is generally prepared indoors. Traditional Cantonese barbeque involves roasting whole ducks, pigs, and chickens in giant vertical gas ovens. Whole roast pigs are often hung in walk-in fridges to dry overnight, allowing as much moisture as possible to drain and evaporate to give the pork its signature delicately crunchy, reddish-brown skin with moist fat underneath. A variety of flavourings are used, such as star anise, Szechuan peppercorn, green onion, ginger, and various fermented sauces.[21]

The cuisine originates from Guangdong, a coastal region that was a commercial hub on the Silk Road and a main trading port with the West, giving it access to a variety of seafood and imported ingredients. Although the tradition of roast and marinated meats dates to as early as the fifth century, it gained popularity during the 1800s.

Barbeque meat is a Cantonese staple, a comfort food often served in a white Styrofoam "rice box" or plated with condiments like minced ginger and plum sauce. Known more commonly as siu mei, Cantonese barbeque is often served on top of steamed jasmine rice, in a bowl of rice noodles, added to crusty-bottomed claypot rice, or in congee (rice porridge). During the 1950s and 1960s, siu mei rice was an affordable staple among the general population in Hong Kong.[22]

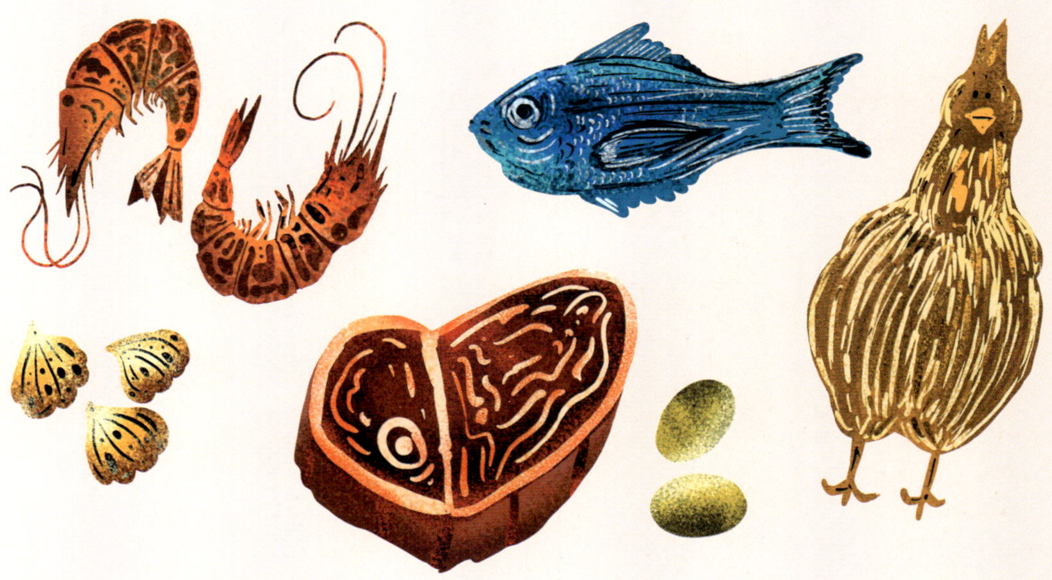

Popular Barbeque Meats

SIU YUK (ROASTED PORK/PORK BELLY)

Siu yuk, or roasted meat, usually pork, is made from a whole pig hung and roasted vertically at high heat. The skin is pierced with hundreds of holes to allow the fat to render as it cooks, resulting in a crunchy skin that leaves the meat tender.

CHAR SIU (BARBEQUE PORK)

Char siu is prepared by marinating long bone-less strips of pork loin in sweet soy, hoisin sauce, fermented soybeans, and rose wine. The meat is skewered on long forks, roasted over fire, and glazed in maltose. This classic can be eaten in steamed buns, in noodle dishes, or with rice.

ROAST DUCK

Duck is marinated in Chinese five-spice powder and cooking wine and hung to air-dry before it's roasted for hours. Served with five-spice sauce and oil and pan drippings.

SLICED WHITE CHICKEN

Chicken is marinated in salt, then poached in broth with ginger and immediately plunged in an ice water bath, giving the skin a filmy texture. Served with a slurry of ginger, green onion, salt, and oil.

SOY SAUCE CHICKEN

Chicken that is poached in seasoned sweet soy sauce with scallions, ginger, and spices. Supple and gelatinous, with the salty, savoury flavour of soy sauce.

CURED PORK BELLY

Usually eaten over rice, cured pork belly is similar to Western bacon but soft and spongy rather than hard and crispy.

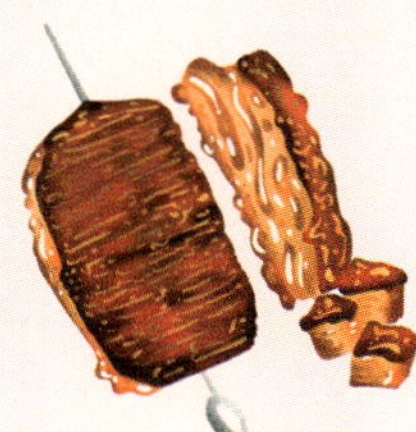

ROAST QUAIL

Quail is prepared with a light marinade of soy and five-spice. Quail bones can be quite brittle, so enjoy with caution.

ROAST GOOSE

Goose is steeped in a saucy marinade and rubbed with vinegar and maltose before being roasted in a charcoal furnace at high temperature and served with sweet plum sauce.

ORANGE CUTTLEFISH

Cuttlefish is prepared with master stock, a savoury soy sauce–based brine made with Chinese spices and dried ingredients. Orange colouring is added for aesthetic purposes.

LAP CHEONG

This salty-sweet dried sausage comes in a variety of flavours using meats such as pork, pig liver, duck liver, and even turkey liver. Have it steamed, fried, or cut up in bits on top of congee.

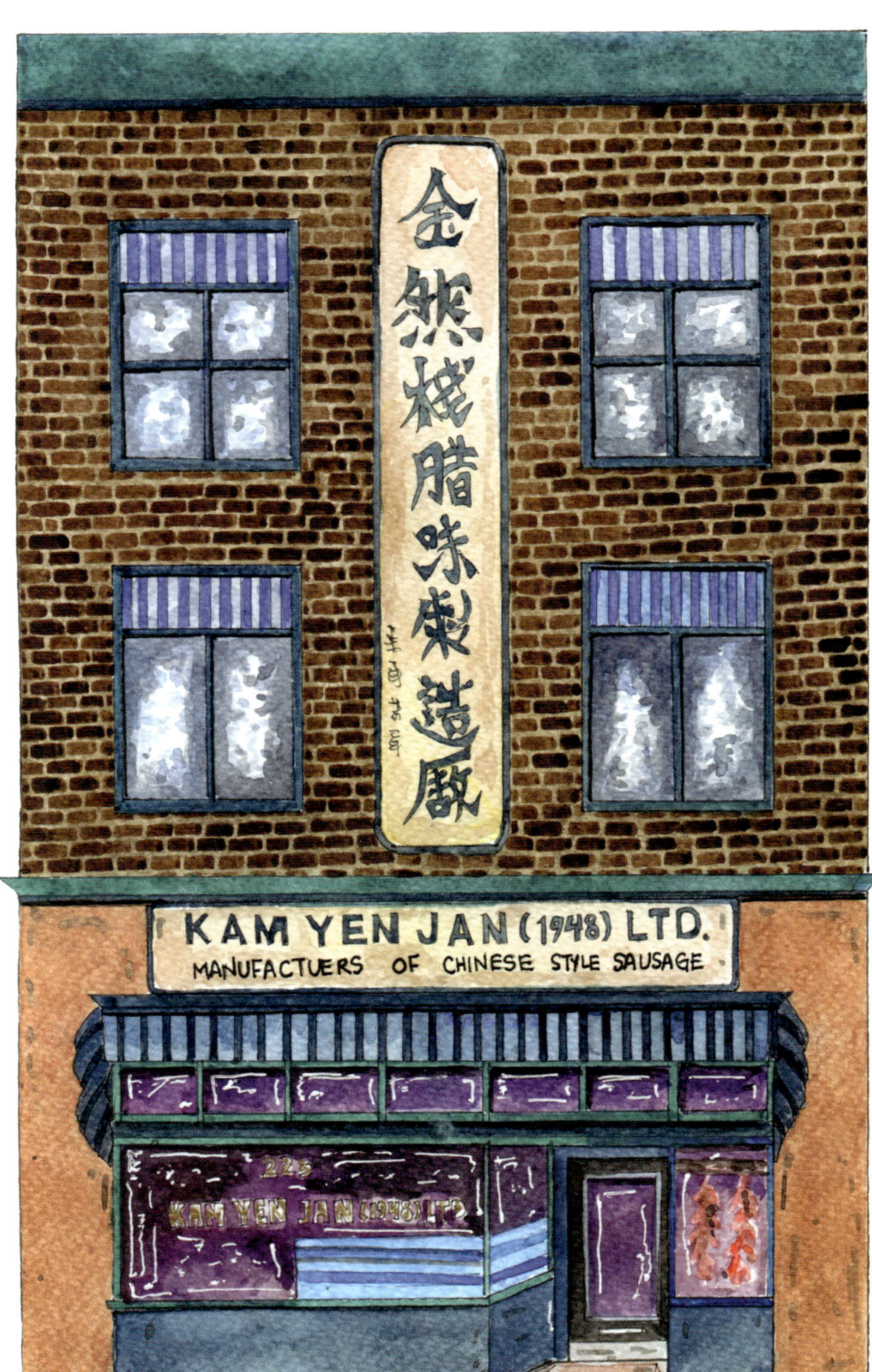

金燉棧臘味製造廠
KAM YEN JAN (1948) LTD.
MANUFACTUERS OF CHINESE STYLE SAUSAGE
225
KAM YEN JAN (1948) LTD.

Kam Yen Jan

223 Keefer Street

The Kam Yen Jan factory started making lap cheong (dried sausages) at 223 Keefer in the 1920s, before moving to Seattle in 1978. The four-storey building on Keefer, which was once a warehouse, has since undergone significant renovations that altered its facade and now houses the Evergreen Taoist Church and offices.

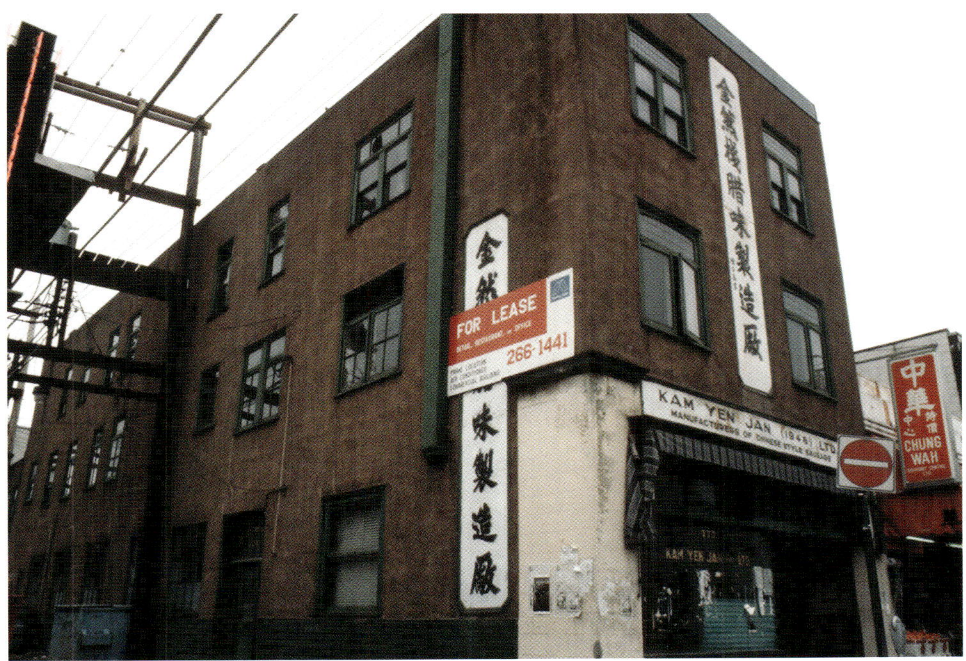

Kam Yen Jan sausage factory in 1981

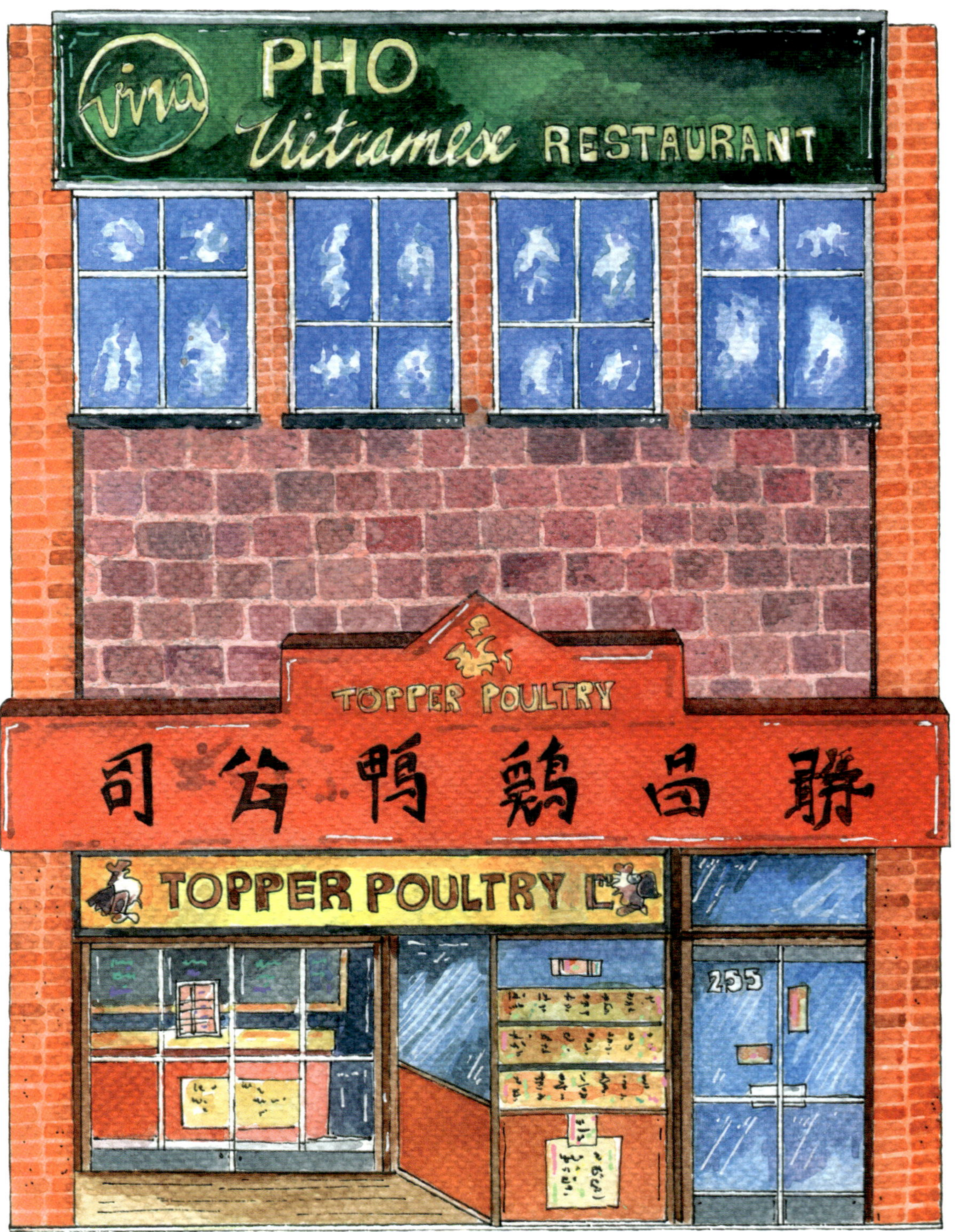
viva
PHO
Vietnamese RESTAURANT
TOPPER POULTRY
司 分 鴨 鷄 昌 聯
TOPPER POULTRY
255

Topper Poultry
253 East Pender
Built 1945

There are some smells that stay with you, like the stench of raw poultry on a warm summer day. On our weekly grocery expeditions to Chinatown, my mother and I would stop at Topper Poultry to pick up a whole chicken or a bag of drumsticks. These days, 253 East Pender is a gym, where yogis practise their namastes surrounded by the ghosts of chicken carcasses. The two-storey brick building was constructed in 1945 and renovated in 1970.[23]

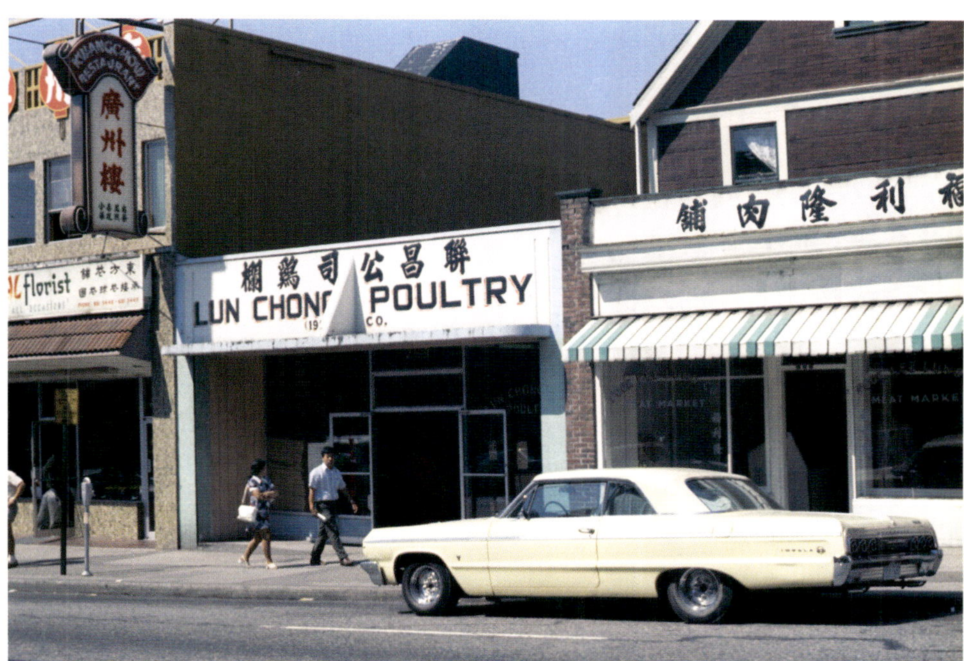

Lun Chong Poultry at 253 East Pender, on the site where Topper Poultry was later established

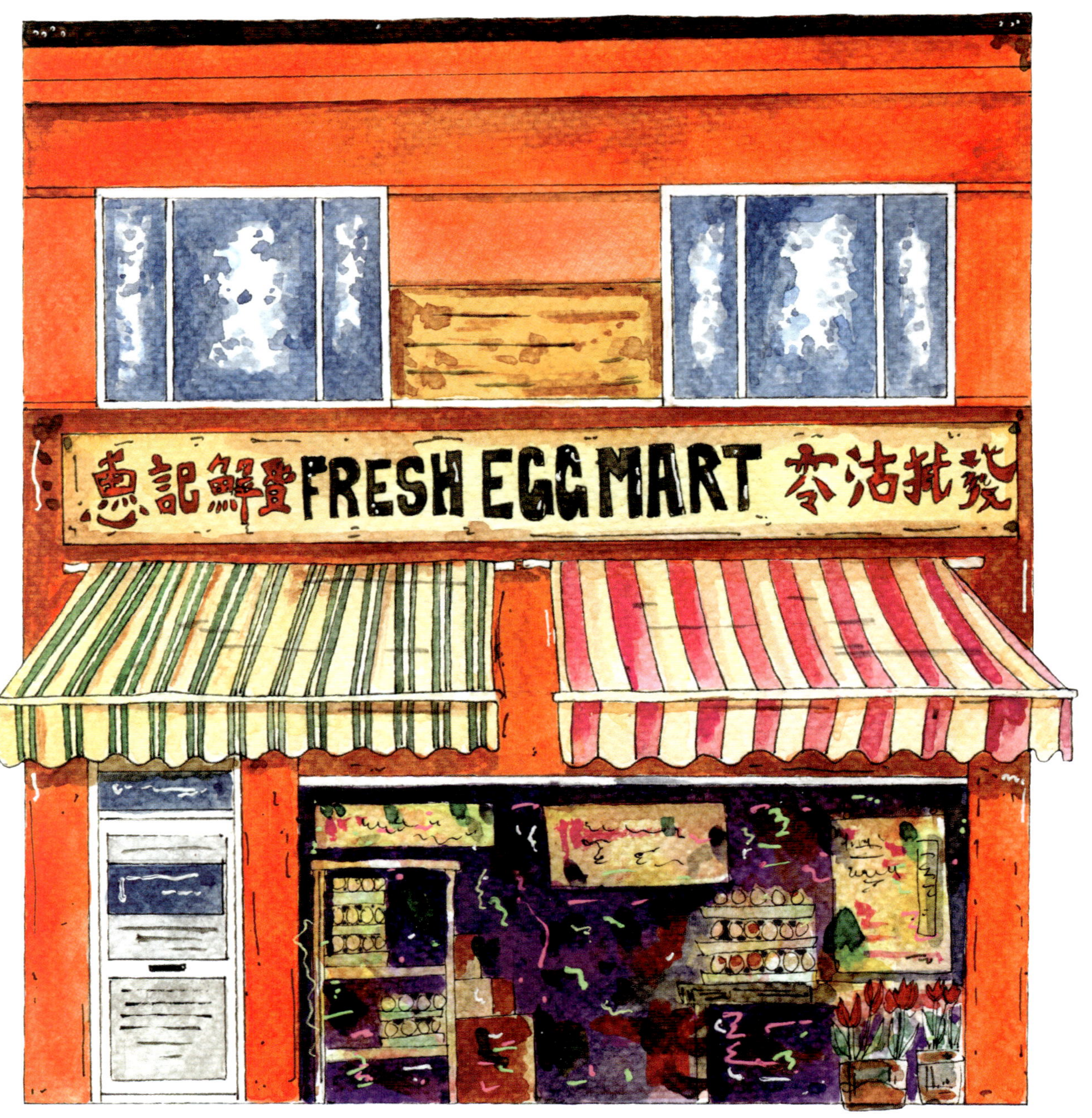

惠記鮮蛋 FRESH EGG MART 零沽批發

Fresh Egg Mart
269 East Georgia

Fresh Egg Mart was an everyday go-to for eggs, but every so often they would sell flowers that decorated the orange facade with an additional splash of colour. The charm of this East Georgia establishment was enhanced by homemade signs written in English and Chinese advertising the latest and greatest egg deals.

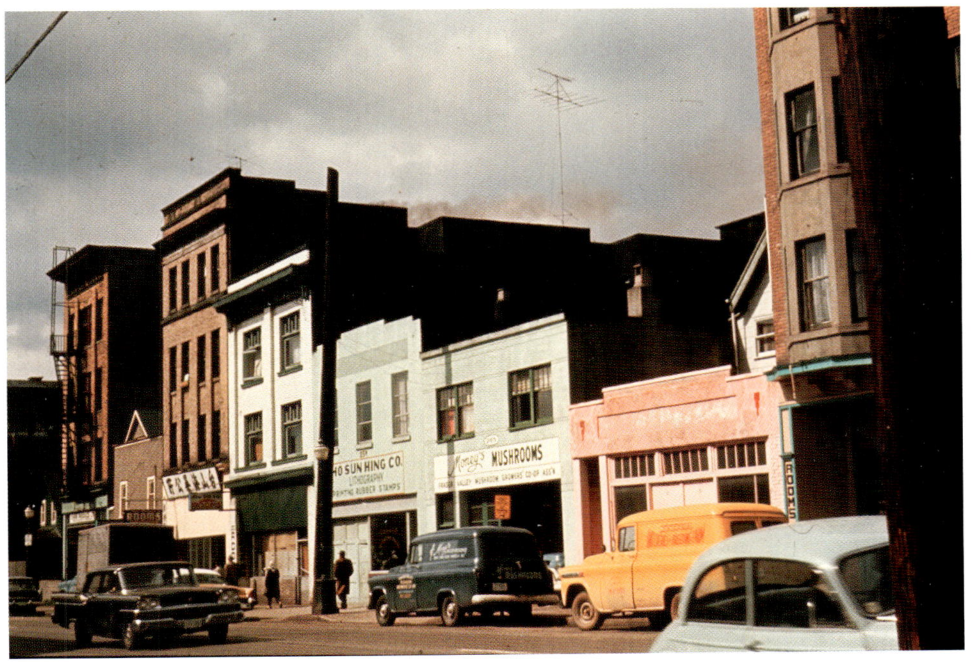

Storefronts along the 200 block of East Georgia in the 1960s

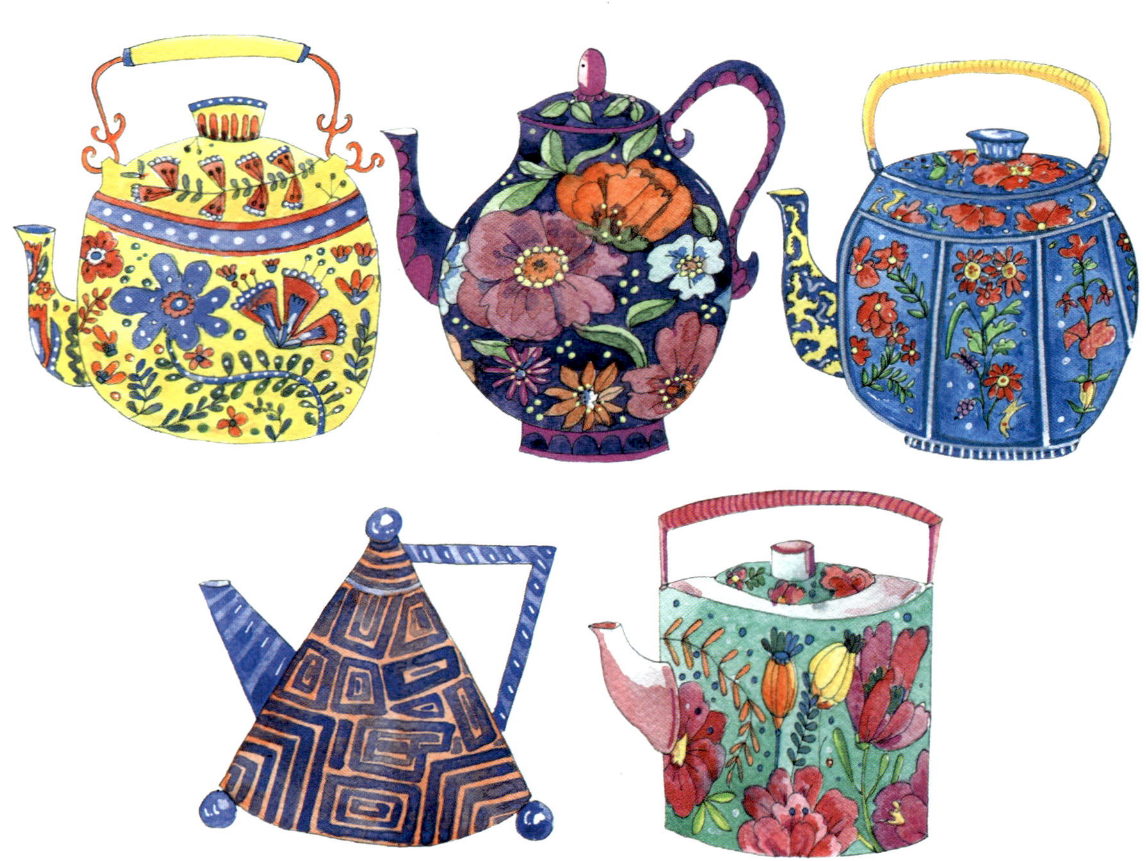

Treasure Green Tea
227 East Georgia
Established 1981

As a local pioneer in Chinese tea imports, Kwok Sun Cheng established Treasure Green Tea in 1981 as a wholesale and retail store where tea drinkers could find ethically sourced, high-quality tea. Initially known as Super Fine Tea Company, the business is now owned by Kwong Sun Cheng's daughter, tea master Olivia Cheng, and is located at 227 East Georgia.

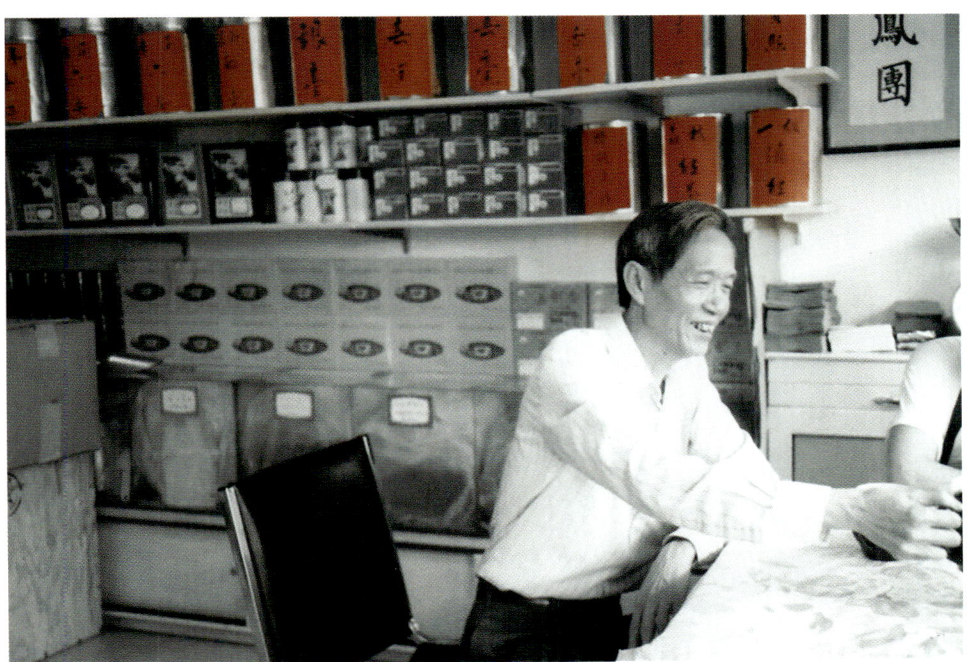

Interior of Super Fine Tea Company at 275 East Georgia before Treasure Green Tea

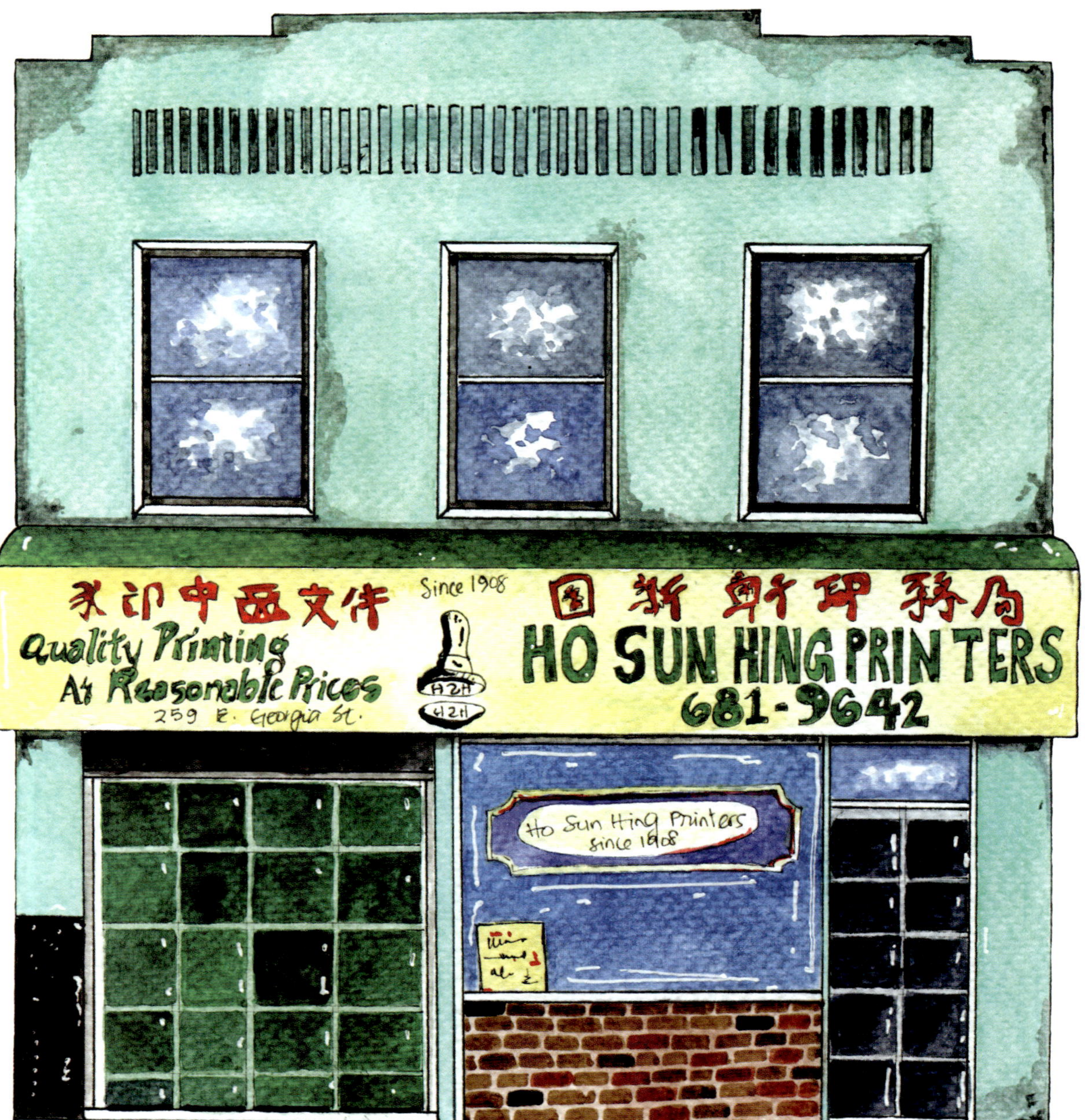
求印中西文件
Quality Printing
At Reasonable Prices
259 E. Georgia St.
Since 1908
HO SUN HING PRINTERS
681-9642
Ho Sun Hing Printers
since 1908

Ho Sun Hing Printer
259 East Georgia
Established 1908

Established in 1908, Ho Sun Hing Printer quietly weathered the digital advancements in the print world from its turquoise art deco home at 259 East Georgia. The generational business started at 205 East Pender before moving to 428 Main Street in 1920. From the mid-1920s, it ran its print business from the basement of 258½ East Pender, until the family purchased 259 East Georgia in 1963. The building, which is six thousand square feet over two floors, provided space for the printshop as well as living quarters for the growing family.

In 1908, Lam Lat Tong left his job as a railway cook to start Ho Sun Hing Rubber Stamp. The shop would become a staple in Chinatown when Lam Lat Tong's son, Fong Lam, expanded the business to provide print services for Chinese restaurants across Canada. The business was left to Fong's wife, Hilda Lam, who closed the shop in 2014, when she turned eighty-one. Highlighting the interconnectedness of generational businesses in Chinatown, Hilda notes that their eight kids "were born here and they were all raised in the printing business."[24]

Hilda grew up in a house on the edge of Chinatown, on the site demolished for the MacLean Park housing development in the 1970s. She was in the same class at Strathcona Elementary School as Angelo Tosi, owner of the legendary Tosi and Company.[25]

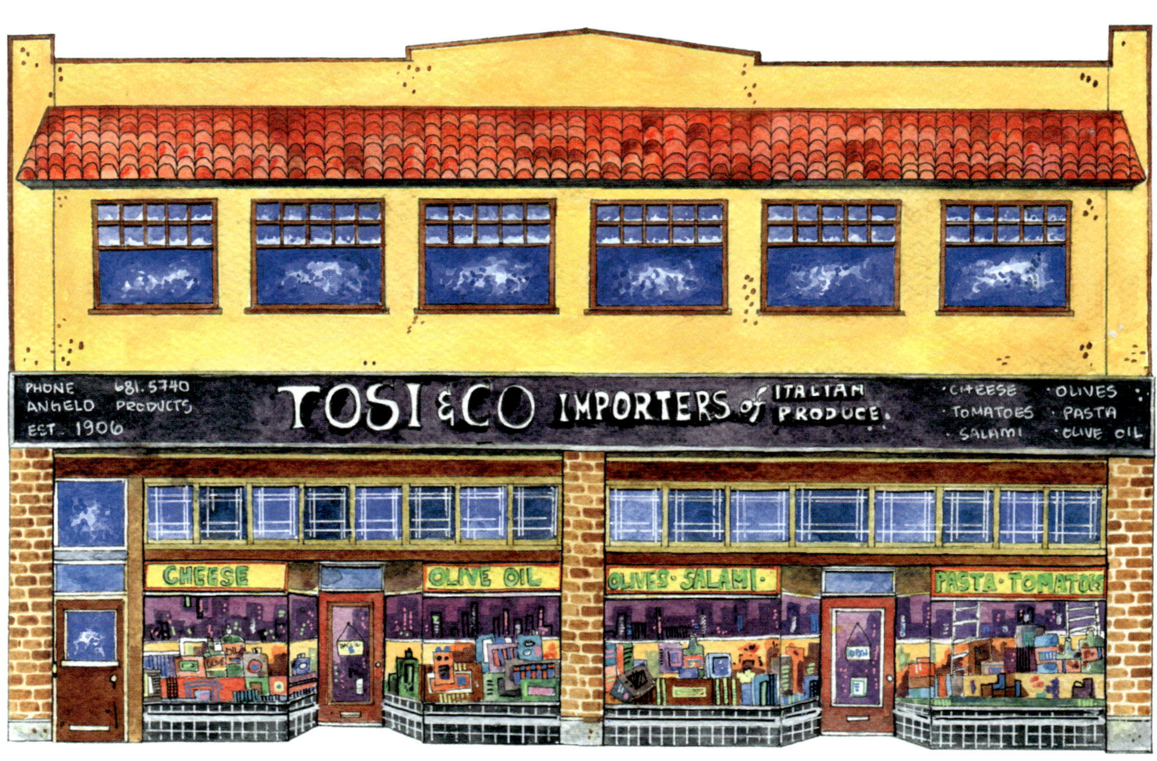
PHONE   681.5740
ANGELO PRODUCTS
EST. 1906
TOSI & CO IMPORTERS of ITALIAN PRODUCE.
CHEESE   OLIVES
TOMATOES   PASTA
SALAMI   OLIVE OIL
CHEESE
OLIVE OIL
OLIVES · SALAMI ·
PASTA · TOMATOES

Tosi and Company
624 Main Street
Established 1906

Ring the bell to be transported to a turn-of-the-century Italian grocery shopping experience. Having served the community since 1906, Tosi and Company is Vancouver's oldest Italian food specialist and importer. Its six-thousand-square-foot warehouse at 624 Main Street is full of Italian specialty products—pasta, risotto, polenta, balsamic vinegar, olive oil, olives, anchovies, and a variety of Italian cheeses and salamis.

Tosi and Company is also one of Chinatown's oldest family-run businesses. The business moved into its current location in the 1930s, but Peter Tosi first opened a butcher shop on Union Street. In 1973, Peter's son, Angelo, took over the business after his father passed away at eighty-nine.[26]

The first Italian immigrants in BC worked to extend the Canadian Pacific Railway from Port Moody to Coal Harbour. Prior to the 1930s, many Italians settled in Strathcona, between Main Street and Clark Drive along East Georgia, Union, Adanac, and Prior Streets, which were close to the places where many worked. In addition to Tosi's, some pioneering Italian businesses that emerged in this area were Crosetti's, Benny's Italian Market, Minichiello's Grocery (later Union Market), and Giuratti's.[27] The Italian community eventually shifted east toward Commercial Drive.

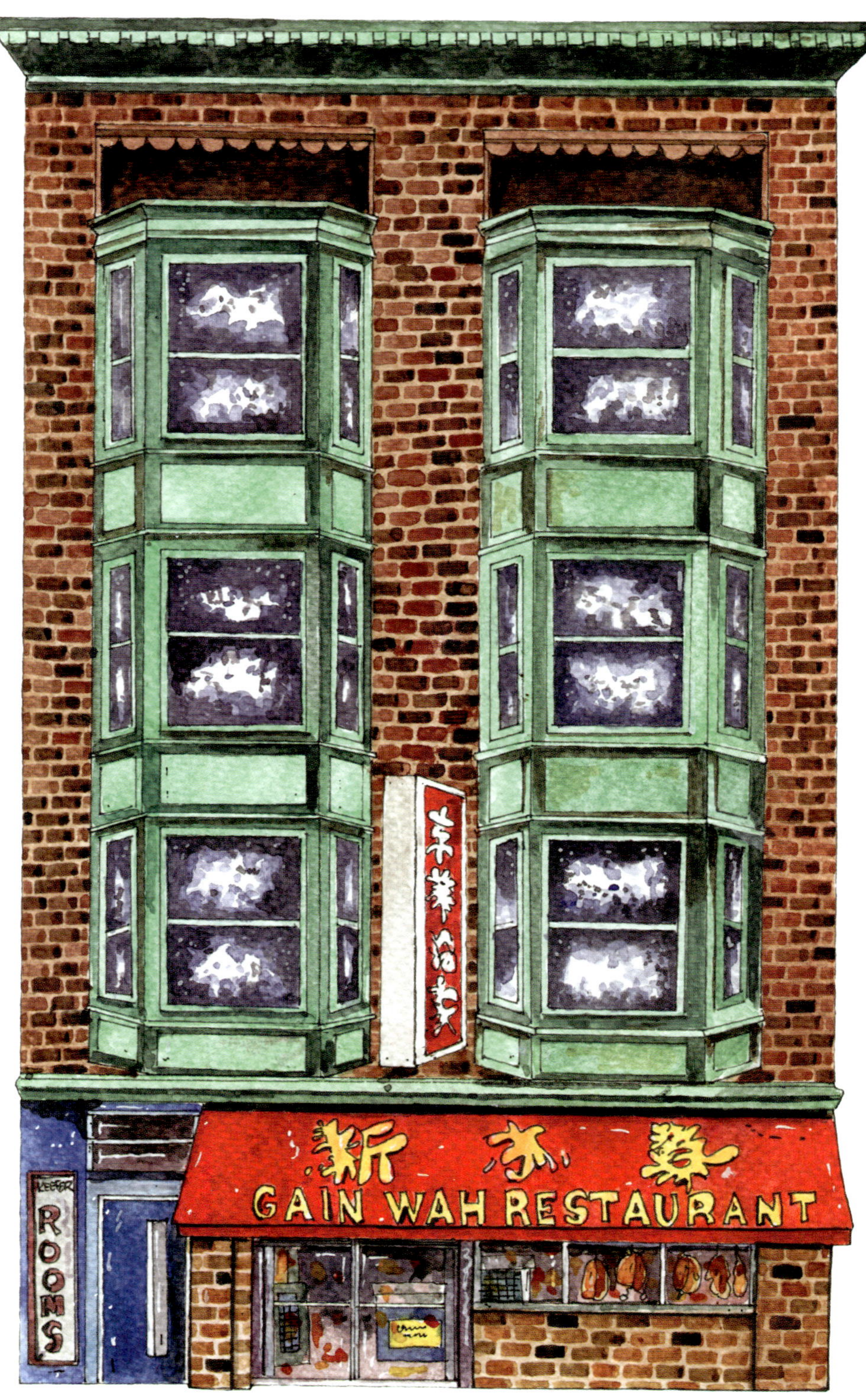
新 亞 華 餐館
GAIN WAH RESTAURANT
KEEFER
ROOMS
CHIU FONG

Gain Wah Restaurant and Keefer Rooms

218 Keefer Street
Built 1912

In 1981, Andrew Leung helped a friend transform the ground floor of 218 Keefer from the Way Inn, a Chinese Canadian café, into Gain Wah Restaurant. Andrew would purchase Gain Wah from his friend in 1989, with the expectation that he would operate it for ten years. He continued to run the restaurant until a kitchen fire destroyed it in 2022.

The restaurant once ran the length of the building and entertained its customers with a décor of mismatched items, such as a painting of former Canuck goalie Roberto Luongo alongside handwritten menus and a portrait of Elvis. Diners enjoyed affordable home-style Cantonese food while sitting on maroon seat cushions at tables clothed in teal. Gain Wah offered Cantonese classics like barbeque meat and American Chinese–style dishes like General Tso's chicken. Gain Wah, like its neighbour Kent's Kitchen, was a key player in Chinatown's community, offering food at affordable prices.[28] In addition to ten-dollar meals, Gain Wah provided Keefer Rooms' residents with coupons they could exchange for food in the restaurant.[29]

The haunting four-storey Keefer Rooms, with its jade-coloured bay windows, was completed by Rogers and McKay in 1912. The brick building was designed with three floors of cabins, or rooming house–type accommodation, and retail on the ground floor. Initially, the rooming house contained seventy-four rooms with shared cooking and bathroom facilities. In 1974, stricter bylaw enforcements and urban renewal projects concerned with overcrowded and poor-quality accommodations forced Keefer Rooms to reduce the number of rooms to forty-five.[30]

Located on the east side of Main Street, the building represents the socioeconomic marginality and diversity of the neighbourhood. During the 1920s and 1930s, a Japanese grocery store (Keefer Grocery) operated from the ground floor, and the upper floors housed Japanese residents. In the 1930s, the ground floor also contained public baths, which were common throughout Chinatown and along Powell Street.

The Japanese first arrived in Canada in the late 1880s and settled in the Powell Street area, northeast of Chinatown, where many established stores, boarding houses, and other businesses like Maikawa department store. Many of the Japanese were employed at the nearby Hastings sawmill. The Japanese also settled on farms in the Fraser Valley, in fishing villages, and in mining, sawmill, and pulp mill towns throughout BC. In 1907, the anti-Asian Riot ripped through Chinatown and Powell Street, targeting both the Chinese and the Japanese communities.

Powell Street, or Paueru Gai, was the largest settlement of Japanese Canadians prior to the Second World War. Shortly after Japan's entry into the war in 1941, the government under the War Measures Act ordered an estimated twenty-one thousand Japanese Canadians to move 160 kilometres inland from the west coast. Most Japanese were initially held in the livestock barns of Hastings Park (Vancouver's Pacific National Exhibition grounds), and then moved to hastily built camps in the BC interior. During the early stages of internment, men were separated from their families and sent to camps in Ontario and on the BC-Alberta border, while women, children, and the elderly were interned in camps in Greenwood, Sandon, New Denver, and Slocan. In order to stay together, some families agreed to work on sugar beet farms in Alberta and Manitoba, where there were labour shortages. Those who resisted were rounded up and incarcerated in a barbed-wire camp in Angler, Ontario.[31]

On April 1, 1949, almost four years after the Second World War ended, all restrictions against Japanese Canadians were finally lifted. The Japanese were given full citizenship rights, including the right to vote and the right to return to the west coast. Having had their property confiscated, however, many did not have homes to return to.

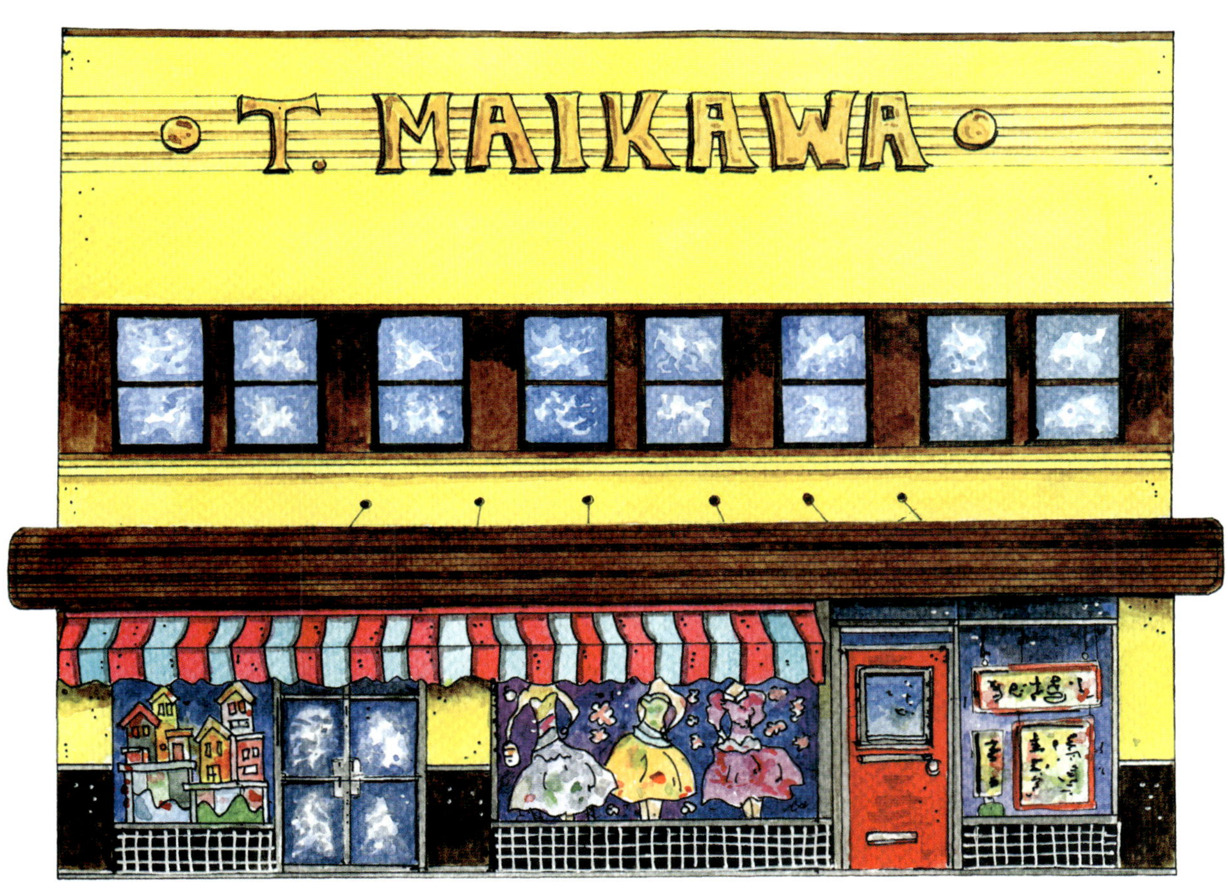

T. MAIKAWA

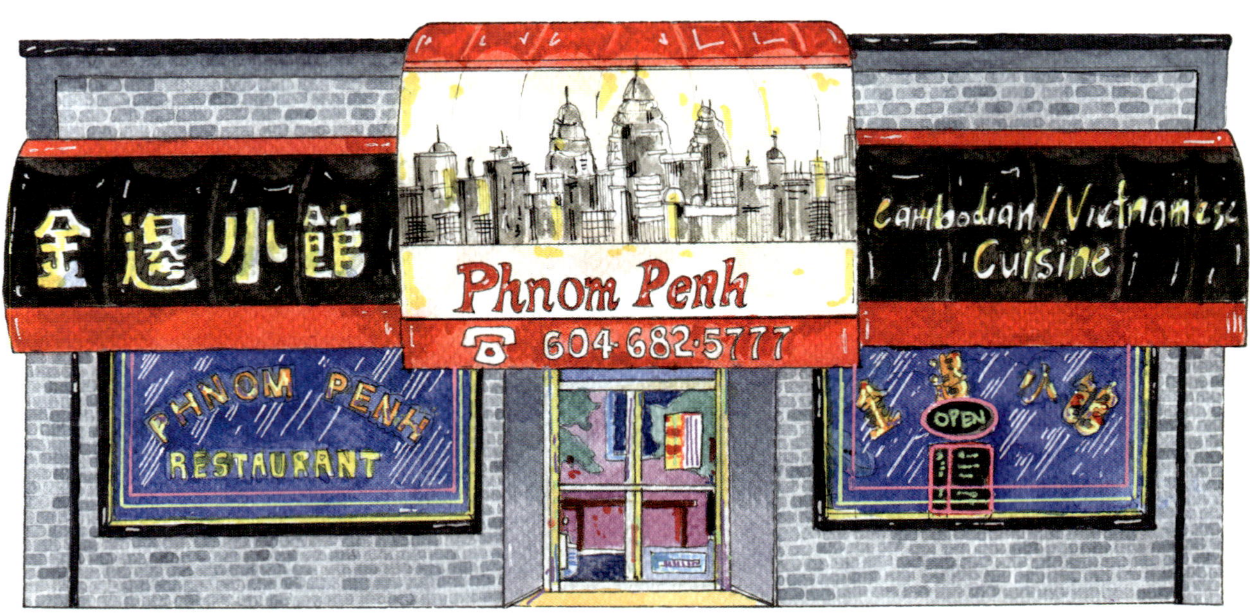

金邊小館
Phnom Penh
☎ 604·682·5777
Cambodian/Vietnamese Cuisine
PHNOM PENH RESTAURANT
OPEN

Phnom Penh Restaurant
244 East Georgia
Established 1982

On any given day, crowds line up along East Georgia or huddle under the black-and-red awning outside the award-winning Phnom Penh Restaurant. Specializing in Cambodian and Vietnamese food, the restaurant is an example of how Chinatown and its surroundings have always been a landing pad for new immigrants. Phnom Penh, with its culinary roots formed in exile, demonstrates how geopolitics aligns with diasporic tastebuds to produce mouth-watering food, like its famous chicken wings.

Phnom Penh Restaurant started as a noodle shop in Phnom Penh, Cambodia, operated by Nam Trieu Humpkik, a Chinese-born chef. Nam Trieu Humpkik's culinary expertise dazzled the locals and undoubtedly influenced dishes such as golden-fried chicken wings and beef luc lac, which have become favourites in Vancouver. In 1975, Nam Trieu Humpkik's shop in Phnom Penh had to close when the Khmer Rouge took over, and his family was forced to flee. They hid in the Cambodian jungle for a month before they were able to cross the border into Vietnam, which was dealing with its own internal political struggles. In Vietnam, the family survived by selling Cambodian-style noodles on the streets and opened a small noodle restaurant. Eventually, Solange Huynh, a daughter of Nam Trieu Humpkik, accompanied a relative to an immigration interview, where she learned that her family could also be granted asylum in Canada.

In 1982, having recently arrived in Vancouver, the family started a small noodle booth in the Vietnam-Chinese Community Services Association on East Georgia, but it was shut down for lack of a permit. The family eventually opened a small noodle shop on East Georgia in 1985 that would be the beginnings of Phnom Penh Restaurant.[32] Phnom Penh's dishes are connected to the family's culinary history and influenced by their grandfather's masterpieces, such as crab roll wrapped in tofu paper and stuffed with jicama, as well as crab and pork with hoisin chili sauce.[33]

As a multigenerational family establishment, the restaurant demonstrates the importance of food to identity, as it provides others in the community with a connection to home.[34] The Huynh family continues to please crowds with their blend of Vietnamese, Cambodian, and Chinese influences born through their resilience and love of food.

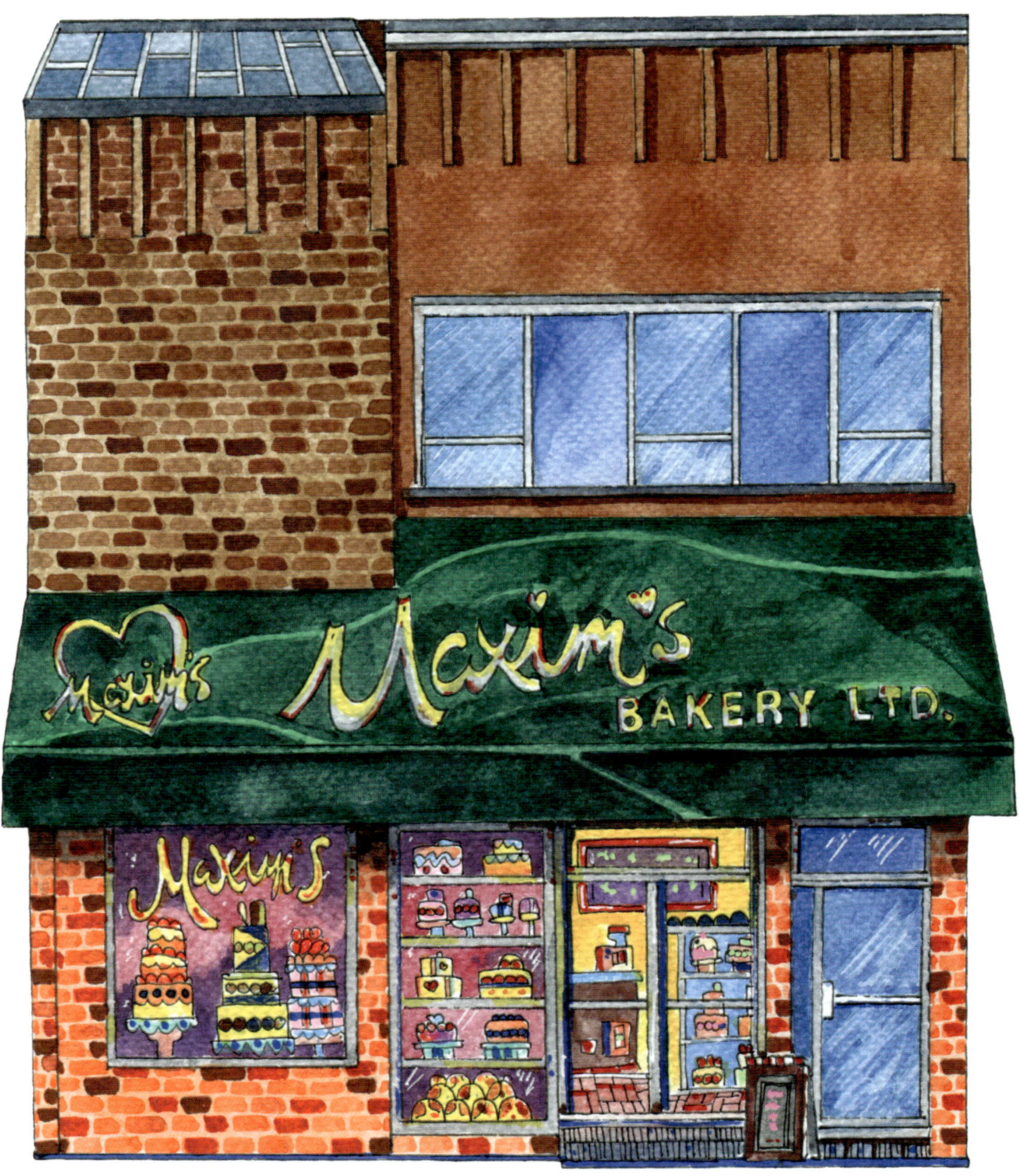
Maxim's
Maxim's
Maxim's
BAKERY LTD.
Maxim's

Maxim's Bakery and Restaurant

257 East Georgia

Established 1979

There aren't many places where you can find ox tongue on spaghetti with a choice of tomato, cream, or soy sauce and have the option to add a flaky pineapple or coconut-filled cocktail bun on the side. With a famous Hong Kong milk tea, you're set for a catch-up session with your best buds or a moment to enjoy your own company with a newspaper in one of Chinatown's cha chaan tengs, or Hong Kong–style cafés, like Maxim's Bakery and Boss Bakery and Restaurant.

Popular in Hong Kong, Macao, and parts of Guangdong, the HK-style café is known for its eclectic, culturally blended food that is best enjoyed with coffee or tea. In Hong Kong, it's not unusual to see a crowded cha chaan teng with hustling waiters serving people seated shoulder to shoulder, devouring bowls of noodles and guzzling cups of coffee.[35] The history of HK-style cafés, however, is steeped in class and colonization. The establishments date back to the 1850s, when the British introduced luxuries such as milk and cakes, which were out of reach for the everyday person.[36]

After the Second World War, cha chaan tengs sprung up in Hong Kong as an affordable food option, often merging local cuisine with inexpensive British foods; for example, adding milk to strong tea and coffee as well as slathering fried toast with butter and sweetened condensed milk. The cafés served what was known as blue-collar food, a mixture of Canto-Western cuisine and drinks at reasonable prices, which led many to call them "cheap Western food" or "soy sauce Western food." Despite their early reputation, these restaurants gained popularity in the 1990s, especially during the 1997 financial crisis, which coincided with Hong Kong's return to China from British rule. As Hong Kong residents emigrated, the cafés became a staple in Chinese diasporic communities.[37]

Menu items in cha chaan tengs range from steak to wonton noodles to sandwiches and HK-style French toast, with some places offering breakfast or lunch set menus that come with a drink. Some of the local cha chaan tengs, like Maxim's Bakery and the Boss Bakery and Restaurant (532 Main Street), also offer buns, pastries, and tarts. Beverages at cha chaan tengs also fuse East and West, with coffee, lemon tea, black cow (coke and ice cream), cream soda with milk, boiled water with egg, red bean ice, Horlicks, and Ovaltine. Two of the most popular drinks are Hong Kong–style milk tea and yuenyeung. HK-style milk tea is soaked in an iron container for several hours to let the flavours of the tea come out. Customers can add condensed milk instead of regular milk. Yuenyeung, which originated in Hong Kong, is a mixture of coffee and tea that allows the combination of "hot" and "cold" as prescribed by traditional Chinese medicine.[38]

Once a neighbourhood favourite, Chinatown's Goldstone Restaurant (139 Keefer) closed in 2020, leaving only a few HK-style restaurants to serve up a mean cup of yuenyeung.

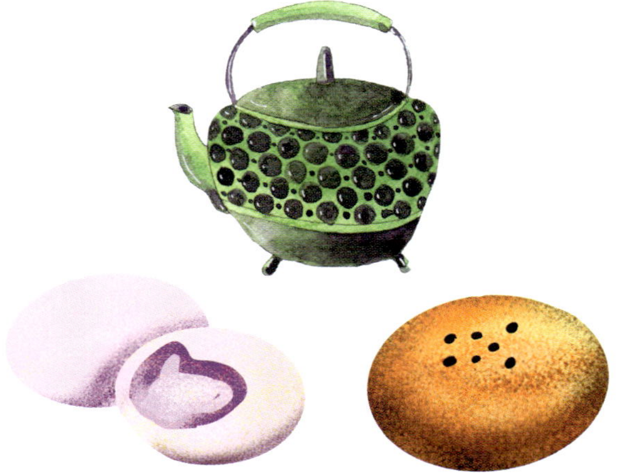

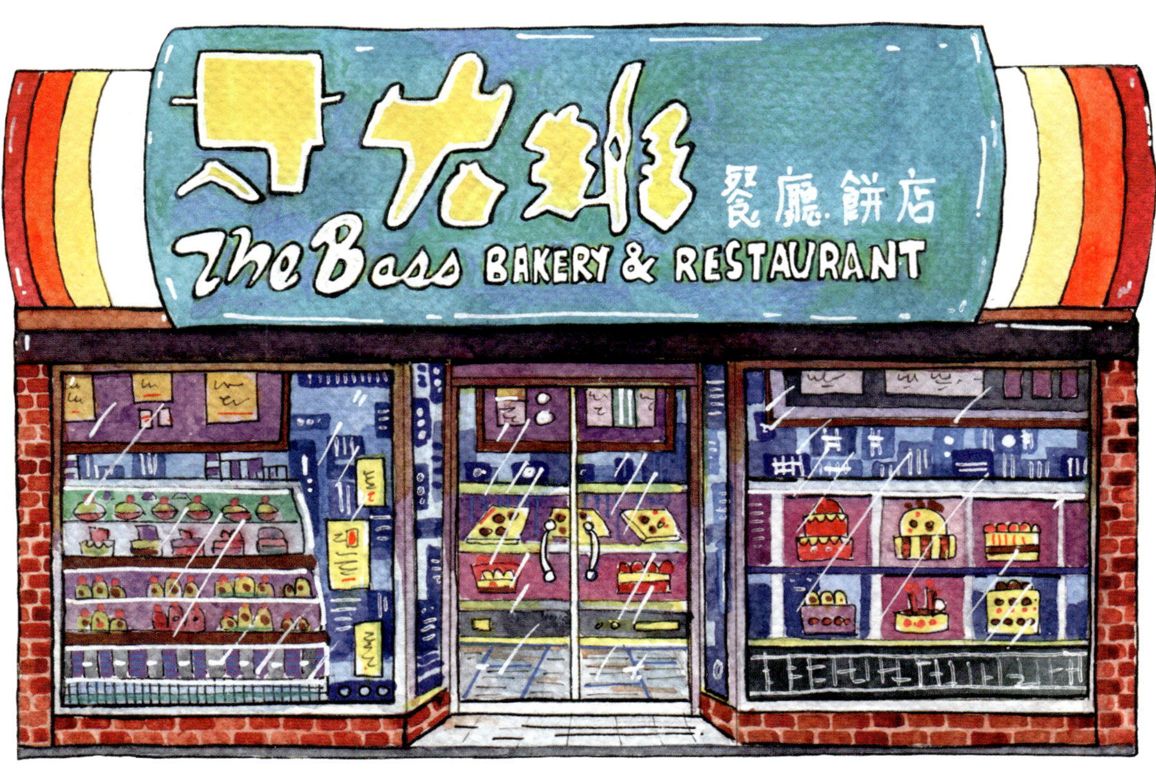
餐廳．餅店
The Bass BAKERY & RESTAURANT

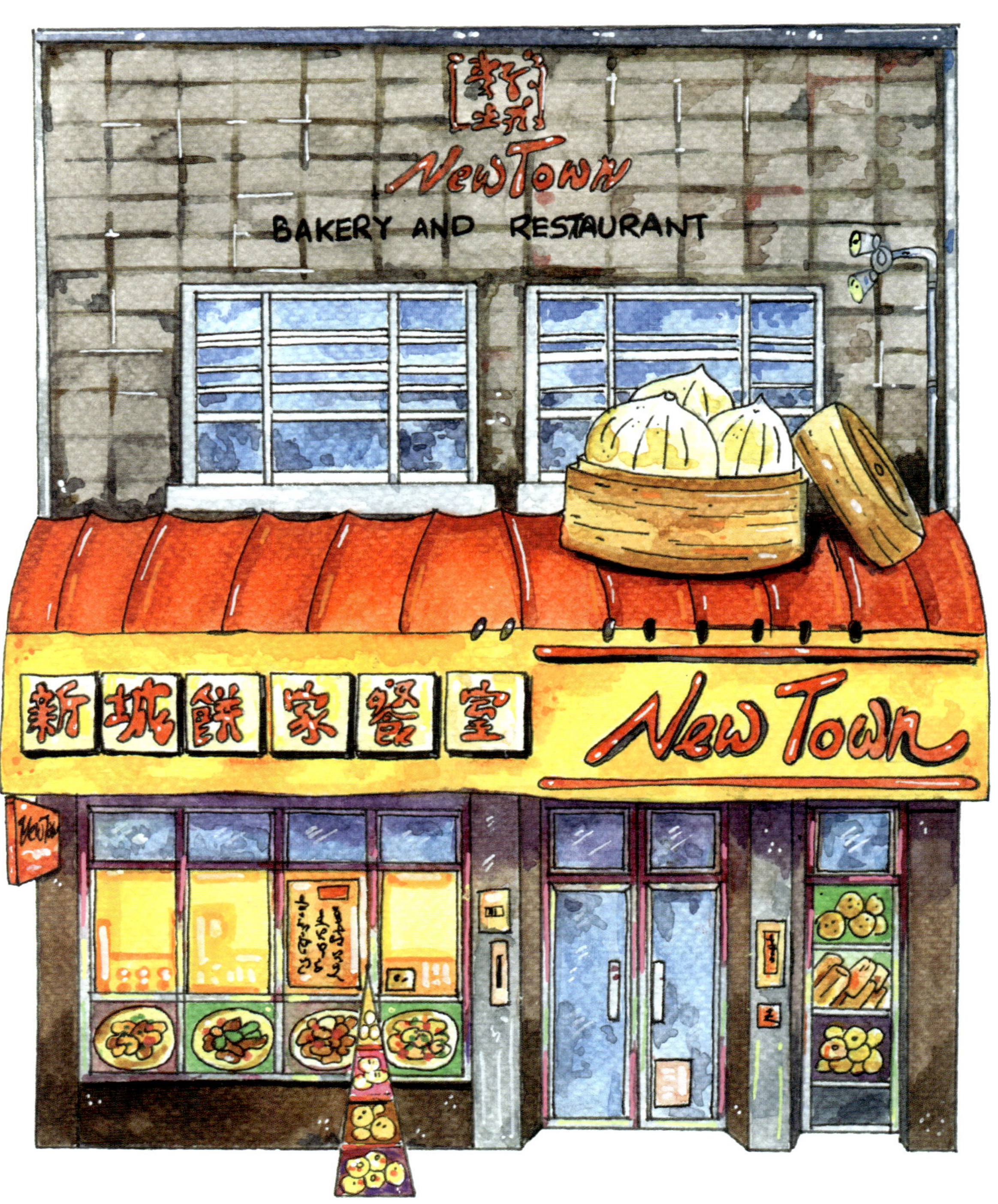

NewTown
BAKERY AND RESTAURANT
新城餅家餐室
New Town

New Town Bakery

148 East Pender
Established 1980

New Town Bakery once served its sweet baked buns from the ground floor of the Chin Wing Chun Society Building before moving several doors down to 148 East Pender. Since 1980, New Town has been the go-to place for comfort foods such as apple tarts, pineapple buns, egg tarts, and steamed meat buns. At the back of the bakery is a Cantonese diner serving homestyle old-school eats like chow mein and wonton soup.[39] In 2019, New Town Bakery was featured in Ali Wong's romantic comedy *Always Be My Maybe*.

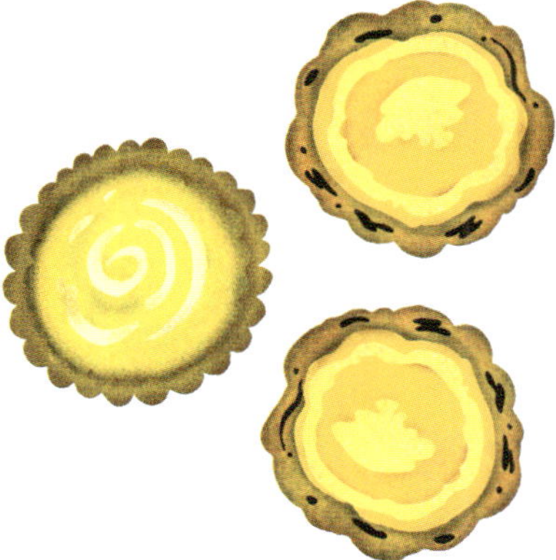

Popular Chinese Pastries

Walk into any Chinese bakery and you'll be greeted with an array of baked goods that reflect the diversity of influences on Chinese tastebuds.

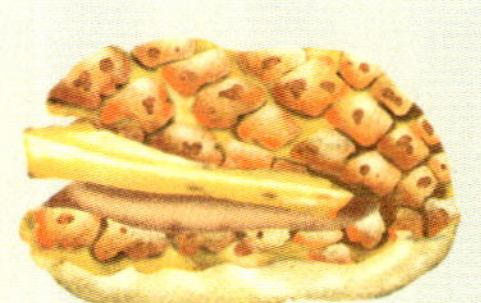

PINEAPPLE BUN

This bun doesn't contain any pineapple. Instead, it's topped with a sweet paste made of sugar, flour, egg, and fat that turns a deep yellow and cracks in the oven to give it the look of a pineapple rind.

COCKTAIL BUN

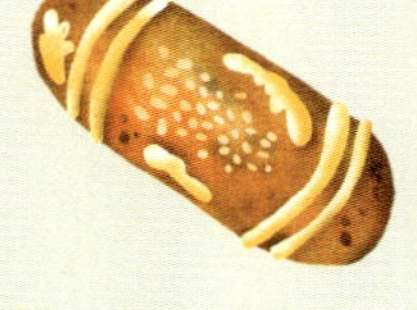

Filled with sweet coconut flakes, these long golden buns are called chicken tail buns in Cantonese. Usually topped with a sprinkling of sesame seeds and doughy stripes made of flour and icing sugar.

COCONUT BUN

Delicate buns that are split down the middle and filled with a salty-sweet cream made of shortening and sugar and topped with coconut flakes.

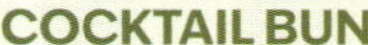

ROAST PORK BUN

Baked buns filled with chopped char siu (barbeque pork) mixed with oyster sauce, hoisin, soy sauce, sugar, and other ingredients.

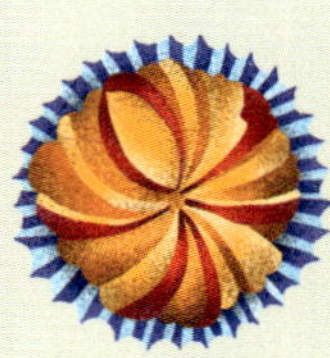

RED BEAN PASTE BUN

A sweet bun made from adzuki beans that are boiled and mashed with sweetener.

HOT DOG BUN

A whole hot dog wrapped in slightly sweet dough and baked.

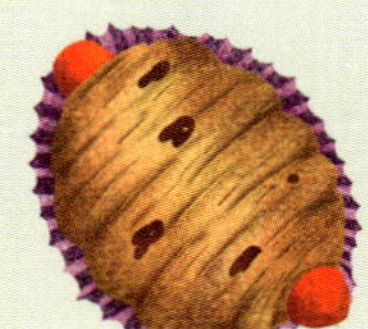

SAVOURY STEAMED BUNS

Savoury buns filled with pork, chicken, or vegetables.

SPONGE CAKES

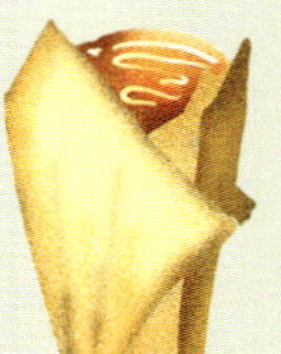

Chinese sponge cakes are airy, more like angel food cake but not as sweet. Often baked in an oval boat shape and wrapped in paper.

SWISS ROLL

Similar to sponge cakes but denser. Baked in a flat sheet, then rolled with a creamy filling in a variety of flavours, such as chocolate, coffee, mango, and green tea.

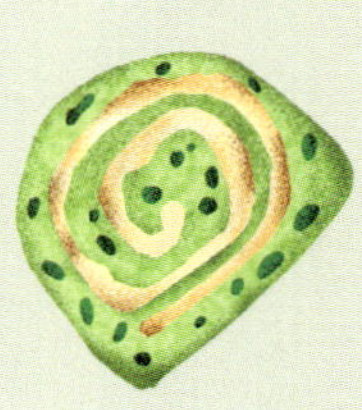

EGG CUSTARD TARTS

Sweet and silky smooth with a slightly wiggly, creamy texture and a strong eggy flavour. Egg tarts originate from Macau but were transformed in Hong Kong with more egg yolks and less dairy and sugar.

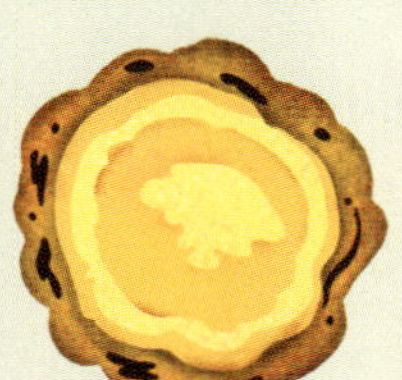

PORTUGUESE EGG CUSTARD TARTS

Similar to the flaky crust of an egg custard tart but with a smoother, lighter filling and a broiled top.

MOONCAKE

A seasonal cake for the Mid-Autumn Festival, with a thin layer of soft pastry surrounding a filling of lotus seed or red bean paste, sometimes with egg yolks in the centre. The cakes are pressed into intricate moulds for a beautifully patterned stamp topping.

TARO BUN

A golden baked bun with the light floral-vanilla flavour of taro, which also gives it a lavender colour.

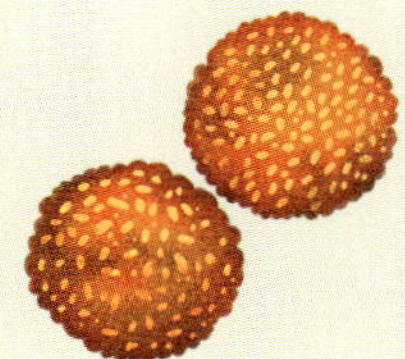

SESAME BALLS

Crispy exterior that tastes of sesame seeds, a chewy layer of glutinous rice dough, and a red bean paste filling.

MOCHI

Borrowed from Japanese cuisine. Soft sticky-rice dough with sweet filling, usually rolled in coconut or finely crushed peanuts. Varieties include taro, mango, green tea, peanut, black sesame, and red bean.

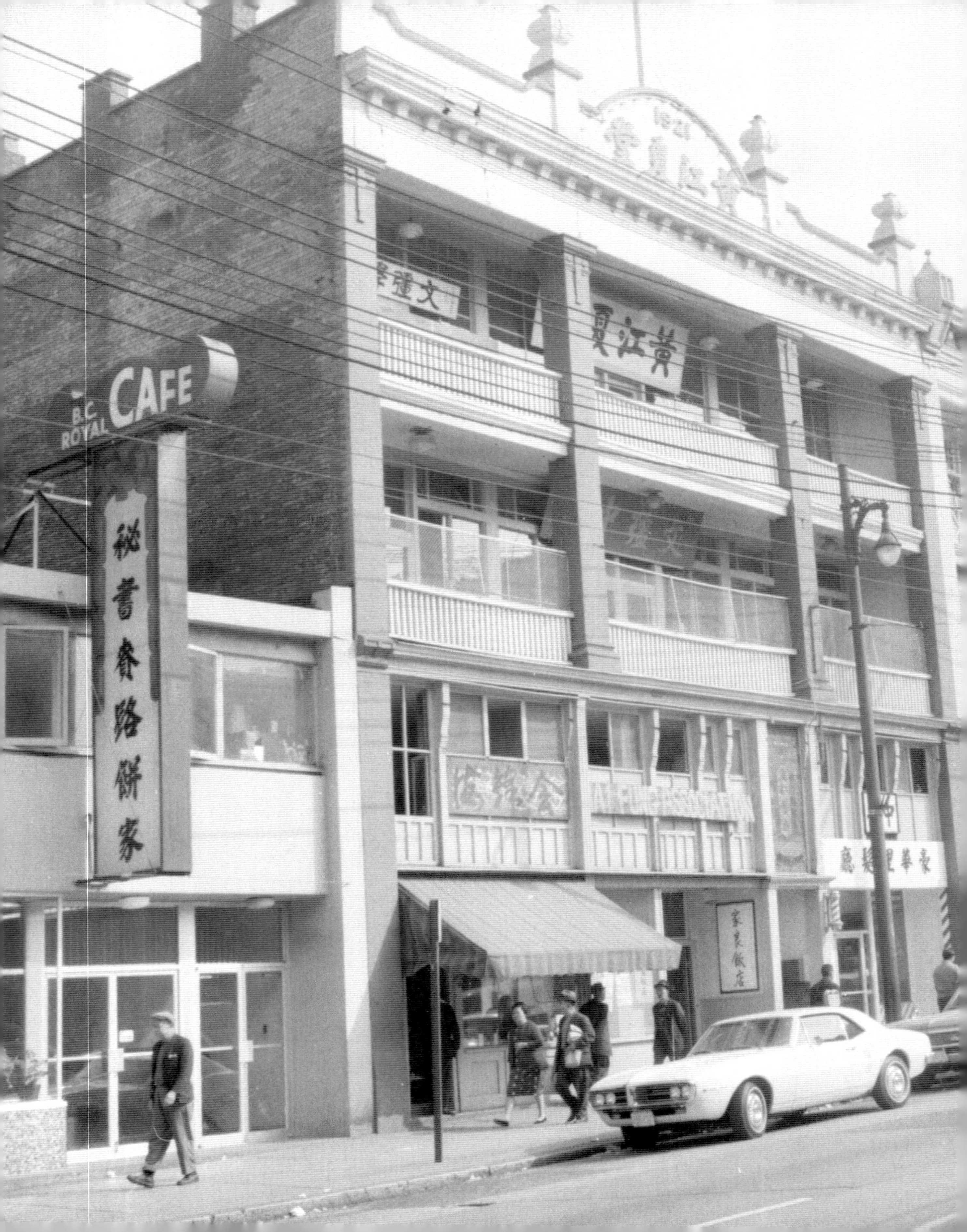

B.C.
ROYAL CAFE
秘書賽路餅家
文蓮榮
華江夏
文庚
金陵灣
BATHURST SUB STATION
豪華理髮廳
家長飯店

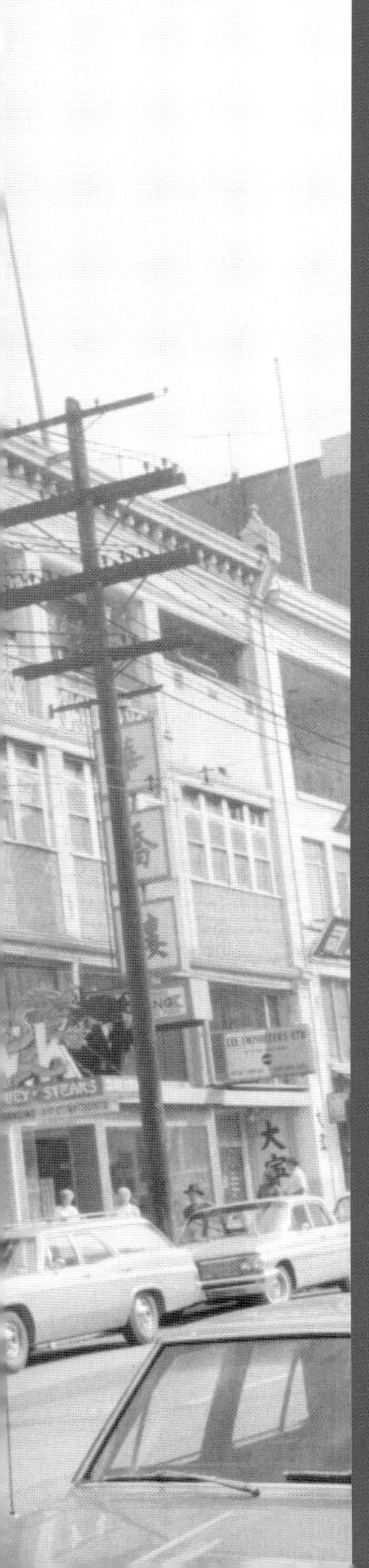

Highways, Gentrification, and Grit

"**W**HERE DO YOU USUALLY shop in Chinatown?" I ask my mother. On the trip in, we weave between construction workers smoking outside a multistorey condo development on Keefer and adrenalin-fuelled kickboxers sipping lime-green protein shakes on East Pender.

"Nowhere!" she says. "Chinatown is no longer tong yan gai. It's now low fan gai! It's for foreigners!" She makes this pronouncement with a look of disappointment that only Chinese seniors can muster—one that criticizes my generation's ignorance of our heritage, our refusal to learn the language, and our preferences for kickboxing and yoga over martial arts.

We arrive at Floata Seafood Restaurant, once a regular haunt for weekly family dim sum outings before the pandemic. The largest restaurant in Chinatown, with space for a thousand guests, Floata was solemnly quiet for a Saturday morning. There were only five or six other tables of diners, most of whom were non-Chinese. Where did all the Chinese seniors go? The ones who spent hours at Floata, gossiping with friends and reading newspapers. After I lose a wrestling match for the bill, my mother and I venture out into Chinatown, where she points out— "Café, dog store, pizza shop, gym, designer clothing. Not Chinese!"

The gentrification of Chinatown has been hard on Chinese seniors like my mother who depend on its intricate ecosystem of affordable goods, community, and village gossip. In 2023, it was estimated that 7,200 seniors above the age of fifty-five lived in and around Chinatown; a significant number were non-English speakers who relied on the cultural and linguistic connections associated with the area.[1] Historically, housing in Chinatown has been a culturally attractive and affordable option for low-income Chinese seniors, who rent rooms for $80 to $420 a month in single-room-occupancy (SRO) units often operated by clan or regional associations.[2] Although the influx of high-end restaurants, cafés, art galleries, and boutiques helps enhance the local economy, it also erases cultural identity, displaces long-term residents and businesses, and alienates existing residents, such as Chinese seniors who cannot afford or see the value in a seven-dollar latte.

Gentrification, urban renewal, and displacement aren't new to Chinatown. In 1912, the city expropriated the original Sam Kee Building to widen a main artery into downtown. The expropriation of Chang Toy's store coincided with the dismantling of a row of wooden buildings for the Great Northern Railway and later the BC Electric Depot. Throughout the 1940s and 1950s, criticisms of the poor living conditions in Chinatown resulted in the destruction of tenement buildings in Shanghai and Canton Alleys, as well as homes throughout Strathcona, displacing thousands of residents. Alternative living accommodations took years, if not decades, to complete, without consideration for the loss of culture and community and the psychological damage that accompanies displacement.[3] A decade later, the city proposed the construction of an elevated off-ramp through the heart of Chinatown as an exit for the planned freeway along Burrard Inlet. Having witnessed how the initial construction of the Georgia and Dunsmuir Viaducts destroyed the Black community of Hogan's Alley,[4] the Chinese community opposed the plan and prevented the freeway from being built.

After the designation of Chinatown as a historic area in 1971, existing buildings were enhanced with "Chinese" design elements such as tiled roofing, lanterns, and signage. The transformation marketed Chinatown as a distinct area, where tourists and locals alike could enjoy its unique architecture and "exotic" flavours—although the motifs were rejected by the community as commercializing culture through narrow representations.

Debates regarding gentrification in Chinatown resurfaced in 2023 when the city approved the controversial development of 105 Keefer, a condominium project located next to the Dr. Sun Yat-sen Classical Chinese Garden and Chinatown Memorial

The residents of Chinatown have always demonstrated ingenuity and weathered the changing landscape.

Square. The development was originally rejected by city council due to its failure to meet technical specifications of the area, including providing much-needed affordable housing for seniors.[5] Local organizations in opposition to 105 Keefer noted how recent condominium developments have not been beneficial to Chinatown's legacy, heritage, culture, and family-owned businesses.[6] Rather they have contributed to the rapid decline of local businesses and the displacement of long-term residents who provide the area with a living history and culture.[7]

Solutions to address gentrification in Vancouver's Chinatown are complicated by its location next to the Downtown Eastside (DTES). These discussions are often fraught, pitting different groups in the community against each other, while further complicating underlying socioeconomic and historical injustices that have plagued Chinatown, the DTES, and surrounding neighbourhoods. Due in part to the significant reduction in foot traffic during the pandemic, the neighbourhood has experienced an increase in vandalism, crime, and violence. A community historically reliant on a self-sufficient governing system is left to reconsider initial criticisms of gentrification and find alternatives to attract outside capital, investment, and government funding to reshape Chinatown.[8]

The residents of Chinatown have always demonstrated ingenuity and weathered the changing landscape. As legacy businesses such as Ming Wo Cookware and Tinland Cookware close, those who remain in Chinatown are reconsidering alternatives to stay afloat. Businesses like Kam Wai Dim Sum have reinvented themselves from providing wholesale and frozen goods to offering eat-in options. Forum Home Appliances is taking a sustainability approach by fixing small appliances to keep them out of the landfill. The Wongs' Benevolent Association is being led by a new generation who have taken to social media to connect with others and highlight the organization's historic contributions. The community has found ways to speak up about the challenges—through political activism, public forums, events, artistic endeavours such as murals, and resistance seen through practising tai chi in public spaces—demonstrating how everyday encounters in complex urban spaces like Chinatown are deeply political.[9] Chinatown is evidence that places are not static but ever-changing and very much alive.

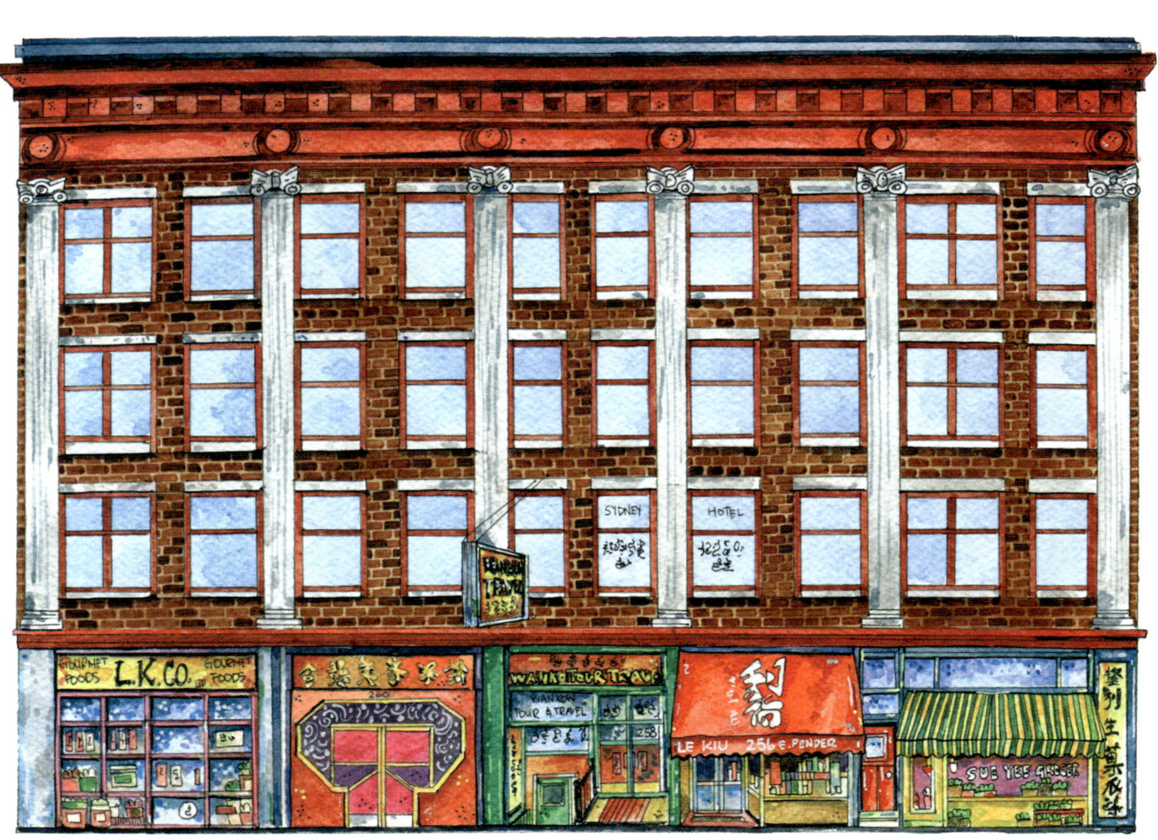

L.K. CO.
GOURMET FOODS
GOURMET FOODS
WAN KW TOUR TRAVEL
WAN KW TOUR & TRAVEL
258
LE KIU   256 E. PENDER
SYDNEY
HOTEL
SUE YEE GINGER

May Wah Hotel
256 East Pender
Built 1913

My grandmother lived most of her life in rural Guangdong and then Hong Kong, before immigrating to Canada in 1986. She lived on her own in a single-room dwelling on the outskirts of Chinatown until she was in her mid-nineties. Each morning, she would eat a simple breakfast before making her way across East Hastings to her clan association on Pender. We could often spot her handmade crocheted hat among the crowd of other Chinatown poh-pohs; its ruffled pompom resembled a daisy in the smoky society halls rustling with mahjong tiles. Often, she blended in with the other grannies in her polyester floral blouse and checkered pants, which she layered with multiple sequined vests and undershirts. Sometimes we would find her drinking watered-down tea at a diner or ordering a takeout container of rice and barbeque pork to share with other poh-pohs at her SRO. Refusing to live with any of her children, she made her home in Chinatown, where she lived within walking distance of a familiar language, affordable food, and a game of mahjong.

The SROs in and around Chinatown were once dormitories for young transient male workers during the early twentieth century. These men largely worked low-paying seasonal jobs as farmhands and railway workers, as well as at sawmills and canneries. Their incomes limited their opportunities for better living conditions, subjecting early migrants to small, poorly designed dorm rooms in crowded tenement buildings along East Pender, as well as Shanghai and Canton Alleys. Most rooming houses in Chinatown consisted of a dorm room with a bed and shared washing and kitchen facilities, but larger residencies such as those built in the Ming Wo Building and Chinese Times Building provided space for families.

Early rooming houses, especially those in older tenement and society buildings, were criticized for being undersized and overpopulated. In 1910, the city's medical officer stated that people in Chinatown lived in crowded spaces that lacked natural light and proper ventilation, which encouraged the transmission of diseases.[10] Learning from countries such as Scotland, Ireland, and England, the city passed a bylaw in 1910 that established criteria for room size, window placement, and amount of ventilation, as well as licencing requirements and maintenance responsibilities.

Known today as the May Wah Hotel, the purpose-built lodging facility at 256 East Pender was a response to the squalid living conditions in existing rooming houses. May Wah, a large neoclassical-style rooming house, stretches across three lots and provides commercial space on the ground floor and in the basement, and residential units above.[11] The five-storey brick building was built in a U-shape and designed to accommodate natural light and ventilation through operable windows on each floor as well as three lightwells that run perpendicular to the street. The hotel contains 130 rooms, with a communal kitchen and bathrooms on each of its four floors. In 2017, the Chinatown Foundation purchased the building and maintains it as housing for seniors.[12]

Even though many seniors expect to live out their lives in Chinatown, the situation is complicated by the lack of adequate housing stock and culturally appropriate care. A 2023 report revealed that out of the 12,788 units of affordable housing in Chinatown and the DTES, only 5,259 are designated for seniors.[13] Of those senior homes, 1,577 are in buildings with some Chinese community affiliation. Of those senior homes with Chinese affiliations, only 504 units offer services that range from assisted living to nurses, cultural programming, and Chinese meal plans.[14]

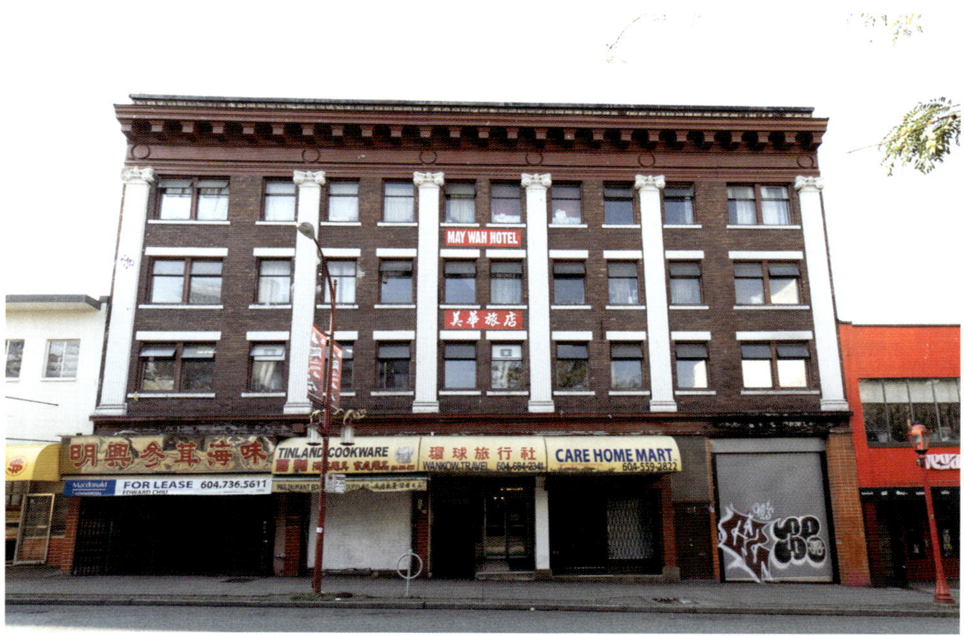

May Wah Hotel in 2023

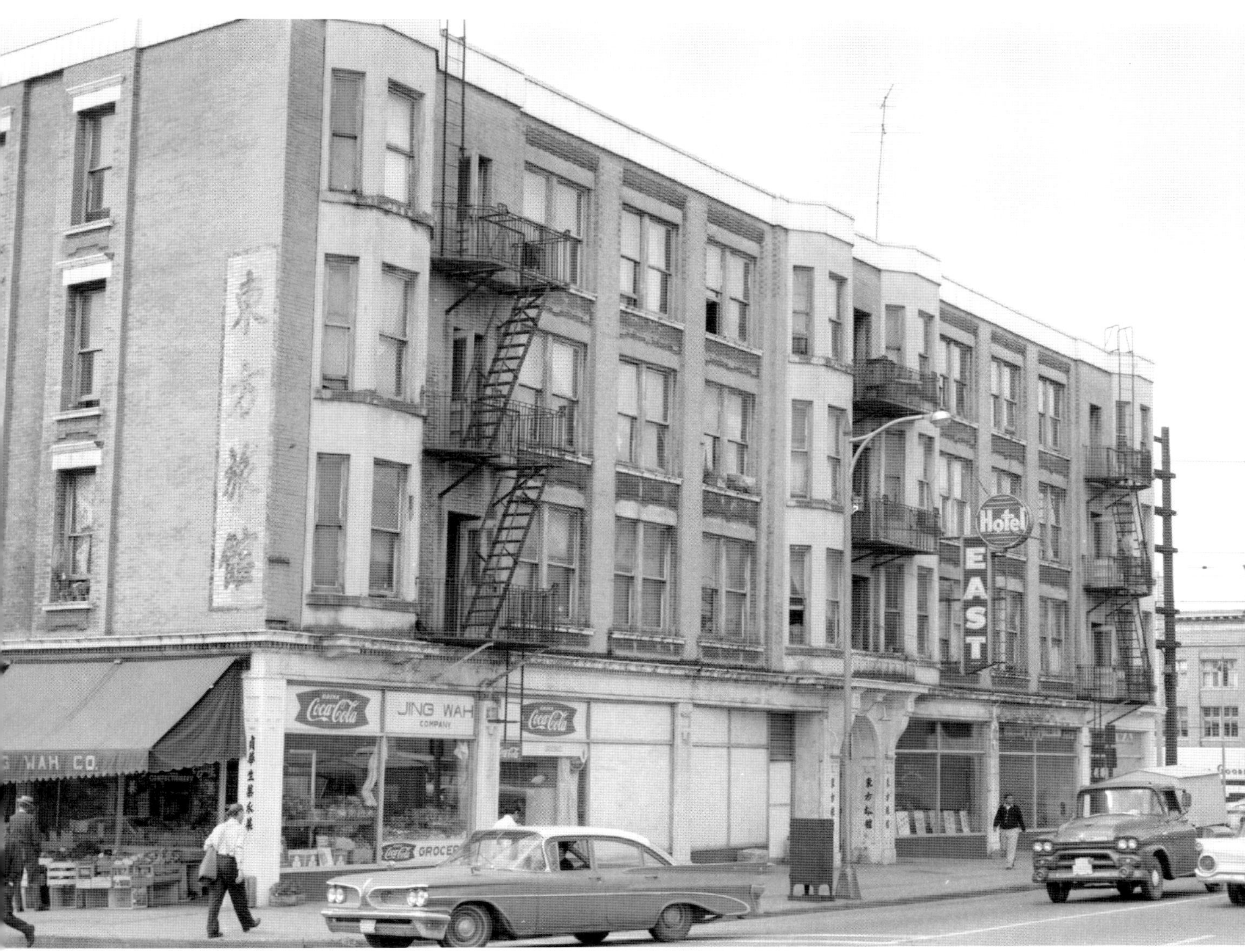

East Hotel at Gore and East Pender in 1968

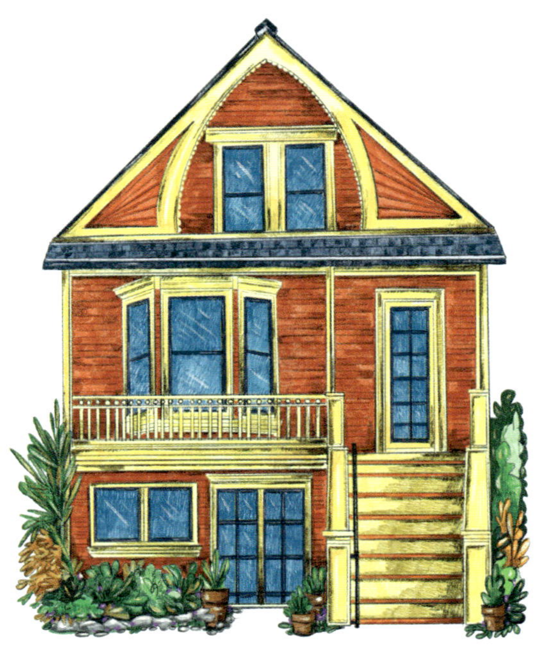
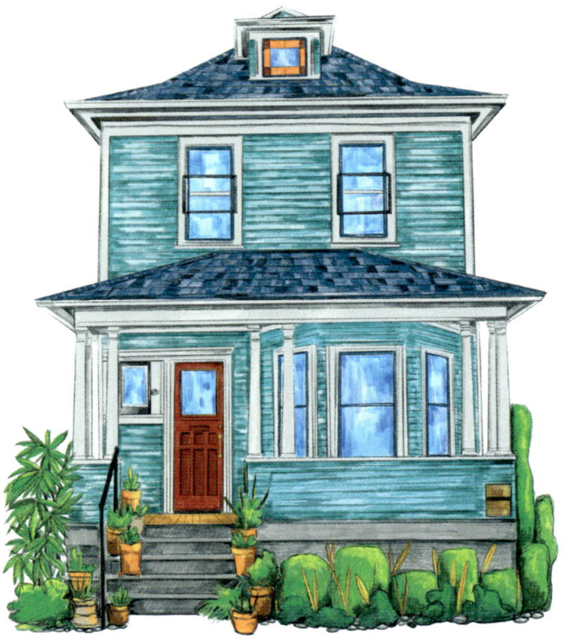
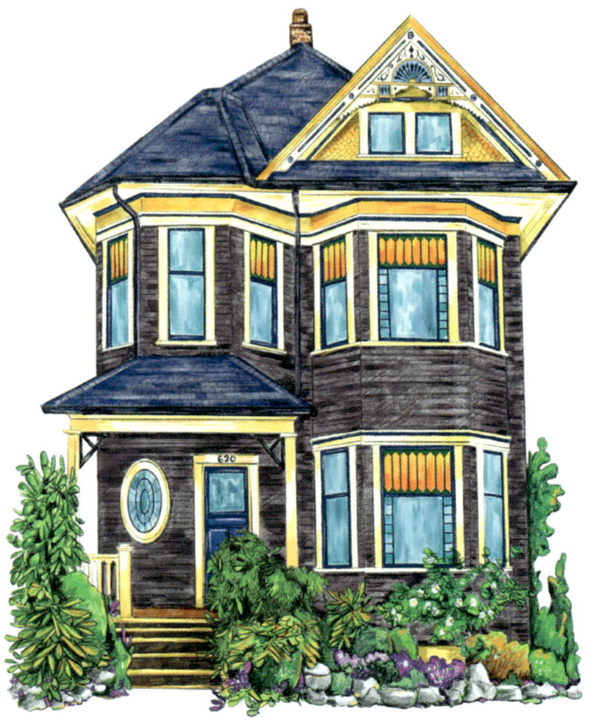
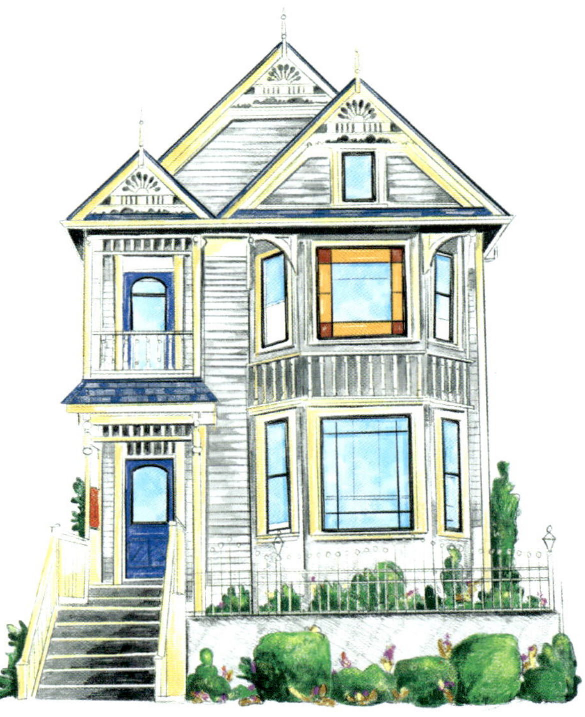

MacLean Park Housing
Union Avenue and Jackson Avenue

Built in phases in the 1960s, MacLean Park Housing, located on the east side of Gore Avenue, was part of the Strathcona redevelopment plan. The project, along with Skeena Terrace, was initially meant to replace three residential blocks and a public park, but most of the planned demolition was never completed after the community objected. The twelve-acre housing project blends public and semiprivate open space around a mix of maisonettes (three- or four-storey attached houses) and towers of one-bedroom apartments. The housing complex, along with later developments such as Mau Dan Gardens (built in 1981), was part of the project to rehouse displaced Chinatown and Strathcona residents during the city's attempt at urban renewal and "slum clearance."

In August 1944, health officials claimed that poor living conditions in Chinatown had led to high rates of death from tuberculosis in the area. This claim, which falsely stated that tuberculosis in Chinatown was six or seven times higher than other parts of Vancouver, was used to justify the condemnation of tenement buildings in Shanghai and Canton Alleys. Long criticized for being filthy and overcrowded, the buildings were demolished in 1949, leading to the displacement of three hundred tenants.[15] Displacement in Shanghai and Canton Alleys coincided with a major redevelopment scheme proposed for Strathcona during the 1940s.

Strathcona is a neighbouring district where early immigrants such as Italians, Jews, Japanese, and Chinese settled because of its affordability and proximity to work such as the Hastings sawmill. The population in Strathcona in the 1940s was approximately seventy-five hundred, made up of an estimated 11 percent Chinese, but by 1957 nearly half of residents were of Chinese origin.[16] In 1949, a report released by Leonard Marsh, a social researcher, noted that 60 percent of Strathcona properties were structurally poor, out of date, or dilapidated. His report characterized the neighbourhood as a "crowded cesspool" with train tracks cutting through what could be residential areas, making it dangerous for residents, especially children. Children, he claimed, resorted to playing in the streets around "pool halls and beer parlours" because the area's "hodge-podge of commerce and small industry" limited official play areas. City council later used Marsh's report to influence its "tear it down and rebuild" redevelopment projects in Strathcona.

The proposed plans for redeveloping parts of Strathcona required the acquisition of dilapidated structures, which would be replaced with housing for ten thousand people in apartments, row housing, and small suites. In the first phase of urban renewal, more than a thousand residents were displaced with the building of MacLean Park Housing and Skeena Terrace. The project demolished historically and culturally important buildings, such as the Hing Mee Society House, where twelve old men had been living together for more than thirty-seven years. By 1965, twenty-four properties, including the well-maintained Christ Church of China, had been appropriated for demolition.

The Chinese community criticized subsequent phases of redevelopment as "unwise, too ambitious and without regard to the human element,"[17] arguing that the proposed apartment complexes were not suitable for the Chinese family system of multiple generations living under one roof. In addition, the redevelopment plans would force Chinese families out of Chinatown, endanger social structures such as Chinese schools and organizations, and scatter the Chinese population.

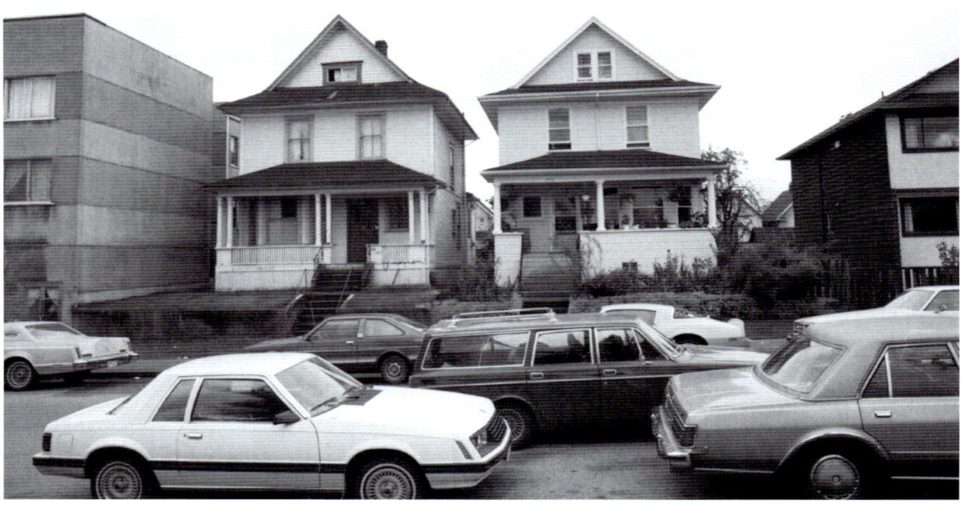

Mary and Walter Chan's house on Keefer Street in 1985

Strathcona Property Owners and Tenants Association (SPOTA)

Mary, Walter, and Shirley Chan

Mary and Walter Chan purchased their house in 1954 for fifteen thousand dollars. When the city announced plans to redevelop Strathcona in 1958, Mary, a garment factory worker and unofficial social worker for the community, launched a campaign to collect signatures to save their community from expropriation. Homeowners like the Chans were given low-ball offers of five to six thousand dollars for their homes, leading them to note that expropriation left inadequate funds to purchase another home in another neighbourhood.[18] Mary recruited her ten-year-old daughter, Shirley, to accompany her door to door and translate the message from Cantonese into English and then from English into Cantonese. In 1959, the city launched its first of three phases of expropriation.

In December 1968, while studying at Simon Fraser University, Shirley co-founded the Strathcona Property Owners and Tenants Association (SPOTA) with her parents. SPOTA protested the destruction of their community and proposed that the city help residents improve existing homes instead of tearing them down. SPOTA highlighted that the city had failed to think critically about the neighbourhood's social problems or consult with the community about the psychological stress and socioeconomic costs associated with being uprooted.[19]

By October 1969, the government recognized SPOTA's efforts. They were invited to form the Strathcona Working Committee to help design the future of the area, favouring rehabilitation of existing homes rather than large-scale acquisition and demolition.[20] Throughout the 1960s and early 1970s, the community opposed further erasure of Chinatown and Strathcona, including the city's plans to build a freeway through Chinatown.[21]

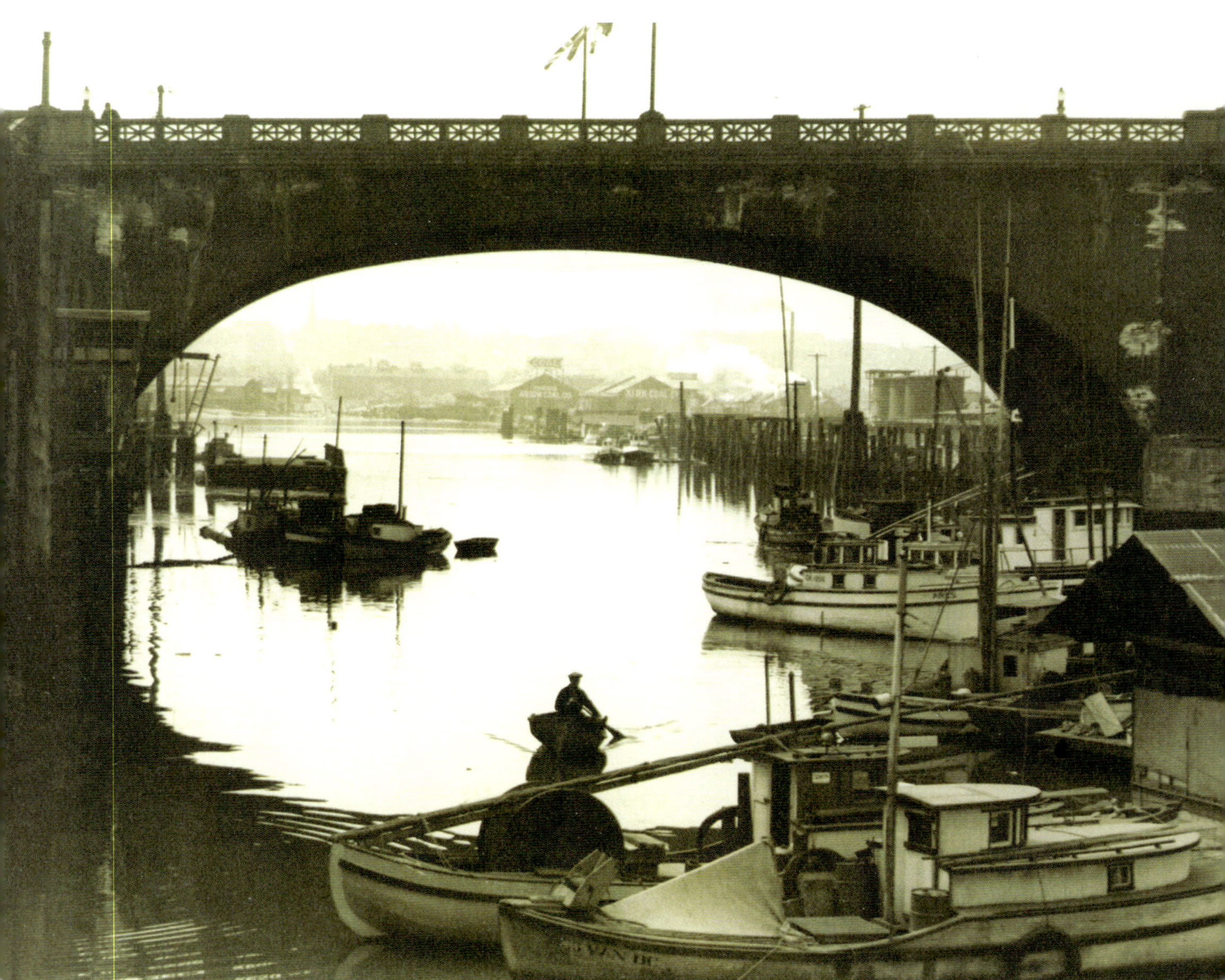

The old Georgia Viaduct in 1939

Georgia Viaduct and Hogan's Alley

During the 1950s and 1960s, the population boom in Vancouver influenced plans that mirrored urban development initiatives in other North American cities, such as Seattle, Toronto, and Montreal. Responding to the growth of the suburbs and increased use of cars, urban planners championed sleek freeways that connected the city's core with the suburbs, trucking routes, and other interurban highways, such as the Trans-Canada Highway.

The subsequent urban redevelopment scheme and construction of the new Georgia and Dunsmuir Viaducts, twin eight-hundred-metre stretches of elevated roadway that connect to the downtown core, destroyed a vibrant Black Canadian community in Hogan's Alley. Hogan's Alley was home to approximately eight hundred residents and many important institutions, such as the African Methodist Episcopal Chapel and a residence for the Brotherhood of Sleeping Car Porters. Vancouver's Black settlement dates back to as early as 1858, when Governor James Douglas introduced a policy welcoming Black Californians to British Columbia.[22] Hogan's Alley was once home to the legendary Vie's Chicken and Steak House, where Jimi Hendrix's grandmother, Nora, a vaudeville performer and choir singer, worked as a cook. A flourishing community in the 1920s, Hogan's Alley was known as an entertainment district and attracted visiting performers like Duke Ellington, Sammy Davis Jr., Ella Fitzgerald, and Louis Armstrong.[23]

In 1967, fifteen city blocks, including the western section of Hogan's Alley, were levelled. Buildings along Main Street were also demolished, including a three-storey brick building belonging to the Chau Luen Society, which had the first London Drugs on the ground floor and a clan-based rooming house for the Chinese community upstairs.[24] The stretch along Main Street was once lined with shops such as Pioneer Junk Co. and Union Laundry, which was one of the last businesses to hold out against expropriation by the city.[25]

The initial plans for a maze of freeways and overpasses would have transformed downtown Vancouver and Chinatown into a concrete rollercoaster. And once again, the city failed to involve the communities affected by the proposed changes. Instead, officials informed Chinatown businesses that land would be acquired and buildings would be demolished for the construction of an off-ramp along Carrall Street, but space would be provided for them underneath the completed exit.[26] In October 1967, protesters marched along Pender with black banners stating the freeway would be the death of Chinatown. The protests united the community, bringing together the Chinese, academics, urban planners, students, and businesses. Initially, protesters were dismissed as "left-wing malcontents—Maoists, communists, pinkos, left wingers, hamburgers."[27] But plans fell through when officials failed to gain funding from the federal and provincial governments. At a public meeting, the audience expressed their desire to preserve Carrall Street as a historic site.

In January 1968, the city finally rescinded its decision to construct the Carrall Street freeway.[28] All proposals for the construction of the freeway were halted in 1972 when a petition signed by twenty-one thousand people pressured the government to withdraw its plans. The Georgia and Dunsmuir Viaducts, which opened in 1972, are the only completed parts of Vancouver's flirtation with urban highways.[29]

In the aftermath of the viaduct fiasco, Chinatown demonstrated renewed life as businesses added "Chinese" elements, such as tiled roofing and signage, to their facades to further distinguish it as a unique area. The distinctive characteristics helped market Chinatown as a tourist attraction and a unique commercial district while demonstrating the community's permanence in Canada.

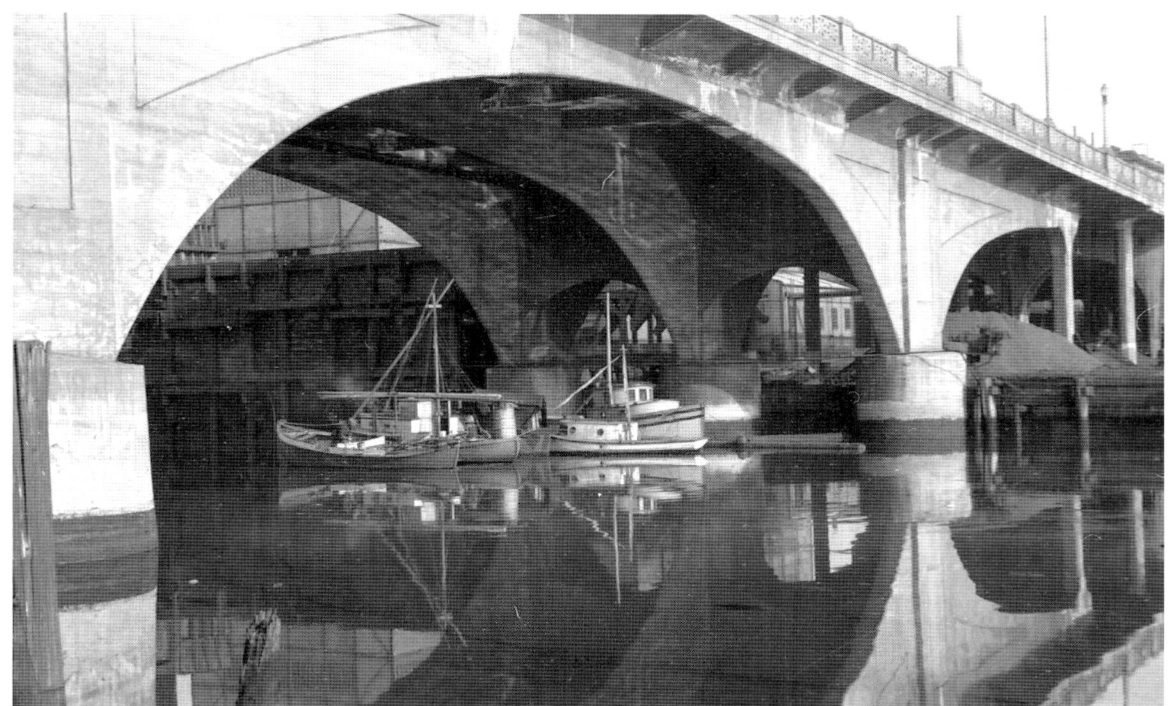

Fishing boats under the old Georgia Viaduct in 1930

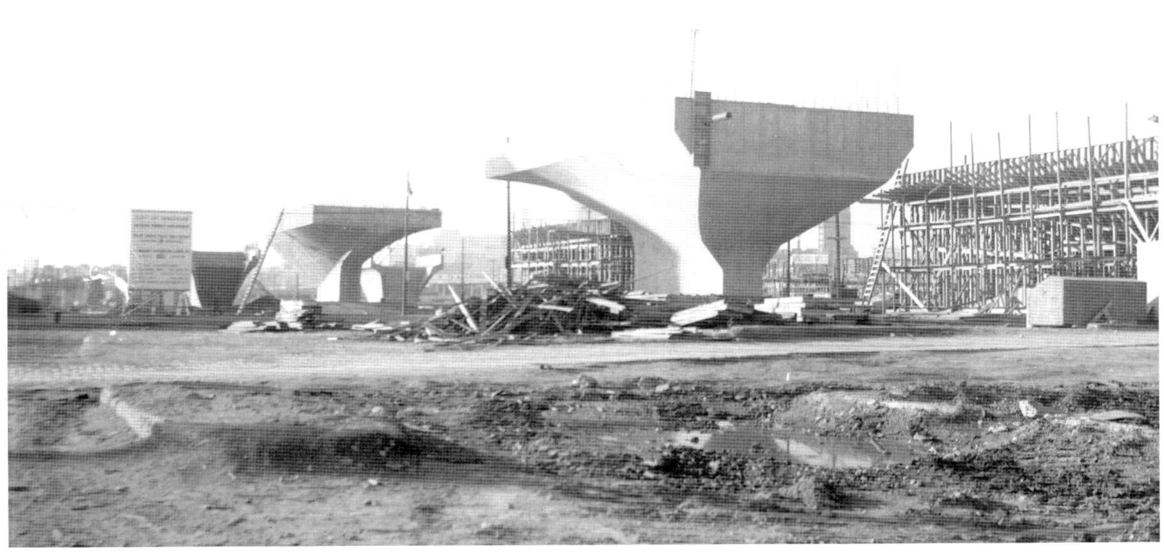

New Georgia Viaduct construction in 1970

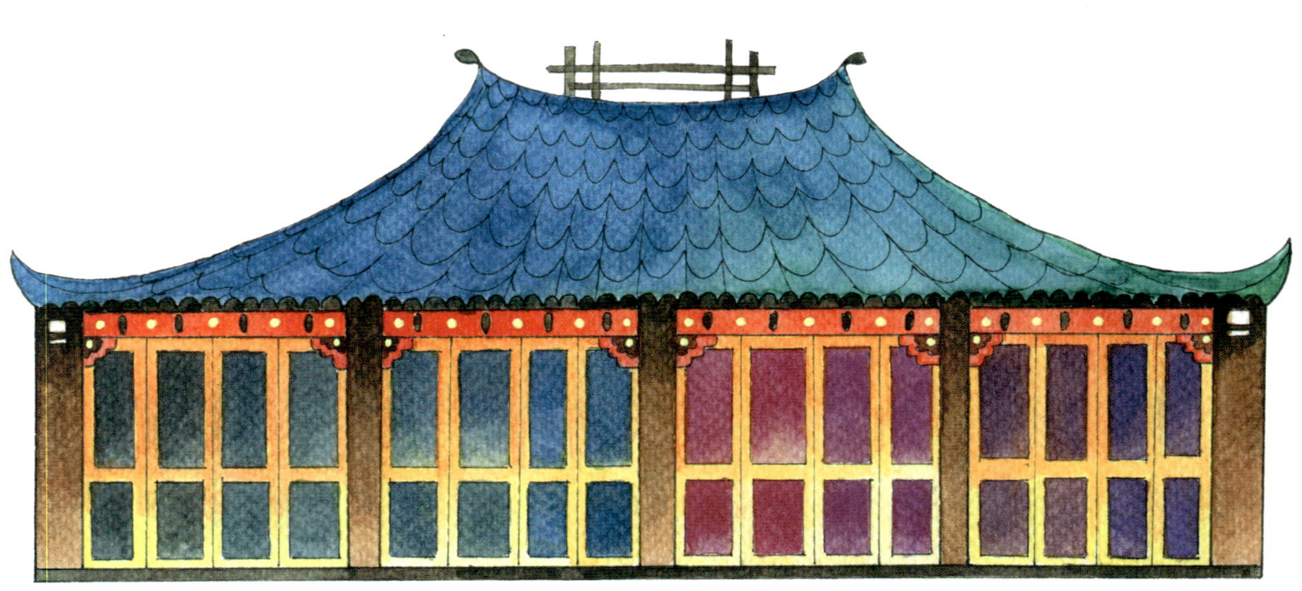

Shell Service Station
231 East Pender
Built 1931

The preservation and interpretation of Chinese culture is interwoven throughout the architecture of Chinatown. During the redevelopment of Strathcona in the 1960s, designers experimented with so-called culturally suitable spaces of small houses and duplexes with moon gate windows and pagoda roofs, as well as small interlocking courtyards. Although the designs aimed to preserve Chinese culture while adding a tourist element, they were criticized as "anti-social and commercial" and a narrow representation of Chinese identity.[30]

After Chinatown was designated a historic district in 1971, Chinese characteristics were added to existing shopfronts, and buildings were deliberately constructed with tiled roofs. Although this tactic was criticized for its commercialization of culture, business owners supported it as a way to transform Chinatown into a designated cultural space that's appealing to both tourists and residents. Recent condo developments in and around Chinatown also include features such as moon gates, lions guarding the entrance, modern wrought-iron railings, and pagodas. The commercialization of culture and its application to architecture isn't a recent phenomenon, as early settlers and businesses experimented with adding cultural elements, as demonstrated in the Shell Service Station in the 1930s.

Opened in 1931, Shell's auto garage on East Pender, which was named the Lion's Gate Service Station, was constructed with an arched tiled roof, carved brackets in the bay corners, and rounded rafter details. Shell had hired architects to develop experimental designs that aligned with the characteristics of Chinatown. Operated by Thomas Chang, son of Chang Toy, the "exotic" station attracted Chinese and non-Chinese customers during the Great Depression and the exclusion era that had depleted the population in Chinatown.[31]

Shell Oil, however, wasn't alone in using cultural marketing techniques to attract wider audiences to Chinatown. As part of Vancouver's 1936 Golden Jubilee celebrations, the Chinese Benevolent Association (CBA) created a "Chinese Village," which featured a bamboo arch from Hong Kong, pagoda, Mandarin Palace, and temple, as well as lectures by Chinese scholars. CBA's educational and celebratory experience introduced

Chinatown's products and services to a non-Chinese audience, but like the roof tiles on building facades, it was read by some as misappropriating Chinese culture.

The service station was eventually renamed Henry's Service Station and closed in the 1970s. These days, a multistorey condo stands in its place with a display of red doors decorating its facade in the alley. Dessert purveyors like Umaluma (closed in 2022) and Mello have found a home on the ground floor.

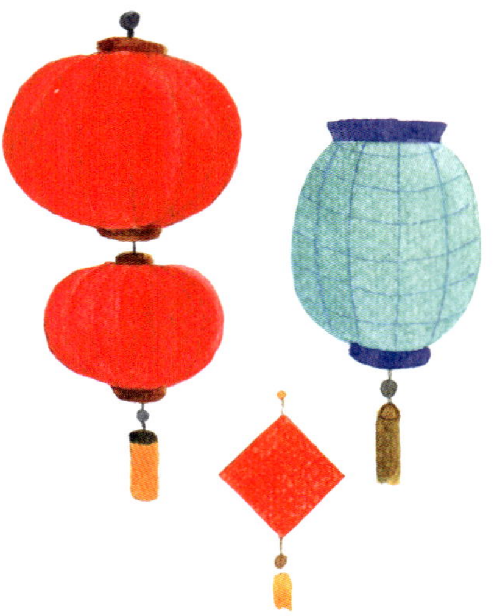

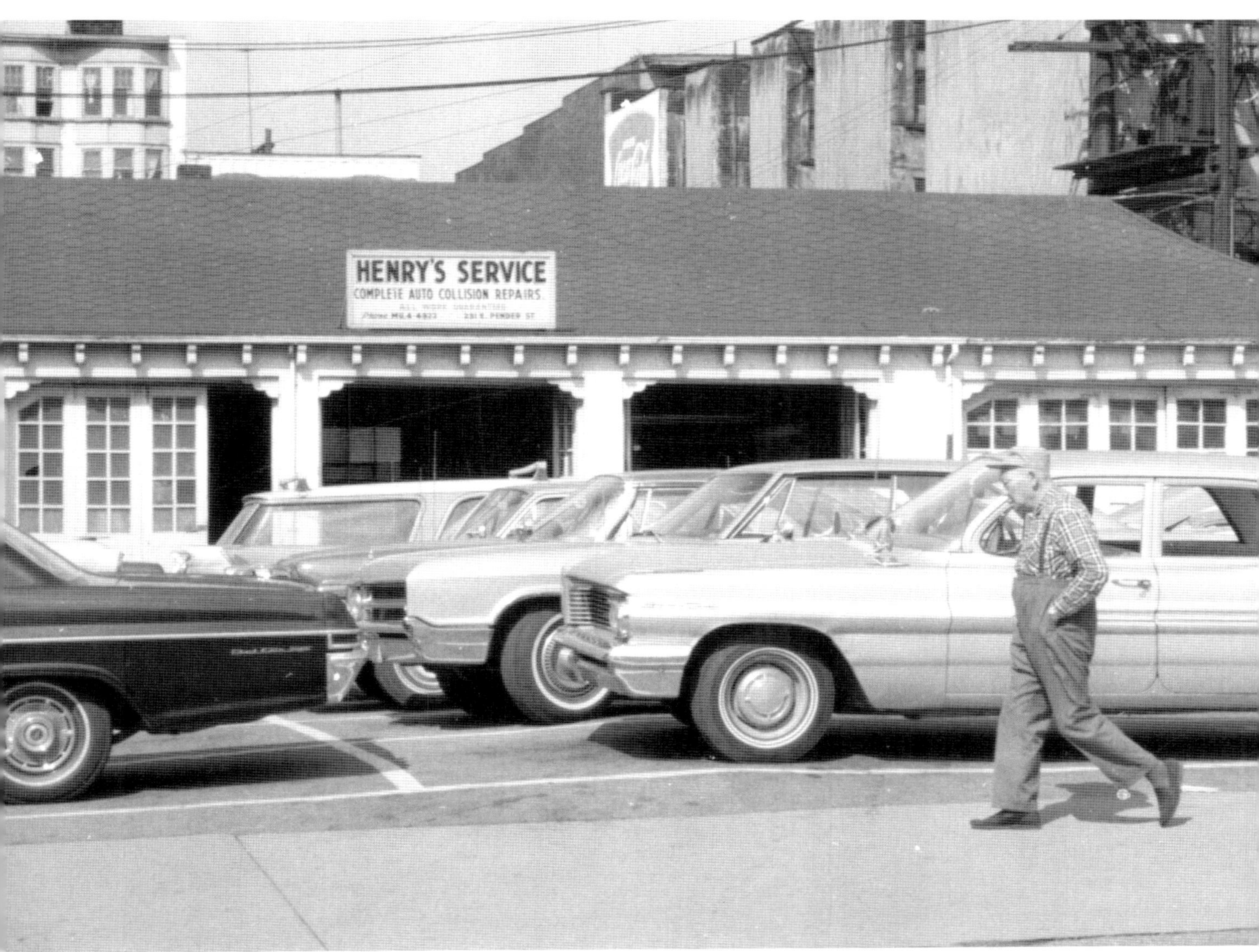

Henry's Service Station in the early 1970s

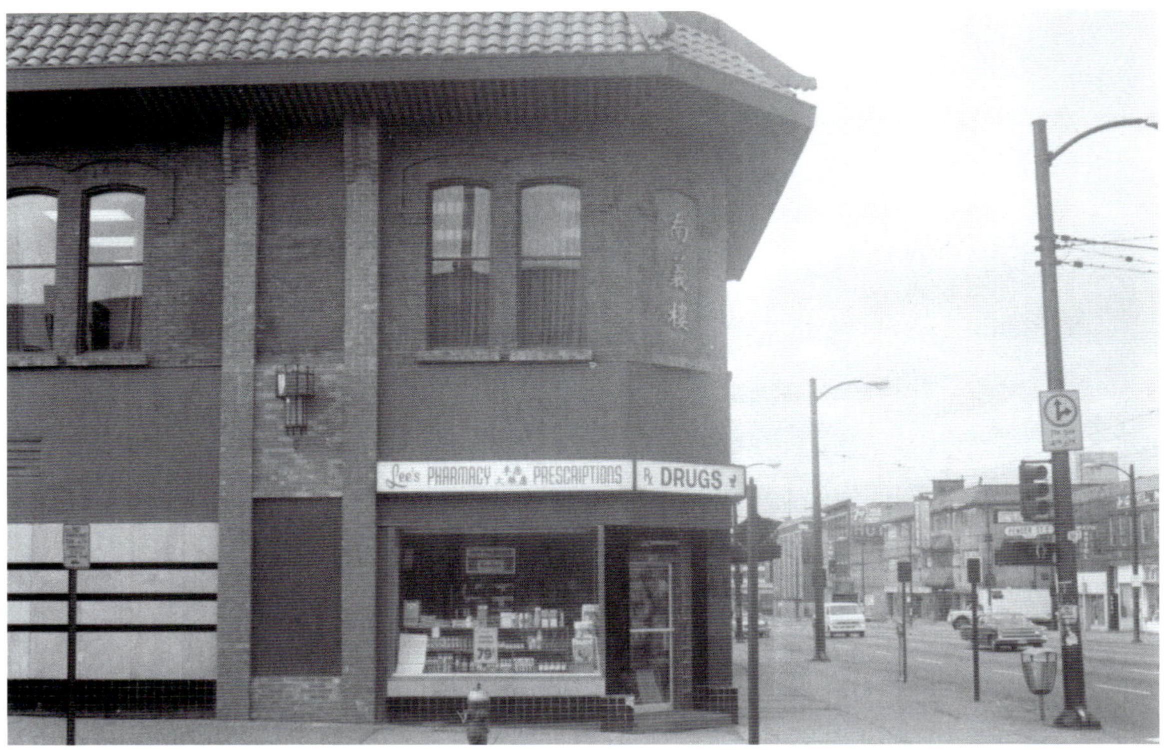

Corner of 500 Main Street in 1968

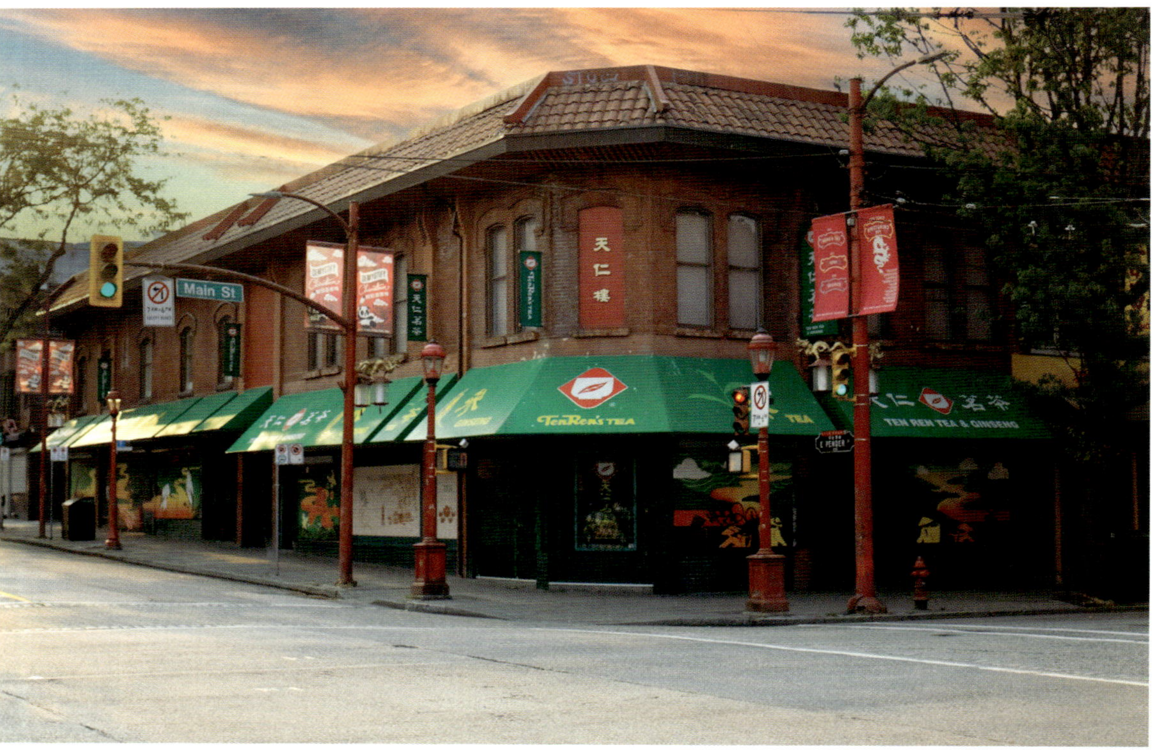

Ten Ren Tea & Ginseng on the corner of Main and East Pender in 2023

Mon Sun Barbershop/ King Hong Chop Suey/ Ten Ren Tea & Ginseng

200 East Pender/500 Main Street
Built 1895/1907/1971

In a grainy black-and-white photograph dated 1973, Mon Sun Barbershop sits quietly next to King Hong Chop Suey at 200 East Pender. Barbershops like Mon Sun, with its telltale red, white, and blue barber pole, once lined the streets of Chinatown, advertising fresh cuts, close shaves, and community gossip. Mon Sun served the community for seventy years from a building originally constructed in 1895.[32]

Built in two phases and altered after Chinatown's historical area designation in 1971, 200 East Pender represents how buildings evolve to suit changes in the urban landscape. The original building consisted of only the front half facing Main Street (then Westminster Avenue). In 1907, an addition was constructed behind the original building to provide more commercial and residential space on the lower and upper floors. In 1919, the owners sold the building to Chinese buyers, further facilitating a shift in the area's demography as Chinese commercial ventures expanded south of Main Street. As the population in Vancouver grew, buildings along Westminster constructed extensions from the main road to the alley.

When you compare a 1973 version of the building to a photograph taken in 1910, the building is almost unrecognizable except for the narrow windows on the second floor. What stands out on the brick corner-lot building is the roof made of intricate terracotta tiles, signifying the area's identity as Chinatown. Historically, the building has been mixed-use with commercial and retail on the ground floor and a mixture of lodging, offices, and meeting rooms occupying the second floor.

Ten Ren Tea & Ginseng is currently located on the ground floor and features a beautiful mural on its shutters depicting oxen, deer, cranes, and peonies. Completed in 2022 by Carolyn Wong with support from the Chinatown BIA and Vancouver Mural Festival as part of an effort to revitalize Chinatown, the artwork celebrates the artist's pride in being Chinese.[33]

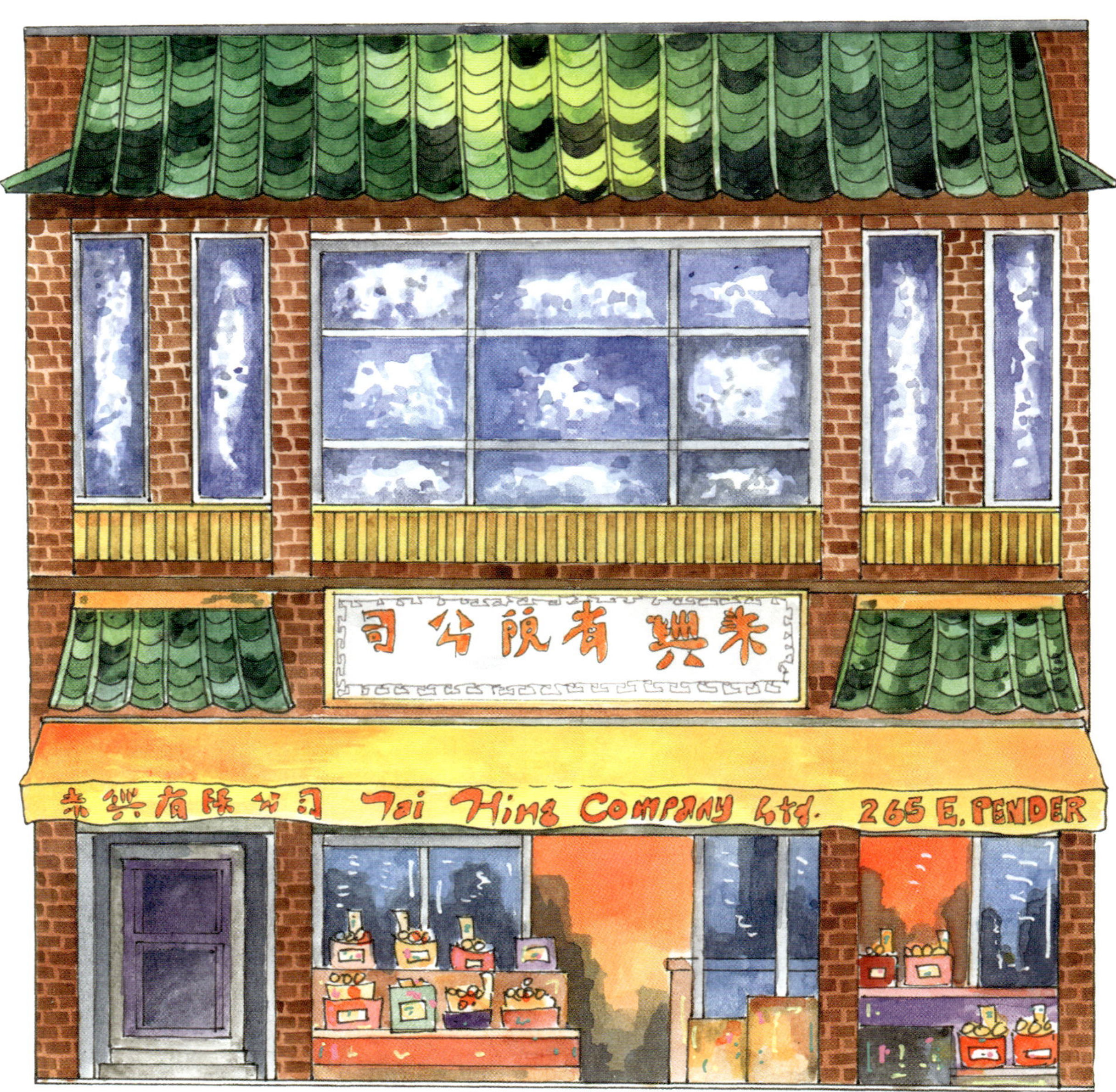
司 分 限 有 興 柒
柒 興 有 限 公 司 Tai Hing Company Ltd. 265 E. PENDER

Tai Hing Company/
Kissa Tanto Restaurant
263–265 East Pender
Built 1973

As I flip through photographs from the 1970s of the 200 block of East Pender, I notice a small group of three houses set behind boxy storefronts, each with its own characteristic awnings and bold signage. The storefronts advertise Fook Lee Lung (261 East Pender), Tai Hing (265 East Pender), and Mary's Fruit and Vegetable (269 East Pender), next to the neon signs hanging off the facades of Nanking Restaurant (245 East Pender) and Kwangchow Restaurant (253 East Pender).

Built in 1973 on the site originally housing Tai Hing Company, 263–265 East Pender is a two-storey building that features two rows of tiled roofing set on brick. Tai Hing, an import-export business, was once located on the ground floor of the original house (built in 1910) and moved into the newly constructed building in the 1970s. From 1976 to 1990, the upper floor was home to Sam Lock Restaurant, which was known for its majestic pagoda-like neon sign.[34]

The building continues its foodie tradition as the home of Kissa Tanto, an upscale Italian-Japanese fusion restaurant. Blending the "delicate flavours of Japan with the warmth of Italian cooking," Kissa Tanto is a reminder of Chinatown's past as a place where immigrant groups such as the Japanese and Italians started. The fusion of Italian and Japanese tastes brings together an elegant blend of "crudo and cruda, crisp exotic salads, playful pastas, and rich, tender meats."[35]

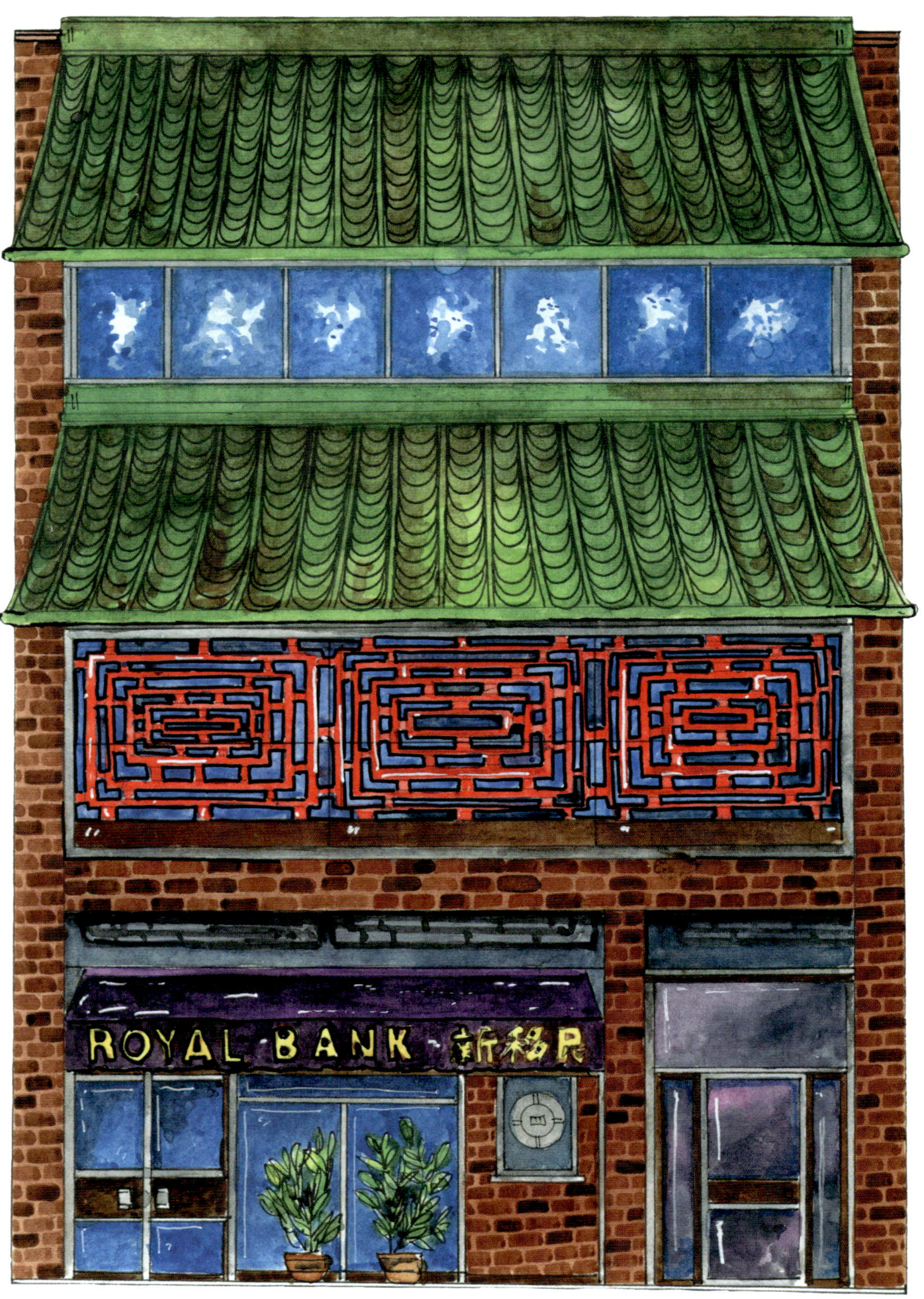

ROYAL BANK 新稳民

Mary's Fruit and Vegetable/ Sing Tao/Royal Bank

269–271 East Pender
Built 1978

The Chinatown streets of my childhood were lined with greengrocers overflowing with fruit, vegetables, and live seafood. On a warm summer's day, the sweet smell of overripe bananas and oranges was intoxicating, trapped under overly large awnings like the one on Mary's Fruit and Vegetable. Constructed in front of a series of houses designed by W. H. Chow in the 1910s, Mary's sheds light on the versatility of space in early Chinatown, where structures served both residential and commercial purposes. Built in 1978, the three-storey brick building that replaced the earlier house shows elements of Chinese architecture, including a modern iron fence, recessed balcony, and shingled roof. From the 1980s to 1990s, the ground floor was occupied by the Royal Bank of Canada, with the *Sing Tao* newspaper on the second floor. [36]

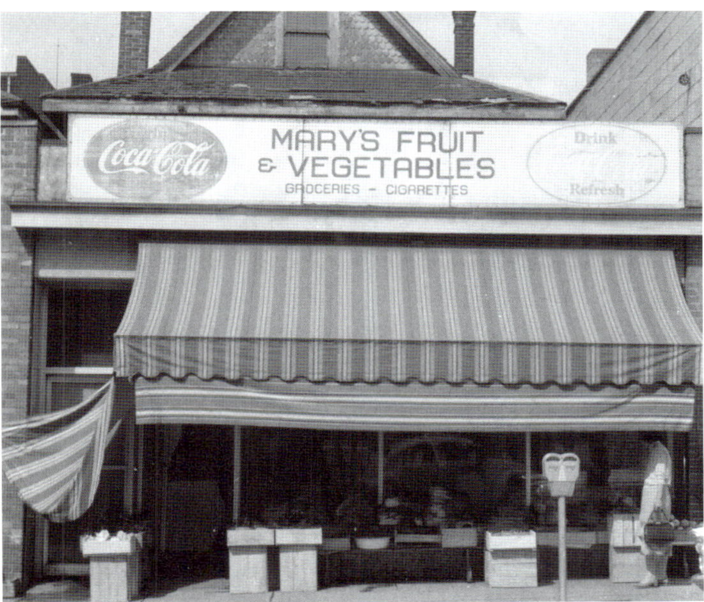

Mary's Fruit and Vegetable in 1970

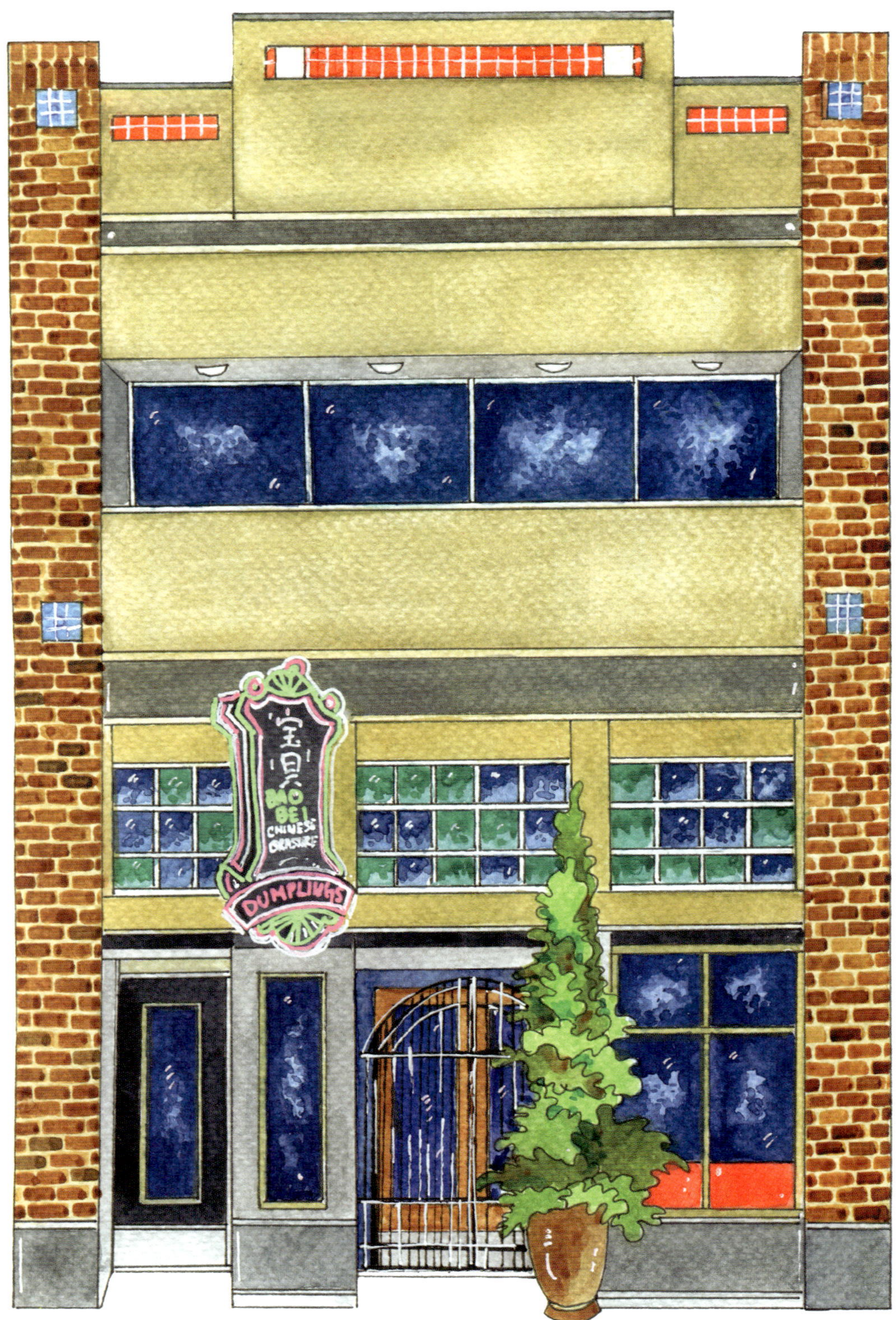

宝貝
BAO BEI
CHINESE
BRASSERIE
DUMPLINGS

Bao Bei Chinese Brasserie
163 Keefer Street
Established 2009

What you value in a culture is deeply personal. If you asked me what it means to be Chinese, I wouldn't know how to answer you. It's like grasping at straws, where I may talk about the sweet crusts on pineapple buns or mouth-watering har gows, stationery from my childhood with wide-eyed characters like Hello Kitty or Keroppi, or Michelle Yeoh's martial arts moves in *Crouching Tiger, Hidden Dragon* or, more recently, *Everything Everywhere All at Once*. My mother has often criticized my interpretation of what it means to be Chinese as some cherry-picked collection of concocted ideas I've borrowed from pop culture and reading *The Joy Luck Club*. But isn't culture, especially for diasporic off-spring like me, always up for interpretation? Where we take the best parts of our heritage and fuse it with our upbringing of Froot Loops and *Saved by the Bell* so it transforms into something even better?

Bao Bei Chinese Brasserie is a culinary masterpiece demonstrative of the ingenuity of cultural fusion and how new generations of Chinese Canadians interpret their heritage. Inspired by her mother's cooking and visits to Chinatown in the 1980s, Tannis Ling created a dining experience that adds a modern spin to traditional Chinese culinary favourites like dumplings, fried rice, and rice cakes. The drink menu is infused with flavours like cardamon, ginger, and osmanthus flower that can be paired with favourites like beef tartare with burnt scallion oil, taro chips, or cumin-flavoured lamb sirloin on sesame flatbread. Bao Bei has been a Chinatown staple since 2009 and is among the new wave of restaurants aiming to preserve the character and flavours of the area. Rather than open in a more upscale neighbourhood, Ling was attracted to Chinatown because of her connection to its heritage, as well as its location among shops, grocers, and herbal stores that are the heart of the restaurant's culinary masterpieces. Located in a modern brick building with a neon sign above its entrance,[37] the restaurant features arches that evoke Chinatown's glory days.

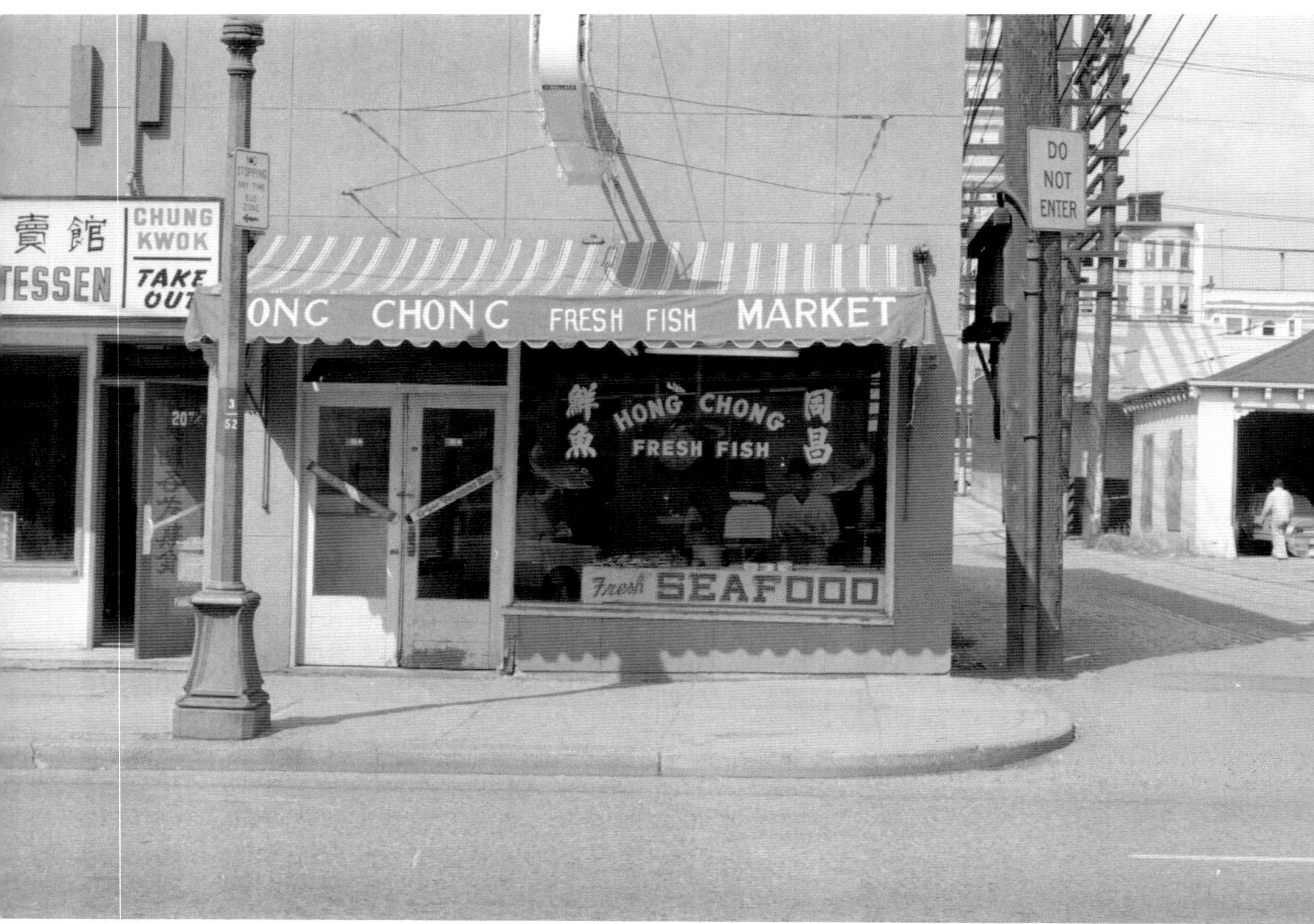

Hong Chong Fish Market in 1969

Propaganda Coffee/
Hong Chong Fish Market
209 East Pender
Established 2015

These days, I can often get a dose of Toisan, or Hoisan, a Cantonese dialect, with my oat latte. The lyrical sounds of Toisan feel like home to me—it is the dialect my parents converse in and was one of the dominant languages spoken in early Chinatowns throughout Canada and the US. On certain days, between the kickboxers, hipsters, and nervous writers scribbling in coffee-stained notebooks, you may notice a group of four or five middle-aged Toisan-speaking men hanging out at Propaganda Coffee. Their Toisan is thick, much thicker than my parents', which I imagine has been watered down with time. From certain angles, they remind me of a younger version of my father and his friends— one with a cigarette stub dangling off the side of his mouth, another sporting a stained polo shirt under a fishing vest, and a loud one who bellows across the coffee shop that his child just got into university. It's odd yet comforting, seeing these men among the hipsters and yogis sipping their matcha lattes and pour-overs in between bites of brown butter chocolate chip cookies.

Co-owned by Will Wang, a third-generation Chinese Canadian, Propaganda Coffee serves a mean latte with its cleverly designed Mod Bar "tap" espresso, a water-delivery system that supplies water volumetrically.[38] Located at 209 East Pender, the café was once home to one of Chinatown's many fishmongers, the Hong Chong Fish Market.

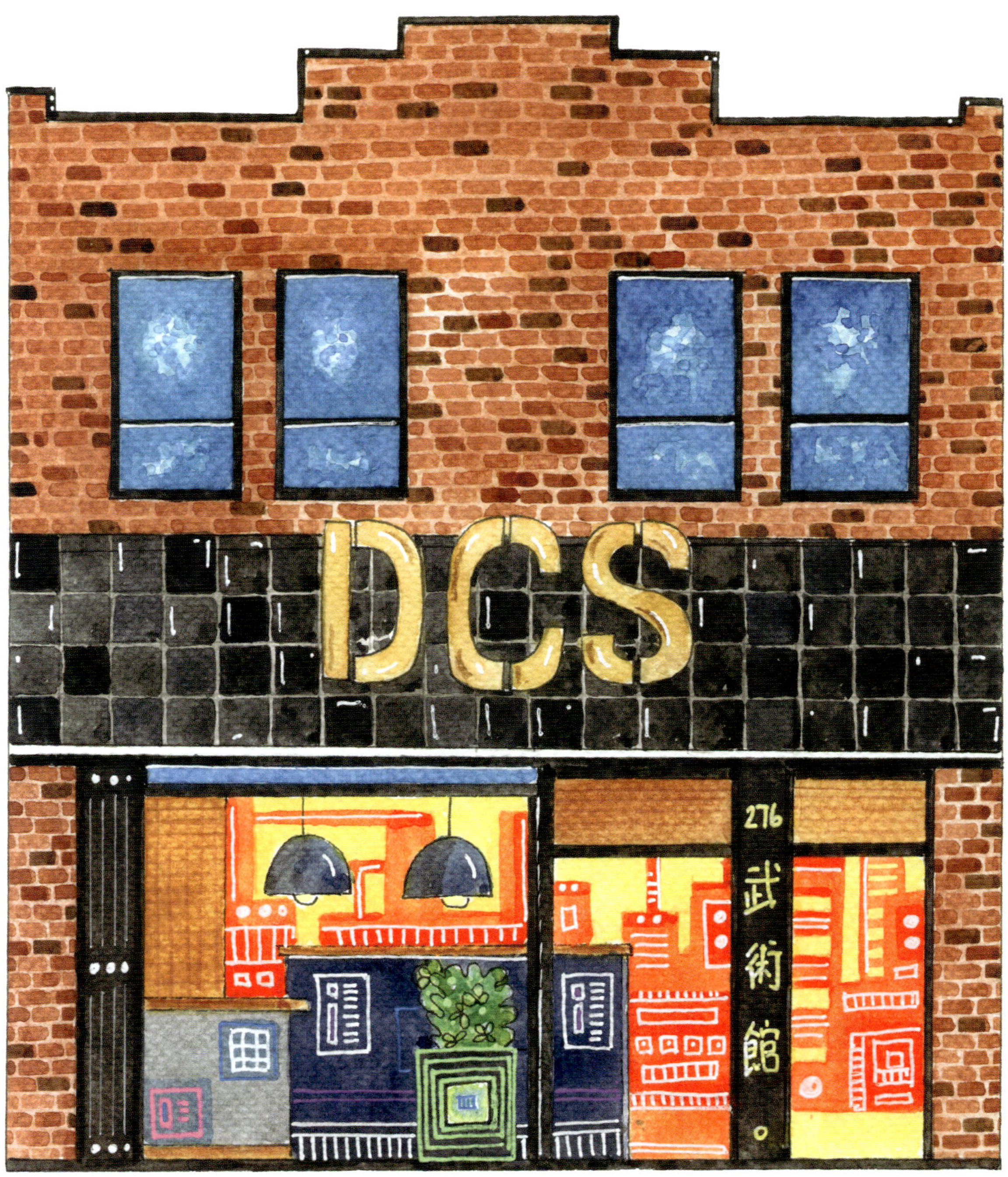

DCS
276
武術館。

Diaz Combat Sports

276 East Pender

Established 2015

Martial arts and athletics have historically been interwoven into the fabric of Chinatown. Whether offered through one of the associations, such as the Mah Society, Hon Hsing Athletic Club, Chinese Freemasons, or as classes at Diaz Combat Sports (DCS), martial arts and athletics provide the community the strength to weather adversity. Created by Ryan "the Lion" Diaz, a two-time mixed martial arts (MMA) world champion, DCS brings together world-class instruction in a modern state-of-the-art facility. Offering classes in Muay Thai kickboxing, boxing, jiujitsu, and conditioning, DCS prides itself on being a friendly, inclusive, and non-intimidating environment that supports beginners and experienced martial artists alike.[39] Echoing the teachings of earlier martial arts masters in Chinatown, DCS recognizes that mental and physical confidence comes with learning martial arts.[40]

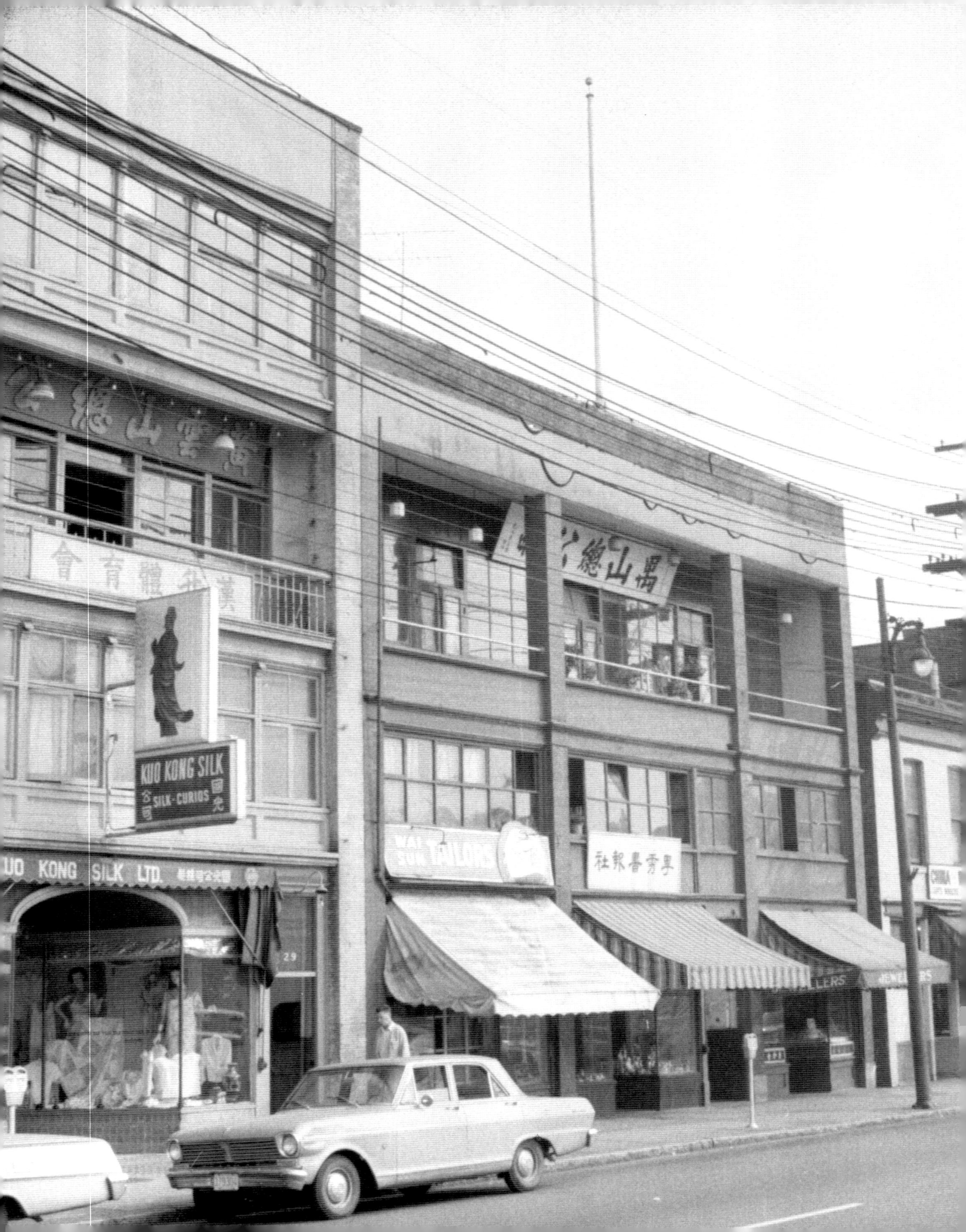
KUO KONG SILK
SILK · CURIOS
KUO KONG SILK LTD.
WAI SUN TAILORS
JEWELLERS
JEWELLERS
CHINA

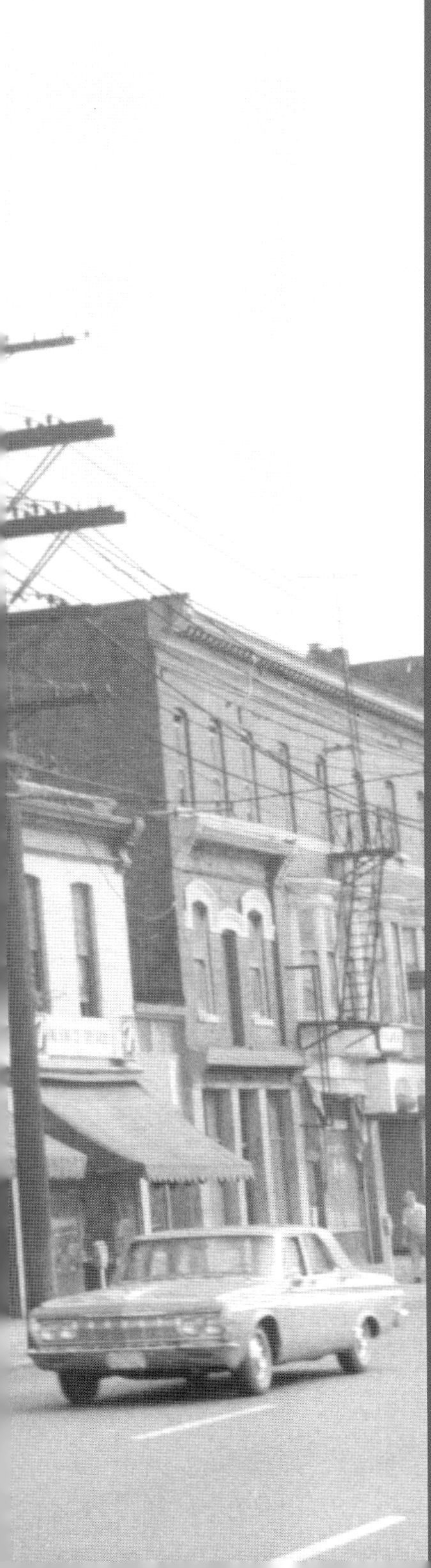

Memory and Place

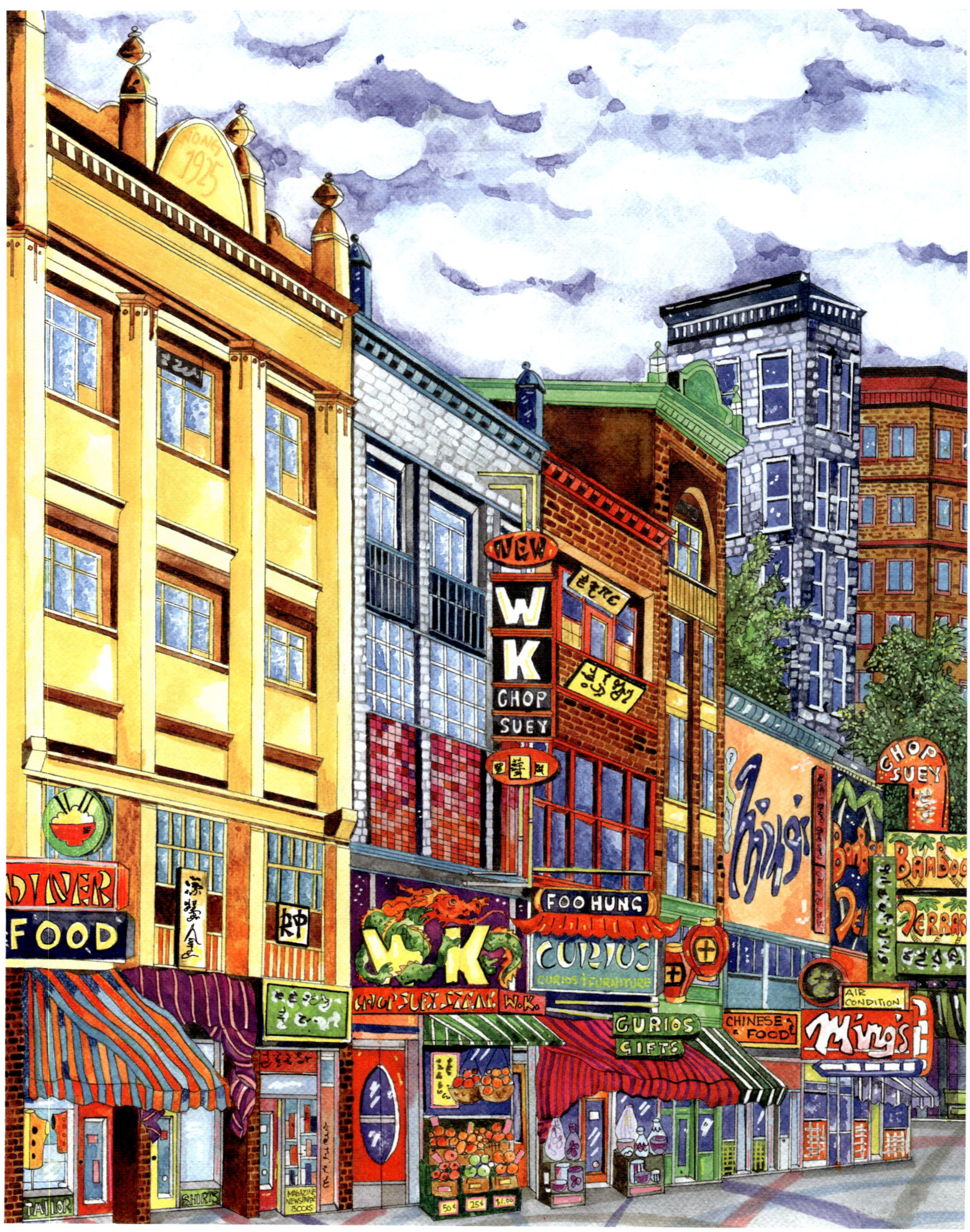

TORONTO
1925
DINER
FOOD
NEW
W K
CHOP
SUEY
FOO HUNG
CURIOS
CURIOS & FURNITURE
W K
CHOP SUEY DINNER W.O.K.
CURIOS
GIFTS
CHOP
SUEY
BAMBOO
TERRACE
CHINESE
FOOD
AIR
CONDITION
Ming's
TAILOR
SHIRTS
MAGAZINE
NEWSPAPER
BOOKS
50¢ 25¢ $1.00

THE LATE JIM WONG-CHU, one of Canada's most celebrated literary pioneers, once commented while dining at Foo's Ho Ho that place offers a connection to memory, that the smell and taste of food sparks something in our brains, and that space acts as a cultural artifact connecting us to the past and, by extension, to who we are.

Ho Ho Chop Suey, or later Foo's Ho Ho, a beloved Chinatown landmark once on the corner of East Pender and Columbia, offered what Jim Wong-Chu called "eating a cultural artifact." Its glowing multi-storey neon sign and comfort food of wok-licking beef chow fun, steaming hot and sour soup, and egg foo young transported more than just tastebuds. The experience was like walking into a time machine, where you were greeted with old-school Cantonese food served among vinyl chairs and faux-wood-panelled walls, taking you back to an era when Chinatown captivated crowds with its neon lights and endless assortment of foods.

What happens when places that unravel our memories and emotions are gone? If a place is lost, what impact does it have on our identities, histories, and heritage?

Place is more than just a physical dot on a map or a collection of buildings; rather, it provides an emotional link to our identities while also connecting us with culture, the past, and the future. Jim Wong-Chu said that experiences such as dining at Ho Ho's, or even simply walking through Chinatown, provide us with sensory cues such as smell, taste, and sight that unravel memories and transport us to a different time and place.

As someone who grew up in the shadows of Chinatown's decline, I realize that my version of a once vibrant Chinatown isn't fully mine; rather, it is imagined and created through the stories told by others and the photographs held in archives and history books. The bustling Chinatown of my childhood is but a fuzzy memory, one I'm not sure really existed until I hear the stories, until others pass down their own memories of Chinatown, until I see the photographs or artifacts at the museum, or when I sit down at a dim sum restaurant.

The histories and illustrations of Vancouver's historic Chinatown attempt to capture some of its tangible and intangible beauty. Most of the illustrations capture the buildings during Chinatown's commercial height in the 1960s and 1970s. In doing so, it serves as a visual archive that hopes to carve out a space for discussion about heritage preservation and the importance of culture for subsequent generations. History remains incomplete without a meaningful inclusion of the experiences of socioeconomically marginalized groups such as the Chinese in Canada.

History is often infused with the politics of power, written by the victors, or those with the power and ability to do so. Often, this one-sided history is limited, as it seeks to encourage collective forgetting of events that may be uncomfortable for some and inconvenient to the current version of history.

Until recently, the history of the Chinese in Canada has existed in the margins. At most, the Chinese have been a short footnote or a face conveniently excluded from a photograph, or at best a minuscule paragraph in a history book. These snapshots rarely honour the life, the messy internal power dynamics, the grief, the loneliness, the friendship and comradery, and the perseverance of the Chinese in Canada.

On July 22, 2006, 121 years after the first Head Tax was passed in 1885, the Canadian government issued a formal apology to Chinese Canadians affected by the discriminatory legislation. Recognizing the generational repercussions of the Head Tax and the Chinese Exclusion Act, the federal government acknowledged that it was an "unfortunate period

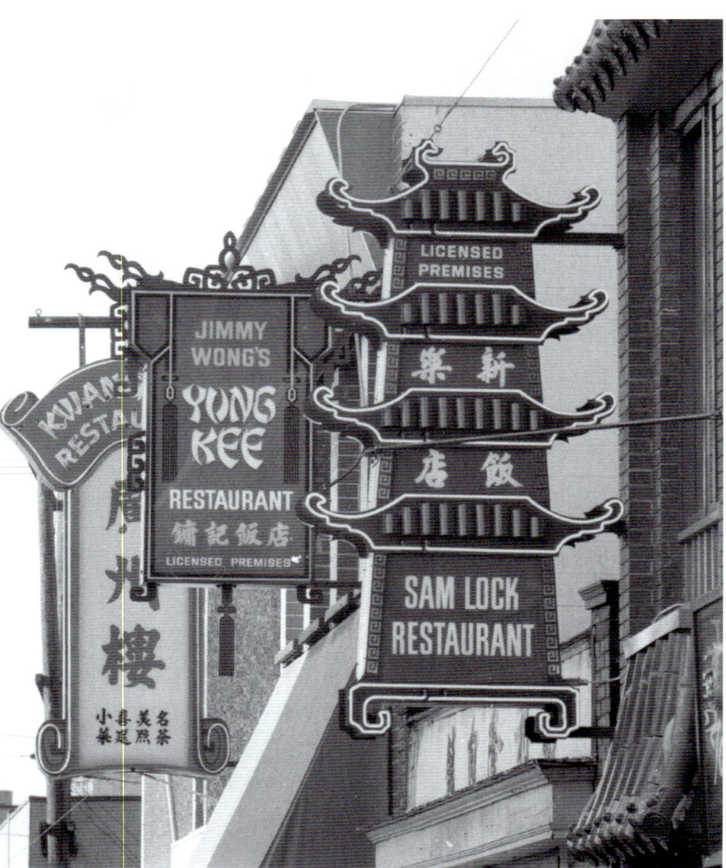

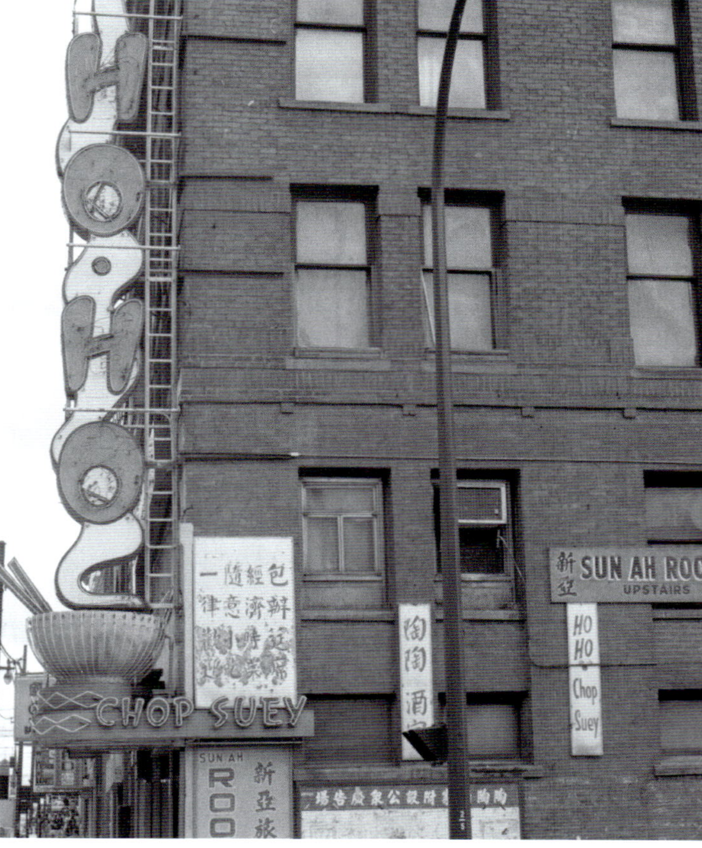

of Canada's past. One during which a group of people—who only sought to build a better life—was repeatedly and deliberately singled out for unjust treatment."[1]

The national apology, however, wasn't an initiative that the federal government spearheaded of its own accord. In 1983, a small group of Chinese Canadians responded to the requests of Dak Leon Mark and Shack Yee, who asked the Canadian government to refund the five-hundred-dollar Head Tax they each paid upon entry into Canada. They were ignored by subsequent Liberal and Conservative governments, until a national apology was finally issued twenty-two years after the initial redress movement had started.

But national apologies are fraught with contentious questions, some of which criticize their performative nature. Critics have also questioned the purpose of an apology, especially when the misdeeds were committed decades earlier, and more importantly, have asked whether the current generation can genuinely understand and acknowledge the pain caused by previous generations.[2]

National apologies are not enough, as the racist belief systems that justified historical wrongs remain deeply ingrained in systemic structures and institutions that continue to sustain inequality between racialized groups. This is where the hard work is. It's easy to utter an apology, but it's much more difficult to ensure that a nation and its people look within themselves to make sure that this kind of injustice never happens again.

Despite the apologies issued by all levels of government and the commitment to recognize the contributions of Chinese Canadians, historic Chinatowns across Canada and the United States continue to struggle. Many Chinatowns, including Vancouver's, have been in decline for years because of the exodus of the Chinese from the area, changing economic priorities, gentrification, and the impacts of the global pandemic. These internal and external forces have been detrimental to the survival of culture and maintenance of Chinatown's unique architecture and life, forcing a number of legacy businesses to make the difficult decision to close their Chinatown location, or to close for good.

Chinatown Vancouver provides a small piece in a big and complex puzzle. The whimsical illustrations and the vision of a reimagined Chinatown blur the present with the past, honouring the stepping stones laid by early Chinese settlers for subsequent generations to succeed.

Acknowledgements

WHEN I SKETCHED MY first building in 2021, I didn't dream of it becoming a book or even a series of paintings documenting Vancouver's Chinatown. It was just a sketch to pass the time during the pandemic. In hindsight, I was an artist before I became an academic. I loved drawing as a kid. In high school, I created a number of pieces in oil paint, soft pastel, pencil, and mixed media, some of which were displayed in school exhibitions. By graduation, I nearly had enough pieces for admission to art school. But as a child of working-class immigrants, I didn't see art as a viable financial option, let alone a career choice. As a result, for more than a decade, I pursued a career as a political scientist that left little room for creativity. Academia made me believe that knowledge creation only existed in university classrooms or stuffy conferences where discussions centred on philosophies written by people who neither look nor grew up like me. More so, academia made me believe that art was something done in secret, a hobby at best, or just a silly doodle in a sketchbook.

Although I didn't realize it immediately, something changed after I posted a painting of Ming Wo Cookware on social media in August 2021. Within minutes, I started receiving comments about Ming Wo, some that hinted that the hardware-turned-cookware store once sold guns and that the building had a secret mahjong hideout for women. I must confess that I didn't know much about the history of Chinatown before I started doing research for this book. Even as a political scientist, my interests were elsewhere because my training taught me that the Chinese weren't part of Canadian history. Even the Canadian history classes I took in university rarely touched upon the Chinese, and if they did, they merely taught us that the Chinese came to Canada to build the railway, and then the Head Tax was passed. The Chinese got a sentence, maybe a paragraph at most. No names or faces, let alone descriptions of Chinatown ladies playing mahjong in a secret clubhouse. But as I posted more paintings throughout 2021 and 2022, I received more and more stories that challenged what academia had taught me. It is these stories that inspired the creation of this book.

Books aren't solitary adventures. The publishing team at House of Anansi were at the heart of putting this book together. Thank you, Shirarose Wilensky, Lucia Kim, Alysia Shewchuk, Karen Brochu, Jenny McWha! I want to especially thank Shirarose for making this all happen—for seeing a book in a series of paintings and for tirelessly transforming these pages into a work of art.

Thanks to the Canada Council for the Arts and the Vancouver Heritage Foundation for funding that assisted with interviews, photography, translation, and my first art exhibition. Thanks to the Vancouver Archives and Vancouver Public Library for maintaining an invaluable collection of historic photographs; many of the images inspired the paintings in this book.

Stories bring history to life and I have an entire community to thank. Thank you, Carol Lee, Lorraine Lowe, Tracy To, Ross Lam, William Liu, Melinda Wong, Keeman Wong, Pearl Louie, David Lee, Janet Lee, Anita Bardel, Sky Lee, Karin Lee, Lincoln Chew, Andy Yan, Olivia Cheng, Suzanna Ng, Cecil Fung, and the Chinese Freemasons for sharing your memories, histories, and photographs. Special thanks to John Atkin for giving advice on dates and reading an early draft. Thank you, everyone in Chinatown for making me feel like I'm part of the community.

Thanks to the many friends, family, and colleagues for the laughter and encouragement. Thanks, Mom and Dad, for taking the risk to come to Canada so we could live better lives. Thanks, Susan, for sharing the kids-of-immigrants experience with me. Thanks to Sherlock for being the resident sock thief. Thank you, Tommy, for always being my biggest advocate.

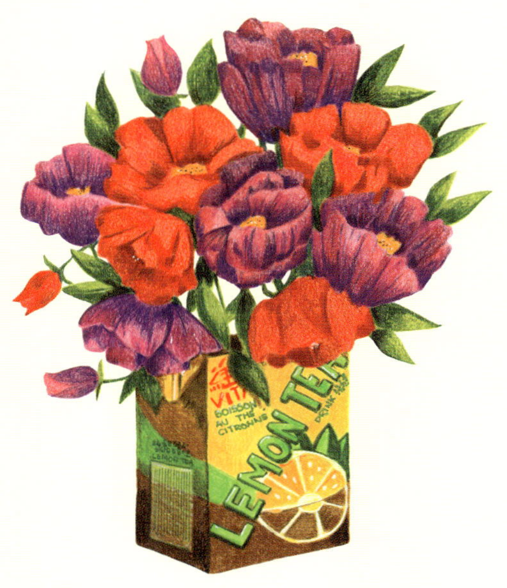

Notes

Introduction

1. Karin Larsen, "Wayward Chinatown Otter Making a Meal of Sun Yat-sen Koi," *CBC News*, November 20, 2018, cbc.ca/news/canada/british-columbia/chinatown-otter-sun-yat-sen-garden-koi-fish-1.4912942.

2. Andrew Weichel, "Chinatown BIA Spending 50% of Budget on Security, President Says in Plea to Vancouver Police," *CTV News*, March 1, 2022, bc.ctvnews.ca/chinatown-bia-spending-50-of-budget-on-security-president-says-in-plea-to-vancouver-police-1.5801933.

Chapter 1

1. Philip Yang, "Sojourners or Settlers: Post-1965 Chinese Immigrants," *Journal of Asian American Studies* 2, no. 1 (1999); Steven B. Miles, *Chinese Diasporas: A Social History of Global Migration* (Cambridge, UK: Cambridge University Press, 2020).

2. Paul Yee, *Saltwater City: An Illustrated History of the Chinese in Vancouver*, rev. ed. (Vancouver: Douglas & McIntyre, 2006); David Chuenyan Lai, *Chinatowns: Towns within Cities in Canada* (Vancouver: University of British Columbia Press, 1988).

3. Lai, *Chinatowns*; Wing Chung Ng, *The Chinese in Vancouver, 1945–80: The Pursuit of Identity and Power* (Vancouver: UBC Press, 1999).

4. Ng, *The Chinese in Vancouver*; Lai, *Chinatowns*.

5. David Chuenyan Lai, "The Visual Character of Chinatowns," *Places* 7, no. 1 (1990).

6. Lai, "Visual Character."

7. Lonely Planet, "Chinatown Millennium Gate," accessed June 29, 2023, lonelyplanet.com/canada/british-columbia/vancouver/gastown-chinatown/attractions/chinatown-millennium-gate/a/poi-sig/1357336/1335106.

8. Yee, *Saltwater City.*

9. Paul Yee, "Sam Kee: A Chinese Business in Early Vancouver," *BC Studies* 69–70 (Spring–Summer 1986).

10. Yee, "Sam Kee."

11. Ashley Moliere, "Built on a Bet: Owner of World-Famous Chinatown Building Says, despite Pandemic, He's Here to Stay," *CBC News*, accessed May 13, 2023, newsinteractives.cbc.ca/longform/sam-kee-building-legacy-chow-family/.

12. Moliere, "Built on a Bet."

13. Frances Hern, *Yip Sang and the First Chinese Canadians* (Victoria, BC: Heritage House, 2011), 40.

14. Hern, *Yip Sang*, 11.

15. Lai, *Chinatowns*; Ng, *The Chinese in Vancouver.*

16. Hern, *Yip Sang*, 55.

17. Canada's Historic Places, "Wing Sang Building," accessed May 13, 2023, historicplaces.ca/en/rep-reg/place-lieu.aspx?id=7835; Heritage Vancouver, "Wing Sang Building," April 16, 2006, heritagevancouver.org/top10-watch-list/2004/6-wing-sang-building-188919011912/; Charlie Smith, "Wing Sang Building Will Become Home to Chinese Canadian Museum with Help from Province and Rennie Family," *Georgia Straight*, February 15, 2022, straight.com/arts/wing-sang-building-will-become-home-to-chinese-canadian-museum-with-help-from-province-and.

18. Interview with Lincoln Chew, March 2023.

19. Canada's Historic Places, "509 Carrall Street," accessed June 2, 2023, historicplaces.ca/en/rep-reg/place-lieu.aspx?id=7899.

20. Yee, *Saltwater City*.

21. Modernize Tailors, "History," accessed May 13, 2023, modernizetailors.com/our-history.

22. Matt Meuse and Gavin Fisher, "Bill Wong, Legendary Vancouver Chinatown Tailor, Dead at 95," *CBC News*, April 16, 2017, cbc.ca/news/canada/british-columbia/bill-wong-obit-1.4072560.

23. Modernize Tailors, "History."

24. Cheryl Rossi, "Advocacy Group Hopes to Save Foo's Ho Ho," *Vancouver Courier*, July 30, 2010.

25. Interview with Pearl Louie, June 2023.

26. Yee, *Saltwater City*; Paul Yee, *Chinatown: An Illustrated History of the Chinese Communities of Victoria, Vancouver, Calgary, Winnipeg, Toronto, Ottawa, Montreal and Halifax* (Toronto: Lorimer, 2005); Jonathan D. Spence, *The Search for Modern China* (New York: W. W. Norton, 1999).

27. Spence, *Search for Modern China*.

28. Victoria's Chinatown, "Chinese Empire Reform Association: The First Worldwide Chinese Political Association," accessed May 13, 2023, chinatown.library.uvic.ca/index.htmlq%3Dchinese_empire_reform_association.html; Canada's Historic Places, "Lim Sai Hor Association Building," accessed May 8, 2023, historicplaces.ca/en/rep-reg/place-lieu.aspx?id=2809; Vancouver Heritage Foundation, "Lim Sai Hor Association Building," *Vancouver Heritage Site Finder*, accessed May 8, 2023, heritagesitefinder.ca/location/525-carrall-st-vancouver-bc/.

29. Chinese Canadian Historical Society, "Historic Study of the Society Buildings in Chinatown" (July 2005).

30. Chinese Canadian Historical Society, "Historic Study."

31. Canada's Historic Places, "Lim Sai Hor Association Building"; Chinese Canadian Historical Society, "Historic Study"; Lim Sai Hor Kow Mock Benevolent Association, "Lim Sai Hor Kow Mock Benevolent Association," accessed May 13, 2023, limassociation.ca.

32. Chinese Canadian Historical Society, "Historic Study ."

33. Fredy Gonzalez, "The Rise and Spread of the Hong Men Chee Kung Tong in the Cantonese Pacific and Beyond," *Pacific Historical Review* 92, no. 1 (2023): 26.

34. Interview with the Chinese Freemasons, September 2022.

35. Norman Shields, "Chee Kung Tong Building, Barkerville, British Columbia," *The Journal of the Society for the Study of Architecture in Canada* 33, no. 2 (2008).

36. Gonzalez, "The Rise and Spread," 26.

37. Canada's Historic Places, "Chinese Times Building," accessed May 8, 2023, historicplaces.ca/en/rep-reg/place-lieu.aspx?id=1187; Vancouver Heritage Foundation, "Chinese Times Building," *Vancouver Heritage Site Finder*, accessed May 8, 2023, heritagesitefinder.ca/location/1-e-pender-st-vancouver-bc/.

38. Dr. Sun Yat-sen Classical Chinese Garden, "Dr. Sun Yat-sen Classical Chinese Garden," accessed May 13, 2023, vancouverchinesegarden.com/.

39. Interview with Lorraine Lowe, July 2023.

40. Chandler Walter, "A Look Inside: $9.5-Million Chinatown Penthouse with Glass-Bottom Pool," *Daily Hive*, August 10, 2017, dailyhive.com/vancouver/vancouver-condo-135-keefer-street-vancouver.

Chapter 2

1. Ng, *The Chinese in Vancouver*, 14.

2. Ng, *The Chinese in Vancouver*.

3. Ng, *The Chinese in Vancouver*.

4. Ng, *The Chinese in Vancouver*, 14; Yee, *Chinatown*; Yee, *Saltwater City*.

5. Canada's Historic Places, "Chinese Benevolent Association Building," accessed May 15, 2023,

historicplaces.ca/en/rep-reg/place-lieu.aspx?id=7800; Vancouver Heritage Foundation, "Chinese Benevolent Association," *Vancouver Heritage Site Finder*, accessed May 15, 2023, heritagesitefinder.ca/location/104-108-e-pender-st-vancouver-bc/.

6. Ng, *The Chinese in Vancouver*, 11.

7. Chinese Canadian Historical Society, "Historic Study ."

8. Ng, *The Chinese in Vancouver*.

9. Chinese Canadian Historical Society, "Historic Study," 29.

10. Wayson Choy, *Paper Shadows: A Chinatown Childhood* (Toronto: Penguin, 2000).

11. Yee, *Saltwater City*, 98.

12. Canada's Historic Places, "Chinese School," accessed May 14, 2023, historicplaces.ca/en/rep-reg/place-lieu .aspx?id=7794.

13. Ng, *The Chinese in Vancouver*.

14. Lai, *Chinatowns*, 195.

15. Chinese Canadian Historical Society, "Historic Study."

16. Canada's Historic Places, "Yue Shan Society Buildings," accessed May 13, 2023, historicplaces .ca/en/rep-reg/place-lieu.aspx?id=11192; Vancouver Heritage Foundation, "Yue Shan Society Buildings," *Vancouver Heritage Site Finder*, accessed May 13, 2023, heritagesitefinder.ca/location/43-47-e-pender/.

17. Ng, *The Chinese in Vancouver*, 70.

18. Ng, *The Chinese in Vancouver*, 70.

19. Chinese Canadian Historical Society, "Historic Study."; Canada's Historic Places, "Mah Society Building," accessed May 14, 2023, historicplaces.ca/en/rep-reg/place-lieu.aspx?id=7802.

20. Bamboo Village, "Bamboo Village," accessed May 14, 2023, bamboovillage.ca.

21. Vancouver Heritage Foundation, "135 E Pender St," *Vancouver Heritage Site Finder*, accessed May 14, 2023, heritagesitefinder.ca/location/135-e-pender-st-vancouver-bc.

22. Bamboo Village, "Bamboo Village."

23. Canada's Historic Places, "Chin Wing Chun Society Building," May 14, 2023, historicplaces.ca/en/rep-reg/place-lieu.aspx?id=7803.

24. John Mackie, "Chinese Society Artifacts a Mountain of Gold for Heritage Buffs," *Vancouver Sun*, October 15, 2022, vancouversun.com/news/local-news/chinese-society-artifacts-a-mountain-of-gold-for-heritage-buffs.

25. Interview with the Chinese Freemasons.

26. Interview with Andy Yan, June 2023.

27. Bob Kronbauer, "This 1987 Vancouver TV Commercial for Acid Wash Jeans!!!," *Vancouver Is Awesome*, August 12, 2014, vancouverisawesome.com/business/this-1987-vancouver-tv-commercial-for-acid-wash-jeans-1929238.

28. Vancouver Heritage Foundation, "110–116 E Pender St," *Vancouver Heritage Site Finder*, accessed May 14, 2023, heritagesitefinder.ca/location/110-116-e-pender-st-vancouver-bc/.

29. Winston Szeto, "Chinese Freemasons Celebrate 160 Years of Community and Cultural Support in Canada," CBC *News*, March 23, 2023, cbc.ca/news/canada/british-columbia/canada-chinese-freemasons-160-anniversary-1.6787635.

30. Lai, *Chinatowns*, 211.

31. Gonzalez, "The Rise and Spread."

32. Interview with the Chinese Freemasons.

33. Edgar Wickberg, "Chinese and Canadian Influences on Chinese Politics in Vancouver, 1900-1947," *BC Studies* 45 (Spring 1980): 46.

34. Stephen Frans Brouwers, "Chinese Architectural Practice and the Spatial Discourse of Vancouver's Chinatown" (master's thesis, University of British

Columbia, 2008); Wickberg, "Chinese and Canadian Influences."

35. Interview with Karin Lee, June 2023.

36. Ng, *The Chinese in Vancouver*, 110.

37. Ng, *The Chinese in Vancouver*, 110.

38. Ng, *The Chinese in Vancouver*, 48–50.

39. Ng, *The Chinese in Vancouver*, 119.

40. Ng, *The Chinese in Vancouver*, 120.

41. Ng, *The Chinese in Vancouver*, 49–50.

42. Ng, *The Chinese in Vancouver*, 113–14.

43. Ng, *The Chinese in Vancouver*, 111.

44. Wing Chung Ng, "Chinatown Theatre as Transnational Business: New Evidence from Vancouver during the Exclusion Era," *BC Studies* 148 (Winter 2005/06): 117–20.

45. Jim Wong-Chu, *Chinatown Ghosts: The Poems and Photographs of Jim Wong-Chu*, rev. ed. (Vancouver: Arsenal Pulp Press, 2018).

46. Interview with Sky Lee, March 2023.

Chapter 3

1. Samantha Barbas, "'I'll Take Chop Suey': Restaurants as Agents of Culinary and Cultural Exchange," *Journal of Popular Culture* 36, no. 4 (2003): 669–86.

2. Andrew Coe, *Chop Suey: A Cultural History of Chinese Food in the United States* (Oxford: Oxford University Press, 2009); Ann Hui, *Chop Suey Nation: The Legion Cafe and Other Stories from Canada's Chinese Restaurants* (Madeira Park, BC: Douglas & McIntyre, 2018).

3. Yee, *Saltwater City*; Yee, *Chinatown*.

4. Tammy Kwan, "Legendary Chinatown Cookware Shop Ming Wo to Close Original Location after More than 100 Years in Business," *Georgia Straight*, January 6, 2020, straight.com/food/1343356/ legendary-chinatown-cookware-shop-ming-wo-close-original-location-after-more-100-years; John Mackie, "After More than 100 Years, Ming Wo Will Close Its Chinatown Kitchen Shop," *Vancouver Sun*, January 7, 2020, vancouversun.com/news/ local-news/after-more-than-100-years-ming-wo-will-close-its-chinatown-kitchen-shop; Michelle Morton, "Ming Wo Cookware's Family-Owned Business in Chinatown Closes Its Doors," *Daily Hive*, March 4, 2020, dailyhive.com/vancouver/ ming-wo-cookware-chinatown-closed.

5. Canada's Historic Places, "Ming Wo Building," accessed May 13, 2023, historicplaces.ca/en/rep-reg/ place-lieu.aspx?id=7833.

6. Yee, *Saltwater City*, 36.

7. Ng, "Chinatown Theatre."

8. Barbas, "'I'll Take Chop Suey.'"

9. J. H. White, "Philanthropist Carol Lee Aims to Reinvent Vancouver Chinatown," *Magnifissance*, January 13, 2020, magnifissance.com/print-edition/ issue-096/vancouver-chinatown/.

10. Canada's Historic Places, "Sun Ah Hotel," accessed May 14, 2023, historicplaces.ca/en/rep-reg/place-lieu.aspx?id=7761; Vancouver Heritage Foundation, "Sun Ah Hotel," *Vancouver Heritage Site Finder*, accessed May 14, 2023, heritagesitefinder.ca/ location/100-e-pender-st-vancouver-bc.

11. Vancouver Heritage Foundation, "Chinese Theatre," *Vancouver Heritage Site Finder*, accessed June 22, 2023, heritagesitefinder.ca/ location/124-e-pender-st-vancouver-bc.

12. Ng, "Chinatown Theatre."

13. Ng, "Chinatown Theatre."

14. Ng, "Chinatown Theatre."

15. Rosanne Amosovs Sia, "Making and Defending Intimate Spaces: White Waitresses Policed in Vancouver's Chinatown Cafes" (master's thesis, University of British Columbia, 2010).

16. Sia, "Making and Defending."

17. Kevin Griffin, "Canada 150: Chu Lai Fought against Anti-Chinese Discrimination and Won," *Vancouver Sun*, June 6, 2017, vancouversun.com/news/local-news/canada-150/canada-150-chu-lai-fought-against-anti-chinese-discrimination-and-won.

18. Victoria Yap, "What Is Dim Sum? Our Beginner's Guide to the Cantonese Cuisine," February 5, 2020, honestfoodtalks.com/dim-sum-guide-yum-cha/; Kat Thompson, "The Essential Guide to Dim Sum," *Thrillist*, May 16, 2022, thrillist.com/eat/nation/best-dim-sum-dishes-food; Huy Vu, "The Ultimate Guide to Chinese Dim Sum (Menu & Ordering Guide)," *Hungry Huy*, April 5, 2021, hungryhuy.com/dim-sum-guide/.

19. Yap, "Dim Sum"; AFP, "The Do's and Don'ts of Proper Dim Sum Etiquette," *Tatler*, February 12, 2013, tatlerasia.com/dining/food/the-do-s-and-don-ts-of-proper-dim-sum-etiquette.

20. University of British Columbia, "Chinese Canadian Stories: Uncommon Histories from a Common Past," accessed July 16, 2023, wayback.archive-it.org/4160/20160413230213/http://ccs.library.ubc.ca/trim/s/en/index.html.

21. University of British Columbia, "Chinese Canadian Stories."

22. Charlie Smith, "The Making of Real-Estate Mogul Robert H. Lee," *Georgia Straight*, October 17, 2012, straight.com/news/making-real-estate-mogul-robert-h-lee.

23. University of British Columbia, "Chinese Canadian Stories."

24. Glen Korstrom, "Philanthropist, Businessman Robert H. Lee Dies at 86," *Vancouver Is Awesome*, February 20, 2020, vancouverisawesome.com/courier-archive/news/philanthropist-businessman-robert-h-lee-dies-at-86-3117340; Smith, "The Making of Real-Estate Mogul Robert H. Lee."

25. Korstrom, "Philanthropist, Businessman Robert H. Lee Dies at 86"; Smith, "The Making of Real-Estate Mogul Robert H. Lee."

26. Canada's Historic Places, "127 East Pender Street," accessed May 14, 2023, historicplaces.ca/en/rep-reg/place-lieu.aspx?id=7801.

27. Interview with Carol Lee, April 2024.

28. Gavin Fisher, "History of Famous Vancouver Chinatown Restaurant Revealed through Collected Menus," CBC *News*, July 24, 2016, cbc.ca/news/canada/british-columbia/history-of-famous-vancouver-chinatown-restaurant-revealed-through-collected-menus-1.3692214.

29. Interview with Carol Lee.

30. Interview with Carol Lee.

31. Yee, *Saltwater City*, 103.

32. Yee, *Saltwater City*, 107.

33. Yee, *Saltwater City*, 108.

34. Interview with Melinda Wong and Keeman Wong, June 2023.

35. Interview with Melinda Wong and Keeman Wong.

36. Interview with David Lee, Janis Lee, and Anita Bardel, November 2022.

37. Lai, *Chinatowns*, 215–16.

38. Interview with David Lee, Janis Lee, and Anita Bardel.

39. Interview with David Lee, Janis Lee, and Anita Bardel.

40. John Mackie, "This Week in History, 1966: The Shanghai Junk Sails into Chinatown," *Vancouver Sun*, February 17, 2023, vancouversun.com/news/this-week-in-history-1966-the-shanghai-junk-sails-into-chinatown.

41. Mackie.

42. Mackie; Vancouver Chinatown Today (blog), "Chinatown History: From Kublai Khan to TD Bank via Shanghai Junk," May 7, 2016, chinatown.today/2016/05/chinatown-history-shanghai-junk/.

43. Mackie, "This Week in History, 1966."

44. Aaron Chapman, *Vancouver After Dark: The Wild History of a City's Nightlife* (Vancouver: Arsenal Pulp, 2020).; Aaron Chapman, "This Legendary Chinatown Hotspot Once Hosted Richard Pryor, Nina Simone," *Vancouver Is Awesome*, November 15, 2019, vancouverisawesome.com/history/this-legendary-chinatown-hotspot-once-hosted-richard-pryor-nina-simone-3111031.

Chapter 4

1. Angela Ho and Alan Chen, "Vancouver Chinatown Food Security Report" (Hua foundation, August 2017).

2. Yee, *Saltwater City*, 58.

3. Yee, *Saltwater City*, 58.

4. Yee, *Saltwater City*, 87.

5. Yee, *Saltwater City*, 87; Lai, *Chinatowns.*

6. Yee, *Saltwater City*, 87.

7. Yee, *Saltwater City*, 92.

8. E. G. Perrault, *Tong: The Story of Tong Louie, Vancouver's Quiet Titan* (Madeira Park, BC: Harbour, 2002).

9. John Mackie, "Canada 150: Tong Louie Built His Family Company into a B.C. Business Empire," *Vancouver Sun*, June 27, 2017, vancouversun.com/news/local-news/canada-150/canada-150-tong-louie-built-his-family-company-into-a-b-c-business-empire.

10. Lai, *Chinatowns*, 85–86.

11. Carlito Pablo, "Renewal Planned for Vancouver Chinatown Site Where Louie Family Business behind London Drugs Began," *Georgia Straight*, October 6, 2020, straight.com/news/renewal-planned-for-vancouver-chinatown-site-where-louie-family-business-behind-london-drugs; Canada's Historic Places, "252 East Georgia Street," accessed June 10, 2023, historicplaces.ca/en/rep-reg/place-lieu.aspx?id=2742.

12. Vancouver Heritage Foundation, "236 E Pender St," *Vancouver Heritage Site Finder*, accessed June 10, 2023, heritagesitefinder.ca/location/236-e-pender-st-vancouver-bc.

13. *Georgia Straight*, "Family-Run Forum Home Appliances in Vancouver Has High-Quality Appliances for Every Budget," November 12, 2021, straight.com/living/family-run-forum-home-appliances-in-vancouver-has-high-quality-appliances-for-every-budget.

14. Interview with Tracy To, Forum Appliances, June 2023.

15. Kam Wai Dim Sum, "Kam Wai Dim Sum," accessed June 10, 2023, kamwaidimsum.ca; Michelle Sproule, "Secrets of Chinatown Shops, with William Liu of Kam Wai Dim Sum," *Scout Magazine*, September 29, 2022, scoutmagazine.ca/2022/09/29/secrets-of-chinatown-shops-with-william-liu-of-kam-wai-dim-sum/; Joanne Lee-Young, "Chinatown Dim Sum Maker Opens Revamped Heritage Business," *Vancouver Sun*, February 8, 2021, vancouversun.com/business/chinatown-dim-sum-maker-opens-revamped-heritage-business; Joshua Berson and Christopher Cheung, "Keeping Calm and Wrapping Dim Sum," *Tyee*, July 17, 2020, thetyee.ca/News/2020/07/17/Kam-Wai-Dim-Sum-Pandemic-Vancouver-Chinatown/.2023.

16. Vancouver Heritage Foundation, "249–251 E Pender St," *Vancouver Heritage Site Finder*, accessed June 10, 2023, heritagesitefinder.ca/location/251-e-pender-st-vancouver-bc.

17. Interview with William Liu, Kam Wai Dim Sum, August 2022.

18. Vancouver Heritage Foundation, "266–272 E Pender St," *Vancouver Heritage Site Finder*, accessed June 10, 2023, heritagesitefinder.ca/location/272-e-pender-st-vancouver-bc.

19. *CBC News*, "Cantonese Barbecue Meat Was Almost Banned in Canada If Not for 'The Good Fight':

Vancouver Island Professor," November 19, 2022, cbc
.ca/news/canada/british-columbia/cantonese-bbq-
meats-banned-vancouver-island-professor-1.6657625.

20. Joanne Lee-Young, "The Demise of Chinatown's
BBQ Meat Shops," *Vancouver Sun*, September
30, 2015, vancouversun.com/news/metro/
the-demise-of-chinatowns-bbq-meat-shops.

21. Karon Liu, "The Relatively Unknown Art of Chinese
Barbecue," *Toronto Star*, May 16, 2018, thestar.com/
life/2018/05/16/the-relatively-unknown-art-of-
chinese-barbecue.html.

22. Clarissa Wei, "A (Very) Comprehensive Illustrated
Guide to Cantonese Barbecue," *Goldthread*,
October 9, 2018, goldthread2.com/food/
comprehensive-cantonese-barbecue-guide/
article/3000169; Gabrielle Caselis, "Hidden Hong
Kong: A History of Cantonese Barbecue (Siu
Mei)," *Localiiz*, August 20, 2021, localiiz.com/post/
food-drink-history-cantonese-barbecue-siu-mei.

23. Vancouver Heritage Foundation, "253 E Pender
St," *Vancouver Heritage Site Finder*, accessed
June 10, 2023, heritagesitefinder.ca/
location/253-e-pender-st-vancouver-bc.

24. Kristen Moran, "Ink Runs Dry on 104-Year-Old
Chinatown Print Shop," *Vancouver Is Awesome*, March
20, 2014, vancouverisawesome.com/courier-archive/
news/ink-runs-dry-on-104-year-old-chinatown-print-
shop-2974910.

25. Kristen Moran, "Chinatown's Ho Sun Hing Printers Shuts Its Doors," *Business in Vancouver*, March
25, 2014, biv.com/article/2014/03/chinatowns-ho-
sun-hing-printers-shuts-its-doors; John Mackie,
"Canada's Oldest Chinese Print Shop Closes at
6 p.m. Today, after 106 Years in Business," *Vancouver Sun*, March 27, 2014, vancouversun.com/
news/metro/last-day-for-a-legend-in-vancouvers-
historic-chinatown.2023, biv.com/article/2014/03/
chinatowns-ho-sun-hing-printers-shuts-its-doors.

26. Tosi & Company, "Tosi & Company," accessed June
10, 2023, tosifoods.com/.

27. John Atkin, "A Brief History of 'Little Italy,'" City of
Vancouver, April 2016, vancouver.ca/files/cov/brief-
history-of-little-italy.pdf.

28. Courtney Dickson, "Closure of Popular, Long-
Running Restaurant Another Blow to Vancouver's
Chinatown," *CBC News*, March 14, 2023, cbc.ca/news/
canada/british-columbia/kent-s-kitchen-vancouver-
chinatown-closing-1.6778600.

29. Christopher Cheung and Joshua Berson, "In
the Pandemic, 'Gain Wah' Keeps Dishing Out
Chinatown Classics," *Tyee*, July 13, 2020, thetyee
.ca/News/2020/07/13/In-The-Pandemic-Gain-
Wah-Keeps-Dishing-Chinatown-Classics/;
Rafferty Baker, "An Affordable Place to Eat in
Vancouver's Chinatown, Gain Wah's Future
Is Now in Peril," *CBC News*, September 17,
2022, cbc.ca/news/canada/british-columbia/
gain-wah-future-uncertain-1.6586572.

30. Canada's Historic Places, "218 Keefer Street,"
accessed June 10, 2023, historicplaces.ca/en/rep-reg/
place-lieu.aspx?id=2746.

31. Japanese Canadian History, "General Overview,"
accessed June 19, 2023, japanesecanadianhistory.net/
historical-overview/general-overview/.

32. Phnom Penh Restaurant, "Phnom Penh Restaurant,"
accessed June 10, 2023, phnompenhrestaurant.ca.

33. Larry Olmsted, "Vancouver's Cambodian-Vietnamese
Eatery Is Worth the Wait," *USA Today*, September
12, 2017, usatoday.com/story/travel/columnist/
greatamericanbites/2017/09/12/phnom-penh-
restaurant-vancouver-canada/653861001/.

34. Mia Stainsby, "Vancouver's Vietnamese
Restaurants—Their Backstories," *Vancouver Sun*,
June 18, 2010, vancouversun.com/news/staff-blogs/
vancouvers-vietnamese-restaurants-their-backstories.

35. Sam Evans, "Why Hong Kong's Cha Chaan Teng Are
Worth Saving—They're 'Essential to the Culture, Like

Pubs Are in the UK,'" *South China Morning Post*, May 6, 2023, scmp.com/magazines/post-magazine/long-reads/article/3219471/essential-culture-pubs-are-uk-why-hong-kongs-cha-chaan-teng-are-worth-saving.

36. Janice Lam, "Hidden Hong Kong: A History of the Cha Chaan Teng, the Humble Hong Kong Tea Restaurant," *Localiiz*, April 22, 2022, localiiz.com/post/food-drink-history-cha-chaan-teng-hong-kong.

37. Viola Gaskell, "Hong Kong's Cha Chaan Tengs," *Whetstone Magazine*, accessed June 27, 2023, whetstonemagazine.com/journal/hong-kongs-cha-chaan-tengs.

38. Man Lai Cheung, Wilson K. S. Leung, Jun-Hwa Cheah, Kian Yeik Koay, and Bryan Cheng-Yu Hsu, "Key Tea Beverage Values Driving Tourists' Memorable Experiences: An Empirical Study in Hong Kong-Style Café Memorable Experience," *International Journal of Culture, Tourism, and Hospitality Research* 15, no. 3 (2021): 355–70; Lam, "Hidden Hong Kong."

39. New Town Bakery & Restaurant, "New Town Bakery & Restaurant," accessed May 14, 2023, newtownbakery.ca/.

Chapter 5

1. Christopher Cheung, "In Chinatown, Precious Few Places for Seniors to Live," *Tyee*, February 8, 2023, thetyee.ca/News/2023/02/08/Few-Places-For-Seniors-Living-In-Chinatown/; Louisa-May Khoo, "January 2023 Vancouver Chinatown Affordable Seniors Housing Inventory: Towards Chinatown as Campus of Care," March 7, 2023.

2. Cheung, "In Chinatown"; Khoo, "Affordable Seniors Housing Inventory."

3. Lai, *Chinatowns*.

4. Friederike Landau-Donnelly, "Ghostly Murals: Tracing the Politics of Public Art in Vancouver's Hogan's Alley," *Environment and Planning: Politics and Space* 41, no. 6 (2023): 1147–65.

5. Bridgette Watson, "6 Years after Its Rejection, Chinatown Condo Project Is Back on the Table and Dividing the Neighbourhood," *CBC News*, May 25, 2023, cbc.ca/news/canada/british-columbia/chinatown-condo-controversy-1.6854765.

6. Christopher Cheung, "Chinatown Condos a Go After Years of Protest," *Tyee*, June 28, 2023, thetyee.ca/News/2023/06/28/Chinatown-Condos-Go-After-Years-Protest/; Mike Howell, "Vote on Controversial Chinatown Condo Project Pushed to June 12," *Vancouver Is Awesome*, May 30, 2023, vancouverisawesome.com/local-news/vote-on-controversial-chinatown-condo-project-pushed-to-june-12-beedie-7071653.

7. Elizabeth McSheffrey and Jasmine Bala, "Debate Heats up in Chinatown as Embattled 105 Keefer St. Development Is Reviewed Again," *Global News*, May 25, 2023, globalnews.ca/news/9723562/opposing-opinions-chinatown-105-keefer-street/.

8. Peter Kwong, *The New Chinatown*, rev. ed. (New York: Hill and Wang, 1996); Him Mark Lai, *Becoming Chinese American: A History of Communities and Institutions* (Lanham, MD: AltaMira, 2004); Laureen D. Hom, "Revitalizing Chinatown for a New Generation: The Community Politics of the Business Improvement District." *Journal of Urban Affairs* (2023): 1–17; Collyn Chan and Amy Zhou, "How to Save Chinatown: Preserving Affordability and Community Service through Ethnic Retail," *Berkeley Planning Journal* 32, no. 1 (2022).

9. Lise Mahieus and Eugene McCann, "'Hot+Noisy' Public Space: Conviviality, 'Unapologetic Asianness,' and the Future of Vancouver's Chinatown," *Urban Planning* 8, no. 4 (2023): 77–88; Diane Wong, "Shop Talk and Everyday Sites of Resistance to Gentrification in Manhattan's Chinatown," *Women's Studies Quarterly* 47, no. 1 & 2 (Spring/Summer 2019): 132–48.

10. Lai, *Chinatowns*.

11. Khoo, "Affordable Seniors Housing Inventory"; Canada's Historic Places, "May Wah Hotel," accessed June 10, 2023, historicplaces.ca/en/rep-reg/place-lieu.aspx?id=7861.2023.

12. Joanne Lee-Young, "COVID-19: Building Manager of Chinatown SRO a Front-Line Worker for Its Vulnerable Seniors," *Vancouver Sun*, April 17, 2020, vancouversun.com/news/local-news/building-manager-of-chinatown-sro-a-front-line-worker-for-its-vulnerable-seniors.

13. Khoo, "Affordable Seniors Housing Inventory."

14. Cheung, "In Chinatown."

15. Lai, *Chinatowns*, 126.

16. Lai, *Chinatowns*, 126.

17. Lai, *Chinatowns*, 129.

18. Don Alexander, "Remembering the Legacy of Shirley Chan: Saving Vancouver's Chinatown Neighborhood," *Planning West* 61, no. 1 (2019): 12–14.

19. Lai, *Chinatowns*, 130–31.

20. Lai, *Chinatowns*, 131–32.

21. Mau Dan Gardens Cooperative, "History of Mau Dan," accessed June 10, 2023, maudancoop.ca/about-the-co-op/history-of-mau-dan.

22. Landau-Donnelly, "Ghostly Murals."

23. John Mackie, "This Week in History: 1948: A Giant 'Slum Clearance' Is Proposed for Strathcona," *Vancouver Sun*, October 18, 2019, vancouversun.com/news/local-news/this-week-in-history-1948-a-giant-slum-clearance-is-proposed-for-strathcona.

24. Christopher Cheung, "Repairing the Damage of 'Slum Clearance' in Vancouver's Inner City," *Tyee*, June 27, 2018, thetyee.ca/News/2018/06/27/Vancouver-Inner-City-Slum-Clearance-Repair/.

25. Cheung, "Repairing the Damage."

26. Maryse Zeidler, "How Nixing a Downtown Freeway 50 Years Ago Made Vancouver One of the World's Most Liveable Cities," CBC News, December 3, 2017, cbc.ca/news/canada/british-columbia/vancouver-freeway-not-built-1.4428986.

27. Tyler Stiem, "Story of Cities #38: Vancouver Dumps Its Freeway Plan for a More Beautiful Future," *Guardian*, May 9, 2016, theguardian.com/cities/2016/may/09/story-cities-38-vancouver-canada-freeway-protest-liveable-city.

28. Lai, *Chinatowns*, 130.

29. Stiem, "Story of Cities #38."

30. Lai, *Chinatowns*, 129.

31. Brouwers, "Chinese Architectural Practice."

32. Vancouver Heritage Foundation, "200 East Pender St," *Vancouver Heritage Site Finder*, accessed June 10, 2023, heritagesitefinder.ca/location/200-e-pender-st-vancouver-bc.

33. Akshay Kulkarni, "New Mural in Vancouver's Chinatown Aims to Help Spark Area's Revitalization," CBC News, May 2, 2022, cbc.ca/news/canada/british-columbia/yvr-chinatown-new-mural-1.6437790.

34. Vancouver Heritage Foundation, "263–265 E Pender St," *Vancouver Heritage Site Finder*, accessed June 10, 2023, heritagesitefinder.ca/location/265-e-pender-st-vancouver-bc.

35. Kissa Tanto, "Kissa Tanto," accessed April 28, 2024, kissatanto.com.

36. Vancouver Heritage Foundation, "269–271 E Pender St," *Vancouver Heritage Site Finder*, accessed June 10, 2023, heritagesitefinder.ca/location/271-e-pender-st-vancouver-bc/.

37. Jamie Mah, "The Story of Bao Bei's Beautiful Neon Sign," *Scout Magazine*, May 16, 2018, scoutmagazine.ca/the-story-of-bao-beis-beautiful-neon-sign/.

38. Brodie Vissers, "Propaganda with Will Wang," *Nomad Barista*, May 13, 2016, thenomadbarista.com/propaganda; Andrew Morrison, "Sleek and Simple: Propaganda Coffee Now Open On East Pender St. in Chinatown," *Scout Magazine*, February 2, 2015,

scoutmagazine.ca/diner-sleek-simple-propaganda-coffee-now-open-on-east-pender-st-in-chinatown/.

39. Diaz Combat Sports, "This $5 Million Martial Arts Facility Will Have Vancouverites Working with World Champion Trainers," *Vancouver Is Awesome*, accessed April 28, 2024, vancouverisawesome.com/sponsored/dcs-diaz-combat-sports-vancouver-2781026.

40. Diaz Combat Sports, "Why DCS," accessed April 28, 2024, diazcombatsports.com/why-dcs/.

Conclusion

1. Government of Canada, "Prime Minister Harper Offers Full Apology for the Chinese Head Tax," *News*, June 22, 2006, canada.ca/en/news/archive/2006/06/prime-minister-harper-offers-full-apology-chinese-head-tax.html.

2. Brian Weiner, *Sins of the Parents: Politics of National Apologies in the U.S.* (Philadelphia: Temple University Press, 2005), 1.

Bibliography

AFP. "The Do's and Don'ts of Proper Dim
    Sum Etiquette." *Tatler*, February 12,
    2013. tatlerasia.com/dining/food/
    the-do-s-and-don-ts-of-proper-dim-sum-etiquette.

Alexander, Don. "Remembering the Legacy of
    Shirley Chan: Saving Vancouver's Chinatown
    Neighborhood." *Planning West* 61, no. 1 (2019): 12–14.

Atkin, John. "A Brief History of 'Little Italy.'" *City of
    Vancouver*. April 2016. vancouver.ca/files/cov/brief-
    history-of-little-italy.pdf.

Baker, Rafferty. "An Affordable Place to Eat in
    Vancouver's Chinatown, Gain Wah's Future
    Is Now in Peril." *CBC News*, September 17,
    2022. cbc.ca/news/canada/british-columbia/
    gain-wah-future-uncertain-1.6586572.

Barbas, Samantha. "'I'll Take Chop Suey': Restaurants as
    Agents of Culinary and Cultural Exchange." *Journal
    of Popular Culture* 36, no. 4 (2003): 669–86.

Baylon, Johna, and Leyland Cecco. "Attacks Make
    Vancouver 'Anti-Asian Hate Crime Capital
    of North America.'" *Guardian*, May 23, 2021.
    theguardian.com/world/2021/may/23/
    vancoucer-anti-asian-hate-crimes-increase.

Berson, Joshua, and Christopher Cheung. "Keeping
    Calm and Wrapping Dim Sum." *Tyee*, July 17, 2020.
    thetyee.ca/News/2020/07/17/Kam-Wai-Dim-Sum-
    Pandemic-Vancouver-Chinatown/.

Brouwers, Stephen Frans. "Chinese Architectural
    Practice and the Spatial Discourse of Vancouver's
    Chinatown." Master's thesis, University of British
    Columbia, 2008.

Canada's Historic Places. historicplaces.ca.

Caselis, Gabrielle. "Hidden Hong Kong: A
    History of Cantonese Barbecue (Siu Mei)."
    Localiiz, August 20, 2021. localiiz.com/post/
    food-drink-history-cantonese-barbecue-siu-mei.

CBC News. "Cantonese Barbecue Meat Was Almost
    Banned in Canada If Not for 'The Good Fight':
    Vancouver Island Professor." November 19,
    2022. cbc.ca/news/canada/british-columbia/
    cantonese-bbq-meats-banned-vancouver-island-
    professor-1.6657625.

Chan, Collyn, and Amy Zhou. "How to Save Chinatown:
    Preserving Affordability and Community Service
    through Ethnic Retail." *Berkeley Planning Journal* 32,
    no. 1 (2022).

Chapman, Aaron. "This Legendary Chinatown Hotspot
    Once Hosted Richard Pryor, Nina Simone."
    Vancouver Is Awesome, November 15, 2019.
    vancouverisawesome.com/history/this-legendary-
    chinatown-hotspot-once-hosted-richard-pryor-
    nina-simone-3111031.

———. *Vancouver After Dark: The Wild History of a City's
    Nightlife*. Vancouver: Arsenal Pulp, 2020.

Cheung, Christopher. "Chinatown Condos a
    Go After Years of Protest." *Tyee*, June
    28, 2023. thetyee.ca/News/2023/06/28/
    Chinatown-Condos-Go-After-Years-Protest/.

———. "In Chinatown, Precious Few Places
    for Seniors to Live." *Tyee*, February 8,
    2023. thetyee.ca/News/2023/02/08/
    Few-Places-For-Seniors-Living-In-Chinatown/.

———. "Repairing the Damage of 'Slum Clearance'
    in Vancouver's Inner City." *Tyee*, June
    27, 2018. thetyee.ca/News/2018/06/27/
    Vancouver-Inner-City-Slum-Clearance-Repair/.

Cheung, Christopher, and Joshua Berson. "In the
    Pandemic, 'Gain Wah' Keeps Dishing Out
    Chinatown Classics." *Tyee*, July 13, 2020. thetyee

.ca/News/2020/07/13/In-The-Pandemic-Gain-Wah-Keeps-Dishing-Chinatown-Classics/.

Cheung, Man Lai, Wilson K. S. Leung, Jun-Hwa Cheah, Kian Yeik Koay, and Bryan Cheng-Yu Hsu. "Key Tea Beverage Values Driving Tourists' Memorable Experiences: An Empirical Study in Hong Kong–Style Café Memorable Experience." *International Journal of Culture, Tourism, and Hospitality Research* 15, no. 3 (2021): 355–70.

Chinese Canadian Historical Society. "Historic Study of the Society Buildings in Chinatown." July 2005.

Choy, Wayson. *Paper Shadows: A Chinatown Childhood.* Toronto: Penguin, 2000.

Coe, Andrew. *Chop Suey: A Cultural History of Chinese Food in the United States.* Oxford: Oxford University Press, 2009.

Cyca, Michelle. "Patricia Massy Is a Book Person." *Tyee,* January 3, 2022. thetyee.ca/Culture/2022/01/03/Patricia-Massy-Book-Person/.

Diaz Combat Sports. "This $5 Million Martial Arts Facility Will Have Vancouverites Working with World Champion Trainers." *Vancouver Is Awesome.* Accessed April 28, 2024. vancouverisawesome.com/sponsored/dcs-diaz-combat-sports-vancouver-2781026.

———. "Why DCS." Accessed April 28, 2024. diazcombatsports.com/why-dcs/.

Dickson, Courtney. "Closure of Popular, Long-Running Restaurant Another Blow to Vancouver's Chinatown." *CBC News,* March 14, 2023. cbc.ca/news/canada/british-columbia/kent-s-kitchen-vancouver-chinatown-closing-1.6778600.

Dr. Sun Yat-sen Classical Chinese Garden. "Dr. Sun Yat-sen Classical Chinese Garden." Accessed May 13, 2023. vancouverchinesegarden.com/.

Evans, Sam. "Why Hong Kong's Cha Chaan Teng Are Worth Saving—They're 'Essential to the Culture, Like Pubs Are in the UK.'" *South China Morning Post,* May 6, 2023. scmp.com/magazines/post-magazine/long-reads/article/3219471/essential-culture-pubs-are-uk-why-hong-kongs-cha-chaan-teng-are-worth-saving.

Fisher, Gavin. "History of Famous Vancouver Chinatown Restaurant Revealed through Collected Menus." *CBC News,* July 24, 2016. cbc.ca/news/canada/british-columbia/history-of-famous-vancouver-chinatown-restaurant-revealed-through-collected-menus-1.3692214.

Gaskell, Viola. "Hong Kong's Cha Chaan Tengs." *Whetstone Magazine.* Accessed June 27, 2023. whetstonemagazine.com/journal/hong-kongs-cha-chaan-tengs.

Georgia Straight. "Family-Run Forum Home Appliances in Vancouver Has High-Quality Appliances for Every Budget." November 12, 2021. straight.com/living/family-run-forum-home-appliances-in-vancouver-has-high-quality-appliances-for-every-budget.

Gonzalez, Fredy. "The Rise and Spread of the Hong Men Chee Kung Tong in the Cantonese Pacific and Beyond." *Pacific Historical Review* 92, no. 1 (2023): 1–29.

Government of Canada. "Prime Minister Harper Offers Full Apology for the Chinese Head Tax." *News.* Last modified June 22, 2006. canada.ca/en/news/archive/2006/06/prime-minister-harper-offers-full-apology-chinese-head-tax.html.

Greedy Panda. "The Origin of the Electric Rice Cooker." Last modified May 18, 2021. greedy-panda.com/2020/08/the-origins-of-electric-rice-cookers/.

Griffin, Kevin. "Canada 150: Chu Lai Fought against Anti-Chinese Discrimination and Won." *Vancouver Sun,* June 6, 2017. vancouversun.com/news/local-news/canada-150/canada-150-chu-lai-fought-against-anti-chinese-discrimination-and-won.

Heritage Vancouver. "Wing Sang Building." April 16, 2006. heritagevancouver.org/

topio-watch-list/2004/6-wing-sang-building-18891901I912/.

Hern, Frances. *Yip Sang and the First Chinese Canadians.* Victoria, BC: Heritage House, 2011.

Ho, Angela, and Alan Chen. "Vancouver Chinatown Food Security Report." Hua foundation, August 2017. huafoundation.org/wp-content/uploads/2020/05/Report_VancouverCTFoodSecurity.pdf.

Hom, Laureen D. "Revitalizing Chinatown for a New Generation: The Community Politics of the Business Improvement District." *Journal of Urban Affairs* (2023): 1–17.

Howell, Mike. "Vote on Controversial Chinatown Condo Project Pushed to June 12." *Vancouver Is Awesome*, May 30, 2023. vancouverisawesome.com/local-news/vote-on-controversial-chinatown-condo-project-pushed-to-june-12-beedie-7071653.

Hui, Ann. *Chop Suey Nation: The Legion Cafe and Other Stories from Canada's Chinese Restaurants.* Madeira Park, BC: Douglas & McIntyre, 2018.

Japanese Canadian History. "General Overview." Accessed June 19, 2023. japanesecanadianhistory.net/historical-overview/general-overview/.

Khoo, Louisa-May. "Vancouver Chinatown Affordable Seniors Housing Inventory: Towards Chinatown as Campus of Care." March 7, 2023.

Korstrom, Glen. "Philanthropist, Businessman Robert H. Lee Dies at 86." *Vancouver Is Awesome*, February 20, 2020. vancouverisawesome.com/courier-archive/news/philanthropist-businessman-robert-h-lee-dies-at-86-3117340.

Kronbauer, Bob. "This 1987 Vancouver TV Commercial for Acid Wash Jeans!!!" *Vancouver Is Awesome*, August 12, 2014. vancouverisawesome.com/business/this-1987-vancouver-tv-commercial-for-acid-wash-jeans-1929238.

Kulkarni, Akshay. "New Mural in Vancouver's Chinatown Aims to Help Spark Area's Revitalization." *CBC News*, May 2, 2022. cbc.ca/news/canada/british-columbia/yvr-chinatown-new-mural-1.6437790.

Kwan, Tammy. "Legendary Chinatown Cookware Shop Ming Wo to Close Original Location after More than 100 Years in Business." *Georgia Straight*, January 6, 2020. straight.com/food/1343356/legendary-chinatown-cookware-shop-ming-wo-close-original-location-after-more-100-years.

Kwong, Peter. *The New Chinatown.* Rev. ed. New York: Hill and Wang, 1996.

Lai, David Chuenyan. *Chinatowns: Towns within Cities in Canada.* Vancouver: University of British Columbia Press, 1988.

———. "The Visual Character of Chinatowns." *Places* 7, no. 1 (1990).

Lai, Him Mark. *Becoming Chinese American: A History of Communities and Institutions.* Lanham, MD: AltaMira, 2004.

Lam, Janice. "Hidden Hong Kong: A History of the Cha Chaan Teng, the Humble Hong Kong Tea Restaurant." *Localiiz*, April 22, 2022. localiiz.com/post/food-drink-history-cha-chaan-teng-hong-kong.

Landau-Donnelly, Friederike. "Ghostly Murals: Tracing the Politics of Public Art in Vancouver's Hogan's Alley." *Environment and Planning: Politics and Space* 41, no. 6 (2023): 1147–65.

Larsen, Karin. "Wayward Chinatown Otter Making a Meal of Sun Yat-sen Koi." *CBC News*, November 20, 2018. cbc.ca/news/canada/british-columbia/chinatown-otter-sun-yat-sen-garden-koi-fish-1.4912942.

Lee-Young, Joanne. "Chinatown Dim Sum Maker Opens Revamped Heritage Business." *Vancouver Sun*, February 8, 2021. vancouversun.com/business/chinatown-dim-sum-maker-opens-revamped-heritage-business.

———. "COVID-19: Building Manager of Chinatown SRO a Front-Line Worker for Its Vulnerable Seniors." *Vancouver Sun*, April 17, 2020. vancouversun.com/news/local-news/building-manager-of-chinatown-sro-a-front-line-worker-for-its-vulnerable-seniors.

———. "The Demise of Chinatown's BBQ Meat Shops." *Vancouver Sun*, September 30, 2015. vancouversun.com/news/metro/the-demise-of-chinatowns-bbq-meat-shops.

Lim Sai Hor Kow Mock Benevolent Association. "The Lim Sai Hor Kow Mock Benevolent Association." Accessed May 13, 2023. limassociation.ca.

Liu, Karon. "The Relatively Unknown Art of Chinese Barbecue." *Toronto Star*, May 16, 2018. thestar.com/life/2018/05/16/the-relatively-unknown-art-of-chinese-barbecue.html.

Lonely Planet. "Chinatown Millennium Gate." Accessed June 29, 2023. lonelyplanet.com/canada/british-columbia/vancouver/gastown-chinatown/attractions/chinatown-millennium-gate/a/poi-sig/1357336/1335106.

Mackie, John. "After More than 100 Years, Ming Wo Will Close Its Chinatown Kitchen Shop." *Vancouver Sun*, January 7, 2020. vancouversun.com/news/local-news/after-more-than-100-years-ming-wo-will-close-its-chinatown-kitchen-shop.

———. "Canada 150: Tong Louie Built His Family Company into a B.C. Business Empire." *Vancouver Sun*, June 27, 2017. vancouversun.com/news/local-news/canada-150/canada-150-tong-louie-built-his-family-company-into-a-b-c-business-empire.

———. "Canada's Oldest Chinese Print Shop Closes at 6 p.m. Today, after 106 Years in Business." *Vancouver Sun*, March 27, 2014. vancouversun.com/news/metro/last-day-for-a-legend-in-vancouvers-historic-chinatown.

———. "Chinese Society Artifacts a Mountain of Gold for Heritage Buffs." *Vancouver Sun*, October 15, 2022. vancouversun.com/news/local-news/chinese-society-artifacts-a-mountain-of-gold-for-heritage-buffs.

———. "This Week in History: 1948: A Giant 'Slum Clearance' Is Proposed for Strathcona." *Vancouver Sun*, October 18, 2019. vancouversun.com/news/local-news/this-week-in-history-1948-a-giant-slum-clearance-is-proposed-for-strathcona.

———. "This Week in History, 1966: The Shanghai Junk Sails into Chinatown." *Vancouver Sun*, February 17, 2023. vancouversun.com/news/this-week-in-history-1966-the-shanghai-junk-sails-into-chinatown.

Mah, Jamie. "The Story of Bao Bei's Beautiful Neon Sign." *Scout Magazine*, May 16, 2018. scoutmagazine.ca/the-story-of-bao-beis-beautiful-neon-sign/.

Mahieus, Lise, and Eugene McCann. "'Hot+Noisy' Public Space: Conviviality, 'Unapologetic Asianness,' and the Future of Vancouver's Chinatown." *Urban Planning* 8, no. 4 (2023): 77–88.

Mau Dan Gardens Cooperative Housing. "History of Mau Dan." Accessed June 10, 2023. maudancoop.ca/about-the-co-op/history-of-mau-dan.

McSheffrey, Elizabeth, and Jasmine Bala. "Debate Heats up in Chinatown as Embattled 105 Keefer St. Development Is Reviewed Again." *Global News*, May 25, 2023. globalnews.ca/news/9723562/opposing-opinions-chinatown-105-keefer-street/.

Meuse, Matt, and Gavin Fisher. "Bill Wong, Legendary Vancouver Chinatown Tailor, Dead at 95." *CBC News*, April 16, 2017. cbc.ca/news/canada/british-columbia/bill-wong-obit-1.4072560.

Miles, Steven B. *Chinese Diasporas: A Social History of Global Migration*. Cambridge, UK: Cambridge University Press, 2020.

Moliere, Ashley. "Built on a Bet: Owner of World-Famous Chinatown Building Says, despite Pandemic, He's Here to Stay." *CBC News*. Accessed May 13, 2023. newsinteractives.cbc.ca/longform/sam-kee-building-legacy-chow-family/.

Moran, Kristen. "Chinatown's Ho Sun Hing Printers
     Shuts Its Doors." *Business in Vancouver*,
     March 25, 2014. biv.com/article/2014/03/
     chinatowns-ho-sun-hing-printers-shuts-its-doors.

———. "Ink Runs Dry on 104-Year-Old Chinatown Print
     Shop." *Vancouver Is Awesome*, March 20, 2014.
     vancouverisawesome.com/courier-archive/news/
     ink-runs-dry-on-104-year-old-chinatown-print-
     shop-2974910.

Morrison, Andrew. "Sleek and Simple 'Propaganda
     Coffee' Now Open On East Pender St. in
     Chinatown." *Scout Magazine*, February 2, 2015.
     scoutmagazine.ca/diner-sleek-simple-propaganda-
     coffee-now-open-on-east-pender-st-in-chinatown/.

Morton, Michelle. "Ming Wo Cookware's Family-Owned
     Business in Chinatown Closes Its Doors." *Daily
     Hive*, March 4, 2020. dailyhive.com/vancouver/
     ming-wo-cookware-chinatown-closed.

Ng, Wing Chung. "Chinatown Theatre as Transnational
     Business: New Evidence from Vancouver during
     the Exclusion Era." *BC Studies* 148 (Winter
     2005/06).

———. *The Chinese in Vancouver, 1945–80: The Pursuit of
     Identity and Power*. Vancouver: UBC Press, 1999.

Olmsted, Larry. "Vancouver's Cambodian-Vietnamese
     Eatery Is Worth the Wait." *USA Today*, September
     12, 2017. usatoday.com/story/travel/columnist/
     greatamericanbites/2017/09/12/phnom-penh-
     restaurant-vancouver-canada/653861001/.

Pablo, Carlito. "Renewal Planned for Vancouver
     Chinatown Site Where Louie Family Business
     behind London Drugs Began." *Georgia Straight*,
     October 6, 2020. straight.com/news/renewal-
     planned-for-vancouver-chinatown-site-where-
     louie-family-business-behind-london-drugs.

Perrault, E. G. *Tong: The Story of Tong Louie, Vancouver's
     Quiet Titan*. Madeira Park, BC: Harbour, 2002.

Premji, Zahra. "3 Years into the COVID-19 Pandemic,
     Anti-Asian Hate Still Prevalent in Metro

Vancouver: Advocates." *CBC News*, January 26,
     2023. cbc.ca/news/canada/british-columbia/
     anti-asian-hate-in-metro-vancouver-2023-1.6725671.

Rossi, Cheryl. "Advocacy Group Hopes to Save Foo's Ho
     Ho." *Vancouver Courier*, July 30, 2010.

Shields, Norman. "Chee Kung Tong Building, Barkerville,
     British Columbia." *The Journal of the Society for the
     Study of Architecture in Canada* 33, no. 2 (2008):
     53–72.

Sia, Rosanne Amosovs. "Making and Defending Intimate
     Spaces: White Waitresses Policed in Vancouver's
     Chinatown Cafes." Master's thesis, University of
     British Columbia, 2010.

Smith, Charlie. "The Making of Real-Estate Mogul Robert
     H. Lee." *Georgia Straight*, October 17, 2012. straight
     .com/news/making-real-estate-mogul-robert-h-lee.

———. "Wing Sang Building Will Become Home to
     Chinese Canadian Museum with Help from
     Province and Rennie Family." *Georgia Straight*,
     February 15, 2022. straight.com/arts/wing-sang-
     building-will-become-home-to-chinese-canadian-
     museum-with-help-from-province-and.

Spence, Jonathan D. *The Search for Modern China*. New
     York: W. W. Norton, 1999.

Sproule, Michelle. "Secrets of Chinatown Shops,
     with William Liu of Kam Wai Dim Sum." *Scout
     Magazine*, September 29, 2022. scoutmagazine
     .ca/2022/09/29/secrets-of-chinatown-shops-with-
     william-liu-of-kam-wai-dim-sum/.

Stainsby, Mia. "Vancouver's Vietnamese Restaurants—
     Their Backstories." *Vancouver Sun*, June 18, 2010.
     vancouversun.com/news/staff-blogs/vancouvers-
     vietnamese-restaurants-their-backstories.

Stiem, Tyler. "Story of Cities #38: Vancouver Dumps
     Its Freeway Plan for a More Beautiful Future."
     Guardian, May 9, 2016. theguardian.com/
     cities/2016/may/09/story-cities-38-vancouver-
     canada-freeway-protest-liveable-city.

Szeto, Winston. "Chinese Freemasons Celebrate 160 Years of Community and Cultural Support in Canada." *CBC News*, March 23, 2023. cbc.ca/news/canada/british-columbia/canada-chinese-freemasons-160-anniversary-1.6787635.

Thompson, Kat. "The Essential Guide to Dim Sum." *Thrillist*, May 16, 2022. thrillist.com/eat/nation/best-dim-sum-dishes-food.

Tosi & Company. "Tosi & Company." Accessed June 10, 2023. tosifoods.com.

University of British Columbia. "Chinese Canadian Stories: Uncommon Histories from a Common Past." Accessed July 16, 2023. wayback.archive-it.org/4160/20160413230213/http://ccs.library.ubc.ca/trim/s/en/index.html.

Vancouver Chinatown Today. "Chinatown History: From Kublai Khan to TD Bank via Shanghai Junk." May 7, 2016. chinatown.today/2016/05/chinatown-history-shanghai-junk/.

Vancouver Heritage Foundation. *Vancouver Heritage Site Finder*. heritagesitefinder.ca.

Victoria's Chinatown. "Chinese Empire Reform Association: The First Worldwide Chinese Political Association." Accessed May 13, 2023. chinatown.library.uvic.ca/index.htmlq%3Dchinese_empire_reform_association.html.

Vissers, Brodie. "Propaganda with Will Wang." *Nomad Barista*, May 13, 2016. thenomadbarista.com/propaganda.

Vu, Huy. "The Ultimate Guide to Chinese Dim Sum (Menu & Ordering Guide)." *Hungry Huy*, April 5, 2021. hungryhuy.com/dim-sum-guide/.

Walter, Chandler. "A Look Inside: $9.5-Million Chinatown Penthouse with Glass-Bottom Pool." *Daily Hive*, August 10, 2017. dailyhive.com/vancouver/vancouver-condo-135-keefer-street-vancouver.

Watson, Bridgette. "6 Years after Its Rejection, Chinatown Condo Project Is Back on the Table and Dividing the Neighbourhood." *CBC News*, May 25, 2023. cbc.ca/news/canada/british-columbia/chinatown-condo-controversy-1.6854765.

Wei, Clarissa. "A (Very) Comprehensive Illustrated Guide to Cantonese Barbecue." *Goldthread*, October 9, 2018. goldthread2.com/food/comprehensive-cantonese-barbecue-guide/article/3000169.

Weichel, Andrew. "Chinatown BIA Spending 50% of Budget on Security, President Says in Plea to Vancouver Police." *CTV News*, March 1, 2022. bc.ctvnews.ca/chinatown-bia-spending-50-of-budget-on-security-president-says-in-plea-to-vancouver-police-1.5801933.

Weiner, Brian. *Sins of the Parents: Politics of National Apologies in the U.S.* Philadelphia: Temple University Press, 2005.

White, J. H. "Philanthropist Carol Lee Aims to Reinvent Vancouver Chinatown." *Magnifissance*, January 13, 2020. magnifissance.com/print-edition/issue-096/vancouver-chinatown/.

Wickberg, Edgar. "Chinese and Canadian Influences on Chinese Politics in Vancouver, 1900–1947." *BC Studies* 45 (Spring 1980).

Wong, Diane. "Shop Talk and Everyday Sites of Resistance to Gentrification in Manhattan's Chinatown." *Women's Studies Quarterly* 47, no. 1 & 2 (Spring/Summer 2019): 132–48.

Wong-Chu, Jim. *Chinatown Ghosts: The Poems and Photographs of Jim Wong-Chu*, rev. ed. Vancouver: Arsenal Pulp Press, 2018.

Yang, Philip. "Sojourners or Settlers: Post-1965 Chinese Immigrants." *Journal of Asian American Studies* 2, no. 1 (1999).

Yap, Victoria. "What Is Dim Sum? Our Beginner's Guide to the Cantonese Cuisine," February 5, 2020. honestfoodtalks.com/dim-sum-guide-yum-cha/.

Yee, Paul. *Chinatown: An Illustrated History of the Chinese
   Communities of Victoria, Vancouver, Calgary,
   Winnipeg, Toronto, Ottawa, Montreal and Halifax.*
   Toronto: Lorimer, 2005.

———. *Saltwater City: An Illustrated History of the Chinese
   in Vancouver.* Rev. ed. Vancouver: Douglas &
   McIntyre, 2006.

———. "Sam Kee: A Chinese Business in Early Vancouver."
   BC Studies 69–70 (Spring-Summer 1986).

Yu, Ida. "The Serious Eats Field Guide
   to Chinese Pastries." *Serious Eats,*
   February 25, 2019. seriouseats.com/
   chinese-bakery-pastries-buns-egg-tarts-guide.

Zeidler, Maryse. "How Nixing a Downtown Freeway 50
   Years Ago Made Vancouver One of the World's
   Most Liveable Cities." *CBC News,* December 3,
   2017. cbc.ca/news/canada/british-columbia/
   vancouver-freeway-not-built-1.4428986.

Illustration and Photograph Credits

City of Vancouver Archives: 20 (*287-2*), 27 (*1095-08980*), 32 (*1095-09741*), 41 (*1095-06783*), 63 (*1095-09724*), 70 (*1095-09664*), 74 (*790-2374*), 109 (*1095-09725*), 117 (*1095-09498*), 127 top (*1095-09745*), 132 top (*1095-09391*), 142 (*1095-11326*), 144 top (*1095-12567*), 147 (*780-335*), 148–49 (*203-9*), 154 (*790-2401*), 166 left (*1095-11255*) and right (*1095-11241*), 167 (*1095-09656*), 173 (*1095-11556*), 196–97 (*1095-14251*), 203 (*1095-10311*), 206 (*790-0728*), 215 (*1095-11258*), 216 top (*1095-08646*), 224 (*1095-11253*), 228–29 (*1095-14315*), 232 left (*1095-11745*) and right (*2008-010.0109*)

City of Vancouver Archives (Photographer: Yucho Chow): 104 top (*2021-034.122*) and bottom (*2021-034.121*)

City of Vancouver Archives (Photographer: James Crookall): 56–57 (*260-452*), 211 top (*260-296*)

City of Vancouver Archives (Photographer: Walter Frost): 211 bottom (*447-374*)

City of Vancouver Archives (Photographer: William Eadington Graham): 175 (*1135-34*)

City of Vancouver Archives (Photographer: James Skitt Matthews): 45 top (*M-14-62*), 208 (*371-2242*)

City of Vancouver Archives (Photographer: Paul Yee): 30 bottom right (*2008-010.0329*), 85 (*2008-010.0522*), 94 (*2008-010.1039*), 171 (*2008-010.0507*), 232 left (*2008-010.0109*)

Donna Seto (author collection): iv, x, 2, 5, 6 left and right, 9, 14, 18, 22 top and bottom, 25, 28, 34, 38, 42, 46, 48, 50, 54, 59 left and right, 60, 64, 66 left and right, 67, 68, 71, 72, 75, 76, 78, 80, 82, 86, 88, 90, 97, 100, 102, 105, 106, 110, 113, 114, 118, 120, 122, 123, 124, 128, 130, 133, 136, 138, 140, 146, 152, 155, 156, 158, 159, 160, 162, 164, 168, 169, 170, 172, 174, 176, 178, 180, 182, 185, 186, 188, 190, 191, 192, 193, 194, 195, 200, 204, 212, 214, 218, 220, 222, 226, 230, 235

David Lee: 143 top left, top right, bottom left, bottom right, 144 bottom

Karen Lee: 93

Lorraine Lowe: 53 top and bottom

Melinda Wong: 132 bottom, 135 left and right

Olivia Cheng: 177

Tommy Seto: 17, 127 bottom, 202, 216 bottom

Vancouver Public Library: 98–99 (*2002*)

Vancouver Public Library (Photographer: Philip Timms): viii–ix (*1904*), xviii–1 (*7234*), 21 top (*939*) and bottom (*6831*), 30 top (*66677*) and bottom left (*78362*), 37 (*5240*), 45 bottom (*940*)

Vancouver Public Library/Canadian Pacific Railway Collection: 10–11 (*1746*)

Index

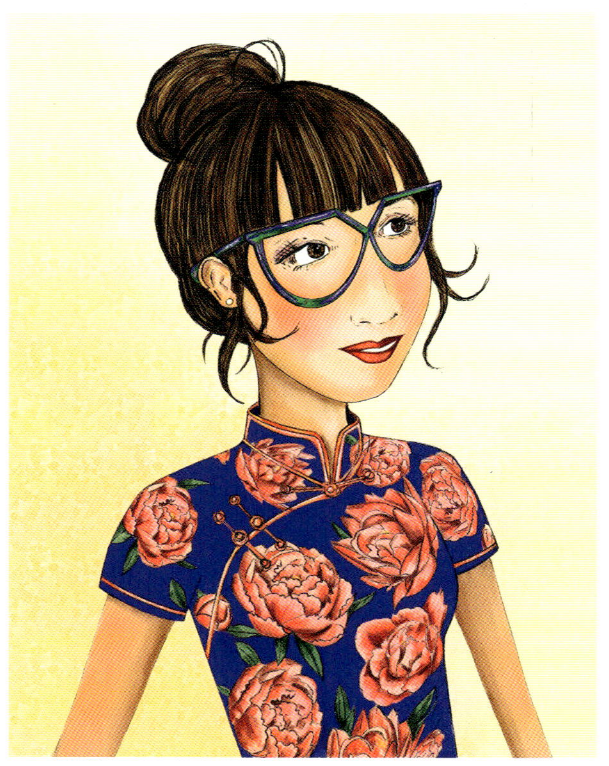

DONNA SETO is a writer, self-taught artist, and occasional academic. Growing up, Donna accompanied her parents on regular ventures through the bustling streets of Vancouver's Chinatown, where they bought groceries, ate dim sum, purchased newspapers, and visited her grandmother. During the pandemic, she revisited her long-lost passion for art and started drawing buildings in Chinatown. Donna has a PhD in politics and international relations. She lives in Vancouver.